구문 독해 204

204개의
핵심 구문을 통한
직독직해
완전정복!

BOOK 2

구문독해 204 BOOK 2

지은이 김상근
펴낸이 임상진
펴낸곳 (주)넥서스

출판신고 1992년 4월 3일 제311-2002-2호 ②-10
10880 경기도 파주시 지목로 5
Tel (02)330-5500 Fax (02)330-5555

ISBN 978-89-6790-773-0 (54740)
ISBN 978-89-6790-771-6 (SET)

가격은 뒤표지에 있습니다.
잘못 만들어진 책은 구입처에서 바꾸어 드립니다.

www.nexusEDU.kr

구문을 알면 독해가 저절로!

구문 독해 204

204개의
핵심 구문을 통한
직독직해
완전정복!

BOOK 2

SENTENCE STRUCTURE
+READING

김상근 지음

NEXUS Edu

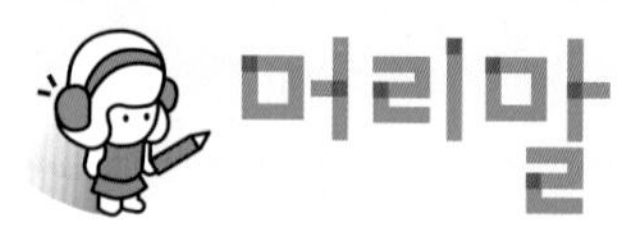

우리나라에서 영어를 잘하는 것은 쉬운 일이 아닙니다. 특히나 긴 글을 단숨에 읽어나가는 건 더더욱 어려운 일입니다. 그래서 영어의 기본기를 다지는 것이 중요합니다. 그 기본기를 다지기에 가장 효과적인 방법은 영어 문장을 분석하고, 그 구조를 파악하는 것입니다.

물론 이러한 구조 파악에는 영문법이 가장 기본이 됨은 말할 것도 없습니다. 영문법에 대한 기본기가 없다면 영어 문장의 구조 파악은 불가능합니다. 그래서 학교에서 학생들이 어려워하고, 시험에 나오면 대부분 틀리는 문법을 정리했고, 그러한 문법이 사용된 문장을 사용하여 204개의 구문 분석으로 엮었습니다. 특히 문장이 길어서 해석이 어려운 것, 주어와 동사 사이에 긴 삽입구가 들어가 해석이 어려운 것, 문장의 주요 성분(주어, 동사, 목적어, 목적격 보어)을 수식해 주는 군더더기가 많아서 해석이 어려운 것 등을 추려 냈습니다.

영문법의 기본을 쌓고, 구문 분석을 꾸준히 하면 문법은 물론 독해 실력까지 향상시킬 수 있습니다. 독해를 잘하지 못하는 학생들의 대부분은 주어와 동사를 잘 찾지 못하고 헤매는 경우가 많습니다. 이러한 현상은 어떤 것이 수식어구인지, 어떤 것이 삽입구인지를 제대로 파악하지 못하기 때문에 일어나는 현상입니다.

영어 문장을 분석하고, 그 구조를 파악하는 연습을 충분히 하고 나면, 나중에는 굳이 문장을 분석하려고 하지 않아도 머리 속에서 저절로 주어, 동사를 파악하고 문장을 이해할 수 있게 됩니다. 이것이 우리가 흔히 말하는 직독직해입니다.

직독직해에 있어서 가장 중요한 것은 주어와 동사를 파악하는 것입니다. 문장의 주요 요소에 포함되는 목적어, 목적격 보어까지 파악하고 나면, 나머지는 그저 문장의 주요 요소를 꾸며주는 수식구들에 불과할 뿐입니다.

〈구문독해 204〉 교재는 주어, 동사를 찾는 구문 풀이의 기본에 충실하면서도 수식어구까지 파악할 수 있도록 자세한 설명을 달았습니다. 구문독해 204를 끝내고 나면 어느 새 영어 문장의 원리를 모두 파악하고 있는 자신을 발견할 수 있도록 충분한 연습문제를 수록했습니다.

구문독해 204를 공부하면 영어 문법은 물론 직독직해에 자신감이 생기리라 자신있게 말씀드릴 수 있습니다.

이 책이 나오기까지 옆에서 늘 응원하고 나에게 힘이 되어주며 여러 가지 충고를 해준 나현 씨에게 고마움을 표합니다.

구성과 특징

Key Sentence

14년간 시험 기출 통계 자료를 통해 엄선된 핵심 구문을 수록했습니다. 문장 구조를 분석해 주는 친절한 해설은 직독직해가 쉬워지는 비결을 제시합니다.

Grammar Point

핵심 구문에서 뽑은 시험에 자주 나오는 문법을 선별하여 정리했습니다.

Check-up

Grammar Point에서 학습한 문법을 간단히 확인할 수 있는 문제를 제공합니다.

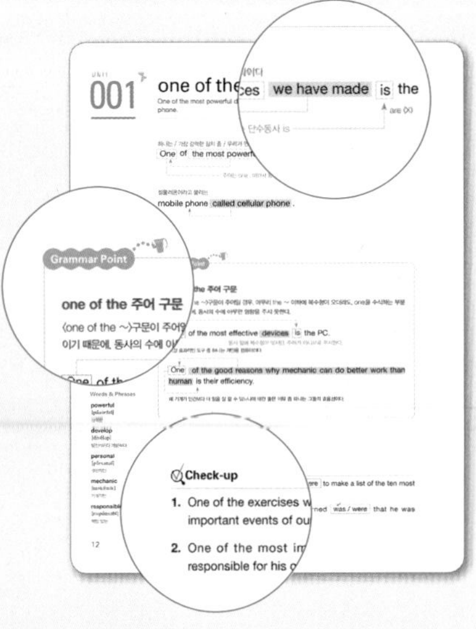

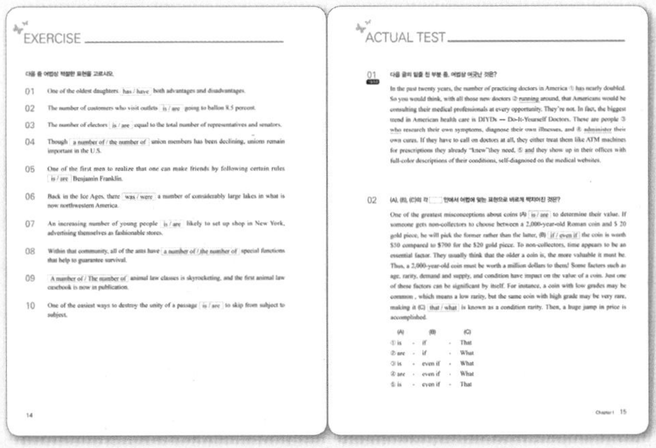

EXERCISE

Key Sentence와 Grammar Point에서 익힌 내용을 점검할 수 있는 연습 문제입니다. 스스로 문장 구조를 파악하며 직독직해를 연습하면 효과는 두 배가 됩니다.

ACTUAL TEST

지문 속에 숨어 있는 어법 문제를 통해 독해와 어법을 동시에 점검할 수 있습니다. EXERCISE에서는 단문을 연습했다면 이를 장문에 적용하여 독해력과 어법 실력을 동시에 향상시킬 수 있습니다.

REVIEW TEST

해당 챕터에서 배운 문법 사항을 점검할 수 있는 심화 어법 문제를 수록했습니다. EXERCISE와는 다른 다양한 유형의 문제를 학습함으로써 문장 구조 파악에 자신감을 가질 수 있도록 구성했습니다.

FINAL CHECK

실제 시험 유형의 장문 어법 문제를 수록했습니다. 실전 독해 장문 문제 풀이를 통해 글 속에 숨어 있는 오류를 찾아내고, 본격적인 직독직해 연습을 해볼 수 있습니다.

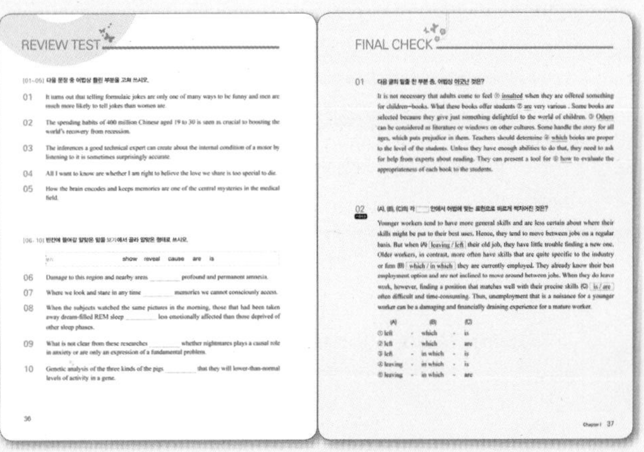

Monthly Planner

		1st	2nd	3rd	4th	5th	6th	7th
First Week	Book 1	Unit 001~005 □ □ □ □	Unit 006~010 □ □ □ □	Unit 011~015 □ □ □ □	Unit 016~020 □ □ □ □	Unit 021~025 □ □ □ □	EXERCISE / ACTUAL TEST □ □ □ □	REVIEW TEST / FINAL CHECK □ □ □ □
	Book 2	Unit 099~103 □ □ □ □	Unit 104~108 □ □ □ □	Unit 109~113 □ □ □ □	Unit 114~118 □ □ □ □	Unit 119~123 □ □ □ □	EXERCISE / ACTUAL TEST □ □ □ □	REVIEW TEST / FINAL CHECK □ □ □ □
Second Week	Book 1	Unit 026~030 □ □ □ □	Unit 031~035 □ □ □ □	Unit 036~040 □ □ □ □	Unit 041~045 □ □ □ □	Unit 046~050 □ □ □ □	EXERCISE / ACTUAL TEST □ □ □ □	REVIEW TEST / FINAL CHECK □ □ □ □
	Book 2	Unit 124~128 □ □ □ □	Unit 129~133 □ □ □ □	Unit 134~138 □ □ □ □	Unit 139~143 □ □ □ □	Unit 144~148 □ □ □ □	EXERCISE / ACTUAL TEST □ □ □ □	REVIEW TEST / FINAL CHECK □ □ □ □
Third Week	Book 1	Unit 051~055 □ □ □ □	Unit 056~060 □ □ □ □	Unit 061~065 □ □ □ □	Unit 066~070 □ □ □ □	Unit 071~075 □ □ □ □	EXERCISE / ACTUAL TEST □ □ □ □	REVIEW TEST / FINAL CHECK □ □ □ □
	Book 2	Unit 149~153 □ □ □ □	Unit 154~158 □ □ □ □	Unit 159~163 □ □ □ □	Unit 164~168 □ □ □ □	Unit 169~173 □ □ □ □	EXERCISE / ACTUAL TEST □ □ □ □	REVIEW TEST / FINAL CHECK □ □ □ □
Fourth Week	Book 1	Unit 076~080 □ □ □ □	Unit 081~085 □ □ □ □	Unit 086~090 □ □ □ □	Unit 091~095 □ □ □ □	Unit 096~098 □ □ □ □	EXERCISE / ACTUAL TEST □ □ □ □	REVIEW TEST / FINAL CHECK □ □ □ □
	Book 2	Unit 174~179 □ □ □ □	Unit 180~185 □ □ □ □	Unit 186~191 □ □ □ □	Unit 192~197 □ □ □ □	Unit 198~204 □ □ □ □	EXERCISE / ACTUAL TEST □ □ □ □	REVIEW TEST / FINAL CHECK □ □ □ □

목차

CHAPTER 10
관계사
Relatives

CHAPTER 11
분사구문
participle constructions

CHAPTER 12
동명사
Gerunds

CHAPTER 13
to부정사
To Infinitives

CHAPTER 14
접속사
Conjunctions

CHAPTER 15
가정법
Subjunctives

CHAPTER 16
강조 · 도치 구조
Stress and Inversion

CHAPTER 17
병렬 구조
Parallel structures

1권 목차

Chapter

Relatives

관계사

사람 선행사 - who

The Pope canonized six new saints, including Portugal's 14th century independence leader and a French monk who died of torture.

교황은 포르투갈의 14세기 독립운동 지도자와 고문으로 죽은 프랑스의 수도승을 포함한 여섯 명의 새로운 성인을 공표했다.

교황은 / 성자로 공표했다 / 여섯 명의 새로운 성인을 /
The Pope canonized six new saints,

포함해서 / 포르투갈의 14세기 독립운동 지도자와 /
including Portugal's 14th century independence leader and

프랑스의 수도승을 // 고문으로 죽은
a French monk who died of torture.

선행사가 사람인 a French monk이고, 관계대명사절에 주어가 없으므로 died의 주어가 되는 주격 관계대명사 who가 온다.

Words & Phrases

Pope [poup] 교황

canonize [kǽnənàiz] 성자로 공표하다

independence [indipéndəns] 독립

monk [mʌŋk] 수도승

torture [tɔ́:rtʃər] 고문, 고통

cherish [tʃériʃ] ~을 소중히 여기다, 아끼다

Grammar Point

선행사가 사람인 관계대명사 who

선행사가 사람이면 관계대명사 who를 사용하고, 관계대명사절에서 생략된 선행사의 격에 따라서 who, whom, whose로 바꿔서 쓴다. 목적격인 whom 대신 who를 쓸 수도 있지만, 전치사 바로 뒤에 목적어로 쓸 경우 whom을 써야 한다.

Check-up

정답 및 해설 p.2

1. Many people [who / which] live in this part of the world are likely to be worried again with the beginning of cold weather. 기출응용

2. My family took a trip to the studio of Jerry Smith, a craftsman [who / whom] made the furniture that our family has cherished for many years.

전치사의 목적어 - whom

She introduced me to her husband whom I tried to look for to decipher some of that language.

그녀는 그 언어의 일부를 해독하기 위해 내가 찾으려고 했던 자신의 남편에게 나를 소개했다.

그녀는 / 소개했다 / 나를 / 그녀의 남편에게 // 내가 찾으려고 했던 /

She introduced me to her husband whom I tried to look for

for who (X)

목적격 관계대명사 whom은 look for의 목적어이다.
전치사 for가 관계대명사 앞으로 나오면 who를 쓸 수 없다.

그 언어의 일부를 해독하기 위해

to decipher some of that language.

Grammar Point

전치사의 목적어로 쓰인 관계대명사

1. 관계대명사가 전치사의 목적어로 쓰인 경우, 전치사가 관계대명사 앞으로 오면 who와 that은 쓸 수 없다. 하지만, 전치사가 관계대명사절의 동사 뒤에 위치한 경우 who와 that도 쓸 수 있다.

She is the actress to whom I was talking.

to who (X) to that (X)

그녀가 나와 이야기를 하고 있던 배우이다.

She is the actress whom I was talking to.

who (O) that (O)

2. 목적격 관계대명사는 생략 가능하지만, 전치사 바로 뒤에 오면 생략할 수 없다.

She is the actress whom I was talking to.

(whom) (O) 관계대명사 생략 가능

She is the actress to whom I was talking.

to (whom) (X) 관계대명사 생략 불가능

Words & Phrases

decipher [disáifər] 해독하다, 풀다

closely [klóusli] 밀접하게

individual [ìndəvídʒuəl] 개인; 개개인의

outraged [áutreidʒid] 분노한

revenge [rivéndʒ] 복수

Check-up

정답 및 해설 p.2

1. Such roles are closely connected to the relationship between an individual and the person to who / whom he or she is speaking.
2. One outraged citizen even called the office and asked where he could find some Iraqi people on who / whom he wanted to take revenge.

EXERCISE

정답 및 해설 p.2

[01-10] 다음 중 어법상 가장 적절한 표현을 고르시오.

01 Jack saw a toll booth attendant [who / which] reminded him of his father.

02 He is bright and can do well in school when he wants to, and he has friends with [who / whom] he enjoys being.

03 기출변형 I would encourage you to request a reference letter from those teachers with [that / whom] you have had the most chance to demonstrate your skills.

04 Alumni can lend money to students with [who / whom] they feel a bond, and the students are required to update their information four times a year for those who support them.

05 In the sixteenth century, situations were very different; spices were a sought-after treasure, bringing wealth and power to [whoever / whomever] could gain them.

06 I saw a news interview with an acquaintance [who / whom] I was certain was going to tell some lies.

07 The good thing about the medical office is that patients [who / which] want to stay longer are allowed to do so.

08 기출응용 People who have large, infrequent meals tend to gain more weight and to have a higher level of fat in the blood than do those [who / which] eat smaller quantities at regular intervals.

09 I can't find your sister in the picture [which / who] I heard was quite pretty.

10 This is the actress [who / whom] my sister claims has attracted her friend.

ACTUAL TEST

정답 및 해설 p.2

01 기출응용

다음 글의 밑줄 친 부분 중, 어법상 어긋난 것은?

When I was a kid, I was always left out when my friends chose players for their baseball teams. In those days, there ① were no baseball gloves for left-handers like me. I was normal in other times, but I ② was considered disabled every time they played a game. Fortunately, my son, who is also one of the left-handers, ③ was born after gloves for left-handers were invented. So he doesn't have to feel ④ what I felt when he wants to play baseball. There are other various inventions which can reduce the condition of disability. Thanks to eyeglasses, I can avoid feeling powerless in this world. Wheelchairs can improve the mobility of the people ⑤ which cannot walk.

02

다음 (A), (B), (C)의 각 [ ] 안에서 어법에 맞는 표현으로 바르게 짝지어진 것은?

Peter's grandmother paused and then replied slowly, "You know, sometimes it may be best (A) [to not have / not to have] a detailed plan. I remember when your grandfather and I first went to New York. We went to museums or concerts every day. We saw festivals and baseball games. We ate wonderful food and met many interesting people. But one of my greatest memories from that trip (B) [was / were] completely unexpected." Grandma paused again and then said, "We had come especially to see the famous works of art, but one day just for a change we went to the zoo. And there I met someone (C) [which / who] had a great effect on me. His name is John Adams," she continued, "and he is a gorilla, a very special albino gorilla, with white fur and pink skin."

	(A)		(B)		(C)
①	to not have	-	was	-	which
②	not to have	-	were	-	which
③	not to have	-	was	-	which
④	to not have	-	were	-	who
⑤	not to have	-	was	-	who

UNIT

101 소유격 관계대명사 - whose

A man whose father is American and mother is French asked his Korean boss what his comment stood for.

아버지가 미국인이고 어머니가 한국인인 한 남자가 한국인 상사에게 그의 말이 무엇을 의미하는지 물었다.

한 남자가 // 그의 아버지가 미국인이고 // 어머니가 프랑스인인 //

A man whose father is American and mother is French

who, whom (X)

한국인 상사에게 물었다 // 그의 말이 무엇을 의미하는지

asked his Korean boss what his comment stood for.

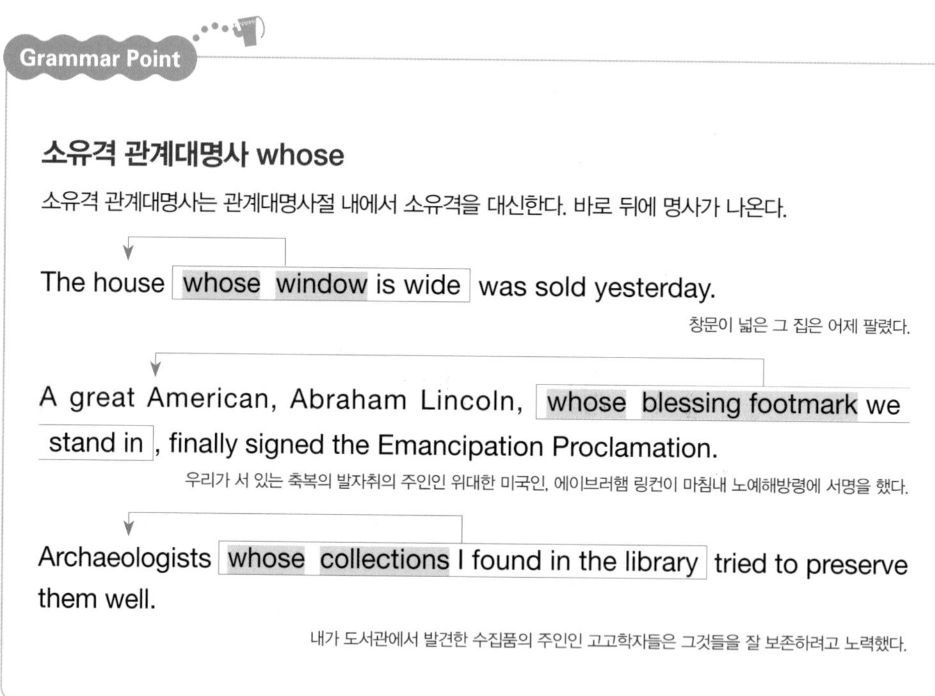

Grammar Point

소유격 관계대명사 whose

소유격 관계대명사는 관계대명사절 내에서 소유격을 대신한다. 바로 뒤에 명사가 나온다.

The house whose window is wide was sold yesterday.

창문이 넓은 그 집은 어제 팔렸다.

A great American, Abraham Lincoln, whose blessing footmark we stand in, finally signed the Emancipation Proclamation.

우리가 서 있는 축복의 발자취의 주인인 위대한 미국인, 에이브러햄 링컨이 마침내 노예해방령에 서명을 했다.

Archaeologists whose collections I found in the library tried to preserve them well.

내가 도서관에서 발견한 수집품의 주인인 고고학자들은 그것들을 잘 보존하려고 노력했다.

Words & Phrases

stand for
의미하다

sign
[sain]
서명하다

preserve
[prizə́:rv]
보존하다

realize
[rí(:)əlàiz]
깨닫다, 실현하다

feed
[fi:d]
먹이다

grain
[grein]
곡물

Check-up

정답 및 해설 p.3

1. There are many truths whose / who meaning cannot be realized until the next day.

2. In the study with a mouse which / whose age was equivalent to humans at sixty or seventy, the scientists fed various grains to the animals.

UNIT 102

사람이 아닌 선행사 - which

Engineering is a field of study which requires a lot of patience and endurance.

공학은 많은 끈기와 인내를 필요로 하는 학문의 한 분야이다.

공학은 / 이다 / 학문의 한 분야 // 요구하는 / 많은 끈기와

Engineering is a field of study which requires a lot of patience

a field of study가 선행사이므로 which가 왔다.

인내를

and endurance.

Grammar Point

사람이 아닌 선행사를 받는 관계대명사 which

which는 사람 이외의 것을 선행사로 받는다.
주격과 목적격의 형태가 동일하고, 소유격일 경우 of which나 whose를 사용한다.

I would like to talk about several problems which I have faced since I moved to this city.

이 도시로 이사 온 이후로 내가 직면한 몇 가지 문제에 대해 얘기하고 싶다.

⇒ which는 several problems를 선행사로 받고, have faced의 목적어가 되는 목적격 관계대명사이다.

Words & Phrases

engineering [èndʒəní(:)əriŋ] 공학

acknowledge [əknɑ́lidʒ] 인정하다

investigation [invèstəgéiʃən] 조사

take part in 참가하다

strike [straik] 파업

Check-up

정답 및 해설 p.3

1. We will acknowledge the police as a main body who / which can begin investigations.

2. Beginning today, the number of workers who / which take part in the strike will dramatically increase because of the support from people.

EXERCISE

정답 및 해설 p.3

[01-10] **다음 중 어법상 가장 적절한 표현을 고르시오.**

01 기출응용 On January 10, 1992, a ship traveling through rough seas lost 12 cargo containers, one of [which / whose] held 28,800 floating bath toys.

02 It wasn't very long before Mike, [who / whose] stage name was "Blind Mike," was earning around $150,000 annually.

03 Someone [whom / whose] we talk with is likely to feel much easier next to us when he think himself heard.

04 James and Carter were called "Tom and Jerry" after TV animation, [who / whose] title was *Tom and Jerry*.

05 기출응용 Dreams have been regarded as prophetic communications [which / whose], when properly decoded, would enable us to foretell the future.

06 Wendy was a famous filmmaker [who / whose] work–such as the highly acclaimed *Joy Luck Club*–deals with the complexities of being Asian in America.

07 A major research recently discovered that those [who / whose] diets are loaded with potassium-rich foods such as bananas, tomatoes, and oranges may be able to cut their risk of stroke by one-third.

08 We have only to watch today's newspaper headlines to discover examples of child athletes and performers [which / whose] parents' ambitions spoiled their children's dreams.

09 기출응용 The audience was made up of many parents and some young people, most of [which / whom] I knew.

10 Duke's deep-pocketed alumni already support an approximately $35 billion scholarship fund, which finances one of the most usual fellowship programs in higher education, promising full tuition to pupils [that / whose] families earn less than $50,000 per year.

ACTUAL TEST

정답 및 해설 p.3

01 다음 글의 밑줄 친 부분 중, 어법상 어긋난 것은?

San Francisco Seaside College is proud once again to open its two-week English Winter Camps for high school students from all over the world ① <u>which</u> are interested in improving their English skills. Classes ② <u>are offered</u> at five levels, from basic to advanced. Students are tested on arrival and placed in the level appropriate to their language ability. Every class ③ <u>has</u> a maximum of 15 students. In the classroom, lessons focus on student interaction while teachers provide feedback and support. If you have to withdraw from the camp after you have been accepted, but ④ <u>no later than</u> November 30, then all the fees you have paid will be returned. If you withdraw after November 30, we regret that we cannot return ⑤ <u>any</u> fees.

02 다음 (A), (B), (C)의 각 [ ] 안에서 어법에 맞는 표현으로 바르게 짝지어진 것은?

There are just 630 species of primates, and (A) [although / despite] one of them is doing fine, with a worldwide population approaching seven billion, more than 300 are threatened with extinction. Last week, a group of zoologists sought to highlight the threat to primates—the biological order which contains monkeys, great apes, gibbons and of course, humans—by naming the 25 species most at risk. The list comprises five species from Madagascar, six from Africa, eleven from Asia, and three from Central and South America. These range from the blue-eyed black lemur, (B) [which / whose] habitat in Madagascar is being destroyed by slash-and-burn agriculture, to the Sumatran orangutan. Numbers of one of the rarest primates, the silky sifaka, a white lemur, (C) [believe / are believed] to be down to around 100.

*lemur : 여우

	(A)		(B)		(C)
①	although	-	which	-	believe
②	although	-	whose	-	are believed
③	although	-	whose	-	believe
④	despite	-	whose	-	believe
⑤	despite	-	which	-	are believed

UNIT

103 문장이 선행사인 관계대명사 - which

It was a very elegant place, and it was always full of interesting people, which was why I liked to go there.

그곳은 굉장히 멋진 장소였고, 항상 재미있는 사람들로 가득 차 있었는데, 그것이 내가 그곳에 가는 것을 좋아하는 이유였다.

그곳은 / 굉장히 멋진 장소였다 // 그리고 / 그곳은 항상 가득 차 있었다 / 재미있는 사람들로 /
It was a very elegant place and it was always full of interesting people ,

그것이 / 였다 // 그곳에 가는 것을 좋아하는 이유
which was why I liked to go there.

who(X)

앞 문장 전체가 선행사이므로 which가 와야 한다.
people이 선행사가 아니므로 who를 쓰지 않도록 주의한다.

Grammar Point

문장을 선행사로 받는 which

관계대명사 which는 문장을 선행사로 받을 수 있고, 〈, which〉의 형태로 쓰인다. 이 경우 관계대명사절 내의 동사의 수 일치에 주의해야 한다. 콤마 뒤에 온 관계대명사절은 선행사를 수식해서 그 의미를 제한하는 것이 아니라, 추가적인 정보를 제공하는 것이다. 관계대명사의 용법에는 선행사를 수식하는 제한적 용법과 선행사에 추가적인 정보를 제공하는 계속적 용법이 있다.

Mrs. Anderson doesn't respond to my letters right away,
which irritates me. my letters를 선행사로 보고 irritate라고 하면 안 된다.

앤더슨 여사는 내 편지에 바로 답장하지 않는데, 그것이 나를 짜증나게 한다.

⇒ 앞 문장 전체가 선행사이므로 관계대명사로 which가왔고 이 자리에 다른 관계대명사는 오지 못한다.

Words & Phrases

elegant [éləgənt] 멋진, 우아한

be full of ~로 가득 차다

respond [rispάnd] 답장하다

found [faund] 설립하다

paradox [pǽrədὰks] 역설

obviously [άbviəsli] 명백하게

Check-up

정답 및 해설 p.4

1. Judy worked hard in her youth, which / who led to found her own company later.
2. Paradoxes of this kind arise when the time traveler tries to change the past, which / what is obviously impossible.

UNIT

104 관계대명사 that의 특수 용법

The first product that had us see inter-Korean ties could develop regardless of the political situation was a pot made in the Gaeseong Industrial Complex.

정치적 상황에 상관없이 남북 관계가 발전할 수 있다는 것을 우리에게 알게 해준 최초의 상품은 개성공단에서 만들어진 냄비였다.

최초의 상품은 // 우리에게 남북 관계가 발전할 수 있다는 것을 알게 한 /

The first product | that had us see inter-Korean ties could develop

선행사가 The first의 수식을 받아서 관계대명사 that이 왔다.

정치적 상황에 상관없이 // 냄비였다 / 만들어진 /

regardless of the political situation | was a pot | made in

개성공단에서

the Gaeseong Industrial Complex.

Grammar Point

관계대명사 that을 주로 사용하는 경우

선행사가 〈사람+비사람〉인 경우, 또한 〈the very, the same, all, any, anything, everything, a few, the only one〉 등의 수식을 받는 경우는 주로 관계대명사 that을 사용하지만, 선행사가 사람인 경우는 who도 사용된다.

Look at the boy and his cute puppy that are jogging in the park.

공원에서 조깅하고 있는 그 소년과 그의 귀여운 강아지를 봐라.

⇒ 선행사가 사람과 강아지(the boy and his cute puppy)이므로 관계대명사로 that이 왔다.

Words & Phrases

regardless of
~에 상관없이

political
[pəlítikəl]
정치적인

industrial
[indʌ́striəl]
산업의, 공업의

complex
[kɑ́mpleks]
공장단지, 복잡한

probably
[prɑ́bəbli]
아마도

animosity
[æ̀nəmɑ́səti]
반감, 적대감

Check-up

정답 및 해설 p.4

1. James is probably the only person whom / who thinks that I have any animosity towards him.

2. Harrisburg was the last town where / that was flooded with many miners.

EXERCISE

정답 및 해설 p.4

[01-10] **다음 중 어법상 가장 적절한 표현을 고르시오.**

01 You can learn other countries' cultures and customs in many different ways, [that / which] may be new to you.

02 The printing industry was not the only one [that / who] benefited from the invention of air conditioning.

03 Estrogen can raise levels of the stress hormone cortisol, [that / which] helps explain the higher rates of depression among women.

04 기출응용 The very technology [that / who] was supposed to free us from mass society has turned out to be as much a fishbowl as an information highway.

05 기출응용 The reason [that / which] we keep making the same error repeatedly is that associations form between the ideas in the chain of thoughts and become firmer each time they are used.

06 You must pay a security deposit equal to three weeks' rent, [that / which] is the standard practice for house rentals in this area.

07 Jack's wife was very intelligent, [which / who] was a source of great pride to him.

08 Look at the girl and the dog [that / which] are running together. They are so fast!

09 One of the students kept laughing, [that / which] annoyed Mr. Smith seriously.

10 Insulation provides basic protection against electric shock, [that / which] allows people to work safely.

ACTUAL TEST

정답 및 해설 p.4

01 다음 글의 밑줄 친 부분 중, 어법상 <u>어긋난</u> 것은?

Taipei is famous to travelers for many traditional Buddhist temples, which ① <u>makes</u> it not widely known for its modern architecture. But Taipei ② <u>does</u> have the very impressive L-shaped Taipei 101 Mall, at 508 meters, which is one of the world's tallest buildings. Recently, the building has become a symbol of Taipei's progress, identity, and vision. You can see the Grand Market in the basement. You then move up to the first floor ③ <u>which</u> a busy shopping mall begins, while the fourth floor, ④ <u>called</u> City Square, offers coffee shops with tables in a central plaza. On the fifth floor ⑤ <u>can you</u> buy tickets for the elevators to the observation deck. They are among the world's fastest, and in no time at all you are at the top of the building. Half a kilometer below, the scene glows orange-pink with city lights. Even after the sun sets, you can still recognize the outline of Taipei's surrounding mountains, blacker than the evening sky.

02  다음 (A), (B), (C)의 각 [ ] 안에서 어법에 맞는 표현으로 바르게 짝지어진 것은?

Because the harp has a wide range of sound, it sends vibrations through the body better than (A) [another / other] musical instruments. Research shows the harp's vibration stimulates the body's organs, which (B) [help / helps] the body's instinct for fighting disease. Sara J. Williams, physical therapist, found that people with a lot of neuromuscular disorders really benefited from the harp. Theories about the harp's effect (C) [is / are] not new. Traditionally called the instrument of a Greek god, or of the angels, the harp has long been an instrument of cure in Western culture.

	(A)		(B)		(C)
①	another	-	help	-	is
②	other	-	help	-	are
③	other	-	helps	-	are
④	other	-	helps	-	is
⑤	another	-	helps	-	is

UNIT 105

선행사가 없는 관계대명사 - what

They want to make sure that what they have to say to other people is true to their lives, too.

그들은 다른 사람들에게 말해야 하는 것이 자신들의 삶에 있어서도 진실이라고 확신하기를 원한다.

그들은 / 확신하기를 원한다 // 그들이 다른 사람들에게 말해야 하는 것이 /

They want to make sure that [what] they have to say to other people

that (X)

앞에 선행사가 없고 뒤에 say의 목적어가 없으므로 관계대명사 what이 온다.

진실이라고 / 그들의 삶에 있어서도

[is] true to their lives, too.

주어가 what절이므로 단수 취급하여 동사는 is가 온다.

Grammar Point

선행사를 포함하는 관계대명사 what

what은 선행사를 포함하는 관계대명사이기 때문에 다른 관계대명사와 달리 선행사가 없다. 〈what = the thing which〉라는 관계가 성립하므로 선행사가 있다면 what이 올 수 없다.

Egyptians were looking for something less dangerous to throw, and they developed [what] were the first balls. 기출응용

이집트인들은 던지기에 덜 위험한 것을 찾고 있었고, 최초의 공을 개발했다.

⇒ 앞에 선행사가 없으므로 what이 온다.

Words & Phrases

make sure
확신하다

apply
[əplái]
적용하다

practically
[prǽktikəli]
실용적으로

relay
[rìːléi]
전달하다, 중계 방송하다; 다시 두다

influence
[ínfluəns]
영향을 주다

Check-up

정답 및 해설 p.5

1. Having returned to the school I attended many years ago, my brain was flooded with images [that / what] I remembered from childhood.

2. A recent food research program relayed surprising news to the public about [what / that] exactly influences the food choices of adults.

UNIT

106 전치사 + 관계대명사

Cell phones are the most useful tool these days for which teenagers want to save money as much as possible.

오늘날 휴대 전화는 (그것을 사려고) 십대들이 가능한 한 많은 돈을 모으기를 원하는 대상이 되는 가장 유용한 도구이다.

휴대 전화는 / 가장 유용한 도구이다 / 오늘날 // 대상이 되는

Cell phones are the most useful tool these days **for which**

여기서 which가 없다면 for는 관계사절의 마지막에 위치해야 한다. 그렇지 않다면 어법상 틀린 부분이 된다.

십대들이 / 돈을 모으기를 원하는 / 가능한 한 많이

teenagers want to save money as much as possible.

Grammar Point

전치사+관계대명사

원래 전치사는 아래 두 번째 문장의 마지막에 있었다. 하지만 전치사는 혼자 있는 것을 싫어하는 특징이 있다. 따라서 아래 마지막 문장을 보면 전치사가 원래 명사가 변한 관계사를 따라서 온 것을 볼 수 있다.

Cell phones are the most useful tool these days.

휴대 전화는 오늘날 가장 유용한 도구이다.

+

Teenagers want to save money as much as possible **for** cell phones.

십대들은 휴대 전화를 (사기) 위해서 가능한 한 많은 돈을 모으기를 원한다.

=

Cell phones are the most useful tool these days **for which** teenagers want to save money as much as possible.

⇒ 〈전치사+관계사 = 관계부사〉의 관계가 성립하며, 뒤에는 완전한 문장이 온다.

Words & Phrases

useful [jú:sfəl] 유용한

save A for B B를 위해 A를 모으다

portrait [pɔ́:rtrit] 초상화

include [inklú:d] 포함하다

saint [seint] 성인

Check-up

정답 및 해설 p.5

1. The Dutch painter Rembrandt painted a portrait of St. Jerome [which / in which] he included eye glasses hanging from the saint's desk. 기출응용

2. The saying [which / for which] I had to find the meaning was: those who live in glass houses shouldn't throw stones.

EXERCISE

정답 및 해설 p.5

[01-10] 다음 중 어법상 가장 적절한 표현을 고르시오.

01 If you have behaved in some way [which / of which] you are not proud, we would be disappointed.

02 She kept large sketchbooks [which / into which] she could paste the results or enter new ideas.

03 They have something a little different, [which / in which] people are encouraged to be proud of their heritage.

04 기출응용 However you might define it, beauty extends far beyond the visual to [what /which] pleases other senses and even the mind.

05 Gaps in intellectual performance are usually much narrower than the disparity in grown-ups' height, [which / in which] the average man is taller than most women.

06 기출응용 The dictionary defines courage as a quality which enables one to pursue a right course of action, [which / through which] one may provoke disapproval, hostility, or contempt.

07 There were no tables or sofas—just two drawers filled with knee-high linoleum-covered platforms [which / on which] we were supposed to lie like hot dogs lined up on a grill.

08 기출응용 These containers, widely used in neighborhoods that lack full sewer networks, are settling tanks buried at shallow depths [which / in which] bacteria decompose the solid waste from household sewage.

09 기출응용 He established the basic laws for the establishment and extinction of [which / what] he called "conditional reflexes," like salivation, that only occurred conditionally upon specific previous experience.

10 Most of her friends thought that she had started behaving in a crazy way, but [that / what] she was really doing was fighting for her life.

ACTUAL TEST

정답 및 해설 p.5

01 다음 글의 밑줄 친 부분 중, 어법상 어긋난 것은?

Do you know why countries want to increase their productivity? Then, what is countries' productivity and how ① can we measure it? At the national level, productivity typically is gauged as the dollar value of output per unit of labor. Productivity measurement depends on the quality of the products and services ② generated in a nation, the rate ③ which goods are produced, and the amount produced, especially in relation to the time, money, and work ④ needed to produce them. National productivity is the major determinant of a nation's standard of living. If the value of yield per work hour rises, the nation benefits from overall high income levels, because employee wages depend on the productivity of human resources. On the other hand, declining productivity lowers the standard of living. Wage or price increases ⑤ not accompanied by productivity increases cause inflationary pressures rather than real increases in the standard of living.

02  다음 (A), (B), (C)의 각 [ ] 안에서 어법에 맞는 표현으로 바르게 짝지어진 것은?

Have you ever had a favorite author and found out later that author wrote books under a different name (A) [which / about which] you knew nothing? Pen names are an absolute necessity for authors who work in more than one genre. This is (B) [why / because] readers of one type of book may be disappointed if they pick up a novel by their favorite author that is entirely different. For a writer who writes in only one genre or very similar genres, however, a pen name can actually be harmful. A pen name (C) [makes / makes it] far more difficult for readers to find the writer. If the genres an author writes in complement each other, such as mystery and thriller, assuming a pen name will only cause him to lose half of his potential readership.

	(A)		(B)		(C)
①	which	-	why	-	makes
②	about which	-	why	-	makes it
③	about which	-	why	-	makes
④	about which	-	because	-	makes it
⑤	which	-	because	-	makes it

UNIT 107

that을 못 쓰는 경우 (1)

Hope, which seems like the thinnest little thread, is an incredibly powerful force leading us from the most horrible problems into a bright new day. Hang on to hope. 기출응용

가장 가늘고 작은 실낱 같은 희망은 우리를 가장 끔찍한 문제로부터 밝은 새날로 이끄는 믿을 수 없을 만큼 강한 힘이다. 희망을 가져라.

희망 // 그것은 / 가장 가늘고 작은 실과 같고 // 이다 / 믿을 수 없을 만큼

Hope, which seems like the thinnest little thread, is an incredibly

that (X)

콤마 뒤에 위치하므로 that은 올 수 없다.

강한 힘 // 우리를 이끄는 / 가장 끔찍한 문제로부터 /

powerful force leading us from the most horrible problems

밝은 새날로 // 희망을 가져라

into a bright new day. Hang on to hope.

Grammar Point

콤마 뒤에 관계대명사 that은 사용 불가

관계대명사 that은 계속적 용법으로 쓰지 못한다. 즉, 콤마 뒤에 올 수 없다.

After mating, [that / which] always takes place in flight, a drone immediately dies.

짝짓기는 항상 비행 중에 이루어 지는데, 수벌은 짝짓기 이후에 바로 죽는다.

⇒ ", (콤마)"가 있는 계속적 용법의 관계대명사절이므로 that은 사용할 수 없다. 따라서 which가 정답이다.

They gradually realize, however, that others are not really interested in them. (O)

하지만 그들은 점차 다른 사람들이 정말로 그것들에 관심이 없다는 것을 깨닫는다.

⇒ that 앞에 콤마가 왔지만, 이 문장의 콤마는 계속적 용법을 의미하는 것이 아니고, however가 삽입구임을 나타내주는 표시이다. 이 외에도 that이 관계대명사가 아닌 경우 콤마 뒤에 올 수 있다.

Words & Phrases

thread [θred] 실

incredibly [Inkredəbli] 믿을 수 없는

horrible [hɔ́(:)rəbl] 끔찍한

hang on ~을 꽉 붙잡다

drone [droun] 꿀벌의 수벌

committee [kəmíti] 위원회

unanimously [ju:nǽnəməsli] 만장일치로

Check-up

정답 및 해설 p.6

1. The groom usually wears a tuxedo, that / which is commonly rented just for his wedding day. 기출응용

2. The members of the committee, which / that has been advancing a plan to introduce a jury trial system here, agreed unanimously on it on Monday.

UNIT **108**

that을 못 쓰는 경우 (2)

Her mother moved with her to Chicago and married a man by whom she was adopted, and she changed her name to Ann Jones.

그녀의 어머니는 그녀와 함께 시카고로 이사를 가서 그녀를 입양했던 남자와 결혼했고 그녀는 자신의 이름을 앤 존스로 바꾸었다.

그녀의 어머니는 그녀와 함께 시카고로 이사했고 / 남자와 결혼했다 //

Her mother moved with her to Chicago and married a man

그녀가 입양 되었던 // 그리고 / 그녀는 자신의 이름을 앤 존스로 바꾸었다

by whom she was adopted, and she changed her name to Ann Jones.

by that (X)

전치사의 목적어 자리이므로 that은 불가.
선행사가 사람이므로 whom이 온다.

Grammar Point

전치사 바로 뒤에 관계대명사 that은 사용 불가

관계대명사 that은 전치사 바로 뒤에서 전치사의 목적어로 쓸 수 없으므로 전치사 바로 뒤에는 whom이나 which가 온다. 단, 전치사와 관계대명사가 떨어져 있는 경우는 전치사의 목적어로 쓸 수 있다.

The Rosetta Stone is a large stone on [which / that] there are three written messages. 기출응용

로제타석은 세 개의 서면 메시지가 있는 커다란 돌이다.

⇒ 앞에 전치사 on이 왔으므로 that은 올 수 없다. 따라서 which가 정답이다. 전치사와 관계대명사가 떨어져 있는 경우는 that을 쓸 수 있으므로 The Rosetta Stone is a large stone that there are three written messages on.이라는 문장은 가능하다.

Cross-pollination is important in that it can lead to variation between the members of its species.

타가 수분은 그 종(種)의 구성원들 간의 다양성을 이끌 수 있다는 점에서 중요하다.

⇒ in that은 '~라는 점에서, ~때문에'라는 의미의 접속사이다.

Words & Phrases

adopt [ədάpt] 입양하다, 채택하다

pollination [pὰlənéiʃən] 수분

variation [vὲəriéiʃən] 다양성

species [spíːʃiːz] 종

abuse [əbjúːs] 학대, (약물 등의) 남용

victim [víktim] 희생자

Check-up 정답 및 해설 p.6

1. People built several houses in [which / that] termites live.
2. The child abuse is done by someone to [whom / that] the victim is close, such as her family, relatives, or a friend of her father.

EXERCISE

정답 및 해설 p.6

[01-10] 다음 중 어법상 가장 적절한 표현을 고르시오.

01 Many scholars made a conclusion that was wrong in [which / that] their premises in the situation were based on the false experiment.

02 WBCs are one of the two kinds of viruses on [which / that] molecular biologists depend when performing gene-transplant experiments.

03 On the east, England is bounded by the North Sea, [which / that] is really nothing but an old depression that has gradually run full of water.

04 This expression shows the general public's disapproval of the vandal who feels he must mark or ruin the appearance of [that / what] belongs to everyone.

05 기출응용 The urbanization of Britain improved the nation's economy in [that / which] it moved workers from regions with low-productivity work to factories with high-productivity work.

06 Just 40 years after the first high-rise building was constructed, many buildings were put up [that / what] rose 100 stories high.

07 One of my friends is from a country, called The Land of the Rising Sun, [that / who] is famous for high technology.

08 The company established the huge shopping center of [that / which] we could be proud.

09 Jenny tore and burnt the letter in [that / which] it could be proof of Jack's cheating.

10 기출응용 Every clan represented in a village has a clanhouse in [that / which] the masks and other sacred items used in the ceremonies are kept when not in use.

ACTUAL TEST

정답 및 해설 p.6

01 다음 글의 밑줄 친 부분 중, 어법상 어긋난 것은?

① What we keep in our mind at second is more complicated than at first. This is related to the strategy and tactics that a company seeks in order to reach its own goals. It is survival that a normal company must achieve first. Of course, not every company ② does have such a goal. For instance, a company designed to perform a task and then end its activities ③ has the survival goal right after a deadline. As expected, most of them could make it. This means that a company performs an internal or external activity if it guarantees an appropriate rise in profit, or cuts down expenses, ④ that are the greatest threat for survival. To issue revenues from one activity can encourage the company to find another profit model for next survival. That is ⑤ why it struggles to cultivate new markets.

02 다음 (A), (B), (C)의 각 [ ] 안에서 어법에 맞는 표현으로 바르게 짝지어진 것은?

In early food production, the way of producing food developed step by step. Not all the necessary techniques were developed within a short time, and not all the wild plants and animals eventually domesticated in a given area (A) [was / were] domesticated at the same time. Even in a hunting-gathering lifestyle, it took thousands of years to move from complete dependence on wild foods to a diet with very few wild foods. Why this transition was gradual (B) [is / to be] that food-production systems evolved as a result of the accumulation of how to allocate time and effort. Foraging humans like foraging animals have finite time and energy, (C) [that / which] they can spend in various ways. Human and animal foragers are constantly making effort-allocation decisions, even if only unconsciously. They concentrate first on favorite foods, or ones that promise the highest payoff. If these are unavailable, they move to less and less preferred foods.

	(A)		(B)		(C)
①	was	-	is	-	that
②	were	-	is	-	which
③	was	-	is	-	which
④	were	-	to be	-	which
⑤	was	-	to be	-	that

UNIT 109

what vs. that

What people see, when they write, can affect the way they think and live.

사람들이 글을 쓸 때 보는 것은 그들이 생각하고 살아가는 방식에 영향을 줄 수 있다.

사람들이 보는 것은 // 그들이 글을 쓸 때 // 영향을 줄 수 있다 / 방식에 //

[What] people see, when they write, can affect [the way]

That (X)

see의 목적어가 없으므로 what이 와야 한다.

the way 뒤에 that 생략

그들이 생각하고 살아가는

[they think and live].

Grammar Point

what vs. that

1. what은 선행사를 포함한 관계대명사이고, '~하는 것'이라고 해석한다.

2. what과 that 중에서 답을 골라야 하는 경우, 앞에 선행사가 없으면서 뒤에 주어나 목적어가 없는 불완전한 문장이 오면 what이, 앞에 선행사가 있거나, 뒤에 완전한 문장이 오면 that이 답이다.

I don't know [what / that] happened to them in the garage.

나는 차고에서 그들에게 무슨 일이 있었는지 모른다.

⇒ 관계대명사 앞에 선행사가 없고, happened의 주어가 없으므로 what이 정답이다.

Words & Phrases

affect [əfékt] 영향을 주다

explain [ikspléin] 설명하다

several times 여러 번

widely [wáidli] 널리

explanation [èksplənéiʃən] 설명

political [pəlítikəl] 정치적인

organization [ɔ̀ːrgənizéiʃən] 조직, 단체

Check-up

정답 및 해설 p.7

1. Although it had been explained to him several times, he still could not see [what / that] the problem was.

2. The most widely accepted explanation is [that / what] O.K. originally stood for the Old Kinderhook Club, a New York political organization of the 1840s.

UNIT

110 what vs. which

As a buyer of those products, you will sometimes need to communicate with a producer when it comes to the quality of what you have bought.

그 상품들의 구매자로서 당신은 구입한 것의 품질에 관하여 생산자와 때때로 의사소통이 필요할 것이다.

그 상품들의 구매자로서 // 당신은 때때로 필요할 것이다 /

As a buyer of those products, you will sometimes need

~로서 * as의 용법 2번 문형 참조

생산자와 의사소통하는 것이 // 품질에 관하여 //

to communicate with a producer when it comes to the quality

~관하여
= about, regarding, as to, when it comes to -ing, in regard to, relative to

여러분이 구입했던 것의

of what you have bought.

which (X)

Grammar Point

what vs. which

〈명사+전치사+관계대명사〉 구조는 대개 which와 what의 대결이다. 앞에 나온 명사가 선행사인지 아닌지 구분하려면 〈명사+전치사〉를 〈전치사+명사〉로 바꿔 문장 뒤로 보내고 말이 되는지 보면 된다. 말이 되면 which가, 어색하면 what이 정답이다.

(X)~ you have bought of quality ~

⇒ '당신이 구입한 것의 품질'이라는 뜻이지, '품질을 구입(?)하다'라는 뜻이 아니므로 the quality는 선행사가 아니다. 따라서 what이 적절하다.

I'd need a very special notebook in [what / which] I can write.

나는 글을 쓸 매우 특별한 공책이 필요하다.

⇒ '내가 글을 쓸 공책'이라는 뜻이므로 I can write in a notebook 정도가 된다. 따라서 which가 적절하다.

Words & Phrases

survivor [sərváivər] 생존자

plane crash 비행기 사고

taste [teist] 맛보다

Check-up

정답 및 해설 p.7

1. There were no survivors from the plane crash, and officials say there is no explanation of [which / what] caused it.
2. There will be opportunities to taste some traditional foods from the region for [which / what] the town is famous.

EXERCISE

정답 및 해설 p.7

[01-10] 다음 중 어법상 가장 적절한 표현을 고르시오.

01 기출응용 I've heard stories of sadness and delight [which / what] would be better than those of well-known TV programs.

02 기출응용 I traded keys with her and told her to drive my car home, while explaining [that / what] I would bring her car home after my class.

03 Those who sleep next to heavy snorers wake up more than ten times per hour, [what / which] seriously reduces the quality and quantity of their sleep.

04 One essential distinction between manufacturing and services is [that / what] the latter cannot make inventories to buffer demand uncertainties.

05 기출응용 They discovered that people who were given popularity rankings were more likely to select [that / what] the website claimed were favorite choices.

06 Conveyed by birds and winds, the seeds of the redwood moved thousands of miles from [which / what] is now the northernmost tip of England to Russia.

07 기출응용 Perhaps [that / what] chatters like best about socializing online is the ability to block unwanted advances from anyone they dislike.

08 Reading for pleasure is different from the reading [that / what] you do for research.

09 Researchers at New York University show [that / what] the more costly areas and institutions furnish a lot more tests, services and intensive hospital-based care than the lower cost centers.

10 This program is intended to help students to realize [that / what] they're passionate about, and to learn how to put themselves into it practically.

ACTUAL TEST

정답 및 해설 p.7

01 다음 글의 밑줄 친 부분 중, 어법상 어긋난 것은?

Dr. Denma Naoki has been a ① highly respected professor in the Department of Education for the past 10 years. He has published many articles and has always been given remarkable teaching evaluations by his students. Some months ago, he won a prize for a paper he wrote. He ② was rewarded with several thousand dollars, and his latest economic writings appeared in a journal. Now university officials have discovered ③ what Dr. Denma copied 5 paragraphs of his article word-for-word from a paper a student ④ had written as a master's thesis. Dr. Denma did not give this student credit as the source of his information. He apologized and promised this ⑤ would never happen again.

02 다음 (A), (B), (C)의 각 [ ] 안에서 어법에 맞는 표현으로 바르게 짝지어진 것은?

There needs to be some limitation to (A) [that / what] students can wear to school. Without a dress code, students could wear any clothing that is offensive, inappropriate, distracting, or threatening. Clothing with offensive slogans and pictures that promote drugs, alcohol and smoking should not be allowed. Pictures and slogans which are offensive to race and gender should not be allowed, (B) [too / either]. Clothing with distracting pictures or writing could take students' attention away from studying, which is why they are there. Clothing with messages, writing or pictures that are threatening to students or teachers shouldn't be worn. Being in a school with no dress code would be very bad. A dress code should be made, (C) [taken / taking] into consideration anyone who studies and works in the school.

	(A)		(B)		(C)
①	that	-	too	-	taken
②	what	-	either	-	taken
③	that	-	either	-	taking
④	what	-	either	-	taking
⑤	what	-	too	-	taken

UNIT 111

what vs. whatever

As you say, whatever the machine does, it's just working according to the material circumstances.

당신이 말한 대로 기계가 무엇을 하든지 간에 그것은 단지 물리적인 환경에 따라 작동하고 있을 뿐이다.

당신이 말한 대로 // 그 기계가 무엇을 하든지 간에 // 그것은 단지 작동하고 있을 뿐이다 /

As you say, whatever the machine does, it's just working

what (X)

뒤에 문장 it's just ~가 나온다. what은 부사절을 이끄는 접속사 역할을 하지 못하므로 whatever가 옳다.

물리적인 환경에 따라서

according to the material circumstances.

Grammar Point

what vs. whatever

what은 '~하는 것'이라는 뜻의 관계대명사나 '어떤'이라는 뜻의 의문사로 사용된다. what은 주어, 목적어, 보어 자리에 올 수 있지만, 부사절을 이끌 수는 없다. 반면, whatever는 '~하는 무엇이든'과 '아무리 ~ 이더라도'의 두 가지 의미를 가지는데, 후자의 경우 부사절을 이끄는 접속사의 역할도 한다.

what		whatever
What절 + 동사	Whatever절 + 동사	
동사 + what절	동사 + whatever절	
What절, 주어+동사 (X)	Whatever절, 주어+동사 (O)	

[What / Whatever] she had done in the workshop, she developed an itchy rash all over her body and her eyes were left streaming.

그녀가 워크숍에서 무엇을 했든지 간에, 온몸에 가려운 발진이 일었고, 눈에서는 눈물이 흘렀다.

⇒ 뒤에 'she developed ~'라는 문장이 접속사 없이 나오므로 부사절을 이끌 수 있는 whatever가 정답이다.

Words & Phrases

material [mətí(:)əriəl] 물질적인, 물리적인

itchy [ítʃi] 가려운

rash [ræʃ] 발진

ancestor [ǽnsestər] 조상

destination [dèstənéiʃən] 목적지

Check-up

정답 및 해설 p.8

1. What / Whatever your family name is, we can know something about your ancestors and their jobs.

2. What / Whatever the coming discussion between the two might be, it is obviously an important matter in their destination.

UNIT

112 부정대명사 + of + 관계사

There are other methods, some of which are now considered to have little scientific value.

다른 방법들이 있는데, 그 중 일부는 현재 과학적 가치가 거의 없다고 여겨진다.

다른 방법들이 있다 // 그들 중 일부는 / 현재 여겨진다 /

There are other methods, some of which are now considered

some of them (X)

〈절+절〉 구조인데 절을 연결하는 접속사가 없으므로 관계대명사가 필요하다.

과학적 가치가 거의 없다고

to have little scientific value.

Grammar Point

부정대명사+of+관계대명사

〈부정대명사+of+관계대명사〉는 〈접속사+대명사〉의 역할을 한다.

They offered us much information, most of which was very useful.

그들은 우리에게 많은 정보를 주었는데, 그것 중 대부분은 매우 유용했다.

= They offered us much information, and most of the information was very useful.

cf.) 접속사나 관계대명사 없이 〈절+절〉의 구조가 되지 않도록 주의해야 한다. 접속사가 있다면 of 뒤에 대명사가, 없다면 관계대명사가 온다.

They offered us much information, most of them was very useful. (X)

Words & Phrases

method
[méθəd]
방법

value
[vælju:]
가치

appearance
[əpí(:)ərəns]
출정; 외모, 외향

Check-up

정답 및 해설 p.8

1. The train was met by a crowd of five hundred people, some of them / whom had been waiting for more than three hours.
2. He scored seven goals in 80 appearances for Chelsea, all of them / which came in his final season.

EXERCISE

정답 및 해설 p.8

[01-10] 다음 중 어법상 가장 적절한 표현을 고르시오.

01 [Who / Whoever] wants to govern in this state has to appeal to different ethnic groups to win election.

02 기출응용 Rain and melted snow flow into dozens of lakes, four of [which / them] are considered sacred by local people.

03 The auditorium was so jammed that students were packed in like sardines, and some of [them / which] had to sit on the floor.

04 기출응용 Logic has an extensive and well-defined set of rules and guidelines, many of [them / which] are all too easy to unintentionally violate.

05 While there are many ways to be rich and powerful in the world, some of [them / which] can lead one to be on the brink of ruin.

06 기출응용 More prolonged levels of cortisol in the bloodstream have negative effects, the very one of [them / which] is to increase abdominal fat.

07 In our modern society, in which knowledge itself is power, [who / whoever] is good at obtaining information is likely to succeed in life.

08 Reputable grading services enjoy the respect of a large number of coin dealers and collectors, some of [them / whom] are accepted blindly.

09 If the present administration is going to help subsidize coverage for millions of uninsured people, it will need to discover significant savings in Medicare spending, at least some of [which / them] should come from reducing over-treatment.

10 기출응용 There are other equally important considerations, [neglect of them / neglect of which] may produce frustration in later years.

ACTUAL TEST

정답 및 해설 p.8

01 다음 글의 밑줄 친 부분 중, 어법상 <u>어긋난</u> 것은?

For warehousing and distribution operations, transportation costs and proximity to markets are very essential. With a warehouse nearby, many companies can hold inventory ① <u>closer</u> to the client, thus reducing promotion sales and delivery time. For instance, Dixie Works of Galveston, Texas, gained a competitive edge in the distribution of home health care items by ② <u>decentralizing</u> inventory into 32 warehouses across the country. Dixie sells hospital beds, wheelchairs, and other patient aids, some of ③ <u>them</u> it buys from other companies, to small dealers who sell to clients. Formerly, the dealers had to wait three weeks for delivery, which meant that a lot of their cash ④ <u>was</u> tied up in inventory surplus. With Dixie's new distribution network, the dealers get daily delivery of products from one company. Dixie's location strategy indicates ⑤ <u>how</u> proper delivery can be a competitive advantage.

02 기출응용

다음 (A), (B), (C)의 각 [ ] 안에서 어법에 맞는 표현으로 바르게 짝지어진 것은?

Malagasy is spoken in the island nation of Madagascar located off the southeastern coast of Africa. Its 15 million speakers include virtually all of the country's population. It would be logical to assume that Malagasy (A) [belongs / is belonged] to one of the African language families. That is not the case, though. It is actually one of the Austronesian languages, the rest of (B) [them / which] are used thousands of kilometers to the east, mainly in Southeast Asia. Malagasy is most closely related to a group of languages (C) [speaking / spoken by] the Dayak people on the island of Borneo in Southeast Asia.

	(A)		(B)		(C)
①	belongs	-	them	-	speaking
②	belongs	-	which	-	speaking
③	belongs	-	which	-	spoken by
④	is belonged	-	which	-	speaking
⑤	is belonged	-	them	-	spoken by

UNIT

113 선행사와 떨어져 있는 관계대명사

The day will surely come when my words will come true and you will regret not believing me.

내 말이 실현되고 네가 나를 믿지 못한 것을 후회할 그날이 반드시 올 것이다.

그날이 / 반드시 올 것이다 // 내 말이 실현되고 /
The day will surely come when my words will come true and

후회할 것이다 / 나를 믿지 못한 것을
you will regret not believing me. → when 이하는 The day를 수식하는 관계부사절이다.
cf.) 시간 부사절(~할 때)에서는 현재 시제가 미래 시제를 대신하므로 will이 나올 수 없다.

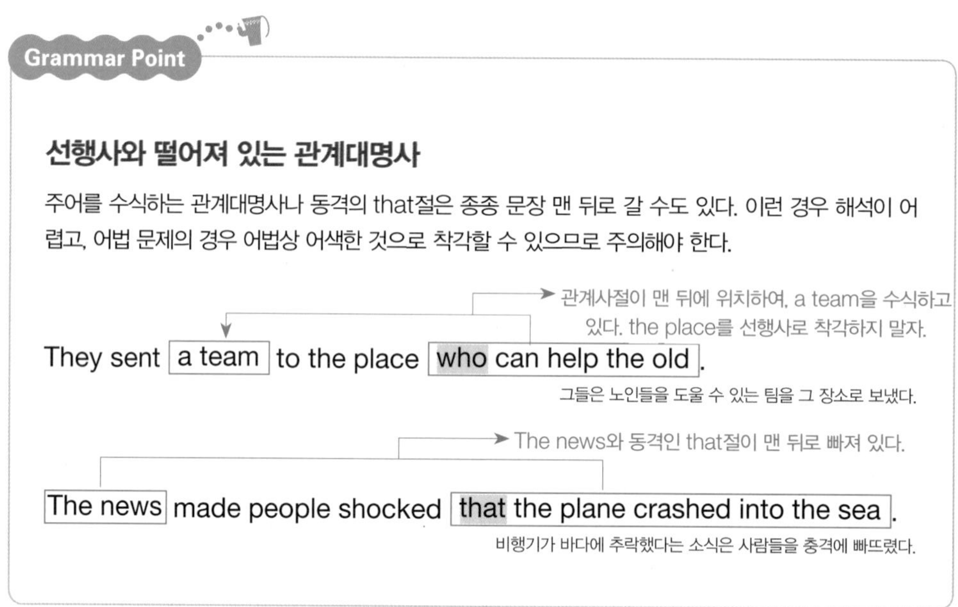

Grammar Point

선행사와 떨어져 있는 관계대명사

주어를 수식하는 관계대명사나 동격의 that절은 종종 문장 맨 뒤로 갈 수도 있다. 이런 경우 해석이 어렵고, 어법 문제의 경우 어법상 어색한 것으로 착각할 수 있으므로 주의해야 한다.

→ 관계사절이 맨 뒤에 위치하여, a team을 수식하고 있다. the place를 선행사로 착각하지 말자.

They sent a team to the place who can help the old.

그들은 노인들을 도울 수 있는 팀을 그 장소로 보냈다.

→ The news와 동격인 that절이 맨 뒤로 빠져 있다.

The news made people shocked that the plane crashed into the sea.

비행기가 바다에 추락했다는 소식은 사람들을 충격에 빠뜨렸다.

Words & Phrases

come true
실현되다

regret
[rigrét]
후회하다, 유감스러워 하다

analyze
[ǽnəlàiz]
분석하다

performance
[pərfɔ́ːrməns]
성취, 성과, (과제 등의) 수행

graceful
[gréisfəl]
우아한

Check-up

정답 및 해설 p.9

1. The research analyzes the performance of students in 15 states [who / which] were in grades one to three during the 2007-8 and 2009-10 school years.
2. Expecting the graceful curves, woody heights, and reflected images along the river [that / what] I remembered from my childhood, I was thrilled at boarding. 기출응용

UNIT
114 관계부사 where

One field where astrology has not been accepted is the academic one, and that is still in progress.

점성학이 받아들여지지 않은 한 분야는 학계이고, 그것은 여전히 그렇다.

한 분야는 // 점성학이 받아들여지지 않은 //

One field | where astrology has not been accepted

주어가 형용사절(관계사절, 분사, 형용사)의 수식을 받을 때 동사의 형태에 주의한다.

동사와 동사가 만나는 지점이 바로 본동사가 있는 장소이다.

학계이며 / 그것은 여전히 진행 중이다

is | the academic one, and that is still in progress.

are (X)

Grammar Point

관계부사 where

앞의 선행사가 장소이고, 뒤에 나오는 문장이 완전한 문장이면 관계부사 where를 쓴다.

where vs. which	
+ 완전한 문장 This is the house [where] she lived. 이것은 그녀가 살았던 집이다. ⇒ 그녀가 살았다: 완전한 문장	+ 불완전한 문장 This is the house [which] she bought. 이것은 그녀가 구입했던 집이다. ⇒ 그녀가 ~을 샀다: 불완전한 문장
+ 수동태 문장 This is the church [where] her great grandparents were buried. 이곳이 그녀의 조부모가 묻혀 있는 교회이다. ⇒ 수동태 문장은 뒤에 주어가 없는 경우를 제외하고, 뒤에 목적어가 없더라도 완전한 문장이다.	전치사 + This is the house [in] [which] she lived. 이 집은 그녀가 살았던 집이다. ⇒ 전치사(in)+관계대명사(which) = 관계부사(where)

Words & Phrases

astrology [əstrálədʒi] 점성학[술]

accept [əksépt] 받아들이다

academic [ӕkədémik] 학계, 학술

in progress 진행 중인

infant [ínfənt] 유아

eye [ai] ~을 주시하다, ~을 눈여겨보다

favorite [féivərit] 우승 후보, 인기 선수

Check-up

정답 및 해설 p.9

1. SIDS is less common in cultures [which / where] infants and parents sleep in the same bed, suggesting that sleeping position may be important.

2. Kim is eyeing the gold at next month's World Championship, [which / where] she is one of the favorites to win.

EXERCISE

정답 및 해설 p.9

[01-10] **다음 중 어법상 가장 적절한 표현을 고르시오.**

01 A young boy appeared at the place [which / where] the sword was plugged in.

02 At one point, Nielsen wrote that Antarctica was a blank slate on [which / where] you could write your soul.

03 There are three main reasons [which / why] pleasure reading is such an effective way to improve your English.

04 기출응용 Sunin's troops retreated, luring We's army into a narrow pass, [which / where] they ambushed and destroyed them.

05 It is a moment of both youthful optimism and expectation that imagines a future [which / where] once-impossible dreams come true.

06 It's not easy for them to organize dances [which / where] the aged can practice their skills.

07 In the southern Indian state of Kerala [which / where] literacy is almost universal, the infant death rate is the lowest in the developing world.

08 Visitors will find 260 guest rooms decorated with Ralph Lauren fabrics and the Piano Bar restaurant [which / where] you'll hear jazz along with old Irish standards.

09 기출응용 In 1762, this island was taken by the English, [who / where] gave it back the following year to the French by the Peace of Paris.

10 We cannot be optimistic about the prospects for intensive agriculture in the tropics, [which / where] the soils will not, with present technology, support intensive agriculture.

ACTUAL TEST

정답 및 해설 p.9

01 다음 글의 밑줄 친 부분 중, 어법상 어긋난 것은?

Politicians have a clear sense of purpose. It would be good to think that political leaders are looking out for the welfare of society as a whole and ① that they are aiming for an optimal combination of efficiency and equity. This saying must be nice to us, but it is not realistic. Selfishness is as ② powerful a motive for political persons as for others. Some politicians are ③ inspired by a desire for reelection and are willing to sacrifice the national interest when doing that ④ strengthens their effect on voters. Other politicians are motivated by simple greed. If you doubt this fact, you should look at poor countries, ⑤ which corruption among government officials is a common obstacle to economic growth.

02 

다음 (A), (B), (C)의 각 [   ] 안에서 어법에 맞는 표현으로 바르게 짝지어진 것은?

Imagine a woman working contentedly at an interesting job for $40,000 a year. A new job opportunity arises (A) [that / what] offers her $60,000. She switches jobs, but, alas, after 6 months, the new company goes under. The old company is happy to take her back, so happy, in fact, that it raises her salary to $45,000. Is she happy with the raise? Will it even feel like a raise? The answer is probably "No." The $60,000 salary, (B) [however / whatever] briefly it was available, may establish a new baseline for her, so that anything less is taken as a loss. Though six months earlier, a raise from $40,000 to $45,000 would have felt (C) [wonderful / wonderfully], now it feels like a cut from $60,000 to $45,000. What was once good enough, or even better than that, isn't good enough any more.

	(A)		(B)		(C)
①	that	-	however	-	wonderful
②	what	-	however	-	wonderfully
③	what	-	however	-	wonderful
④	what	-	whatever	-	wonderfully
⑤	that	-	whatever	-	wonderful

UNIT 115

관계대명사 vs. 대명사

These things are demonstrated well enough in several other publications, some of which I have already pointed out.

이것들은 몇몇 다른 출판물에 충분히 잘 설명되어 있으며 그중 일부는 내가 이미 지적했던 것들이다.

이런 것들은 / 충분히 잘 설명되어 있다 /
These things are demonstrated well enough

몇몇 다른 출판물에 / 그리고 그중 일부는 / 내가 이미 /
in several other publications, some of which I have already

which — thom (X)

〈절 + 절〉 구조이지만 절 사이에 접속사가 없으므로 관계대명사 which가 왔다.

지적했다
pointed out.

Grammar Point

관계대명사 vs. 대명사

관계대명사와 대명사 중 고르는 문제는 접속사의 유무로 판단하면 된다. 관계대명사와 접속사는 상극이므로 서로 어울리지 못한다. 따라서 접속사가 있다면 대명사가 정답이다.

There are various types of trains, and some of [which / them] are not documented on the official web site.

다양한 형태의 기차가 있고 그들 중 일부는 공식 웹사이트에 기록되어 있지 않다.

⇒ 접속사 and가 있으므로 관계대명사 which는 올 수 없다. 따라서 대명사 them이 온다.

Words & Phrases

demonstrate [démənstrèit] 설명하다, 시위하다

publication [pʌ̀bləkéiʃən] 출판물, 출판, 발표

point out 지적하다

subcontract [sʌ̀bkɑ́ntrækt] 하도급을 받다

answerable [ǽnsərəbl] 대답 가능한

Check-up

정답 및 해설 p.10

1. It is said that the system is too complicated and associated with too many companies, and some of them / which were subcontracted.
2. You'd likely have more questions, 70% of them / which might be answerable by folks here.

UNIT 116

종속절의 주어가 관계대명사인 경우

In his culture, it is polite to wait until the third or fourth offer, which he knows will come.

그의 문화에서는 세 번째나 네 번째 제안까지 기다리는 것이 예의인데, 그는 (세 번째, 네 번째) 제안이 있을 것을 안다.

그의 문화에서는 / 기다리는 것이 예의이다 / 세 번째나 네 번째 제안까지 //
In his culture, it is polite to wait until the third or fourth offer,

will come의 주어이다

he knows that the third or fourth offer will come 구문이지만, 선행사가 the third or fourth offer이므로 주격 관계대명사가 선행사 가까이 있기 위해 he knows 앞으로 나갔다.

그는 (제안이) 올 거라는 것을 안다
which he knows will come.

Grammar Point

종속절의 주어가 관계대명사인 경우

두 문장을 관계대명사로 연결할 때, 선행사가 두 번째 문장의 종속절의 주어와 일치하는 경우, 선행사 가까이 위치하기 위해 관계대명사가 주절 앞으로 나가기도 한다. 이때, 해석과 수 일치에 주의해야 한다.

Winchester has written several books about women.
윈체스터는 여성들에 대한 책을 몇 권 썼다.

+

He found that women are not interested in what their husbands are doing.
그는 남편이 하는 일에 관심이 없는 여성들을 찾았다.

⇩

Winchester has written several books about women who he found are not interested in what their husbands are doing.
윈체스터는 자신이 찾은 남편이 하는 일에 관심이 없는 여성에 대한 책을 몇 권 썼다.

⇒ 얼핏 보면 are의 주어가 없는 것처럼 보이지만, women이 선행사이고, who가 주격 관계대명사이다. he founds를 가려보면 주어와 동사를 쉽게 찾을 수 있다.

Words & Phrases

claim [kleim] 주장하다

belong to ~소유(것)이다

saint [seint] 성자

Check-up

정답 및 해설 p.10

1. In 1425, at the age of thirteen, Martin claimed to hear voices [whom / that] he believed belonged to the early Christian saints.
2. He didn't pay the cost, [which / what] he guessed would be about $5.

EXERCISE

정답 및 해설 p.10

[01-10] **다음 중 어법상 가장 적절한 표현을 고르시오.**

01 Jack is the only one of the boys [who / whom], as you know, is not eligible.

02 The seminar, [which / whose] I think is scheduled to take place next week, has now been postponed until the end of next month.

03 MAC has branches in 20 countries and employs 100,000 people, most of [them / whom] live outside major metropolitan areas.

04 The dialogue between the two men was full of pointless rhetoric, and both of [them / whom] knew nothing about the topic at hand.

05 Who looked at a white mass [that / where] he thought was the great white whale?

06 Our understanding of the past is mostly based on written records, and all of [them / which] must be interpreted by many experts.

07 Mrs. Porter began making little bears and dogs, among [them / which] the bears became a big hit in America.

08 I read various science fiction books such as *Tarzan of the Apes* and *At the Earth's Core*, all of [them / which] were written by Edgar Rice.

09 Besides humor and love, the musical provides other themes, and one of [them / which] is to listen to your own voice.

10 WHO reported that there were 7.1 million cases leading to approximately 100,000 deaths last year, most of [them / which] took place in underdeveloped countries.

ACTUAL TEST

정답 및 해설 p.10

01 **다음 글의 밑줄 친 부분 중, 어법상 어긋난 것은?**

Most directors make at least some changes to the originals in order to make them more ① appropriate to today's society. While this means that some of the originals' meaning may ② be lost, the final result could be more effective ③ because of the omission of those elements which are unfamiliar to a modern audience. Yet this gives the director more range to add his own interpretation of the play, which could distort the originally intended meanings and effects. Though much of the original script ④ is preserved in Paolo Pasolini's *Oedipus Rex*, many changes are made, ⑤ it changes the original meaning and adds meanings which are specific to his own experiences.

02  **다음 (A), (B), (C)의 각 [ ] 안에서 어법에 맞는 표현으로 바르게 짝지어진 것은?**

Often in social scientific practice, even (A) [which / where] evidence is used, it is not used in the correct way for adequate scientific testing. In much of social science, evidence is used only to affirm a particular theory — to search for the positive instances (B) [that / what] uphold it. But these are easy to find and lead to the familiar dilemma in the social sciences where we have two conflicting theories, each of (C) [them / which] can claim positive empirical evidence in its support but which come to opposite conclusions. How should we decide between them? Here the scientific use of evidence may help. For what is distinctive about science is the search for negative instances — the search for ways to falsify a theory, rather than to confirm it. The real power of scientific testability is negative, not positive. Testing allows us not merely to confirm our theories but to weed out those that do not fit the evidence.

	(A)		(B)		(C)
①	which	-	what	-	them
②	which	-	that	-	them
③	where	-	what	-	which
④	where	-	that	-	which
⑤	where	-	what	-	them

REVIEW TEST

정답 및 해설 p.11

[01-05] 다음 문장 중 어법상 틀린 부분을 고쳐 쓰시오.

01 In the specific circumstance which a man was talking to a woman, the men laughed 10 percent less than their partners.

02 기출응용 This is the guy whom 1988 book *A Brief History of Time* proved the biggest unread bestseller of all time.

03 It's a relatively novel and youth-oriented phenomenon in Vietnam, which consumerism has launched only as the country has shifted from central planning to capitalism and begun to grow.

04 The common trait of an inference is what it is a declaration about matters which are not directly known.

05 The research team asked the English students to read a collection of German sentences, some of them contained words that look similar and have the same meanings in both languages.

[06-10] 다음 빈칸에 들어갈 알맞은 말을 보기에서 골라 알맞은 형태로 쓰시오.

보기	where	what	which	them	whose

06 If I assign fifty students a five-page essay on the subject of why the Roman Empire fell, most of __________ are likely to say it was a combination of economic and social causes ultimately leading to a weakening of the frontiers.

07 The Manchester United man revealed his class in __________ will be his final tournament on the international stage.

08 기출응용 People do their best to create enjoyable and protective environments __________ children feel comfortable and safe.

09 The professor made inquiries __________ answers confirmed the guess that the first group was warm and the second cold.

10 The excavations uncovered that there are at least 20 installations, __________ in archeological terms can be called temples.

FINAL CHECK

정답 및 해설 p.11

01 **다음 글의 밑줄 친 부분 중, 어법상 어긋난 것은?**

Research has revealed ① why mammoths became extinct 21,000 years ago. To date, people have believed that mammoths, which were relatives of elephants, died out because they ② were hunted to extinction. According to this research led by the UK's Durham University, they ran out of grass, ③ which resulted from global warming. As the Earth became warmer, the mammoths lost lands on which to graze. The study warned ④ that happened to the mammoths could happen to today's large herbivores, grass-eating animals. "Major environmental change and losses of habitat could lead to the extinction of huge animals like elephants. Moreover, the situation becomes worse. As humans tried to develop the forest to expand cropland, we are making large herbivores ⑤ suffer a similar fate. Human-caused habitat change could be an environmental disaster," said one of the researchers.

02 **다음 (A), (B), (C)의 각 [ ] 안에서 어법에 맞는 표현으로 바르게 짝지어진 것은?**

Scientists learn about the universe by the light (A) [that / what] we can see. The light is in the form of radio waves and X-ray and gamma-ray emissions. But what if there is material that does not glow? How will we ever know it is there? Such material is called dark matter, and astronomers now believe that most of the material in the universe (B) [is / are] made of this stuff. It is material that does not emit sufficient light for us to directly detect it. However, there are a variety of ways that we can indirectly detect it. (C) [Most / The most] common method involves the fact that the dark matter has a gravitational pull on both the light and the sources of light. This allows us to measure how heavy dark matter is.

	(A)		(B)		(C)
①	that	-	is	-	Most
②	what	-	are	-	The most
③	what	-	is	-	The most
④	that	-	is	-	The most
⑤	what	-	are	-	Most

03 기출응용

다음 글의 밑줄 친 부분 중, 어법상 어긋난 것은?

We students are not sufficiently provided with opportunities for ① learning through trial and error. This is one of the reasons for my opposition to school uniforms. We do not make mistakes in choosing ② that we wear because we do not choose at all. All we have to do ③ is wear the same uniform every day. ④ Without the school uniform, we would have to make a choice. And sometimes we would find our choices ⑤ incorrect or out of place. We would learn from it. School uniforms have deprived us of a precious opportunity to learn from our mistakes.

04

다음 (A), (B), (C)의 각 [ ] 안에서 어법에 맞는 표현으로 바르게 짝지어진 것은?

The brain is a survival instrument and its various capacities—reason, intuition, perception, emotion—are techniques that must (A) [consider / be considered] in terms of the roles they have played in helping each organism to survive. Like every other organ in the body, the brain has been formed by evolutionary processes. At each stage of evolution, the brain was designed by natural selection to bless our ancestors with the ability to utilize the environment and take proper action. The key word here is action. The brain's basic design pursues the physical points: to find food and shelter for self and family, to succeed in reproduction, to protect family, to make friends, to get high status, and to control the surroundings as (B) [far / further] as possible. The brain was not designed for philosophic speculation, spiritual contemplation, financial dealings or to take an economics exam. In other words, the brain is now carrying out various operations for (C) [which / what] it was not originally designed.

	(A)		(B)		(C)
①	consider	-	far	-	which
②	consider	-	further	-	what
③	be considered	-	far	-	what
④	be considered	-	further	-	what
⑤	be considered	-	far	-	which

Chapter X

05 다음 글의 밑줄 친 부분 중, 어법상 어긋난 것은?

Unfortunately, retirement savings have not been immune to the economic volatility of recent years. And the nearer you are to retirement, ① the more worried you've become about your investments ② being hit by some of the big stock market drops. At times like this, people are looking for more guarantees and less risk, basically a safe haven for their money. At our company, it is our belief that a pension is still one of ③ the best ways to save for your retirement. For example, optimists will like the fact that we offer a choice of places to invest depending on your appetite for risk. Obviously the value of your particular plans may fluctuate, and there could be times ④ which you don't get back the full amount of your original investment. Concerned or worried people tend to gravitate to our fund with a guarantee option, so ⑤ invest your money with us. You can be sure of getting at least your original investment back and fewer charges.

06 다음 (A), (B), (C)의 각 [ ] 안에서 어법에 맞는 표현으로 바르게 짝지어진 것은?

기출응용

It is clear that TV activates an intrinsic response in the human brain. There is nothing particularly unhealthy with this response, but it can become problematic. Studies have been performed to determine (A) [how / however] people respond to television both physiologically and behaviorally. These studies show that people feel relaxed, passive, and less alert while watching television. The feeling of relaxation ends immediately when the set is turned off. The feeling of passivity and the diminished level of alertness, however, persist. As such, the action of turning on the set is positively reinforced with the positive feeling of relaxation, but (B) [turning it off / turning off it] is unpleasant because the feeling of relaxation is removed while the other negative feelings persist. This is (C) [that / what] makes some behavior addictive; it is very difficult to stop, and it takes control of people's lives. This definition seems to apply to television viewers.

	(A)		(B)		(C)
①	how	-	turning it off	-	that
②	however	-	turning it off	-	that
③	how	-	turning it off	-	that
④	however	-	turning it off	-	what
⑤	how	-	turning it off	-	what

participle constructions

분사구문

UNIT

117 분사구문

Standing in the middle of the crowd, I could feel a sense of embarrassment and frustration.

군중 가운데 서 있었을 때, 나는 당혹감과 좌절감을 느낄 수 있었다.

군중 가운데 서 있었을 때 // 나는 느낄 수 있었다 /

[Standing] in the middle of the crowd, I could feel

└ 원래 문장은 When I stood in ~ 이다. 부사절의 주어가 주절의 주어와 동일하므로 생략하고, 접속사도 생략한 뒤, 본동사를 분사(standing)로 만들어 준다.

당혹감과 좌절감을

a sense of embarrassment and frustration.

분사구문

분사구문이란 일반적으로 분사(-ing / -ed)가 이끄는 구를 지칭한다. 대개 주어가 생략되어 있고, 그 경우 주절의 주어와 동일하다. 또한 접속사가 남아 있기도 하다.
다음의 사항에 주의해서 분사구문을 살펴보도록 하자.

* 분사의 형태가 능동형인가? 수동형인가?
* 분사의 형태가 단순형인가? 완료형인가?
* 분사구문의 주어와 주절의 주어는 일치하는가?

I ate a burger for lunch while I was driving to my office.

→ I ate a burger for lunch, [driving to my office].

나는 사무실로 운전하면서 점심으로 버거를 먹었다.

⇒ 분사의 형태는 능동형이고, 단순형이며 분사구문의 주어와 주절의 주어가 일치한다.

Words & Phrases

crowd [kraud] 군중, 관중

embarrassment [imbǽrəsmənt] 당황

frustration [frʌstréiʃən] 좌절

cross [krɔ(:)s] 건너다

on one's way 도중에

disappointment [dìsəpɔ́intmənt] 실망

Check-up

정답 및 해설 p.12

1. While [crossing / crossed] the street on my way to school, I met with an accident.

2. [Examined / Examining] its surface with care, they showed their disappointment at its quality.

UNIT 118

수동 분사구문

Left alone at a young age, the politician Winston Churchill quickly learned how to survive in London's political world.

어린 나이에 혼자 남겨졌기 때문에, 정치인 윈스턴 처칠은 런던의 정계에서 살아남는 방법을 빨리 배웠다.

홀로 남겨져서 / 어린 나이에 // 정치인 윈스턴 처칠은 /

Left alone at a young age, the politician Winston Churchill

주어는 주절의 the politician Winston Churchill이므로, 주어의 입장에서 남기는 행위가 아닌 남겨지는 상태로 봐야 한다. 따라서 수동태인 left가 옳다.

빨리 배웠다 / 살아남는 방법을 / 런던의 정계에서

quickly learned how to survive in London's political world.

Grammar Point

수동 분사구문

일반적으로 분사구문의 주어는 주절의 주어와 동일하므로 해석을 통해서 분사구문의 내용이 수동인지, 능동인지 파악할 수 있다.

[Fettering / Fettered by] convention, we sometimes find it hard to act in our own way.

관습에 얽매여 있기 때문에 우리는 때때로 우리만의 방식으로 행동하는 것이 어렵다는 것을 깨닫는다.

⇒ 우리가 관습을 속박하는 것이 아니라 관습에 의해 우리가 속박을 받는 것이므로 수동태인 Fettered by가 정답이다.

Words & Phrases

fetter
[fétər]
~을 구속하다, 속박하다

convention
[kənvénʃən]
관습, 관례; 집회, 협정

attract
[ətrǽkt]
마음을 끌다

resemble
[rizémbl]
닮다

정답 및 해설 p.12

Check-up

1. Brightly [painting / painted] in many colors, the house attracted a lot of attention.
2. [Watching / Watched] from various angles, such a happening here would resemble a fast-forwarded video.

EXERCISE

정답 및 해설 p.12

[01-10] 다음 중 어법상 가장 적절한 표현을 고르시오.

01 India is the second largest producer of tea, [exports / exporting] 400 million pounds each year.

02 기출응용 Students [interesting / interested] in the position will talk to their classmates.

03 A promotion [giving / gives] the car's gas mileage or repair frequency would be more important to a buyer.

04 기출응용 That is why movie stars prefer to have this side of their face [photographing / photographed].

05 기출응용 If you feel threatened when your rival does well, [remind / reminding] yourself of your own strengths and successes.

06 [Follow / Following] a period of decline that began when industrial interests headed toward design after World War II, Kevin's company now thrives as a destination for creative architecture.

07 The business constraints [imposing / imposed] on the workforce schedule are the resources and the requirements of the staffing plan.

08 The entire schedule of courses can now be produced in only three hours, which includes time [needing / needed] to resolve conflicts with faculty preferences.

09 The consumption of tea, now the second most common beverage after water, expanded from Asia to the rest of the world starting in the 19th century with trade [promoted / promoting] by the British East India Company.

10 기출응용 [Found / Finding] in a variety of habitats in both Africa and Asia, the Jerboa is a small rodent distinguished by its light to dark sandy coat.

ACTUAL TEST

정답 및 해설 p.13

01 다음 글의 밑줄 친 부분 중, 어법상 <u>어긋난</u> 것은?

The thought of "short" or "easy" ① <u>being</u> among the general standard used in choosing what to read, but some people think this means laziness. They consider a short or easy book as not a good ② <u>one</u>. However, this may encourage students away from reading books. For instance, many students purposely choose short books in order to be able to read them during their bus ride to school. Students ③ <u>take it</u> for granted to let such things be part of their book selection process. To let books be books without imposing special meaning on them ④ <u>is</u> less complicated for general readers. If someone stresses the number of pages when it comes to ⑤ <u>selecting</u> books, it can discourage students from reading.

02 기출응용 다음 (A), (B), (C)의 각 [ ] 안에서 어법에 맞는 표현으로 바르게 짝지어진 것은?

A primary source of environmental problems (A) [is / are] the fact that pure air, clean rivers, and other environmental resources are public, not private, goods. Suppose you are raising sheep, and you and your neighbors share a common piece of land for grazing. To increase your income, you want to raise more sheep and graze them on the land. If you do, you may damage the land by overgrazing, but you will gain the entire benefit of raising additional sheep and share only part of the cost of the damage (B) [doing / done] to the common property. So you add another sheep to your herd and then perhaps another. Everyone else using the shared land makes the same calculation, however, and in their own self-interest, they add to their herds. Eventually, overgrazing is severe enough to destroy the commons. In Aristotle's words, "(C) [That / What] is common to the greatest number gets the least amount of care."

	(A)		(B)		(C)
①	is	-	doing	-	That
②	are	-	doing	-	That
③	is	-	done	-	What
④	are	-	done	-	What
⑤	is	-	done	-	That

UNIT 119

주어가 다른 분사구문

The inscription deciphered by a team of archaeologists, the director of the project emphasized that the tablets would provide important insights about ancient Egyptians.

고고학자 팀에 의해 비문이 해독되었을 때, 그 프로젝트의 관리자는 그 현판이 고대 이집트인에 대한 중요한 통찰력을 제공할 것이라고 강조했다.

비문이 / 해독되었을 때 / 고고학자 팀에 의해서 //

The inscription deciphered by a team of archaeologists,

- 비문이 해독되는 것이므로 수동태가 온다.
- 주절과 분사구문의 주어가 서로 다르므로, 분사구문의 주어를 써주어야 한다.

그 프로젝트의 관리자는 / 강조했다 // 그 현판이 /

the director of the project emphasized that the tablets

중요한 통찰력을 제공할 것이다 / 고대 이집트인에 대한

would provide important insights about ancient Egyptians.

Grammar Point

주어가 다른 분사구문

분사구문의 주어가 주절의 주어와 다를 경우, 그 다른 주어를 분사구문 앞에 써주어야 한다. 의미가 없는 There, It 등도 생략할 수 없다. 단, 분사구문의 주어가 일반적인 사람일 경우는 생략이 가능하다.

두 문장의 주어가 다르므로 두 개의 주어를 모두 써준다. 이 경우에는 분사구문의 주어를 생략할 수 없다.

The weather permitting, we are going to leave tomorrow.
날씨가 허락한다면, 우리는 내일 떠날 것이다.

Judging from her accent, she seems to be from Scotland.
그녀의 억양으로 판단하건대, 그녀는 스코틀랜드 출신인 것 같다.

⇒ Judging from~은 원래 If we judge from~으로 주어가 일반적인 사람인 we이므로 주절의 주어인 she와 달라도 생략이 가능하다.

cf.) 막연한 일반인이 생략된 분사구문은 비인칭 독립분사 구문이라고 한다.
strictly / frankly / generally speaking : 엄격히 / 솔직히 / 일반적으로 말해서
talking of something: ~의 말이 나왔으니 말인데
considering: ~을 고려하면

Words & Phrases

inscription [inskrípʃən] 비문
decipher [disáifər] 해독하다
archaeologist [a:rkiá:lədʒist] 고고학자
emphasize [émfəsàiz] 강조하다
tablet [tǽblit] 현판
insight [insàit] 통찰력
permit [pə:rmít] 허락하다

Check-up

정답 및 해설 p.13

1. There being / Being no bus service in the town, we had to walk an hour to school.

2. Tom Clancy writing / Writing his novels in essay style, his many works attract a number of readers.

being 생략 분사구문

Aggressive and strong, his attack didn't cause any damage to the champion, and he received a counterattack.

그의 공격은 저돌적이고 강했지만 챔피언에게 어떤 해도 주지 못했으며 그는 반격을 당했다.

저돌적이고 강했지만, // 그의 공격은 어떤 해도 주지 못했다 /
Aggressive and strong, his attack didn't cause any damage

= Being aggressive and strong, his attack ~

형용사만 나와 있지만, 앞에 being이 생략된 구문이다. 따라서 이 부분에 밑줄이 그어져 있더라도 어법상 옳은 문장임을 잊지 말자.

챔피언에게 // 그리고 그는 반격을 당했다
to the champion, and he received a counterattack.

Grammar Point

being 생략 분사구문

분사구문에서는 주로 being이 생략되지만 일반적으로 많이 쓰는 구문은 아니다.
〈-ed, 형용사, 명사〉로 시작하고, 그 뒤에 콤마(,)가 나오는 구문에 주의하자. 특히, 형용사로 시작하는 분사구문의 어법성 판단을 물을 경우 맞는 구문이라는 것을 명심하자.

앞에 being이 생략된 분사구문이다. 따라서 어법에 맞는 표현이다.
= Being an excellent speaker, he was never at a loss for words.

An excellent speaker, he was never at a loss for words.

그는 뛰어난 웅변가로 결코 말 실수를 하지 않았다.

Words & Phrases

aggressive [əgrésiv] 공격적인

damage [dǽmidʒ] 손해, 피해

counterattack [káuntərətæ̀k] 반격, 역습

patient [péiʃənt] 환자; 인내심 있는

serious [sí(:)əriəs] 심각한, 진지한

Check-up 정답 및 해설 p.13

다음 문장을 읽고, 해석하시오.

1. Happy, Barry Grazer tried to find another adventure by traveling to Harper's Island.

2. An able physician, Dr. Gray has never failed to treat his patients and dealt with serious diseases.

EXERCISE

정답 및 해설 p.13

[01-10] **다음 중 어법상 가장 적절한 표현을 고르시오.**

01 [The royal family having / Having] reached and taken seats prepared for them, the opening ceremony started.

02 Those seated in an exit row get extra legroom but also the responsibility of opening the emergency exit door if [needing / needed].

03 Strictly [speaking / spoken], you did violate the regulation but we decided to give you one more chance to make up for your mistake.

04 [Judging / Judged] from the behavior of the friends Tony is hanging out with, he must be headed for trouble.

05 [Considering / Considered] the weak consumer confidence, the government finds it has no choice but to take more aggressive steps to revive the economy.

06 [Being written / Been written] in simple English, the book was easy for children to read.

07 He [very rich / being very rich] and gentle, Julie wanted to marry him.

08 [Being / It being] fine yesterday, we went on a picnic and had a good time with the children.

09 [Informing / Informed] immediately, the computer repair technician will restore lost and damaged data by this evening.

10 [There being / Being] no definite evidence for or against the existence of gods, science cannot judge which is right.

ACTUAL TEST

정답 및 해설 p.14

01 다음 글의 밑줄 친 부분 중, 어법상 어긋난 것은?

Imagine that you are on the beach and hear the crash of the ocean waves. They come up to your bare feet, and the water tries to take the sand out from under ① them as it retreats into the sea. The transparent window of the beach house reflects the clouds on the blue sky. Girls and boys play in the sand ahead of you using their bright yellow bucket and red shovel to build a sand castle ② decorated with seashells. ③ The evening sky blazing orange over the sky-blue water, you turn your stare out to the sunset. Half of mankind lives near the sea. ④ Even if I live far from the ocean, it's one of my favorite places to visit and therefore paint. Many artists have a spiritual, mystical enchanting, compelling urge to paint water. Maybe it's ⑤ why our own bodies are mostly water. Whatever the reason, watercolor is made for painting water.

02 다음 (A), (B), (C)의 각 [ ] 안에서 어법에 맞는 표현으로 바르게 짝지어진 것은?

As a twelve-year-old boy in 1972, I was (A) [excited / exciting] that I could go and watch a baseball game in the stadium. My father, who worked hard with a heavy six-day-a-week schedule, took a day off and took me to the game. As we reached the stadium, the side doors near the left-field bleachers opened to bring some equipment. Scores of fans rushed to the doors, some (B) [commenting / commented] loudly about a free baseball game. Thinking we could enjoy the game for free, I was about to join the group. But my father determined that we shouldn't, so we continued to stand in line for tickets. The action on the field and the winner of the game (C) [forget / are forgotten] soon, but not the silent message of honesty from a loving and disciplined father.

*bleacher : 외야석

	(A)		(B)		(C)
①	excited	-	commented	-	forget
②	exciting	-	commenting	-	are forgotten
③	excited	-	commenting	-	are forgotten
④	exciting	-	commented	-	forget
⑤	excited	-	commented	-	are forgotten

UNIT 121

문장 뒤에 오는 분사구문

A ball flew into the living room, breaking the vase on the table.

공이 거실로 날아들어와 탁자 위의 꽃병을 깨뜨렸다.

공이 거실로 날아들어왔다 / 깨뜨렸다 / 탁자 위의 꽃병을

A ball flew into the living room , breaking the vase on the table.

broke(X), broken(X)

콤마 뒤에 분사구문으로 연속 동작을 의미한다. (~ and broke the vase ~)
공이 꽃병을 깬 것이므로 '-ing' 형이 왔다.

Grammar Point

문장 뒤에 오는 분사구문

문장 뒤에 콤마로 이어진 분사구문은 주로 앞 문장에 연결되어 'and 동사'의 동시 동작 또는 연속 동작을 나타내거나 바로 앞의 단어를 수식하는 형용사 역할을 한다. 의미상 자연스러운 쪽으로 해석한다.

The dog wandered around my house, barking loudly.

그 개는 크게 짖으면서 우리 집 주변을 맴돌았다

⇒ 앞 문장의 주어와 연결되어 동시 상황을 나타낸다. The dog wandered around my house and barked loudly.라는 문장으로 이해할 수 있다.

Words & Phrases

wander [wάndər] (정처 없이) 돌아다니다

affect [əfekt] ~에 영향을 미치다

open up (가능성을) 열다

steamy [stí:mi] 수증기의

settlement [sétlmənt] 정착; 정착지

Check-up

정답 및 해설 p.14

1. When you are shocked, you should breathe more deeply, making / made your body relaxed.

2. Air conditioning affected where Americans lived, opening / opened up the steamy South and the desert Southwest for settlement.

UNIT 122

명사 + 분사

The first preserved example of Greek alphabetic writing, scratched onto an Athenian wine jar of about 740 B.C., is a line of poetry announcing a dancing contest. 기출응용

그리스 문자로 쓰인 글이 최초로 보존된 예는 기원전 약 740년의 아테네의 와인 항아리에 긁어서 쓴 것인데 댄스 대회를 알리는 시 구절이다.

첫 번째 보존된 예는 / 그리스 문자로 쓰인 글의 //

The first **preserved** example of Greek alphabetic writing,

preserving (X)

예가 보전하는 것이 아니라 보전된 것이므로 수동

아테네의 와인 항아리에 긁어서 쓴 / 기원전 약 740년 경의 // 이다

scratched onto an Athenian wine jar of about 740 B.C., is

scratch, scratching (X)

예가 긁어서 쓴 것이 아니라 긁어서 쓰여진 것이므로 수동

시 구절 / 댄스 대회를 알리는

a line of poetry **announcing** a dancing contest.

announce / announced (X)

시가 댄스대회를 알리는 것이므로 능동

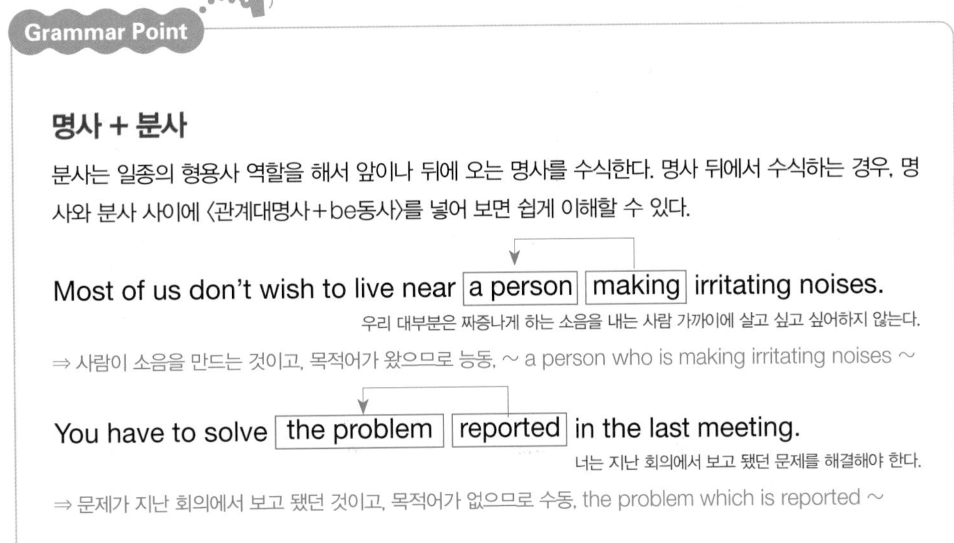

Grammar Point

명사 + 분사

분사는 일종의 형용사 역할을 해서 앞이나 뒤에 오는 명사를 수식한다. 명사 뒤에서 수식하는 경우, 명사와 분사 사이에 〈관계대명사+be동사〉를 넣어 보면 쉽게 이해할 수 있다.

Most of us don't wish to live near a person making irritating noises.
우리 대부분은 짜증나게 하는 소음을 내는 사람 가까이에 살고 싶어하지 않는다.

⇒ 사람이 소음을 만드는 것이고, 목적어가 왔으므로 능동. ~ a person who is making irritating noises ~

You have to solve the problem reported in the last meeting.
너는 지난 회의에서 보고 됐던 문제를 해결해야 한다.

⇒ 문제가 지난 회의에서 보고 됐던 것이고, 목적어가 없으므로 수동. the problem which is reported ~

Words & Phrases

preserve [prizə́ːrv] 보존하다, 보호하다

alphabetic [æ̀lfəbétik] 알파벳으로 된

scratch [skrætʃ] (긁어서) 쓰다, 그리다

poetry [póuitri] 시

announce [ənáuns] 알리다

volcanic eruption 화산 폭발

Check-up

정답 및 해설 p.14

1. English is the number one language speaking / spoken all over the world.
2. Ash from volcanic eruption continued to fall for a week, completely cover / covering the great city of Pompeii.

EXERCISE

정답 및 해설 p.14

[01-10] **다음 중 어법상 가장 적절한 표현을 고르시오.**

01 Most of the mobile devices [offering / offered] with low-cost plans are either fairly basic or relatively cheap.

02 Under his leadership, the country passed new laws [designing / designed] to promote racial equality.

03 A parent [taking / taken] a leave of absence from work is entitled to 100% pay for 3 months.

04 기출응용 Supporters say it's merely legalizing a practice already [carrying / carried] out by many doctors.

05 기출응용 This result proved the role of water in the spread of cholera, [pointed / pointing] the way toward protection against it.

06 The first experience lastingly changes the chemistry and function of the genes inside cells, [leading / led] to special behavioral effects.

07 기출응용 The word 'courage' takes on added meaning if you keep in mind that it is derived from the Latin word 'cor' [means / meaning] 'heart.'

08 The new girl's attitude was very poor, [contaminating / contaminated] the other students in English class.

09 Our world is only one of nine planets [revolving / revolved] around a star we call the sun.

10 The hurricane hit the south coast of the United States, [causing / caused] enormous damage and [causing / caused] hundreds of deaths.

ACTUAL TEST

정답 및 해설 p.15

01 기출응용

다음 글의 밑줄 친 부분 중, 어법상 어긋난 것은?

Emotional eaters manifest their problem in lots of different ways. For many people, one of the classic signs of emotional eating is night eating. Night eaters are often ① eating in response to anxiety or to the emotional turmoil they've experienced throughout the day. Boredom and loneliness are also more likely to come to the surface when the rush of the day is ② done and the night stretches ahead. Sometimes emotional eating is a reaction to a specific situation. You had a bad day at work. The kids have been so ③ demanding that you are completely worn out. You and your significant other are fighting. It doesn't matter ④ what the circumstances are; the end result is that 99 times out of 100 you end up on the couch with a bowl of chips or bag of cookies in your hand, ⑤ told yourself it's the only way you can relax.

02 기출응용

다음 (A), (B), (C)의 각 [ ] 안에서 어법에 맞는 표현으로 바르게 짝지어진 것은?

Uranium is a resource in France because electricity is generated in nuclear power plants. However, uranium is not a resource to an isolated person (A) [living / lived] in the remote Highlands of Irian Jaya. In a similar way, a bicycle is a resource to an 8-year-old boy in a city, but it would be of (B) [most / almost] no use to a Highlander who lives in Irian Jaya. There steep narrow trails with sharp rocks, crossing creeks and climbing steep mountains, make (C) [to use / using] a bicycle impossible. Small sticks are a resource to Bushmen in South Africa. However, they are of little use to most urbanized people in the world. For them, twigs are worthless.

	(A)		(B)		(C)
①	living	-	most	-	to use
②	lived	-	most	-	using
③	living	-	almost	-	using
④	lived	-	almost	-	to use
⑤	living	-	almost	-	to use

UNIT 123

with+명사+분사구문

The innovational plan was accused of failing the brightest schoolchildren, with one in seven pupils marked as gifted and talented failing to get five good points.

혁신적인 계획은 천부적이고 재능이 있다고 인정받은 일곱 명 중 한 명 꼴로 5점이라는 좋은 점수를 받지 못하게 하여 가장 똑똑한 학생들을 실패하게 했다고 비난을 받았다.

혁신적인 계획은 / 비난을 받았다 / 가장 똑똑한 학생들을 실패하게 했다고 /
The innovational plan was accused of failing the brightest schoolchildren,

한 명 꼴로 / 일곱 명 학생 중 / 천부적이고 재능있다고 인정받은 /
with one in seven pupils marked as gifted and talented

with 다음에 명사(one)가 오고 동사가 오면 동사는 분사의 형태를 띈다. 학생이 성적을 받는 데 실패한 것이므로 failing이 왔다.

5점이라는 좋은 점수를 얻는 것을 실패하게 하여
failing to get five good points.

fails / failed (X)

Grammar Point

with+명사+분사구문

〈with+명사+-ing/-ed〉 구문은 일종의 분사구문이다. with를 붙여줌으로써 동시 상황을 강조한 것이고, 명사를 주어로, 분사구문을 동사로 이해하면 된다.

He stood there, with his eyes closed. 그는 눈을 감은 채 거기에 서 있었다.

With July approaching, we need to set up this year's vacation schedule. 7월이 다가옴에 따라, 우리는 휴가 계획을 세워야 한다.

with+명사+형용사/to부정사

Don't speak with your mouth full. 입에 음식물을 가득 넣은 채로 말하지 마라.

With no children to inherit, her estate passed to her younger sister. 상속받을 자식이 없어서 재산은 그녀의 여동생에게 물려졌다..

Words & Phrases

be accused of ~으로 비난 받다; ~으로 고소 당하다

pupil [pjú:pəl] 학생

gifted [gíftid] 천부적인, 재능 있는

inherit [inhérit] 상속하다

take effect 효력을 나타내다

arise [əráiz] 발생하다

Check-up

정답 및 해설 p.15

1. With the new rule taking / taken effect in five months, concerns over non-English speaking players in the league are arising. 기출응용

2. With dark night coming / come on, the cold wind began to blow and the rain began to fall.

UNIT

124 감정동사의 분사형

After having a long promotion meeting, we decided to place colorful displays in astonishing spots to catch the customers' attention.

장시간의 홍보 회의 후, 우리는 고객의 관심을 끌기 위해 깜짝 놀랄 만한 장소에 다채로운 전시물을 설치하기로 결정했다.

장시간의 홍보 회의 후에 / 우리는 / 설치하기로 결정했다 /
After having a long promotion meeting, we decided to place

다채로운 전시물을 / 깜짝 놀랄 만한 장소에 /
colorful displays in astonishing spots

astonished (X)

spots가 놀라움을 느끼는 것이 아니라 놀랍게 만드는 것이므로 능동인 astonishing이 왔다.

고객의 관심을 끌기 위해
to catch the customers' attention.

Grammar Point

감정동사의 분사형

감정과 관련된 동사들(surprise, please, shock, excite)의 능동 또는 수동을 고르는 문제는 수식의 여부, 주체가 되는 대상이 그러한 감정을 주는지 혹은 받는지 여부에 따라 고르면 된다. 감정을 주면 -ing, 감정을 느끼면 -ed를 사용한다.

주체가 되는 대상인 nothing이 surprise라는 감정을 주는 것이므로 능동형인 surprising이 온다.

There's nothing surprising in your presentation, so we are disappointed.

당신의 프레젠테이션에는 놀라운 점이 없어서 우리는 실망했다.

주체가 되는 대상인 we가 disappoint라는 감정을 받게되는 것이므로 수동형인 disappointed가 온다.

Words & Phrases

display [displéi] 전시하다; 전시물; 진열

disappointed [dìsəpɔ́intid] 실망한

resident [rézidənt] 거주자

get along with ~와 잘 지내다

calculation [kæ̀lkjəléiʃən] 계산

Check-up

정답 및 해설 p.15

1. What is surprising / surprised is that most residents don't try to get along with each other in the city.

2. Your teacher may be surprising / surprised at how fast you can make the calculations for this question.

EXERCISE

정답 및 해설 p.15

[01-10] **다음 중 어법상 가장 적절한 표현을 고르시오.**

01 With my back [easing / eased] into my favorite rocking chair and my feet eased up from it, I feel like I am in heaven.

02 His strategy is that he leaned against the ropes until his opponent was [exhausting / exhausted] from throwing punches.

03 That can be a very [surprising / surprised] experience, especially if you are moving at a high speed.

04 Almost all of our students are quite [satisfying / satisfied] due to the fact that the quality of our lectures has been improved.

05 [Irritating / Irritated by] a tradition that required students to wear uniforms in school, they decided to challenge it.

06 Jupiter was very [displeasing / displeased], for he loved humankind, but could not refuse the request because of his promise.

07 "Honestly, this kind of situation is [embarrassing / embarrassed]," said Lt. Kevin Wilson, a 20-year veteran of the New York Police Department.

08 기출응용 I find myself sitting next to someone who's quite talkative. This is often a [pleasing / pleased] experience for me because I enjoy meeting people.

09 With night [come / coming] on, we started to tremble with fear of a vampire.

10 For the past 10 years, there has been [amazed / amazing] progress in cancer research and treatment in Korea.

정답 및 해설 p.16

01 다음 글의 밑줄 친 부분 중, 어법상 어긋난 것은?

If you chew gum habitually, you have to pay attention to this. Some cosmetic surgeons suggest that those who chew gum ① <u>are</u> likely to develop wrinkles around their mouths. According to Dr. Carl Kent of the University of Nebraska, many of his patients who have chewed gum ② <u>have</u> a certain pattern of wrinkles around their mouths. He showed the gum caused it to some degree. Though no studies have yet to show a link between chewing gum and wrinkles, some bloggers do indicate that chewing gum causes people ③ <u>to overuse</u> their jaw muscles. In fact, it is likely that chewing gum promotes muscle over-activity and potentially breaks down support tissue within the skin, with this ④ <u>triggered</u> the loss of skin elasticity. There are, however, bright sides to chewing gum. A study in Germany reported that chewing gum had a significant and positive effect on concentration performance and ⑤ <u>decreasing</u> stress.

02  다음 (A), (B), (C)의 각 [ ] 안에서 어법에 맞는 표현으로 바르게 짝지어진 것은?

Our lives are interwoven with numbers. We use them to mark significant events such as birthdays and wedding anniversaries, as a means of identification like social security numbers. Also they are used as a way of ranking and comparison: most students prefer a test average of 98 in math over an average of 68. In addition, they help us (A) [tracking / to track] the condition of the economy, and keep the score in sports. They even tell us our height, weight, and waist size. Most students accept them as a part of life (B) [with / without] knowing their true significance. However, they will be (C) [surprised / surprising] to realize just how much they rely on numbers.

	(A)		(B)		(C)
①	tracking	-	with	-	surprised
②	to track	-	with	-	surprising
③	to track	-	without	-	surprising
④	tracking	-	without	-	surprising
⑤	to track	-	without	-	surprised

UNIT 125

분사구문의 부정

When the earth releases that heat in the form of infrared radiation, the greenhouse gases retain the heat very efficiently, not allowing it to escape out into space.

지구가 그 열을 적외선의 형태로 방출할 때, 온실 가스들은 그 열이 우주 밖으로 빠져나가는 것을 막으면서 아주 효율적으로 그 열을 유지한다.

지구가 그 열을 방출할 때 / 적외선의 형태로 //
When the earth releases that heat in the form of infrared radiation,

온실 가스들은 / 그 열을 아주 효율적으로 유지한다 /
the greenhouse gases retain the heat very efficiently,

허용하지 않으면서 / 그것이 우주 밖으로 빠져나가는 것을
not allowing it to escape out into space.

allowing not (X)

분사구문의 부정은 not을 분사 앞에 놓는다.

Grammar Point

분사구문의 부정

분사구문을 부정할 경우, not을 분사구문 앞에 놓는다.

Not grabbing his board, he ran into the waves and missed it shortly.

그는 보드를 꽉 움켜쥐지 않은 채 파도로 뛰어들어 갔고, 곧 보드를 놓쳤다.

⇒ 분사구문의 부정은 not을 분사 앞에 둔다. grabbing not이 되지 않도록 주의한다.

Words & Phrases

release [rilíːs] 배출하다, 방출하다; 내놓다

infrared [ìnfrəréd] 적외선의

radiation [rèidiéiʃən] 방사선, 복사

retain [ritéin] 유지하다, 보유하다

escape [iskéip] 빠져나오다, 탈출하다

sacrifice [sǽkrəfàis] 희생하다

Check-up

정답 및 해설 p.16

1. Not knowing / Knowing not what to do, she handed the coin to him and asked nervously, "Want to buy a fresh red rose?" 기출응용

2. Never accepting / Accepting never what she says, I think she'll sacrifice herself for her friends.

UNIT 126

본동사 vs. 분사구문

Any product containing asparagus, which has an anti-cancer effect, can be profitable to our company.

항암 효과를 가지는 아스파라거스를 포함하는 상품은 어떤 것이라도 우리 회사에 이익이 될 수 있다.

어떤 상품도 / 아스파라거스를 포함하는 // 항암 효과를 가지는 //

Any product containing asparagus, which has an anti-cancer effect,

contains (X)

뒤에 본동사가 있으므로 contains가 되서는 안 된다.

which ~ effect가 asparagus에 추가 정보를 제공한다.

우리 회사에 이익이 될 수 있다

can be profitable to our company.

Grammar Point

본동사 vs. 분사구문

본동사와 분사구문을 묻는 문제가 종종 출제되고 있다. 분사구문이 주어를 수식하고 있을 때, 이 분사구문을 본동사와 혼동하지 말아야 한다. 그 반대의 경우도 마찬가지이다. 본동사를 분사구문으로도 혼동하지 말아야 한다. 이는 구문 풀이와 해석을 통해서 풀어야 한다. 하나의 절에는 하나의 본동사만 온다.

Psychologists point to decades of research and more than a thousand studies that [demonstrating / demonstrate] a link between media violence and real aggression. 기출응용

심리학자들은 미디어 폭력과 실제 폭력 사이의 연결고리를 증명하는 수십 년 간의 연구와 천 건 이상의 연구를 지적했다.

⇒ 주격 관계대명사 that 이후에 본동사가 없으므로, 본동사 demonstrate가 와야 한다

Words & Phrases

anti-cancer
항암의

profitable
[práfitəbl]
이익이 나는

aggression
[əgréʃən]
공격성

conference
[kánfərəns]
회의

attend
[əténd]
참가하다

board
[bɔːrd]
이사회

Check-up

정답 및 해설 p.16

1. At the conference, the children [attended / attending] educational sessions, taking field trips to museums and listening to presentations from other children. 기출응용

2. I expect the review to make recommendations about the effectiveness of risk-management by bank boards, [include / including] how pay affects risk-taking.

EXERCISE

정답 및 해설 p.16

[01-10] 다음 중 어법상 가장 적절한 표현을 고르시오.

01 Although [not known / known not] as a famous composer, he wrote many pieces of music.

02 기출응용 The Cambridge University physicist, widely [regards / regarded] as the greatest cosmic thinker since Albert Einstein, is attempting nothing less than a complete understanding of the universe.

03 Many areas that have sought gender equality for the past ten years [have / having] finally gained that equality.

04 Before long, he became an addict and drugs took over his life, [alienates / alienating] him from family, friends, and school.

05 A student [ask / asking] for help is a 23-year-old neurobiology major at Yale, and she is requesting a loan from Yale alumni.

06 기출응용 Clearly, parents make a distinction between violence on a screen and violence [acts / acted] out with plastic guns.

07 기출응용 Imaginative readers can create at least an imitation of the experience they might have [watching / watched] a performance on stage.

08 기출응용 When the fuel cell becomes the automotive engine of choice, the car companies [focused / focusing] on increasing the efficiency of the internal combustion engine may find themselves left behind.

09 Ashley drank some coffee with delicious cookies, [worked / working] until late at night.

10 [Compare / Compared] with life in Seoul, life here is inconvenient in many ways.

ACTUAL TEST

정답 및 해설 p.17

01 기출응용 **다음 글의 밑줄 친 부분 중, 어법상 어긋난 것은?**

Advertisers love to inform us when a product is the ‘fastest-growing’ or ‘largest-selling’ because they do not have to convince us directly that the product is good; they need only say that many others think so, which seems ① proof enough. The producers of charity telethons devote excessive amounts of time to the continuous listing of viewers ② who have already pledged contributions. The message ③ is communicated to the hesitaters is clear: “Look at all the people who have decided to give. It ④ must be the correct thing to do.” Salespeople are taught to emphasize their sales with numerous accounts of individuals who have purchased the product. Sales and motivation consultant Robert Cavett captures the principle ⑤ nicely in his advice to sales trainees: “People are persuaded more by the actions of others than by any proof we can offer.”

02 **다음 (A), (B), (C)의 각 [ ] 안에서 어법에 맞는 표현으로 바르게 짝지어진 것은?**

All of the general Greek tragedies were written for the Dionysia, a festival in honor of Dionysus, (A) [who / which] was celebrated by four full days of theatrical performance of tragedies, satire plays, and comedies. This implies that the plays had a definite religious purpose: to celebrate and worship the god Dionysus. The poet was often thought of as a “teacher of the people” and the success of a Greek tragedy was based on the poet’s success in achieving his role as religious teacher. This means that common themes found in Greek tragedies (B) [being / are] usually moral or religious, such as the relationship between gods and people, and the power of the gods and divine justice. It is also essential to notice that the religious ideas the poets were teaching (C) [was / were] very different from those found in the majority of modern religions.

	(A)		(B)		(C)
①	who	-	being	-	was
②	which	-	being	-	were
③	which	-	are	-	was
④	which	-	are	-	were
⑤	who	-	are	-	was

REVIEW TEST

정답 및 해설 p.17

[01-05] 다음 문장 중 어법상 틀린 부분을 고쳐 쓰시오.

01 His science literature has stated that stress resulted from lasting white noise can cause the release of cortisol-hormone leading to stress.

02 Jerry LeVias, scanned the crowd for both supporters and opponents, needed to know who might vote for him on election day.

03 Most chimps predominantly used their right hands when communicated with others.

04 The unique method using for the preservation of the temple has really been the key to the survival of this amazing place.

05 Statements that some members with a history of alcoholism can safely engage in controlled drinking having generated a hot controversy.

[06-10] 다음 주어진 단어를 어법과 문맥에 맞게 고쳐 쓰시오.

06 __________ as the generation of the coupon, young people are shifting how business is done in the Chinese economy. (know)

07 Christine found herself __________ with the thought of lying alone in a room while being stuck by a dozen needles. (confuse)

08 __________ a new form of the optical image device, Dylan and his associates observed neurons as they were stimulated by an electrode. (use)

09 Students __________ a ladder repeatedly looked up and down to make sure of their progress. (climb)

10 A skydiver starts to fall, moving through the air with the parachute tightly __________. (pack)

FINAL CHECK

정답 및 해설 p.18

01 기출응용

다음 글의 밑줄 친 부분 중, 어법상 어긋난 것은?

I taught debating and argumentation in college. Since then, I ① have listened to, criticized, engaged in, and watched the effects of thousands of arguments. As a result of it all, I have come to the conclusion that ② there is only one way to get the best of an argument and that is to keep away from it. Nine times out of ten, an argument ends with each of the contestants ③ are more firmly convinced than ever that he is absolutely right. You can't win an argument ④ even though you win it. Why? Well, ⑤ suppose you triumph over the other man. You'll feel fine. But what about him? You have hurt his pride. He will resent your triumph.

02

다음 (A), (B), (C)의 각 [ ] 안에서 어법에 맞는 표현으로 바르게 짝지어진 것은?

Your Ultra Pepper Grinder is warranted to the original owner for one year from the date of purchase against defects in material and workmanship under normal use and service. (A) [Your Ultra Grinder should / Should your Ultra Grinder] prove defective within one year from the date of purchase, return the defective part or unit along with an explanation of the claim to Ultra Grinder. Under this warranty, our company will repair or replace any parts (B) [find / found] to be poorly made due to a manufacturer's defect. This warranty extends only to personal use and does not extend to any product (C) [that / what] has been put to commercial or rental use.

	(A)		(B)		(C)
①	Your Ultra Grinder should	-	find	-	that
②	Should your Ultra Grinder	-	find	-	what
③	Your Ultra Grinder should	-	found	-	what
④	Should your Ultra Grinder	-	found	-	that
⑤	Should your Ultra Grinder	-	found	-	what

03 다음 글의 밑줄 친 부분 중, 어법상 어긋난 것은?

One thing that can make you motivated is the book review. Book reviews — a form of writing a ① little different from a simple summary or a plain report — can ② be given to students as a special assignment, or for the school newspaper. Teachers can encourage schools to have annual book-review contests. Some institutes hold a kind of composition competition. They invite teachers to turn in their students' work. The winners of the contest usually ③ receive books and the satisfaction of seeing their work ④ publishing in a teachers' newsletter. Since they are written for public reading, book reviews can move the written report from the field of teacher-student interaction into the reading community ⑤ itself. This can lead to follow-up activities such as student oral reports.

04 다음 (A), (B), (C)의 각 [ ] 안에서 어법에 맞는 표현으로 바르게 짝지어진 것은?

Deep inside an ancient pyramid in Peru, a female archaeologist noticed rectangular patches of soft clay — a telltale sign of a grave. She was examining a sacred location. After weeks of careful digging, she looked through the ancient dust. A mummy (A) [lay / laid] in front of her. As she unwrapped the bundled layers, hundreds of treasures were revealed, including gold, sparkling crowns, and huge war clubs usually (B) [reserving / reserved] for the greatest warriors. But (C) [lifting / lifted] a gold bowl covering the mummy's face, the archaeologist found the biggest surprise yet. The mummy wasn't a king or a male warrior; it was a young woman. She was covered in mysterious tattoos!

	(A)	(B)	(C)
①	lay	- reserving	- lifted
②	lay	- reserved	- lifting
③	lay	- reserved	- lifted
④	laid	- reserving	- lifted
⑤	laid	- reserved	- lifting

05 다음 글의 밑줄 친 부분 중, 어법상 어긋난 것은?

It is more expensive than any other crime to investigate white-collar crime. Investigating a theft may include interviewing some witnesses and writing a police report—nothing too time-consuming. Yet investigating even a simple bribe case from small businesses ① involves not only more work but also more time. Like with a theft, the police must interview the owner of the business and all witnesses, of course. But he/she must also get duplicates of all pertinent financial records and do a complete ② analysis of them. A police chief has only a limited number of detectives to address all specific cases, so he/she is usually reluctant ③ to allot this long-term financial case to one detective. However, ④ what frequently happens in this situation, as you know, is that the detective simply turns down taking the case, ⑤ used the most common avoidance in law enforcement: "It looks like a civil affair."

06 다음 (A), (B), (C)의 각 [ ] 안에서 어법에 맞는 표현으로 바르게 짝지어진 것은?

기출응용

The concept of seasonal fruit is starting to fade away, as consumers are getting (A) [offering / offered] fruits from all seasons all year round. Who do you thank for this? The freezer and advanced packaging. Owing to the latest technologies, retailers are capturing the taste, smell and freshness of just ripe fruits and bringing them to shoppers throughout the year. For consumers, this is a fruity delight. These iced packages let us forget the old days, when we were only limited to fruit harvested during the season. Industry experts say that frozen fruits will become more popular and (B) [wide / widely] consumed as the global climate change impacts and damages regular fruit harvests. In addition, high health-consciousness contributes to the popularity of frozen fruits while people are throwing junk food, rather (C) [turn / turning] to frozen healthy snacks.

	(A)		(B)		(C)
①	offering	-	widely	-	turning
②	offered	-	wide	-	turning
③	offering	-	wide	-	turn
④	offered	-	widely	-	turning
⑤	offering	-	widely	-	turn

gerunds

Chapter 12

동명사

UNIT 127

동명사 vs. 명사

This is one of way of avoiding criticism of our plan which may some day turn over the world.

이것은 언젠가 세상을 뒤집을 지도 모르는 우리의 계획에 대한 그들의 비판을 피하는 일종의 방식이다.

이것은 일종의 방식이다 / 우리의 계획에 대한 그들의 비평을 피하는 // 그것은

This is one of way of [avoiding criticism] of our plan which may

of avoidance criticism (X)

전치사 뒤에 위치하므로 명사와 동명사 모두 올 수 있지만, 뒤에 critic이라는 명사가 나오므로 목적어를 취할 수 있는 동명사가 왔다.

언젠가 세상을 뒤집을지도 모른다

some day turn over the world.

Grammar Point

〈전치사/동사 + 명사/동명사〉구문

명사, 대명사, 동명사는 전치사나 동사 뒤에 올 수 있다. 명사나 동명사 중 옳은 것을 선택하는 문제가 종종 출제되는데, 뒤에 목적어가 오면 동명사를, 전치사가 오면 명사를 선택하면 된다.

The tools [for analysis of] the last year's data weren't even available until Wednesday.

작년 자료의 분석을 위한 도구들은 수요일까지 이용 조차 가능하지 않았다.

⇒ 뒤에 전치사 of가 오므로 for 뒤에 명사인 analysis가 온다.

You need to submit the form within a week [of receiving this].

양식을 받으면 일주일 안에 제출해야 한다.

⇒ 뒤에 목적어 this가 오므로 of 뒤에 동명사인 receiving이 온다.

Words & Phrases

avoid [əvɔ́id] 피하다

turn over 뒤집다

individuality [ìndəvìdʒuǽləti] 개성

liquefy [líkwəfài] 액화하다

offshore [ɔ́(:)fʃɔ́:r] 앞바다의, 연안의

gas field 가스전

Check-up

정답 및 해설 p.19

1. We tend to believe that our taste in music is a great way of [expressing / expression] our individuality. 기출응용
2. This year, the country made big success and started [producing / production] of liquefied natural gas from its first offshore gas field in the East Sea.

UNIT

128 전치사+-ing

By studying pre-Columbian cultures, scientists were beginning to see just how highly complex they were.

콜럼버스가 미대륙을 발견하기 이전의 문화를 연구함으로써 과학자들은 그 문화가 얼마나 많이 복잡한지 겨우 알기 시작했다.

콜럼버스가 미대륙을 발견하기 이전의 문화를 연구함으로써 / 과학자들은 / 시작했다 //

By studying pre-Columbian cultures, scientists were beginning

By study (X)

전치사의 목적어이고 뒤에 목적어가 나오므로 studying이 되어야 한다.

알기 / 겨우 / 그들이 얼마나 많이 복잡한지

to see just how highly complex they were.

highly는 추상적 의미로 '매우'를 의미하고, high는 측정 가능한 '높이'를 의미한다.

Grammar Point

전치사의 목적어가 되는 동명사

전치사 뒤에 동사가 목적어로 오면 동명사(-ing)의 형태가 된다.

I thought about [correct / correcting] him, but he can't hear me because he has earphones on.

나는 그에게 지적하려고 생각했지만, 그는 이어폰을 꽂고 있어서 내 말을 들을 수가 없다.

⇒ 전치사 about 뒤에 나오는 동사이므로 동명사 correcting이 되어야 한다.

Words & Phrases

complex [kámpleks] 복잡한

conversation [kànvərséiʃən] 대화

tumor [tjú:mər] 종양

molecule [málәkjù:l] 분자

Check-up

정답 및 해설 p.19

1. With text messages, you can have entire conversations without ever reach / reaching anyone.
2. It was about understand / understanding how tumors work at the cellular level, then making drugs that play a role like smart bombs to target only the molecules which lead to the problem.

EXERCISE

정답 및 해설 p.19

[01-10] 다음 중 어법상 가장 적절한 표현을 고르시오.

01 기출응용 A job is like a marriage or [having / to have] a spouse.

02 기출응용 The class will then vote by [mark / marking] their choices on ballots.

03 You can play more effectively and contribute to [succeeding / the success] of your teams.

04 As a starting point for [an analysis / analyzing] of financial markets, we discuss the key variables in this meeting.

05 The Quality Control Department has been waiting anxiously for [arriving / the arrival] of the new devices which were ordered 2 weeks ago.

06 What they don't realize is that by [executing / execution] criminals, the state practices the kind of behavior it wants to punish.

07 We need an unusually gifted teacher to solve this sensitive problem without [creation / creating] any trouble.

08 Prior to [the creation / creating] of the utility, it had been necessary to check the air in the building.

09 When David Beckham spoke at New York University last summer about New York [is / being] a model multicultural community for the rest of the country, it raised several questions.

10 기출응용 Despite several emperors' [attempt / attempting] to colonize it, Petra remained largely in the Nabataeans' hands until around 100 A.D., when the Romans took over.

ACTUAL TEST

01 기출응용

다음 글의 밑줄 친 부분 중, 어법상 어긋난 것은?

The introduction of the player piano in the United States at the turn of the 20th century had been accompanied by ① fairly critical comments. Player pianos produced music mechanically through a set of instructions stored on a music roll. ② Although proponents of the player piano such as piano manufacturers and publishers of sheet music thought that it would lead to 'an ③ almost universal music education,' many music teachers, musicians, and composers opposed it. Opponents claimed that one could copy sound, but not interpretation, and ④ that mechanical instruments reduced the expression of music to mathematical systems. For this reason, they believed that mechanized music lessened the ideal of beauty by '⑤ production the same after same, with no soul, no joy, no passion,' and that the introduction of the player piano would lead to the disappearance of amateur players.

02

다음 (A), (B), (C)의 각 [ ] 안에서 어법에 맞는 표현으로 바르게 짝지어진 것은?

Recently, China's open media, which are now more commercially driven because of the retraction of government subsidies, have been straying into once-forbidden fields. (A) [Despite / Although] the growing activity and reliability of at least a few open publications, the secret media have shown no sign of disappearing and some of (B) [them / which] have found new ways of making money. China's rapid (C) [adopting / adoption] of the Internet has even furnished abundant material for a whole new genre of reporting. And China's leaders seem to be absorbing it.

	(A)		(B)		(C)
①	Despite	-	them	-	adopting
②	Although	-	them	-	adopting
③	Despite	-	them	-	adoption
④	Although	-	which	-	adoption
⑤	Despite	-	which	-	adopting

UNIT 129

동명사를 목적어로 취하는 동사

Developing countries refused to consider limiting their greenhouse gas emissions.

개발 도상국은 온실가스 배출량 제한에 대해 고려할 것을 거절했다.

개발 도상국은 / 거절했다 / 제한하기를 고려하는 것을 /
Developing countries [refused] to [consider limiting]

consider to limit (X)

refuse는 to부정사를 목적어로 취하는 동사이다.

consider는 동명사를 목적어로 취하는 동사이므로 limiting이 온다.

그들의 온실가스 배출량을
their greenhouse gas emissions.

Grammar Point

동명사를 목적어로 취하는 동사

다음의 동사는 동명사를 목적어로 취하는 동사들이다. 암기하도록 하자.

avoid, enjoy, can't help, deny, consider, mind,
keep, practice, quit, suggest, postpone + 동명사(-ing)

I [can't help] [thinking] that her decision was not legitimate at all.

나는 그녀의 결정이 전혀 합리적이지 않았다는 생각을 떨칠 수가 없다.

⇒ can't help는 동명사인 thinking을 목적어로 취했다.

Words & Phrases

refuse [refjúːz] 거절하다

greenhouse gas 온실 가스

emission [imíʃən] 배출, 방출

legitimate [lidʒítəmit] 합리적인, 정당한; 합법적인

Check-up

정답 및 해설 p.20

1. Tommy quit [checking / to check] the products and tried to find another job.
2. The students loved to practice [to throw / throwing] pieces of paper into the basket.

UNIT 130

동명사의 부정

Scientists have discovered that for some students, not getting enough rest does not necessarily mean that their grades will fall.

과학자들은 일부 학생들에게 있어서 충분한 휴식을 취하지 못하는 것이 꼭 성적이 떨어짐을 의미하는 것은 아니라는 점을 발견했다.

과학자들은 / 발견했다 // 일부 학생들에게 있어서 /
Scientists have discovered that for some students,

얻지 못한 것이 충분한 휴식을 / 꼭 의미하는 건 아니다 //
not getting enough rest does not necessarily mean

getting not (X)
동명사의 부정은 앞에 not을 붙이므로 not getting이 왔다.

그들의 성적이 떨어질 것이다
that their grades will fall.

Words & Phrases

discover [diskʌ́vər] 발견하다

necessarily [nèsəsérəli] 꼭

grade [greid] 성적, 등급

discourage [diskə́:riʤ] 낙담시키다

advertise [ǽdvərtàiz] 광고하다

appreciate [əprí:ʃièit] 감사하다; 평가하다

come under fire 비난을 받다

reveal [riví:l] 밝히다

efficiency [ifíʃənsi] 효율성

Grammar Point

동명사의 부정

동명사를 부정하기 위해서는 동명사 앞에 not을 붙인다. 즉, 〈not+-ing〉 형태로 만들어준다.

Governments can discourage smoking and encourage healthier eating—for example, by [not allowing / allowing not] tobacco industries to advertise unhealthy products.

정부는 예를 들어 담배 산업이 건강에 해로운 상품을 광고하지 못하게 함으로써 흡연을 못하게 하고 건강식을 권장할 수 있다.

⇒ 동명사의 부정은 not을 동명사 앞에 위치시킨다. 따라서 not allowing이 정답이다.

Check-up 정답 및 해설 p.20

1. I appreciated your [not leaving / leaving not] me although there was heavy rain.
2. The department came under fire for [not revealing / revealing not] the result of the research about efficiency of this system.

EXERCISE

정답 및 해설 p.20

[01-10] 다음 중 어법상 가장 적절한 표현을 고르시오.

01 As Ben pointed out, it is the easiest thing in the world to give up [to smoke / smoking].

02 People who enjoy [feeling / to feel] this rush are often thrill seekers who are not doing something more valuable by putting things off.

03 Women are more likely to succeeding quitting [smoking / to smoke] if they start on a day when their natural progesterone levels are high.

04 If you have a rare coin, when should you consider [submitting / to submit] it to a grading service?

05 Some experts suggested [to create / creating] a more level playing field by using the same system that limits some dealers to certain designated geographical areas.

06 He considered [going not / not going] to school today, but his idea was ignored by his mother.

07 A panda spends most of its waking hours eating and keeps [to eat / eating] all year round.

08 Hopkins used illegal information to avoid [to pay / paying] a $1,000 fine, and he happened to be arrested.

09 To be honest with you, I don't feel like [to keep / keeping] our relationship anymore.

10 If you don't want to waste your time in writing, your pencil needs [to sharpen / sharpening].

ACTUAL TEST

정답 및 해설 p.20

01 다음 글의 밑줄 친 부분 중, 어법상 <u>어긋난</u> 것은?

Women who delay ① <u>having</u> children may be increasing their risk of having a child with autism. A research of all births that occurred in California in the 1990s suggests that the risk ② <u>increases</u> by 18% for every five-year increase in maternal age — and that by the time a woman is 40, she is 50% more likely to have an autistic child than a woman in her late twenties, and 77% more likely than a woman under 25. The research, which ③ <u>involving</u> 12,000 children with autism and a control group of around five million, revealed that paternal age is also a factor. A man in his forties ④ <u>does</u> have an increased risk of having an autistic child. ⑤ <u>Only if</u> his partner is over 30 does the additional risk die out.

*autism : 자폐증

02 다음 (A), (B), (C)의 각 [ ] 안에서 어법에 맞는 표현으로 바르게 짝지어진 것은?

Your heart rate is influenced by your physical condition, the air temperature, the level of stress in your life, etc. The rate (A) [which / at which] your heart can pump rests with so many factors that you really are better off (B) [not knowing / knowing not] your heart rate when training or competing. Heart rate monitors can be valid and useful tools. Athletes have been training with them, and certainly this has improved their level of fitness. But heart rate is just one small piece of the puzzle. How fast your heart is pumping (C) [is / are] a response to a stimulus. Think of your heart rate as being similar to the rpm dial in your car. The more you step on the gas pedal, the higher the rpms go.

	(A)		(B)		(C)
①	at which	-	not knowing	-	are
②	at which	-	not knowing	-	is
③	which	-	not knowing	-	are
④	at which	-	knowing not	-	is
⑤	at which	-	knowing not	-	are

UNIT

131

동명사의 의미상 주어

Please stop the dog's barking. It will wake the baby who fell asleep some minutes ago.

제발 개가 짖지 않도록 해 주세요. 그 소리는 몇 분 전에 잠이 든 아기를 깨울 거예요.

제발 멈춰 주세요 / 개가 짖는 것을 // 그것은 그 아기를 깨울 거예요 //

Please stop [the dog's] [barking]. It will wake [the baby]

the dog (X)

동명사의 의미상의 주어는 소유격을 쓰므로 the dog's가 온다.

몇 분 전에 잠이 든

[who fell asleep some minutes ago].

Words & Phrases

bark [bark] 짖다

fall asleep 잠이 들다

ethics [éθiks] 윤리학

conscious [kánʃəs] 의식있는

behave [bihéiv] 행동하다

mind [maind] 꺼리다

Grammar Point

동명사의 의미상 주어

동명사의 의미상 주어는 원칙적으로 소유격을 사용하지만, 일상체에서는 목적격도 쓴다.

Ethics begins with [our] being conscious that we select how to behave.

윤리학은 우리가 어떻게 행동할지를 선택하는 데 있어 의식을 가지는 것에서 시작한다.

Check-up

정답 및 해설 p.21

다음 주어진 대명사를 알맞게 바꿔 문장을 완성하시오.

1. Would you mind ________ opening the window? (I)

2. According to his father, ________ going to fine art school is just another example of how he doesn't listen. (he)

UNIT 132

동명사의 시제

This navigation error was brought about by having sailed too far south, despite accurate interpretation of the map given by the first officer.

이 항해 오류는 일등 항해사에 의한 정확한 지도 해석에도 불구하고 남쪽으로 너무 멀리 항해했기 때문에 일어났다.

이 항해 오류는 / 야기되었다 / 항해함으로써 /
This navigation error was brought about by having sailed

항해 오류가 야기된 것보다 남쪽으로 항해를 한 것이 먼저 발생한 사건이므로 완료형인 having sailed가 왔다.

남쪽으로 너무 멀리 / 정확한 지도 해석에도 불구하고 /
too far south, despite accurate interpretation of the map

일등 항해사에 의해서 주어진
given by the first officer.

Grammar Point

동명사의 시제

동명사의 시제가 본동사의 시제보다 앞선다면 having p.p.의 형태가 된다. 동명사의 기본 형태가 -ing이므로 과거를 나타내는 시제를 만들기 위해서는 완료형을 써야 한다.

I feel ashamed for not having visited my grandparents for the last three years.

나는 지난 3년 동안 조부모님을 방문하지 않았던 것이 부끄럽다.

⇒ 내용상 feel ashamed한 것보다 방문하지 않은 것이 먼저 발생했기에 having visited와 같은 완료형이 왔다.

Words & Phrases

navigation [nævəgéiʃən] 항해

bring about ~을 야기하다

accurate [ǽkjərit] 정확한

interpretation [intə̀ːrpritéiʃən] 해석

ashamed [əʃéimd] 부끄러운

commission [kəmíʃən] 위원회

Check-up

정답 및 해설 p.21

1. You and your team are the key to [finishing / having finished] this project one month ago.

2. The commission's [investigating / having investigated] the cases yesterday may play a crucial role in settling this scandal.

EXERCISE

정답 및 해설 p.21

[01-10] **다음 중 어법상 가장 적절한 표현을 고르시오.**

01 [We / Our] writing, while reading promotes concentration, increases comprehension and ensures remembering.

02 The manager is suspected of [embezzling / having embezzled] large amounts of money.

03 Robin is proud of his son, Tony [being / having been] a boxing champion last year.

04 I'm sorry for not [making / having made] suggestions for improving the volume of imported car sales in the last conference.

05 Captain Thomson is very nervous because of [never speaking / having never spoken] in public until now.

06 The CIA was convinced of [she / her] being a spy, so they searched her house to find clear evidence.

07 I'm now considering [he / his] joining a football team and competing in a tournament.

08 Judy adamantly denied [cheating / having cheated] on the last final exam.

09 Due to [securing / having secured] quite a few contracts with major corporations here, Leon is expected to be promoted to the vice president.

10 His roommates thank him for simply his [helping / having helped] them although he was very busy.

ACTUAL TEST

정답 및 해설 p.21

01 다음 글의 밑줄 친 부분 중, 어법상 어긋난 것은?

Students often learn the pronunciation of individual words in isolation and ① are unable to recognize them in a connected utterance. ② Having learned a word in its isolated form, students fail to recognize it in an utterance, when changes have ③ taken place in the vowels or in the final consonant, or when a sound is ④ missing altogether. In their own speech, students tend to separate words instead of joining them. They also tend to over-pronounce each syllable and tend not to shorten, compress or reduce unstressed syllables. To understand native speakers better, students need to focus more on how words sound different along with others when ⑤ listened and spoken.

02 다음 (A), (B), (C)의 각 [ ] 안에서 어법에 맞는 표현으로 바르게 짝지어진 것은?

The scientists discovered that women (A) [regular / regularly] wearing high heels suffered from more muscle pains when taking their shoes off. This is because their muscles do not have time to relax and are being overstretched for long periods. According to Dr. Boris Johnson, it was harder for women to stretch their feet out in removing their shoes. He did recommend that women do simple stretching exercises to relieve the pain. "If you stand on your tip toes and lower your heels up and down again, it will stretch out the fibers, (B) [making it / making] easier to walk without heels," he said. He did not suggest women stop wearing high heels but advised (C) [them / their] wearing flat shoes a little more often. "Fashion is intended to be uncomfortable and none of the women in the study planned to give up their high heels," he said.

	(A)		(B)		(C)
①	regular	-	making it	-	their
②	regular	-	making	-	them
③	regularly	-	making	-	their
④	regularly	-	making	-	them
⑤	regularly	-	making it	-	their

UNIT
133 -ing의 관용적 표현

Charlie did not have time to go to the party last night because he was busy preparing for his exam for graduation.

찰리는 졸업 시험을 준비하느라 바빠서 어젯밤에 파티에 갈 시간이 없었다.

찰리는 / 시간이 없었다 / 어젯밤에 파티에 갈 //
Charlie did not have time to go to the party last night

그는 시험을 준비하느라 바빴기 때문에 / 졸업을 위한
because he was busy preparing for his exam for graduation.

to prepare (X)
be busy –ing '~하느라 바쁘다'라는 구문이므로 preparing이 옳다.

Grammar Point

-ing의 관용적 표현

아래는 뒤에 -ing를 취하는 표현들이다. 시험에 출제되기도 하고 독해에서도 중요한 역할을 하므로 암기하도록 하자.

be busy -ing	~ 하느라 바쁘다
It is no use -ing	~ 해도 소용이 없다
It goes without saying that ~	~ 은 말할 필요도 없다
There is no -ing	~ 할 수 없다
cannot help -ing	~ 하지 않을 수 없다
feel like -ing	~ 하고 싶다
be worth -ing	~ 할 가치가 있다

Words & Phrases

graduation [grӕ̀dʒəwéiʃən] 졸업

witness [wítnis] 목격자

currently [kə́:rəntli] 현재

Check-up 정답 및 해설 p.22

1. The witness could not help [to talk / talking] about what he saw last Saturday.
2. It is worth [of knowing / knowing] that many, perhaps a majority, of Venezuelans currently oppose the measures.

UNIT

134 전치사+-ing

Certainly no one would object to having enough in the bank to keep them fed for the rest of their lives.

분명 어느 누구도 은행에 여생을 먹을 수 있을 만큼 충분히 가지는 것을 반대하지는 않을 것이다.

분명 / 어느 누구도 / 반대하지는 않을 것이다 / 은행에 충분히 가지는 것을 /

Certainly no one would **object to having** enough in the bank

to have (X)

object to는 '~에 반대하다, 싫어하다'라는 뜻이고 쓰이며 뒤에는 (동)명사가 온다.

그들이 계속 먹을 수 있도록 / 그들의 삶의 나머지를

to keep them fed for the rest of their lives.

Grammar Point

전치사 + -ing

보통 to 다음에는 동사원형이 와서 to부정사로 사용된다. 하지만 to가 전치사로 사용되어 뒤에 동사가 올 경우 동명사가 와야 하는 경우도 있다. 이런 것은 암기하도록 하자.

be used to	~에 익숙해지다	be accustomed to	~하는 데 익숙하다
with a view to	~을 위하여	be committed to	~에 전념하다
contribute to	~ 에 공헌하다	devote oneself to	~ 에 전념하다, 헌신하다
key to	~대한 핵심	look forward to	~ 을 기대하다
from A to B	A에서 B까지	pay attention to	~에 주의를 기울이다
object to	~에 반대하다	be opposed to	~에 반대하다
in addition to	~와 더불어	when it comes to	~에 관하여
thanks to	~ 덕분에	come close to	거의 ~할 뻔하다
due to	~ 때문에	as opposed to	~와는 대조적으로
owing to ~	~ 때문에		

Words & Phrases

feed
[fi:d]
먹이다

supplement
[sʌ́pləmənt]
보충제; 추가

garlic
[gɑ́:rlik]
마늘

Check-up

정답 및 해설 p.22

1. In addition to [take / taking] vitamin supplements, you should eat a lot of garlic, broccoli, and cauliflower.

2. I was so hurried I came close to [hit / hitting] pedestrians crossing the street.

EXERCISE

정답 및 해설 p.22

[01-10] **다음 중 어법상 가장 적절한 표현을 고르시오.**

01 If you are accustomed to [use / using] forks and knives, you can find it difficult to use chopsticks.

02 기출응용 When it comes to [buy / buying] clothes, shoppers can feel overwhelmed by the choices.

03 Others have no assets left in their homes due to [decline / declining] housing prices.

04 Some heritages that are worth [saving / to save] are important not only for how they look but for what they mean.

05 기출응용 It covered every situation, from constructing boats, huts, and tents in a hurry to [catching / catch] fish without a line.

06 Modern people are generally busy [trying / to try] to fit more and more activities into less and less time to enjoy their happy lives.

07 When they are so committed to [improve / improving] their physical ability and skill on the field that they use muscle-building drugs, young players become deviant.

08 The chip is used to [store / storing] information to positively identify the cardholder.

09 Amie is used to [look / looking] after a little child because she has 3 younger sisters.

10 It was time to pay more attention to [stabilize / stabilizing] the country and improving the quality of life.

정답 및 해설 p.22

01 기출응용

다음 글의 밑줄 친 부분 중, 어법상 어긋난 것은?

We are familiar with the story of Johnny Appleseed, who traveled the frontiers of America in the 1840s. To reforest the land ① where earlier pioneers had cut off all trees, he carried a sack of apple seeds and planted them wherever he went. However, it seems that he was as ② much an innocent polluter as a conservationist. In addition to ③ plant apple seeds, Johnny planted all along his wandering way a weed called dog fennel, believing that this could be used ④ to cure malaria. He was wrong about that. There are only two obvious things about dog fennel: it spreads like any other weed, and it stinks badly. So, for years after Johnny ⑤ had passed, angry farmers were holding their noses and desperately rooting out dog fennel.

*dog fennel : 개꽃

02

다음 (A), (B), (C)의 각 [ ] 안에서 어법에 맞는 표현으로 바르게 짝지어진 것은?

Joao da Silva is one of the most famous environmental activists. He was born in the Amazon region in 1954 to a poor Brazilian family that had farmed rubber from rubber trees for many generations. They loved the rainforest and used its resources in a way (A) [which / that] people did not destroy it. However, cattle ranchers and mining companies started destroying the Amazon rainforest which is more than 180 million years old. They burned and cut down hundreds of thousands of trees, (B) [endangered / endangering] the living environment of the people there. Da Silva began a movement that organized ordinary workers to oppose (C) [performance / performing] those harmful practices. The movement eventually spread to other parts of the world, as Da Silva's efforts led people in other countries to protect the earth's forests and the forests' native residents.

	(A)		(B)		(C)
①	which	-	endangered	-	performance
②	that	-	endangered	-	performing
③	which	-	endangering	-	performance
④	that	-	endangering	-	performing
⑤	that	-	endangering	-	performance

UNIT 135

동명사 주어

Giving people the latitude and flexibility to use their judgment and apply their talents rapidly accelerates progress. 기출응용

사람들에게 자신의 판단을 적용하고, 재능을 활용할 수 있는 자유와 융통성을 주면 진행이 급속도로 빨라진다.

사람들에게 자유와 융통성을 주는 것은 / 그들의 판단을 사용하고 /
Giving people the latitude and flexibility to use their judgment and

Giving이 이끄는 동명사구가 주어이므로 단수 동사인 accelerates가 왔다.

그들의 재능을 적용할 / 급속하게 / 앞당긴다 / 진행을
apply their talents rapidly accelerates progress.

talents는 함정이다
accelerate (X)

Words & Phrases

latitude [lǽtətjùːd] (행동·사상 등의) 자유

flexibility [flèksəbíləti] 융통성, 유연성

rapidly [rǽpidli] 급속하게

accelerate [əksélərèit] 빠르게 하다, 앞당기다

identify [aidéntəfài] 식별하다

molecular [moulékjələr] 분자의

generic [dʒenérik] 유전자의

diagnosis [dàiəgnóusis] 진단

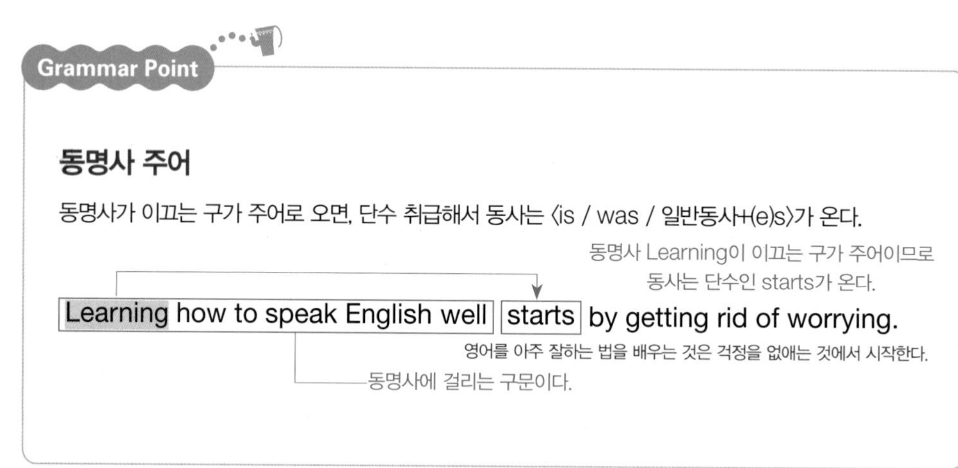

Grammar Point

동명사 주어

동명사가 이끄는 구가 주어로 오면, 단수 취급해서 동사는 〈is / was / 일반동사+(e)s〉가 온다.

동명사 Learning이 이끄는 구가 주어이므로 동사는 단수인 starts가 온다.

Learning how to speak English well starts by getting rid of worrying.

영어를 아주 잘하는 법을 배우는 것은 걱정을 없애는 것에서 시작한다.

동명사에 걸리는 구문이다.

Check-up

정답 및 해설 p.23

1. Fighting an army of diseases as varied as cancers [mean / means] first being able to identify the enemy at the molecular level.

2. Stamping someone's illness with the generic diagnosis "tumor" [doesn't / don't] help the treatment process.

UNIT 136

5문형에서의 동명사 목적어

You want a road bike with narrow, smooth tires that decrease drag and ground friction as well as a light frame that will make going up hill easier. 기출응용

당신은 언덕을 올라가는 것을 더 쉽게 만들어 줄 가벼운 몸체뿐 아니라 저항과 지면 마찰을 줄여 줄 좁고 부드러운 타이어를 갖춘 로드 바이크를 원한다.

당신은 / 로드바이크를 원한다 / 좁고 부드러운 타이어를 갖춘 /

You want a road bike with narrow, smooth tires

저항과 지면 마찰을 줄여주는 / 가벼운 몸체뿐 아니라 //

that decrease drag and ground friction as well as a light frame

언덕 올리가는 것을 더 쉽게 만들어 줄

that will make going up hill easier.

5문형의 목적어 자리에 going이 왔다.

make to go up hill easier (X)

Words & Phrases

narrow [nǽrou] 좁은

smooth [smu:ð] 부드러운

drag [dræg] (자전거의) 타이어 저항

friction [fríkʃən] 마찰

frame [freim] 구조

witness [wítnis] 목격자

settle [sétl] 해결하다

criminal [krímənəl] 범죄자

Grammar Point

5문형에서의 동명사 목적어

5문형에서는 목적어 자리에 동명사는 올 수 있지만 to부정사는 오지 못한다.
to부정사의 경우 가목적어 it을 대신 사용한다.

~ it easy to learn how to read (O)
~ to learn how to read easy (X)

Educational screensavers have made learning how to read easy.

교육적인 화면 보호기로 읽는 법을 쉽게 배울 수 있다.

Check-up

정답 및 해설 p.23

1. The students found studying / to study English conversation by themselves difficult in the classroom.

2. Rin's witness made settling / to settle this case easy, and finally we arrested the real criminal.

EXERCISE

정답 및 해설 p.23

[01-10] 다음 중 어법상 가장 적절한 표현을 고르시오.

01 With smaller herds, Ecto found [to survive / surviving] more difficult.

02 기출응용 People in Himalayas enjoy a warm climate year-round that makes [living / to live] here pleasant.

03 This can broaden the airways, causing shortness of breath and making [breathing / to breathe] difficult.

04 Watching these programs [seems / seem] to motivate and enhance speaking and talking in English among young students.

05 Setting such a positive and friendly working environment [enhances / enhance] productivity because it puts people in high spirits.

06 Taking advantage of all the resources the Internet has to offer [is / are] the smartest way to help streamline work of all kinds.

07 The technologies which are designed to separate us from the public make [watching / to watch] our behavior possible.

08 기출응용 Comparing ourselves with other students [is / are] natural and can be encouraging, but too much of it causes envy, especially if we are ungenerous toward ourselves.

09 Using the graphics and referring to them [is / are] encouraged, so please do it in presentations, web pages, newspapers, blogs and reports.

10 Because of the low cost of living, making ends meet in Asia [is / are] easier than in Europe.

ACTUAL TEST

정답 및 해설 p.23

01 기출응용 다음 글의 밑줄 친 부분 중, 어법상 어긋난 것은?

Visual Regression means you continually go back to read words or phrases ① that have already been completed. It might sound like this: The... The dog... The dog ate... The dog ate a bone. Unfortunately, this is ② done at the expense of your reading speed. This can quickly be overcome by using hand motions during reading. Using hand motions quickly ③ increase your reading speed by making your eyes ④ view text more visually, as well as it helps overcome several habits that can slow down reading speed. ⑤ Take a simple step to begin increasing your reading speed with your fingers placed at the start of a line, and quickly move them toward the right margin.

02 다음 (A), (B), (C)의 각 [ ] 안에서 어법에 맞는 표현으로 바르게 짝지어진 것은?

Some people can go to the gym as often as they like, but it won't do much for their health. New research has shown that around 20% of us carry genes that make (A) [to absorb / absorbing] oxygen difficult and therefore render aerobic exercise all but useless, as far as keeping away heart disease and other disorders (B) [is / are] concerned. According to this study, scientists subjected 500 volunteers to a five-month-long program of aerobic exercise. By the end, most showed some significant drop in their VO2 max — a measure of the ability of oxygen to get to the muscles (C) [which / where] it is needed, since their DNA prevented it. Those people should forget jogging and aim to keep their hearts healthy by other lifestyle changes, such as eating a healthy, balanced diet.

	(A)		(B)		(C)
①	to absorb	-	is	-	where
②	absorbing	-	is	-	where
③	to absorb	-	are	-	where
④	absorbing	-	are	-	which
⑤	to absorb	-	is	-	which

UNIT 137

부사의 동명사 수식

Hastily rebuilding the old houses could destroy our tradition and our way of life, so we should reconsider the plan for reconstruction.

성급하게 그 오래된 집들을 재건축하는 것은 우리의 전통과 삶의 방식을 파괴할 수 있기 때문에 재건축 계획을 다시 고려해야 한다.

성급하게 / 그 오래된 집들을 재건축하는 것은 / 파괴할 수 있다 /

Hastily rebuilding the old houses could destroy

Hasty (X)

동명사 rebuilding을 수식하므로 부사인 Hastily가 온다.

우리 전통과 삶의 방식을 // 그래서 우리는 다시 고려해야 한다 /

our tradition and our way of life, so we should reconsider

재건축 계획을

the plan for reconstruction.

Words & Phrases

hastily [héistəli] 성급하게

destroy [distrɔ́i] 파괴하다

tradition [trədíʃən] 전통

reconstruction [rìːkənstrʌ́kʃən] 재건축

immediate [imíːdiət] 즉각적인

thirsty [θə́ːrsti] 갈증이 나는

severely [sivíərli] 심하게, 엄격하게

Grammar Point

부사의 동명사 수식

동명사는 명사의 성격을 띠지만, 실제로는 동사의 역할을 하므로 부사가 수식을 한다. 하지만 목적어가 없는 동명사 즉, 동사의 역할을 하지 않는 동명사는 형용사가 앞에서 수식한다.

We have several rules, including that talking loudly is not allowed in this hall.

우리는 몇 가지 규칙이 있는데, 이 강당에서는 크게 말하는 것이 허용되지 않는다는 것을 포함한다.

⇒ 동명사 talking을 수식하므로 부사 loudly 뒤에서 수식하고 있다.

Check-up

정답 및 해설 p.24

1. Immediate / Immediately drinking water when you are thirsty can cause you to cough severely.
2. He thought that dreams were a way of safe / safely releasing desires.

UNIT 138

have trouble + -ing

Jim was having trouble dealing with his part-time job at the restaurant and his acting at night at the same time.

짐은 식당 아르바이트를 하고 동시에 밤에 연기 활동을 해나가는 데 어려움을 겪고 있다.

짐은 / 해나가는 데 어려움을 겪고 있다 / 그의 아르바이트

Jim was [having trouble dealing] with his part-time job

to deal (X)

have trouble –ing '~하는데 어려움을 겪다'

식당에서 / 밤에 그의 연기 활동을 / 동시에

at the restaurant and his acting at night at the same time.

Grammar Point

have trouble [hard time / difficulty] + –ing

'~ 하는 데 어려움을 겪다'를 의미하는 〈have trouble[hard time / difficulty]〉 구문 다음에 전치사 in이 생략되었다고 볼 수 있기 때문에 동사가 올 경우 -ing형이 온다.

Some patients with swallowing troubles have difficulty [feeding / to feed] themselves.

삼키는 데 문제가 있는 일부 환자들은 먹는 데 문제가 있다.

⇒ 〈have difficulty –ing〉 구문이므로 feeding이 옳다.

Words & Phrases

deal with
다루다

at the same time
동시에

prosecutor
[prásəkjù:tər]
검사

sum
[sʌm]
합계

Check-up

정답 및 해설 p.24

1. We had a lot of trouble [finding / to find] people whose hobby is making model airplanes.

2. Prosecutors have had difficulty [to find / finding] out how the money was spent, as the whole sum was given in cash.

EXERCISE

정답 및 해설 p.24

[01-10] 다음 중 어법상 가장 적절한 표현을 고르시오.

01 기출응용 [Active / Actively] practicing gratitude on a regular basis will keep you in touch with the very best of your possibilities.

02 One of them may have difficulty [organizing / to organize] work and may lose direct contact with colleagues.

03 기출응용 Rice has proved hard to enrich without [negative / negatively] affecting its appearance or flavor.

04 Those who do that may have trouble [finding / to find] a bank willing to hand out home equity loans that they can use to pay for college.

05 The author is primarily concerned with discovering methods of eliminating harmful microorganisms without [subsequent / subsequently] generating drug-resistant bacteria.

06 The rescue team had a hard time [sort / sorting] out English names from the victims of the crash.

07 Judy ended up escaping from the sticky situation by [careful / carefully] plotting her scheme.

08 Samuel was a French writer whose stories were famous for their [careful / carefully] plotting.

09 The members of the marketing department have to consider [active / actively] promoting the new products.

10 [Successful / Successfully] managing financial resources is crucial in novel and expanding fields.

ACTUAL TEST

정답 및 해설 p.24

01 다음 글의 밑줄 친 부분 중, 어법상 어긋난 것은?

A study revealed that drivers who were distracted by calling or sending a message killed approximately 16,000 people from 2001 to 2007, in America. This result suggested that ① rapid surging in texting volume has led to thousands of additional road deaths in the United States. During this period, the volume of the texting increased by several hundred percent from 1 million to 110 million texts. This study showed that ② despite using a hands-free device, just talking on a cell phone can distract a driver. Also, smart phones providing e-mail access and other applications could take the problem to a new level. In 2008, ③ when sales of smart phones started increasing, roughly 1 in 6 fatal car accidents resulted from a driver distracted by texting. It was found that 5,870 people died in accidents ④ attributed to distracted driving. Due to this situation, 30 states banned texting while driving, and some cities and states required hands-free devices for drivers ⑤ using mobile telephones.

02 다음 (A), (B), (C)의 각 [ ] 안에서 어법에 맞는 표현으로 바르게 짝지어진 것은?

Certain fears are normal during childhood. That is (A) [why / because] fear can be a natural reaction to feeling unsure and much of what children experience is unfamiliar. Young children often have fears of the dark, being alone, strangers, monsters, or other scary imaginary creatures. School-aged children might be afraid when it is stormy or at a first sleep-over. As they grow and learn, with the support of adults, most children are able to slowly conquer these fears and outgrow them. Some children are more sensitive to fears and may have a tough time (B) [to overcome / overcoming] them. When fears last beyond the expected age, it might be a sign that someone is overly fearful, worried, or anxious. People (C) [who / whose] fears are too intense or last too long might need help and support to overcome them.

	(A)		(B)		(C)
①	why	-	to overcome	-	who
②	why	-	overcoming	-	whose
③	because	-	overcoming	-	who
④	because	-	overcoming	-	whose
⑤	because	-	to overcome	-	who

REVIEW TEST

정답 및 해설 p.25

[01-05] 다음 문장 중 어법상 틀린 부분을 고쳐 쓰시오.

01 His research also showed that people tend to laugh more when they are speaking as opposed to listen.

02 This survey suggests that excessive exercising mice and obese mice may be less sensitive to the rewards of physical activity and food, respectively.

03 These statements date back at least to Aristotle, who observed that viewing tragic plays offer the opportunity for catharsis.

04 Controlled drinking can be especially worth to consider for patients for whom abstinence-oriented programs have failed to work over and over.

05 As teens address their increasingly complex daily lives, they need more sleep than younger kids or older adults, and so not getting enough sleep for months are problematic.

[06-10] 다음 빈칸에 들어갈 말을 보기에서 골라 알맞은 형태로 바꿔 쓰시오.

보기	receive	reflect	look	they	assess

06 기출응용 Greenhouse gases have been known to absorb heat and hold this heat in the atmosphere, instead of __________ it back to space.

07 Science can and should guide judicial processes to enhance the accuracy and __________ of what our eyes recognize.

08 It is no use __________ for adventure or for wealth, for they have already felt contented in their lives.

09 I'm sure of __________ deforesting more and more forests to produce more provisions for feeding the expanding population.

10 For decades, she has been used to __________ the royal treatment from European leaders.

FINAL CHECK

정답 및 해설 p.25

01 기출응용

다음 글의 밑줄 친 부분 중, 어법상 어긋난 것은?

I took a room in the Draco Hotel, a pleasant hotel and a pleasant room: small but comfortable, with a telephone, a small color television, and ① <u>its own bathroom</u>. I was highly pleased and full of expectations ② <u>about being</u> in a new place. I dumped my things and went out to look around the town. I soon came to be grateful for ③ <u>living not there</u>. It was entirely the opposite of my expectations. The hotel was in a dark neighborhood of shipping offices and warehouses. There were also a couple of banks, a very large police station with its paint ④ <u>peeling off</u>, and a weather-beaten post office with a row of telephone booths in front. I noticed that the telephone books in the booths ⑤ <u>had been torn</u> or burned and hung from their chains.

02

다음 (A), (B), (C)의 각 [ ] 안에서 어법에 맞는 표현으로 바르게 짝지어진 것은?

What color were dinosaurs? The truth is that no one knew. But now palaeontologists have found a way of (A) [analysis / analyzing] the pigments preserved in certain fossils, and their findings suggest that some dinosaurs (B) [be / were] not grey and scaly but remarkably colorful. For example, it was revealed earlier this year that the *Sinosauropteryx* had an orange-and-white striped tail. And now, researchers have for the first time uncovered the colors of a complete dinosaur, *Anchiornis huxleyi*, and found evidence that this dinosaur was even more striking-looking, with a reddish-brown Mohican, and white feathers with black tips on its wings and legs. Overall, it looked like a large, exotic chicken. In this research, palaeontologists used an electron microscope to study the structure of microscopic pigment in the fossils. By comparing the structure with (C) [modern birds / those of modern birds], the scientists could work out what *Anchiornis huxleyi* looked like when it was alive.

*palaeontologist : 화석을 연구하는 사람

	(A)		(B)		(C)
①	analysis	-	be	-	modern birds
②	analyzing	-	be	-	those of modern birds
③	analysis	-	were	-	modern birds
④	analyzing	-	were	-	those of modern birds
⑤	analyzing	-	were	-	modern birds

03 다음 글의 밑줄 친 부분 중, 어법상 어긋난 것은?

Crown rot is one of the most destructive diseases for waterplants. It spreads by infected plants ① being introduced to a pond. According to experts, there is no solution except ② destruction infected plants. This sounds bad, but a number of waterplants are resistant and show little effect from the infection, but those that are susceptible are ③ seriously affected. Yellowing leaves in summer and no new growth ④ are indicators of the disease as well as the crowns eventually rotting away. If this takes place, buy a different variety and go on. If you grow a waterplant as a hobby, to avoid this problem you should choose very small plants, wash them free of soil, and ⑤ soak them in a kind of fungicide.

04 다음 (A), (B), (C)의 각 [ ] 안에서 어법에 맞는 표현으로 바르게 짝지어진 것은?

There are some benefits of a bike lane. First, (A) [it / they] can help promote an orderly flow of traffic and increase the predictability of both motorists and bicyclists. Second, it helps decrease the stress level of bicyclists riding in traffic, and signal motorists that cyclists have a right to the road. Moreover, cyclists using the street with it were less likely to ride on the sidewalk and were less likely to ride against the flow of traffic. Also, by bicyclists (B) [not blocking / blocking not] it, drivers and riders can go to their destination faster. Lastly, several studies have found that cyclists are more comfortable and think streets having it (C) [provide / provides] a better level of service for them.

	(A)		(B)		(C)
①	it	-	not blocking	-	provide
②	it	-	not blocking	-	provides
③	it	-	blocking not	-	provide
④	they	-	blocking not	-	provides
⑤	they	-	not blocking	-	provides

05 다음 글의 밑줄 친 부분 중, 어법상 어긋난 것은?

If suddenly one gas station increased its price of oil by 10%, its sales would ① considerably fall and become damaged in its profit. Raising the price or the cost ② come to hurt the station rather than benefit it. On the other hand, in the case of water, the situation turns around. If a water company raised the price of city water by 10%—even 20%—there would be just a little drop in sales. This is ③ because the number of companies ④ decides market structure and has a deep impact on price and production. Customers could move to other gas stations which supply gas at a low price. There, however, is only one city water company. ⑤ What most of customers can do is to complain about the hike in prices. That is, the difference between the gasoline market and the city water market controls the decision of the prices.

06 다음 (A), (B), (C)의 각 [ ] 안에서 어법에 맞는 표현으로 바르게 짝지어진 것은?

The (A) [producing / production] of sex hormones fluctuates over the course of a life time. The amount of hormone can vary from day to day and even from hour to hour. Output of it usually starts getting a spike in infancy and early childhood and invigorates in the teen years, announcing the start of puberty. The amount of sex hormones drops down gradually from the late teens to the early or mid-50s, in which women enter menopause, (B) [which / after which] estrogen production declines steeply, and men enter a state many doctors are calling climacterium, marked by a sharp drop in output of testosterone. In men and women (C) [like / alike], scientists have connected the depleted hormone levels of old age to memory loss, cognitive decline and even extreme depression.

*climacterium : 갱년기

	(A)		(B)		(C)
①	producing	-	which	-	like
②	production	-	which	-	alike
③	producing	-	after which	-	alike
④	production	-	after which	-	alike
⑤	producing	-	after which	-	like

To Infinitives

to부정사

UNIT 139

to부정사의 의미상 주어

It is impossible for these children to deal with the social problems, although they are promising and gifted.

아무리 이 아이들이 전도유망하고 재능이 있다고 하더라도 그들이 사회적 문제를 다루는 것은 불가능하다.

불가능하다 / 이 아이들이 / 사회적 문제를 다루는 것은 //

It is impossible for these children to deal with the social problems,

That / There (X)　　to부정사의 의미상 주어

It은 문장의 형식적인 주어 역할을 하는 가주어이며, 실질적인 주어 역할을 하는 진주어는 to deal ~ problems이다.

아무리 그들이 전도유망하고 재능이 있더라도

although they are promising and gifted.

Grammar Point

to부정사의 의미상 주어

〈It is+형용사+to부정사〉 구문은 it을 형식적인 주어로 내세우고 to부정사는 문장의 뒤로 보낸 것이다. 이때 it을 가주어라고 부른다. 진주어인 to부정사의 의미상 주어는 to부정사 앞에 for와 함께 쓰인다. 단, 형용사가 칭찬이나 비판의 의미일 때는 for 대신 of를 쓴다.

for	of
easy, difficult, hard, necessary, important, essential, possible, impossible, pleasant, a pity, convenient	kind, smart, stupid, foolish, generous, clever, polite, wrong, good, considerate, careful, careless, cruel

1. It is necessary for Jane to finish this step. 　제인은 이 단계를 끝내야 한다.
   = This step is necessary for Jane to finish.
   ⇒ to부정사의 목적어를 주어로 만드는 것이 가능하다.

2. It is kind of Jane to help the old. 　노인들을 돕다니 제인은 친절하다.
   = Jane is kind to help the old.
   ⇒ to부정사의 의미상 주어를 주어로 만드는 것이 가능하다.

Check-up

정답 및 해설 p.26

1. It was very nice of / for you to show me around the country.
2. It is natural of / for him to pass the MCAT and become a doctor.

Words & Phrases

impossible [impάsəbl] 불가능한

deal with 다루다

although [ɔːlðóu] 비록 ~ 이더라도

promising [prὰmisiŋ] 전도유망한

gifted [gíftid] 우수한, 재능이 있는

generous [dʒénərəs] 관대한

show A around B A에게 B를 구경시켜 주다

UNIT 140

to부정사의 의미상 주어 vs. 목적어

An allowance is a way for children to learn about handling money and about saving or spending.

용돈은 아이들이 돈을 다루는 것과 저축 또는 소비에 대해 배울 수 있는 한 방법이다.

용돈은 / 한 방법이다 / 아이들이 / 배울 수 있는 /
An allowance is a way [for children] [to learn]

children to learn (X)
to learn의 의미상 주어로 for children이 온다.

돈을 다루는 것과 / 저축 또는 소비에 대해
about handling money and about saving or spending.

Grammar Point

to부정사의 의미상 주어 vs. 목적어

어법 문제에서 to부정사 앞에 목적어와 〈for/of+의미상 주어〉 중에 선택해야 할 경우, 대부분 〈for/of+의미상 주어〉가 정답인 경우가 많다. 하지만, 전체적인 의미와 문장의 구조를 통해 to 앞의 (대)명사가 to부정사의 의미상 주어인지 〈동사+목적어+목적격 보어〉의 구조인지 따져보아야 한다.

The girl is very little, and the doorbell is too high [her / for her] to reach.

그 소녀는 너무 작고, 초인종은 그녀가 닿기에 너무 높다.

⇒ 구조상 high 뒤에 her는 올 수 없으며, for her가 의미상 주어로 쓰여 to부정사의 주어 역할을 할 수 있다.

Words & Phrases

allowance [əláuəns] 용돈, 승인
handle [hǽndl] 다루다
educator [édʒukèitər] 교육가
acquire [əkwáiər] 습득하다, 배우다
command [kəmǽnd] (언어) 구사력
comparison [kəmpǽrisən] 비교

Check-up

정답 및 해설 p.26

1. According to local educators, it is much easier [younger children / for younger children] to acquire a good command of English.
2. Her playing experience in the two countries enables [her / for her] to make a sharp comparison of different ping-pong styles.

EXERCISE

정답 및 해설 p.26

[01-10] 다음 중 어법상 가장 적절한 표현을 고르시오.

01 In addition, the dominant scholars did not think it was appropriate [for /of] females to study these areas.

02 It was pleasing [for /of] you to accept the proposal offered from the Major Leagues.

03 기출응용 It's time [for /of] the government to increase the budget for foreign language services online.

04 It was very pleasant [for /of] them to see their children singing and dancing on the stage.

05 In this station, there are two spaces for work, and all the devices and life-support systems are necessary [researchers / for researchers] to live and study.

06 The principle is to present sounds in context and to provide chances [students / for students] to learn sounds in connected streams of speech.

07 It is important [for /of] young people to support the proposal for a mandatory community service program so that they will learn the value of giving to others.

08 As technology advances, it is possible [for /of] businessmen to run their companies from remote places.

09 It's dangerous [for /of] children to play with matches. So keep them away from children.

10 It takes [him / for him] 2 hours to get to his destination by KTX.

정답 및 해설 p.27

01 기출응용 **다음 글의 밑줄 친 부분 중, 어법상 어긋난 것은?**

Any kid ① working in a garage knows you can't pump more gas into a full tank. If you add more gas, it splashes onto the ground. Likewise, your listener's brain is always full of her own thoughts, worries, and enthusiasm. If you pump your ideas into your listener's brain, ② which is full of her own notions, you'll get a polluted mixture, then a spill. If you want ③ for your ideas to flow into her tank, drain her tank completely first. ④ Whenever you are discussing emotionally charged matters, let the speaker finish completely before you jump in. Count to ten if you must speak. It will seem like an eternity, but letting the angry speaker finish ⑤ is the only way that she'll hear you when it's your turn.

02 **다음 (A), (B), (C)의 각 [ ] 안에서 어법에 맞는 표현으로 바르게 짝지어진 것은?**

Although 30% of American high school graduates enter college, it is not high school graduates who have recently dominated the college campuses. Grown-ups of various ages return to college, not only for new job skills but also for self-improvement. For example, about 20% of American college students are over age 35. The number older than 50 on the many campuses (A) [is / are] close to 600,000. We can see American faith in the value of education from the (B) [rising / raising] number of Americans who have a bachelor's degree. College is not available only to the rich and the talented. It is open to anyone. (C) [People / For people] to handle college-level work, many colleges give extra classes involved in business, economics, and marketing.

	(A)		(B)		(C)
①	is	-	rising	-	People
②	is	-	rising	-	For people
③	are	-	rising	-	People
④	are	-	raising	-	For people
⑤	is	-	raising	-	People

UNIT
141 to부정사의 부정

They have the faulty gene that causes Huntington's disease, and some of them decided not to have children.

그들은 헌팅턴병을 유발하는 결함이 있는 유전자를 가지고 있으며 그들 중 일부는 아이를 가지지 않기로 결정했다.

그들은 / 지니고 있다 / 결함이 있는 유전자를 / 헌팅턴병을 일으키는 //
They have the faulty gene [that causes Huntington's disease],

그리고 그들 중 일부는 / 아이를 가지지 않기로 결정했다
and some of them decided [not to have] children.

to not have (X)
→ to부정사의 부정은 to 앞에 not을 붙인다.

Words & Phrases

faulty
[fɔ́:lti]
결함이 있는

gene
[dʒi:n]
유전자

impede
[impí:d]
~을 방해하다

resident
[rézidənt]
거주민

district
[dístrikt]
구역

persuade
[pərswéid]
설득하다

coastal
[kóustəl]
해안의

Grammar Point

to부정사의 부정

to부정사를 부정할 경우 not을 to 앞에 놓는다. not to do가 되어야지 to not do가 되어서는 안 된다. to부정사뿐만 아니라, 동명사와 분사구문의 부정 역시 앞에 not이 오게 된다.
e.g.) not doing, not done

You said you wanted to learn [to not work / not to work] for money.
당신은 돈을 위해 일하지 않는 법을 배우기를 원한다고 말했다.
⇒ to부정사의 부정은 not to do의 형태가 되어야 하므로 not to work가 정답이다.

Check-up

정답 및 해설 p.27

1. Charles' parents tried to walk silently [in order not to impede / not in order to impede] him.
2. A number of residents of that district have been trying to persuade coastal communities [to not destroy / not to destroy] the forests along the coast.

UNIT 142

to부정사의 시제

The Sun, which lies at the center of the solar system, seems to have been formed when the universe was already 10 billion years old.

태양계의 중심에 놓여 있는 태양은 이미 우주가 100억 살이었을 때 형성되었던 것으로 보인다.

태양은 // 놓여있는 / 태양계의 중심에 //
The Sun, which lies at the center of the solar system,

같다 / 형성되었던 것 // 우주가 이미 100억 살이었을 때
seems to have been formed when the universe was already

to be formed (X)
태양이 생성된 때는 과거이므로
to have p.p.의 형태로 써준다.

10 billion years old.

Grammar Point

to부정사의 시제

to부정사는 to 다음에 동사원형이 오는 구조이다. 하지만, to부정사의 내용이 과거를 의미할 경우 과거형 -ed 대신에 to have p.p.의 완료형을 사용한다.

We expect you to have completed your university studies with a doctoral degree in economics last year.

우리는 당신이 작년에 경제학 박사 학위를 받고 대학을 마쳤기를 기대한다.

⇒ to부정사 안의 시제가 과거를 의미하므로 to부정사는 완료형을 써야 한다.

Words & Phrases

solar system
태양계

doctoral degree
박사 학위

alien
[éiljən]
외계의

hover
[hʌ́vər]
맴돌다

Check-up

정답 및 해설 p.27

1. He is happy to finish / have finished his report last night.
2. A woman in London claims to see / have seen an alien spaceship hovering over Golders Green when the show was televised nation-wide.

EXERCISE

정답 및 해설 p.27

[01-10] 다음 중 어법상 가장 적절한 표현을 고르시오.

01 You're very lucky [to find / to have found] such a good job last month.

02 Jesus is said [to feed / to have fed] five thousand people with just two fishes and five loaves of bread.

03 기출응용 The general was determined [to not allow / not to allow] the enemy's forces a return voyage.

04 His brother warned Jack [to not leave / not to leave] his car unlocked as there had been a lot of stealing from cars.

05 She's such a natural for organizing international conventions that you may wonder why no one seems [to think / to have thought] of her before.

06 기출응용 Wise people learn [to not dread / not to dread] but actually to welcome problems and the chance to solve them.

07 A strike occurs when union members decide [to not return / not to return] to work until their employer gives in to some or all of their demands.

08 기출응용 The earliest map is thought [to be made / to have been made] in 7000 B.C. in an ancient city in what is now present-day Turkey.

09 기출응용 In China, it has never been rare for emperors to paint, but Huizong took it so seriously that the entire Northern Song Dynasty is thought [to fall / to have fallen] because of it.

10 Ms. Miller, who met James at the party, seems [to discover / to have discovered] the perfect spouse.

ACTUAL TEST

정답 및 해설 p.28

01 기출응용

다음 글의 밑줄 친 부분 중, 어법상 어긋난 것은?

The yo-yo is believed to ① originate in China about 2,500 years ago. Explorers have even found drawings of yo-yos on ancient Egyptian temples. Back then they were not plastic, of course, but ② were made of wood or clay and were just called "discs." Today we think of a yo-yo as ③ being a child's toy, but in the late 1700s a French king played with a toy "Emigrette"—a yo-yo made of glass and ivory. When the yo-yo was introduced to the United States, it became ④ widely popular, especially among children. It seemed that ⑤ there was a yo-yo on every corner and in every home in the USA. Indeed, many adults were still playing with yo-yos.

02 기출응용

다음 (A), (B), (C)의 각 [ ] 안에서 어법에 맞는 표현으로 바르게 짝지어진 것은?

The dream of employing beams of energy is actually not new. The concept of using rays as a practical weapon is shown through history and in old films. In 214 B.C., Archimedes is believed to (A) [create / have created] large batteries of solar reflectors that focused the sun's rays onto the sails of enemy ships. Ray guns burst onto the science fiction scene in 1898 with H. G. Wells's classic *War of the Worlds*, (B) [which / in which] aliens from Mars devastate entire cities by shooting beams of heat energy. During World War II, the Nazis experimented with various forms of ray guns. Weapons (C) [made / making] from focused light beams entered the public imagination with the James Bond movie *Goldfinger*, the first Hollywood film to feature a laser.

	(A)		(B)		(C)
①	create	-	which	-	made
②	create	-	which	-	making
③	have created	-	in which	-	made
④	have created	-	in which	-	making
⑤	create	-	in which	-	made

UNIT 143

가주어 it

It is advised that everyone over the age of twenty-five should have a regular physical examination. 기출응용

25세 이상의 모든 사람들은 정기검진을 받아야 한다고 권고 받는다.

권고 받는다 // 모든 사람들은 / 25세 이상의 /

It | is advised | that everyone over the age of twenty-five

뒤에 나오는 that절을 받는 가주어로 쓰였다.

정기 검진을 받아야 한다

should have a regular physical examination.

Grammar Point

가주어 it

'it'으로 시작하고 뒤에 형용사나 say, think, believe, advise 등의 수동형이 나오고 뒤에 to부정사나 that절이 나오면 'it'은 가주어일 확률이 높다. 뒤에 진주어가 있다면 주어 자리에는 가주어 it이 와야 한다.

It would be difficult for players to be calm while playing.

선수들이 경기 중 침착하기란 어려울 것이다.

⇒ 가주어는 it, 진주어는 to be 이하로 의미상의 주어는 for players이다.

It was said that James would be one of the most famous actors in ten years.

제임스가 10년 동안 가장 유명한 배우 중 한 명일 것이라고 말했다.

⇒ 가주어는 it, 진주어는 that절 이하다.

Words & Phrases

advise [ədváiz] 조언하다, 권고하다

physical [fízikəl] 신체적인, 물리적인

examination [igzæ̀mənéiʃən] 검진, 조사

satisfactory [sæ̀tisfǽktəri] 만족스러운

contract [kántrækt] 계약하다, 수축하다

construct [kánstrʌkt] 건설하다

Check-up

정답 및 해설 p.28

1. It / That is very satisfactory to know that I can help so many children become skilled and educated adults.

2. It / There is an important person who must sign the contract before we can start to construct the library.

UNIT 144

가목적어 it

Nasal congestion could have made it very hard for Christine to speak the words accurately.

코가 막혀서 크리스틴이 그 단어들을 정확하게 말하는 것이 어려웠을 수도 있다.

코 막힘이 / 만들었을 수도 있다 / 매우 어렵게 / 크리스틴이 /
Nasal congestion could have made [it] very hard for Christine

to부정사는 5형식의 목적어 자리에 올 수 없으므로 가목적어 it이 왔다.

말하는 것을 / 그 단어들을 / 정확하게
[to speak the words accurately.]

Grammar Point

가목적어 it

1. 동사의 목적어 자리에 to부정사나 that절이 올 경우 문장 중간이 길어지기 때문에 문장의 맨 뒤에 진목적어를 위치시키고 원래 자리에는 가목적어로 it을 둔다.

I found [it] difficult [to finish the task in two hours].

나는 2시간 안에 그 일을 끝내기가 힘들다는 것을 알았다.

We took [it] for granted [that you would pass the exam].

우리는 당신이 시험에 통과하는 것을 당연시했다.

2. 동사의 목적어 자리에 동명사가 올 경우는 가목적어를 쓰지 않아도 된다.

Warm weather made [living / to live] here pleasant. 기출응용

따뜻한 날씨 덕분에 여기서 사는 것이 즐거워졌다.

⇒ made 다음에 동사 live와 연결되는 here가 나왔고, 보어인 pleasant가 존재하므로 목적어의 형태는 동명사 living이 된다. to부정사의 목적어 자리에는 가목적어 it이 대신 온다는 것을 잊지 말자.

Words & Phrases

accurately [ǽkjuritli] 정확하게

take A for granted A를 당연시하다

pleasant [plézənt] 즐거운

confront [kənfrʌ́nt] 직면하다

collective [kəléktiv] 집합적인; 공동체

expose [èkspouz] 경험하게 하다, 접하게 하다

Check-up

정답 및 해설 p.28

1. The world today [finds it hard / finds hard] to confront its collective aging in addition to the political and economic choices. 기출응용

2. If you don't laugh enough, find out what you [find / find it] funny and expose yourself to that as much as possible.

EXERCISE

정답 및 해설 p.28

[01-10] 다음 중 어법상 가장 적절한 표현을 고르시오.

01 기출응용 The dog knows that [it / there] is food to be had but has no idea which of the cups hold the prize.

02 Only time will tell whether it's really worthwhile [pay / to pay] extra money for a brand name.

03 기출응용 However, this lack of time for relaxation makes it more difficult [get / to get] the most out of your studies.

04 It is advisable [that / which] colleges provide a well-rounded education which can cultivate the "whole student."

05 Once upon a time, they [took / took it] for granted that we were to spend much of our time in the shop.

06 [It / There] was mysterious that she made herself a strange figure by not appearing at the meeting.

07 Mrs. Porter [found / found it] cheerful to have meals with her children in her room.

08 [It / This] is possible for even children to use guns, so gun control should become more strict.

09 New plans for school investigations published today will [make / make it] harder for schools to be classified as good by focusing more on raw exam results.

10 Her clear explanation made [understanding / to understand] what was going on much easier.

정답 및 해설 p.29

01 다음 글의 밑줄 친 부분 중, 어법상 어긋난 것은?

He's describing everything that ① occurred more than 25 years ago, but the memory still keeps him ② irritated. At that point he found ③ most important to make money in order to get back to school. He was willing to go into town every day and did ④ whatever he had to do just to be a student again, but the school authorities were unwilling to do anything for him. And that was the point he decided he could do what he hoped without the higher education system. Even if he couldn't do without a diploma, it was sufficiently unpleasant to him ⑤ that he wouldn't do it anymore. So he dropped out of school.

02 기출응용 다음 (A), (B), (C)의 각 [ ] 안에서 어법에 맞는 표현으로 바르게 짝지어진 것은?

Some universities require students to keep a record of when they met with their supervisor, what was discussed, and what was the agreed next course of action. For advanced research programs, such as a Ph.D., keeping these records up to date (A) [is / are] a requirement for progression from one stage of the program to another. Seeing your supervisor regularly is one of the best ways of making sure that your dissertation is of the very highest possible standard. Yet you would be surprised how many students see their supervisor as little as possible. Although your supervisor will probably ask to see you if you have been invisible for a long period, (B) [it / that] is normally up to you to arrange such meetings. You should do this as (C) [regular / regularly] as possible whenever you have something to discuss.

	(A)		(B)		(C)
①	is	-	it	-	regular
②	are	-	that	-	regularly
③	is	-	that	-	regular
④	are	-	it	-	regular
⑤	is	-	it	-	regularly

UNIT
145 가목적어 it을 취하는 동사

The loss of the fund, owing to the raised exchange rate, has made it impossible for them to go abroad for their vacation.

오른 환율로 인한 기금 손실이 그들이 외국으로 휴가 가는 것을 불가능하게 했다.

기금 손실은 / 오른 환율 때문에 /

The loss of the fund, owing to the raised exchange rate,

만들어 왔다 / 불가능하게 / 그들에게 있어서 / 외국으로 휴가 가는 것을

has [made] [it] impossible for them [to go abroad for their vacation.]

made impossible to go abroad ~ (X)

앞에 동사 made가 있고 뒤에 to부정사가 있으므로 가목적어 it이 나왔다.

가목적어 it을 취하는 동사

keep, take, consider, think, make가 5문형으로 사용될 경우 뒤에 가목적어 구문이 많이 온다. 따라서 문제에서 ⟨동사 + [it / that] + 형용사 + to부정사 / that절 / 동명사⟩의 구조를 보이면 가목적어 it이 정답이다.

Recently, I've found [it / that] far easier to check something uncertain than to fix or repair it later.

최근에 나는 후에 해결하거나 고치는 것보다 확실하지 않은 것을 점검하는 게 훨씬 더 쉽다는 것을 깨달았다.

⇒ 뒤에 to check라는 to부정사가 나오므로, 이를 받는 가목적어 it이 필요하다.

Words & Phrases

loss [lɔ(:)s] 손실, 상실

owing to ~때문에

exchange rate 환율

abroad [əbrɔ́:d] 외국으로

confidence [kánfidəns] 자신감, 신뢰, 비밀

Check-up

정답 및 해설 p.29

1. The system has helped [make it possible / make possible] to buy products with confidence.

2. You will find [it / that] very nice to take an early morning walk around White Rock Lake in Dallas.

UNIT

146 가목적어 it을 취하지 않는 경우

I believe that artistic phenomena are included in this redemption and that this makes possible a renewal in artistic life which again brings glory to God.

나는 예술적 현상이 이 구원 안에 포함되며 이것이 예술적 삶 속에서 신께 다시 한번 영광을 가져다 줄 부활을 가능하게 한다고 생각한다.

나는 생각한다 // 예술적 현상은 / 포함된다 /
I believe [that] artistic phenomena are included

이 구원에 // 그리고 이것은 / 부활을 가능하게 한다 /
in this redemption and [that] this [makes possible a renewal]

makes it possible a renewal (X)
makes possible 다음에 명사가 오면 가목적어를 사용하지 않는다.

예술적 삶 속에서 // 다시 한번 신께 영광을 가져다 줄
in artistic life which again brings glory to God.

Grammar Point

가목적어 it을 취하지 않는 경우

make possible [impossible, easy, difficult] 구문 뒤에 명사(구)가 올 경우 목적어(명사)와 목적격 보어(형용사)가 도치된 경우이므로 가목적어 it을 취하지 않는다.

In 1775, Daniel Boone opened the Wilderness Road and [made possible the first settlement in Kentucky.]

1775년 다니엘 분은 와일더니스 로드를 개통했고, 켄터키에서의 첫 번째 정착이 가능토록 했다.

⇒ 목적어인 the first ~ Kentucky가 너무 길어서 목적격 보어인 possible과 자리를 바꾼 것이다.

Words & Phrases

artistic [ɑːrtístik] 예술적인

redemption [ridémʃən] 구원, 되찾기

renewal [rinjúːəl] 부활, 갱신

advance [ədvǽns] 발전

diagnosis [dàiəgnóusis] 진단

condition [kəndíʃən] 질병; 상태

considerable [kənsídərəbl] 상당한

Check-up

정답 및 해설 p.29

1. Advances in technology have [made possible / made it possible] the early diagnosis of conditions that may cause serious problems later.

2. You'll [make possible / make it possible] to focus your considerable creative energy on achieving the highest and best of your dreams. 기출응용

EXERCISE

정답 및 해설 p.29

[01-10] **다음 중 어법상 가장 적절한 표현을 고르시오.**

01 My new sneakers gave me blisters, and they [make / make it] a problem to work.

02 The final development of a hydrogen-burning engine can make [possible / it possible] a change in driving habits.

03 Maui [found / found it] rather strange the scene in which Romeo and Juliet died.

04 They'll end up doing things that make college last longer and that just [make more expensive / make it more expensive] to be in the university.

05 You helped [make possible / make it possible] for us to continue offering our students free education.

06 As a child you consistently do well in sports but [find / find it] hard to be part of a team.

07 Most of the villagers considered [unbelievable / it unbelievable] the growth of the small and beautiful flower on the wall.

08 The policymakers usually consider [desirable / it desirable] for women to require their husbands to share childcare duty.

09 Tom himself believed [impressive / it impressive] for her to concentrate on her research thoroughly under that situation.

10 This disaster made [possible / it possible] his research on the relationship between hurricanes and rapid urbanization.

ACTUAL TEST

정답 및 해설 p.30

01 다음 글의 밑줄 친 부분 중, 어법상 어긋난 것은?

After choosing a topic, you can start constructing the body of your presentation. Fundamentally, you develop the body by breaking down your topic into several main points. You then support each main point with specific information such as examples, explanations, facts, and details. In developing your topic, ① it is important to use from two to five main points. ② By limiting the number of main points, you will ③ make easier for listeners to understand and remember the information you present. If you use more than five main points, your listeners may have difficulty ④ trying to follow your ideas. Many topics divide naturally into several main points: advantages, disadvantages, causes, effects, solutions, reasons and so on. In other cases, however, you may need to spend some time sorting through your ideas to organize ⑤ them into two to five main points.

02 기출응용 다음 (A), (B), (C)의 각 [ ] 안에서 어법에 맞는 표현으로 바르게 짝지어진 것은?

Animals went to space before people did, serving as test pilots who (A) [made evident / made it evident] that space and rocket travel would be safe for humans. In the 1950s, no one knew what would happen to living things in space. Scientists wanted as much information as possible before sending a human there. So 'dognauts' and 'chimpnauts' (B) [recruited / were recruited] as the first true space pioneers. The first animal in space was a Soviet dog named Laika, who traveled aboard Sputnik II in 1957. America's National Aeronautics and Space Administration put chimpanzees into orbit in 1959. One chimp spent a year training for his flight! Today creatures from bees to bullfrogs to jellyfish (C) [become / becomes] space cadets so astronauts can study their behavior and the effect of weightlessness.

*cadets : 사관생도

	(A)		(B)		(C)
①	made evident	-	recruited	-	become
②	made evident	-	were recruited	-	becomes
③	made it evident	-	were recruited	-	become
④	made evident	-	were recruited	-	becomes
⑤	made it evident	-	recruited	-	become

UNIT 147

be to 용법

Imagine that it's Friday and you are to go to the movies with your fiancée at COEX in the evening.

금요일이고, 당신은 저녁에 약혼자와 함께 코엑스로 영화를 보러 갈 예정이라고 상상해 봐라.

상상해 봐라 // 금요일이고 // 당신은 영화를 보러 갈 예정이다 /
Imagine that it's Friday and you [are to go] to the movies

당신의 약혼녀와 함께 / 저녁에 코엑스로
with your fiancée at COEX in the evening.

Grammar Point

be to 용법

⟨be+to+동사원형⟩ 구문은 주로 '~할 운명이다', '~하기로 예정되어 있다', '~해야 한다', '~할 수 있다'로 해석된다. 헷갈릴 경우 '~할 예정이다'로 해석하는 게 좋다.

He [is to die] at a young age. 그는 어려서 죽을 운명이다.

Jane [was to arrive] here at 7. 제인은 7시에 여기에 도착할 예정이었다.

You [are to listen] to others. 너는 다른 사람의 말을 들어야 한다.

Nothing [was to be seen] here. 여기서 아무것도 볼 수가 없었다.

be to 용법 vs. 주격 보어

1. 주어와 to부정사의 주술관계가 성립하면 be to용법

Shawn was to be the king. 숀은 왕이 될 운명이었다.

⇒ Shawn is the king이 된다.

2) ⟨주어 = to부정사⟩의 관계가 성립하면 주격 보어

His hobby is to read books. 그의 취미는 책을 읽는 것이다.

⇒ His hobby = to read many books가 성립한다.

Words & Phrases

essential [əsénʃəl] 중요한

make a plan 계획을 세우다

lung [lʌŋ] 폐

cancer [kǽnsər] 암

Check-up

정답 및 해설 p.30

1. The most essential thing you can do for your wife is [made / to make] a plan for the wedding anniversary she really wants.

2. You are [to stop / stopping] smoking. If not, you may get lung cancer.

UNIT 148

본동사 vs. be to 동사원형

To focus on the differences between the sisters is to miss a more essential similarity.

자매들 사이의 차이점에 집중하는 것은 더 본질적인 유사성을 놓치고 있는 것이다.

차이점에 집중하는 것은 / 자매들 사이의 /
To focus on the differences between the sisters

놓치고 있는 것이다 / 더 본질적인 유사성을
is to miss a more essential similarity.

misses (X)
'초점은 놓치고 있다'보다는
'초점은 놓치고 있는 것이다'가 더 자연스럽다.

Grammar Point

일반동사 vs. be to 동사원형

주어로 to부정사나, what절, that절 등이 나올 경우 본동사의 형태는 해석에 따라서 일반동사 또는 be to부정사(~하는 것이다)가 될 수 있다. 따라서, 전체적으로 보다 자연스러운 해석이 되는 것을 답으로 골라야 한다.

Schubert spent his whole life in poverty. But he had one noble purpose in life. That [was to write / wrote] down the beautiful note. 기출응용

슈베르트는 일생을 가난하게 살았다. 하지만, 그는 삶에 한 가지 숭고한 목적을 가지고 있었다. 그것은 아름다운 곡을 쓰는 것이었다.

⇒ 슈베르트가 가지고 있던 목적을 지칭하므로, 목적을 설명하는 보어 to write(쓰는 것)이 온다. 목적이 곡을 쓰지는 않는다.

Words & Phrases

essential [əsénʃəl] 본질적인

similarity [sìməlǽrəti] 유사성

poverty [pávərti] 가난

noble [nóubl] 숭고한

purpose [pə́:rpəs] 목적

treatment [trí:tmənt] 치료, 대접

sort A into B A를 B로 분류하다

genotype [dʒénətàip] 유전자형

Check-up

정답 및 해설 p.30

1. One more thing you need to do [find / is to find] the real partner who will stay with you for the rest of your days.

2. Golub's goal [uses / is to use] this treatment to sort cancer into genotypes rather than phenotypes.

*phenotype : 표현형

EXERCISE

정답 및 해설 p.30

[01-10] 다음 중 어법상 가장 적절한 표현을 고르시오.

01 The best way to look successful [buys / is to buy] an expensive car and a nice house.

02 One of the membership conditions of this club [has / is to have] assets which are worth more than $10 million.

03 Kevin's first goal in his life will [earn / be to earn] $100 thousand before marrying Tracy.

04 The worst way to do your homework [copies and pastes / is to copy and paste] necessary information from the Internet.

05 One way to enjoy football [participates / is to participate] in a real game in the playground with other fellows.

06 The lifestyle change you have to make in order to lose weight [exercises and runs / is to exercise and run] regularly.

07 The best advice for making listeners focus on your presentation [gazes / is to gaze] into their eyes as you communicate with them.

08 One common mistake that students will make [assumes / is to assume] that others are the same.

09 The next thing that you will need to do [searches / is to search] for unfamiliar words in a dictionary.

10 What we must do today [watches / is to watch] the literal raw material of Brazilian cuisine and the rich amalgam of European cooking traditions serving up everything from pizza to sausage.

*amalgam : 혼합

ACTUAL TEST

정답 및 해설 p.31

01 다음 글의 밑줄 친 부분 중, 어법상 어긋난 것은?

The surest way to be healthier and happier ① is to do less work. One in six Britons works more than 60 hours a week, significantly increasing their chances of suffering a heart attack or stroke. However, these days people are finding ways to cut back. Two years ago, the governor of Utah stumbled across a simple policy that lashes greenhouse gas emissions, cuts congestion, and ② makes workers happier. ③ Trying to find a way to cut the cost of heating and lighting state buildings, he decided to pass a law changing the working hours of state employees. ④ Instead of coming in from nine to five, five days a week, they now work from eight to six four days a week, and everyone takes Fridays off. This tiny tinker with work routines ⑤ have had amazing benefits: 82% of workers say they love the new hours; staff sick days have fallen; efficiency is up. The good life is not beyond our reach: it just requires some imaginative thinking.

02 기출응용

다음 (A), (B), (C)의 각 [ ] 안에서 어법에 맞는 표현으로 바르게 짝지어진 것은?

These days, job hunting needs more systematic efforts. The first step (A) [determines / is to determine] what kind of job you want and make sure that you have the right education for it. Rapid changes in technology and science (B) [is / are] creating many professions that never existed until recently. It is important to learn about them because one might be the perfect profession for you. The fastest-growing areas for new jobs are in health services and computer science. Jobs in these fields usually require specific skills, so you need to find out exactly (C) [that / which] skills and degrees are necessary.

	(A)		(B)		(C)
①	determines	-	is	-	that
②	is to determine	-	is	-	that
③	is to determine	-	are	-	which
④	is to determine	-	are	-	that
⑤	determines	-	are	-	which

UNIT
149 to부정사를 목적어로 취하는 동사

Many college presidents believe that current laws not only fail to deter this dangerous problem, but they actually make it worse.

많은 대학의 학장들은 현행 법이 이 위험한 문제를 막는 데 실패할 뿐 아니라 실제로 더 악화시킬 거라고 생각한다.

많은 대학의 학장들이 / 생각한다 // 현행 법이 /
Many college presidents believe that current laws

이 위험한 문제를 막는 데 실패할 뿐만 아니라 //
not only fail to deter this dangerous problem,

fail deterring (X)
fail은 to부정사를 목적어로 취하는 동사이다.

실제로 그것을 더 악화시킨다
but they actually make it worse.

Grammar Point

to부정사를 목적어로 취하는 동사

다음의 동사들은 to부정사를 목적어로 취하는 동사들이다. 암기하도록 하자.

afford, agree, attempt, beg, care, choose, decide, expect, fail, happen, hope, learn, manage, offer, pretend, promise, plan, refuse, seem, seek, tend, want, wish	+ to부정사

Words & Phrases

current [kɔ́:rənt] 현재의

deter [ditɔ́:r] 막다

actually [ǽktʃuəli] 사실

can't afford 여유가 없다

significant [signífikənt] 특이한; 심각한

related to ~과 관련된

Check-up

정답 및 해설 p.31

1. We can't afford [to worry / worrying] about something that may not be a significant problem.

2. Government officials refused [to reveal / revealing] more details of the project related to the new town.

UNIT 150

to부정사와 동명사를 모두 목적어로 취하는 동사

If you make a conscious decision to become a less aggressive driver, you begin using your time in the car to relax. 기출응용

만약 당신이 덜 난폭한 운전자가 되겠다고 의식적으로 결정을 내린다면 차 안에서 있는 시간을 휴식을 취하는 데 사용하기 시작할 것이다.

만약 당신이 의식적으로 결정을 내린다면 / 덜 난폭한 운전자가 되겠다고 //
If you make a conscious decision to become a less aggressive driver,

당신은 사용하기 시작할 것이다 / 차 안에 있는 시간을 / 쉬기 위해
you begin using your time in the car to relax.

to use (O)

begin은 목적어로 to부정사와 동명사 모두를 취할 수 있으므로 using과 to use 둘 다 올 수 있다.

Grammar Point

to부정사와 동명사 모두를 목적어로 취하는 동사

다음의 동사들은 to부정사와 동명사 모두를 목적어로 취하며, 그 의미 또한 거의 같다. 이러한 동사 뒤에 나오는 목적어에 밑줄이 그어져 있다면 정답일 확률은 거의 없다.

begin, start, love, like, intend, prefer, hate, continue	+	to부정사 / -ing

Check-up 정답 및 해설 p.31

1. Children are less likely to enjoy going to the library and more likely to prefer [surfing / to surf] the Internet to reading various books.
2. They discouraged other netizens from calling the company to pressure it to continue [placing / place] ads in the papers.

Words & Phrases

conscious [kánʃəs] 의식하고 있는, 의식적인

aggressive [əgrésiv] 난폭한

discourage [idskə́:ridʒ] 낙담시키다

pressure [préʃər] 압력을 가하다

EXERCISE

정답 및 해설 p.31

[01-10] 다음 중 어법상 가장 적절한 표현을 고르시오.

01 The publishing company cannot afford [pay / to pay] overtime.

02 She doesn't consider [visiting / to visit] the campus library or the bookstore.

03 They failed [take / to take] pleasure in their potential sources of happiness that were all around them.

04 Union wages in the United States have risen so high that few firms can afford [hire / to hire] American workers.

05 This essay fails [focusing / to focus] upon a particular aspect or make a main point about its subject.

06 African-Americans refused [riding / to ride] the buses until they were desegregated, and their campaign was successful.

07 To encourage the assembly line to perform more efficiently, the institute suggested [enhancing / to enhance] the quality of the device.

08 If you want to cut back your cost of oil, discontinue [using / to use] it immediately and try something new.

09 Shawn lived with his parents until he was 19 and then decided [challenging / to challenge] himself and come to the city.

10 Several different departments refused [changing / to change] the target market.

정답 및 해설 p.32

01 기출응용 다음 글의 밑줄 친 부분 중, 어법상 어긋난 것은?

Overgrazing of the savanna is one of ① the biggest factors in the shrinking of the lake, according to the scientists, Cole and Foley. "As the climate became drier, the vegetation that supported grazing livestock began ② to disappear. Vegetation has a big influence, especially in semiarid regions, in determining weather patterns," said Foley. "The loss of vegetation ③ in itself contributed to a drier climate." The situation is a "domino effect," Cole said. Overgrazing reduces vegetation, ④ which in turn reduces the ecosystem's ability to recycle moisture back into the atmosphere. That contributes to ⑤ retreat the monsoons. The consequent drought conditions have triggered a huge increase in the use of lake water for irrigation, while the Sahara has gradually edged southward.

*semiarid : 반 건조성의

02 다음 (A), (B), (C)의 각 [ ] 안에서 어법에 맞는 표현으로 바르게 짝지어진 것은?

According to studies, European-Americans who are more forgiving experience less stress and less hostility, (A) [what / which] are fatal factors for heart disease. European-Americans who imagine forgiving their offenders show immediate improvement in their cardiovascular, muscular, and nervous systems. Even those who have experienced devastating losses report feeling better psychologically and emotionally when they forgive. On the other hand, European-Americans who fail (B) [forgiving / to forgive] have higher incidences of illnesses such as cardiovascular disease and cancer. European-Americans who imagine (C) [forgiving not / not forgiving] someone who has wronged them show negative changes in blood pressure, muscle tension, and immune response. In short, forgiveness has a positive influence on our body.

*cardiovascular : 심장 혈관의

	(A)		(B)		(C)
①	what	-	forgiving	-	forgiving not
②	which	-	forgiving	-	not forgiving
③	what	-	to forgive	-	not forgiving
④	which	-	to forgive	-	not forgiving
⑤	what	-	to forgive	-	forgiving not

UNIT 151

to부정사와 동명사가 올 때 의미가 다른 동사

While your company suggested a 15% commission for this project, we regret to say that our team won't accept your proposal.

당신의 회사가 이 프로젝트에 대해 15%의 수수료를 제안했음에도 불구하고, 우리 팀이 당신의 제안을 받아들이지 않을 거라고 말하게 되어 유감스럽다.

당신의 회사가 15%의 수수료를 제안했음에도 불구하고 / 이 프로젝트에 대해 //

While your company suggested a 15% commission for this project,

우리는 / 말하게 되어 유감스럽다 // 우리 팀이 / 당신의 제안을 받아들이지 않을 것이다

we regret to say that our team won't accept your proposal.

saying (X)

과거에 말한 것을 후회하는 것이 아니라 유감을 표하는 것이므로 to say가 온다.

to부정사와 동명사가 올 때 의미가 다른 동사

다음의 동사들은 목적어로 to부정사와 동명사가 올 때 그 의미가 달라지므로 꼭 숙지하도록 하자.

remember / forget	to : 미래 (아직 안 함)	-ing : 과거 (이미 함)
regret	to : 유감스럽다	-ing : 후회하다
try	to : 노력하다	-ing : 한번 해보다, 시도하다
mean	to : 의도하다	-ing : 의미하다

Words & Phrases

suggest [sədʒést] 제안하다

commission [kəmíʃən] 수수료

regret [rigrét] 유감스럽게 생각하다

proposal [prəpóuzəl] 제안

blame [bleim] 비난하다

Check-up

정답 및 해설 p.32

1. Jack Bauer was blamed for losing the design maps because he forgot [to lock / locking] the door of the office yesterday.

2. The salesperson forgot [to give / giving] me his business card and gave it to me again.

stop to부정사 vs. stop -ing

The students occasionally stop to think about language-related problems—i.e., gaps in their language knowledge, to resolve their misunderstandings in communication.

학생들은 때때로 언어 지식에서의 차이와 같이 의사소통에서의 오해를 해결하기 위해서 언어와 관련된 문제를 생각하려고 멈춘다.

학생들은 때때로 생각하기 위하여 멈춘다 /
The students occasionally stop to think about

thinking (X)
뒤의 내용이 의사소통문제를 해결하는 것이므로 언어와 관련된 문제를 생각해야지, 그것을 멈추면 안되므로 stop to think가 온다.

언어와 관련된 문제들을 / 즉 자신들의 언어 지식에서의 차이와 같은 /
language-related problems—i.e., gaps in their language knowledge,

해결하기 위하여 / 그들의 의사소통에서의 오해를
to resolve their misunderstandings in communication.

Grammar Point

stop+to부정사 vs. stop+-ing

stop 다음에는 동명사(~하는 것을)나 to부정사(~하기 위하여)가 올 수 있다. stop 뒤에 온 동명사는 stop의 목적어이지만 to부정사는 부사로 쓰인 것이다.

stop	+	-ing	'~하는 것을 멈추다'
		to부정사	'~하기 위하여 멈추다'

I could read the expression on his face, and I stopped [talking / to talk] at that point and changed the subject.

나는 그의 얼굴 표정을 읽을 수 있었고, 그 시점에서 나는 말하는 것을 멈추고 주제를 바꿨다.

⇒ '주제를 바꾼다'라는 내용이 나오므로, '말하는 것을 멈춘다'라는 의미가 자연스럽다. 따라서 talking이 옳다.

Words & Phrases

occasionally [əkéiʒənəli] 때때로

related [riléitid] 관련된

resolve [rizɑ́lv] 해결하다

misunderstanding [mìsʌndərstǽndiŋ] 오해

breathe [bri:ð] 숨을 쉬다

Check-up

정답 및 해설 p.32

1. Finally, Simba stopped [to breathe / breathing]. The doctor said, with tears in his eyes, "I regret to tell you of his death." 기출응용

2. Jamie felt thirsty, so she stopped [to drink / drinking] a bottle of water.

EXERCISE

정답 및 해설 p.32

[01-10] **다음 중 어법상 가장 적절한 표현을 고르시오.**

01 When you are surprised at something, your internal organs stop [moving / to move] momentarily and all activities related to digestion pause.

02 I forgot [to lock / locking] the door, so I should return to my house.

03 기출응용 It is not as addictive as other drugs, but it can be difficult to stop [taking / to take] caffeine once you're a regular coffee drinker.

04 The fish have stopped [to develop / developing] their eyes since they live in such dark water that they no longer have any use for them.

05 We regret [informing / to inform] you that your position has been eliminated, so you should clear your desk before 5 o'clock today.

06 Couples grow apart when they stop [talking and listening / to talk and listen] to each other.

07 The policeman stopped [reading / to read] the magazine to look out for suspects.

08 The news reported that the Korean foreign minister is going to meet Japan's prime minister in Seoul in order to ask him to stop [visiting / to visit] Yasukuni Shrine.

09 When Adam saw Ellen passing by the bank, he stopped [talking / to talk] to her again.

10 I forgot [bringing / to bring] the recommendation letter for him. I should return to the office.

ACTUAL TEST

정답 및 해설 p.33

01 **다음 글의 밑줄 친 부분 중, 어법상 어긋난 것은?**

① Compared to the students of today, I think I could do many things at home and also have enough free time to play outside. It did not take me more than two hours to do my homework. I remember ② to play baseball with my friends at the playground all afternoon almost every day. However, my son complains that he has to spend too much time doing his homework because the reading passage is too difficult for him ③ to read and there are a large number of unfamiliar words to look up. "I wish my school days would pass quickly, so I can stop ④ doing homework," he says. I feel sorry for him and hope that he tries ⑤ to enjoy his school days. Looking back on my school days, I used to live in a world of freedom and joy.

02 기출응용 **다음 (A), (B), (C)의 각 ☐ 안20에서 어법에 맞는 표현으로 바르게 짝지어진 것은?**

The town I live in was built on logging. In the 1980s, we had a lot of jobs—and a lot of money for the town. Our town was full of life. But by 1992, the number of trees we were cutting (A) was / were drastically decreasing. Why? Because the northern spotted owls were found and people who just care about the owls stopped us from doing our jobs. They convinced the government that the company should stop (B) logging / to log trees. Consequently, over 30,000 jobs have been lost. People have a hard time putting food on their table. Our town is a third of the size that it (C) was used / used to be. I'm not against the spotted owl, but saving the owl is hurting people. What is more important, a few owls or the lives of thousands of hardworking families?

	(A)		(B)		(C)
①	was	-	logging	-	was used
②	was	-	to log	-	was used
③	was	-	logging	-	used
④	were	-	to log	-	used
⑤	were	-	logging	-	was used

UNIT

153 forget, remember+to부정사 vs. -ing

She had a very good voice, except that some of her high notes tended to sound like a gate which someone had forgotten to oil. 기출응용

그녀는 고음 중 일부에 누군가 기름칠 하는 것을 잊어버린 문처럼 소리가 나는 경향이 있다는 점을 제외하고는 굉장히 좋은 목소리를 지니고 있다.

그녀는 굉장히 좋은 목소리를 지니고 있다 // 제외하고는 // 그녀의 고음 중 일부가 /
She had a very good voice, except that some of her high notes

문처럼 소리나는 경향이 있다 // 누군가가 기름칠할 것을 잊어버린
tended to sound like a gate which someone had [forgotten to oil].

forgotten oiling (X)
기름칠을 하지 않은 것이므로 to oil이 왔다.

Grammar Point

forget, remember+to부정사 vs. –ing

forget, remember 뒤에 to부정사가 오면 미래(아직 안 함)를 나타내고, -ing가 오면 과거(이미 함)를 나타낸다. 반드시 해석을 통해 풀어야 한다.

forget, remember	forget to turn on the TV : TV를 아직 안 켰음 to부정사 – 미래 (아직 안 했음)
	forget turning on the TV : TV를 이미 켰음 동명사 – 과거 (이미 했음)

I think it gives you big chance, but I expect that you will spoil the work if you forget [to check / checking] it.
나는 그것이 너에게 굉장한 기회라고 생각하지만, 만약 네가 그것을 점검하는 것을 잊는다면, 그 일을 망칠 거라고 예상해.
⇒ 내용상 아직 점검하지 않은 것을 의미하므로 to check이 옳다.

Words & Phrases

except [iksépt] 제외하고

tend [tend] 경향이 있다

reportedly [ripɔ́:rtidli] 전하는 바에 의하면

Check-up

정답 및 해설 p.33

1. The guests had arrived, and the wine was warm. Once again, I'd forgotten [to refrigerate / refrigerating] it.
2. When students were found with a cell phone turned on during the test, they reportedly said they forgot [to turn / turning] their phones in before the exam.

to부정사를 목적격 보어로 취하는 동사

When one plants peas, one must expect peas to grow, not carrots or lilies.

완두콩을 심으면 당근이나 백합이 아니라 완두콩이 자랄 것을 기대해야 한다.

사람이 완두콩을 심으면 // 사람은 기대해야 한다 / 완두콩이 자라기를 /

When one plants peas, one must **expect** peas **to grow**,

grow, growing (X)

expect는 목적격 보어로 to부정사를 취하는 동사이다.

당근이나 백합이 아니라

not carrots or lilies.

Grammar Point

to부정사를 목적격 보어로 취하는 동사

다음의 동사들은 to부정사를 목적격 보어로 취하는 동사들이다. 암기하도록 하자.

advise, allow, ask, beg, cause, convince encourage, enable, expect, forbid, force, get, invite, lead, need, order, permit, persuade, promise, remind, require, teach, tell, urge, want, warn	+ 목적어 + to부정사

Words & Phrases

expect [ikspékt] 기대하다, 예상하다

colorful [kʌ́lərfəl] 화려한

urge [əːrdʒ] 재촉하다

pumpkin [pʌ́mpkin] 호박

Check-up

정답 및 해설 p.33

1. Police advise hikers [to wear / wearing] bright, colorful clothing during hunting season. 기출응용

2. He urges pumpkin buyers [creating / to create] their own zoos this Halloween. 기출응용

EXERCISE

정답 및 해설 p.33

[01-10] 다음 중 어법상 가장 적절한 표현을 고르시오.

01 The students were relieved because Mrs. Lee forgot [giving / to give] them homework.

02 기출응용 He found that the British film-making style allowed everyone [have / to have] an opinion.

03 기출응용 This messaging enables spatially-separated insects [avoiding / to avoid] each other, so that they do not unintentionally compete for the same plant.

04 Jim failed history class because he forgot [submitting / to submit] the final report about Rome.

05 When her old friend Ben urged my son [accepting / to accept] the cake, it was more than he could bear.

06 To help your hair grow long naturally, remember [getting / to get] your hair cut every 6 to 8 weeks to remove split ends.

07 Because she forgot [donating / to donate] 3 million won for the orphanage last month, Jasmine gave 3 million won to the orphanage again.

08 The computer's mouse permits the computer operator [move / to move] the cursor on the video display.

09 The statement says perhaps the worst move is to forbid a student [applying / to apply] for a dream school simply on account of financial problems.

10 The children had a good time with you. They will never forget [visiting / to visit] this amusement park.

ACTUAL TEST

정답 및 해설 p.34

01 **다음 글의 밑줄 친 부분 중, 어법상 <u>어긋난</u> 것은?**

It ① <u>sounds like</u> something out of a fairy tale: a beautiful girl who sleeps for days at a time. However, there is no Prince Charming to wake her up to someone who suffers from Sleeping Beauty disease, a rare illness known as Kleine-Levin Syndrome ② <u>that</u> afflicts an estimated 1,000 people in the world. Sufferers have normal sleep patterns for long periods, and then they'll go to sleep for days or weeks. One girl's longest bout in bed has been 13 days. During these prolonged naps, her parents force her ③ <u>get up</u>. Otherwise, she would be dead to the world. Kleine-Levin Syndrome is still little-understood by doctors. Some think it is hereditary; others say it is the result of an auto-immune disorder. Most link it with a malfunctioning hypothalamus, the area of the brain ④ <u>which</u> regulates sleep and appetite. The good news ⑤ <u>is</u> that it usually fades with adulthood, and in the meantime the symptoms can be alleviated by drugs.

*hypothalamus : 시상하부

02  **다음 (A), (B), (C)의 각 [ ] 안에서 어법에 맞는 표현으로 바르게 짝지어진 것은?**

Leadership is becoming more (A) [important / importantly] in this era of change. A lot of leadership development programs have been created out of a mistaken identity between leadership and management. Leadership is not simply a matter of memorizing financial facts and adopting strategies of the past. A good leader can allow each member to share goals and encourage them (B) [participating / to participate] in decision-making regardless of their status within an organization. Leadership is an influence relationship between leaders and followers, not an authority relationship between so-called superiors and subordinates. There are no cookbooks on the (C) [invention / inventing] of leadership for the future, but understanding the true nature of leadership as a democratic attitude will guide you in the right direction.

	(A)		(B)		(C)
①	important	-	participating	-	inventing
②	important	-	to participate	-	inventing
③	important	-	to participate	-	invention
④	importantly	-	to participate	-	inventing
⑤	importantly	-	participating	-	invention

to -ing

When it comes to buying something, most of us have an idea in our minds of how much we're willing to spend.

무언가를 구매할 때 우리 대부분은 기꺼이 소비하고자 하는 금액에 대해 마음 속으로 생각하는 것이 있다.

무언가를 구매할 때 / 우리 대부분은 / 생각이 있다 /

When it comes **to buying** something, most of us have an idea

to buy (X)

전치사 to 뒤에 동명사인 making이 왔다.

우리 마음 속에 // 우리가 기꺼이 소비하고자 하는 금액에 대해

in our minds of how much we're willing to spend.

Grammar Point

to –ing

보통 to 다음에 동사원형이 와서 to부정사를 이루지만, to가 전치사라면 명사나 동명사가 와야 한다. 다음의 to는 전치사이므로 반드시 암기해야 한다.

be/get used to	~에 익숙해지다	come close to	거의 ~할 뻔 하다
look forward to	~하기를 고대하다	key to	~대한 핵심
contribute to	~에 공헌하다	when it comes to	~에 관하여
devote oneself to	~에 전념하다, 헌신하다	with a view to	~을 위하여
object to	~에 반대하다	in addition to	~와 더불어
be opposed to	~에 반대하다	be accustomed to	~에 익숙해지다

Words & Phrases

have an idea 생각이 있다; 알다

be willing to 기꺼이 ~하다

contact [kάntækt] 접촉하다

client [kláiənt] 고객

invest in ~에 투자하다

Check-up

정답 및 해설 p.34

1. Because Jessica had two young children to care for, she wasn't sure she could devote two years to [train / training].

2. Our mission is to contact companies which our clients invest in, with a view to [improve / improving] things by keeping them informed.

UNIT
156 be used to 동사원형 vs. be used to -ing

This recently completed plant will have an annual output of about 200,000 cars and be used to produce models only for the American market.

최근에 완공된 이 공장은 연간 약 20만 대의 자동차를 생산하게 될 것이고, 미국 시장만을 겨냥한 모델을 생산하는 데 이용될 것이다.

최근에 완공된 이 공장은 / 가질 것이다 / 연간 생산량을 /
This recently completed plant will have an annual output of

약 20만 대의 자동차 / 그리고 모델을 생산하는 데 이용된다 /
about 200,000 cars and be used to produce models

to producing (X)

주어가 plant이므로 '익숙하다'보다는 '이용되다'로 해석하는 게 자연스럽다. 따라서 동사원형인 produce가 온다.

미국 시장만을 위한
only for the American market.

Grammar Point

be used to 동사원형 vs. be used to –ing

be used to는 뒤에 동사원형이 오느냐 동명사(-ing)가 오느냐에 따라 의미가 달라진다. 〈be used to+동사원형〉은 use의 수동태 구문으로 '~하는 데 이용되다'라는 의미이다. 반면에 〈be used to+-ing〉는 하나의 숙어로 '~하는 데 익숙하다'라는 의미이다. 〈be used to+동사원형/-ing〉 문제는 해석으로 해결해야 한다.

This medicine, released yesterday, is used to [treat / treating] acne and scars.

어제 출시된 이 약은 여드름과 상처 치료에 이용된다.

⇒ 약은 상처를 치료하는 데 익숙한 것이 아니라, 상처를 치료하는 데 이용된다. 따라서 treat이 정답이다.

Words & Phrases

complete [kəmplíːt] 완성하다, 끝내다

annual [ǽnjuəl] 연간

output [áutpùt] 생산량; 생산하다

acne [ǽkni] 여드름

scar [skɑːr] 흉터

experimental [ikspèrəméntəl] 실험의

Check-up 정답 및 해설 p.34

1. These researches can be used to [predict / predicting] experimental results including given physical situations.

2. Our director is used to [give / giving] a presentation on new products to the investors.

EXERCISE

정답 및 해설 p.34

[01-10] 다음 중 어법상 가장 적절한 표현을 고르시오.

01 The game begins with a coin toss, which is used to [determine / determining] which team would go first.

02 기출응용 The white blood cells are injected back into the body, and a special camera is used to [pick / picking] up signals from the indium-111.

03 When someone is about to attack, this tool may be used to [warn / warning] the rest of the people.

04 My kids are already looking forward to [spend / spending] their summer vacation on the beach in Hawaii.

05 기출응용 This constant temperature can be used to [cool and heat / cooling and heating] buildings by using a heat pump.

06 Michelle has been in Korea for about two years, so she's used to [eat / eating] Korean food.

07 There has been heated debate over gambling addiction, and many people are opposed to [legalize / legalizing] gambling.

08 For example, in fast food restaurants, quick tempo music is used to [shorten / shortening] the time of eating and get more customers.

09 The task the professor gave to me was too difficult to complete by myself, so I came close to [give up / giving up] several times.

10 The law will contribute to [discourage / discouraging] people from doing something wrong.

ACTUAL TEST

정답 및 해설 p.35

01 기출응용

다음 글의 밑줄 친 부분 중, 어법상 어긋난 것은?

When a person moves from a cool, rainy, and coastal region to a hot, dry, and mountainous area, a number of physiological changes must ① be undergone that allow survival in the new environment. The human body changes in order to regulate body temperature more ② efficiently. To keep from overworking the heart, the body's heart rate slows down. Additionally, the body perspires less to prevent dehydration. Furthermore, people who are unaccustomed to ③ live in high altitudes usually have trouble ④ breathing because of the decreased oxygen levels. So the human body causes an increase in red blood cells, which ⑤ makes it possible for humans to breathe at higher altitudes.

*dehydration : 건조, 탈수

02 기출응용

다음 (A), (B), (C)의 각 [ ] 안에서 어법에 맞는 표현으로 바르게 짝지어진 것은?

Children at the Heritage Lakes School in Carol Stream, Illinois, decided to help the environment. The students collected old rubber-soled shoes and sneakers that could be used to (A) [make / making] bouncy playground surfaces. Many playgrounds are cushioned with wood chips. The students learned they could recycle rubber from old shoes to make a safer, more Earth-friendly surface. The project saved trees by (B) [creation / creating] a replacement for wood chips. And it used old shoes which (C) [might be / might have been] dumped in landfills. The class sent 471 pairs of shoes to be cut into tiny rubber chips. The rubber chips cover new playgrounds. Somewhere, children are playing on Carol Stream's old shoes.

	(A)		(B)		(C)
①	make	-	creation	-	might be
②	make	-	creating	-	might have been
③	make	-	creating	-	might be
④	making	-	creating	-	might have been
⑤	making	-	creation	-	might be

UNIT

157 to부정사의 수동태

Many people are relying on the government for help, and several steps need to be taken to create jobs to make them independent.

많은 사람들이 정부의 도움에 의존하고 있고, 그들을 자립시킬 일자리를 만들기 위해서 몇 가지 절차들이 시행돼야 한다.

많은 사람들이 / 정부에 의존하고 있다 / 도와달라고 // 그리고 몇 가지

Many people are relying on the government for help, and several

절차들이 시행될 필요가 있다 / 일자리를 만들기 위해 / 그들을 자립하게 만들어줄

steps need to be taken to create jobs to make them independent.

to take (X) — 절차(steps)가 시행하는 것이 아니라 시행되는 것이므로 수동형이 왔다.

Grammar Point

to부정사의 수동태

to부정사가 내용에 따라 수동태로 사용될 경우 〈to be p.p.〉나 〈to have been p.p.〉로 쓰인다. 다른 능동태와 수동태를 구분하는 문제처럼 동사의 의미 파악(타동사/자동사 여부)과 목적어 유무 등을 확인하여 문제를 푼다.

This invention allowed songs [to distribute / to be distributed] all around world much faster.

이 발명품이 전 세계로 노래가 배포되는 것을 훨씬 더 빠르게 만들었다.

⇒ distribute는 목적어를 필요로 하는 타동사인데, 뒤에 목적어가 없으므로 수동태인 be distributed가 옳다. 또한 노래가 배포하는 것이 아니라 배포되는 것이다.

Check-up

정답 및 해설 p.35

1. The steel giant Andrew Carnegie handed over $500,000 to charity groups to use / to be used for academic projects.
2. One main decision to make / to be made in tomorrow's meeting will affect our stance regarding your suggestion for preserving this forest.

Words & Phrases

rely on
의존하다, 신뢰하다

distribute
[distríbju:t]
~을 배포하다, 분배하다

hand over
넘겨주다

charity
[tʃǽrəti]
자선단체

stance
[stæns]
입장, 자세

preserve
[prizə́:rv]
보존하다

UNIT 158

의문사+to부정사

By taking this class, most of the students can learn how to develop logical thinking through discussion of a variety of issues.

이 수업을 들음으로써 대부분의 학생들은 다양한 주제에 대한 토론을 통해 논리적인 생각을 발전시키는 법을 배울 수 있다.

이 수업을 들음으로써 / 대부분의 학생들은 / 배울 수 있다 / 발전시키는 법을 /
By taking this class, most of the students can learn how to develop

what to develop (X)
how developing (X)

논리적인 생각을 / 토론을 통해서 / 다양한 주제에 대한
logical thinking through discussion of a variety of issues.

Grammar Point

의문사+to부정사

의문사 뒤에 to부정사가 와서 〈의문사+S+should+동사원형〉과 같은 의미를 지니게 된다. 단, why와는 함께 쓰지 않는다. 이때 각각의 의문사가 맞게 들어 갔는지(what vs. how), 뒤에 to부정사가 오는 지를 살펴보아야 한다.

The intent is definite if one knows [what / how] to address the agenda.

누군가 그 의제를 다루는 방법을 안다면 그 의미는 명확하다.

⇒ to address 뒤에 목적어 the agenda가 있으므로, 명사를 묻는 what이 아니라 정도나 방법을 묻는 how가 적절하다.

Words & Phrases

take a class
수업을 듣다

logical
[ládʒikəl]
논리적인

intent
[intént]
취지, 의미; 의도, 의향

definite
[défənit]
명확한

predict
[pridíkt]
예견하다

expect
[ikspékt]
예상하다

Check-up

정답 및 해설 p.35

1. Blair learned [how to use / what to use] a digital camera from her brother and her father, and now she handles it very well.

2. Their actions are also easy to predict, so everyone knows [what / how] to expect.

EXERCISE

정답 및 해설 p.35

[01-10] 다음 중 어법상 가장 적절한 표현을 고르시오.

01 Based on scripts and dialogues to [memorize / be memorized], language classes feature teacher-led presentations of language samples.

02 기출응용 The discovery of the maps makes one thing certain: humans have long desired to [represent / be represented] their physical surroundings.

03 If the computer doesn't start and the programs are not loaded, an operating system will need to [install / be installed] again.

04 기출응용 In this digital age, images are essential units of information, and knowing [how / what] to use photography effectively is more important than ever.

05 All of the products need to [inspect / be inspected] thoroughly before putting them on the market.

06 Consumers who want to [receive / be received] enough information about products they buy can ask about them at the call center.

07 The animals to [find / be found] in the reservation are endangered in the wild.

08 Frozen pork is placed directly into the oven to [roast / be roasted] until brown.

09 It remains to [see / be seen] whether Julia can master the new computer her father bought her for Christmas.

10 I can't decide [what / whether] to drive to the party or take a taxi.

ACTUAL TEST

정답 및 해설 p.36

01 기출응용

다음 글의 밑줄 친 부분 중, 어법상 어긋난 것은?

When we think of leaders in marketing and branding sectors, Disney comes to our first. Disney has geniuses in promoting ① its brand, magnificent marketers, leaders in the theme park industry, and a universally recognized brand. Then what could possibly go wrong with its expansion into Hong Kong and the Asia-Pacific market? It was cultural misunderstanding ② which led Disney to unpredicted headaches and problems when expanding into global markets and ③ work with other cultures. The lesson to ④ be learned here is to spend time and money in understanding your overseas markets and the culture ⑤ where you will be doing business.

02

다음 (A), (B), (C)의 각 [ ] 안에서 어법에 맞는 표현으로 바르게 짝지어진 것은?

The compulsive clown is finding some kind of recognition or attention. The sadness is (A) [that / what] he thinks he can receive attention only by playing the fool for others. Deeper than this, it may be that he identifies with his playing and tries to ignore the real world by taking nothing seriously. Clowning is sometimes an escape device. The clown doesn't know how (B) [dealing / to deal] with himself in a serious situation, so he adopts an attitude of irresponsible cheerfulness. In handling others, his clowning serves as a sufficient defensive mask to keep others (C) [knowing / from knowing] who he is. He would rather laugh and joke than confront the blue realities of life.

(A)		(B)		(C)
① that	-	dealing	-	knowing
② what	-	dealing	-	from knowing
③ that	-	to deal	-	from knowing
④ what	-	to deal	-	knowing
⑤ that	-	to deal	-	knowing

REVIEW TEST

정답 및 해설 p.36

[01-05] 다음 문장 중 어법상 틀린 부분을 고쳐 쓰시오.

01 It was careless for you to write such a letter to her when we all were in that situation.

02 In fact, to forget something is essential because it makes easier to recall new memories.

03 Beginning in the 1980s, most inspections have failed revealing that matching teaching styles to learning styles works.

04 The newly constructed plant will have an annual output of about 150,000 autos and be used to producing models exclusively for the European market.

05 June urges people with breast cancer to adopt an attitude of watchful realism and to not bury themselves under a cosmetic veil of cheer.

[06-10] 다음 보기에서 알맞은 단어를 골라 문장을 완성하시오. (단, 필요하면 형태를 바꾸시오.)

보기	tell	write	make	detect	sit

06 From preschool onward, teachers encourage children __________ still rather than run and go around.

07 It is impossible for the naked eye __________ the exact location of the sun close to the horizon.

08 I needed a pen __________ with, but I couldn't find one and finally failed to fill out the questionnaire.

09 I forgot __________ my partner something important about the contract, so I should call him for another meeting.

10 The high-tech way was used to __________ a successful bid for the construction of the building in Singapore.

FINAL CHECK

정답 및 해설 p.36

01 기출응용

다음 글의 밑줄 친 부분 중, 어법상 어긋난 것은?

In the Middle Ages, horses were mainly used ① to carrying armored warriors with shields and weapons. They ② were considered the tanks of that time. Later, people bred horses for farm work and for hauling wagons. Clydesdales, ③ referred to as "draft" horses, were extremely strong horses used for pulling heavy loads. The name Clydesdale was derived from the Clydesdale area in Scotland ④ where the breed was developed. They originated in the 1700s when imported Flemish male horses were bred with Scottish mares. The Industrial Revolution brought about the decline of Clydesdales as carrying machines. They hit their lowest number in the 1950s. Clydesdales have made a comeback as parade horses for special occasions such as weddings. Their high-stepping walk ⑤ is eye-catching and a crowd pleaser.

02

다음 (A), (B), (C)의 각 [ ] 안에서 어법에 맞는 표현으로 바르게 짝지어진 것은?

A skeleton unearthed in southern Italy and dating back to the first century AD has been identified as (A) [a man / that of a man] with East Asian ancestry. The remains, the first known evidence of an Asian living in Italy during that period, (B) [was / were] dug up in a cemetery at Bagnari near Bari. An examination of the oxygen isotopes in the surviving teeth showed that the man was not originally from southern Italy, while a study of his DNA revealed his East Asian origins. There is no way of knowing whether he travelled to Italy himself or his ancestors had settled there. However, the simplicity of his grave (C) [makes obvious / makes it obvious] that he wasn't an aristocratic diplomat. This discovery poses many questions about globalization and the movement of people in Roman times.

	(A)		(B)		(C)
①	a man	-	was	-	makes obvious
②	that of a man	-	was	-	makes it obvious
③	a man	-	were	-	makes obvious
④	that of a man	-	were	-	makes it obvious
⑤	that of a man	-	were	-	makes obvious

03 다음 글의 밑줄 친 부분 중, 어법상 어긋난 것은?

Eye contact plays an important role in holding your listeners' interest. ① By moving your eyes from person to person, you can offer listeners the feeling that you are talking to ② them as individuals. You can also see whether or not people are understanding your message by watching their faces. With a large group, you have to move your eyes slowly from one section of the room to ③ another while you are speaking. Be careful ④ not to focus all your attention on only one person—such as the president—or on only a few people. You need ⑤ including all the people in your audience by looking at them directly.

04 다음 (A), (B), (C)의 각 [ ] 안에서 어법에 맞는 표현으로 바르게 짝지어진 것은?

기출응용

A *nocebo effect* is a bad effect caused by the belief (A) [that / which] something is harmful although it has no effect. An experiment done by Japanese researchers proved this. They tested 57 high school boys for their sensitivity to allergens. The boys filled out questionnaires about past experiences with lacquer trees, which can cause an itchy rash. Boys who reported having severe reactions to the poisonous trees were blindfolded. Researchers brushed one arm with leaves from a lacquer tree but told the boys they were chestnut tree leaves, and rubbed (B) [another / the other] arm with chestnut tree leaves but said they came from a lacquer tree. Surprisingly, the arm that the boys believed to (C) [have exposed / have been exposed] to the poisonous tree began to develop a rash. In most cases the arm that had contact with the actual poison did not react.

*lacquer tree : 옻나무

	(A)		(B)		(C)
①	that	-	another	-	have exposed
②	that	-	another	-	have been exposed
③	which	-	the other	-	have been exposed
④	which	-	another	-	have exposed
⑤	that	-	the other	-	have been exposed

05 

다음 글의 밑줄 친 부분 중, 어법상 어긋난 것은?

When I teach introductory astronomy on the first day of class, I make the following announcement, "Obviously, I am not going to intentionally give you false information." Then, I add, "The problem for both of us ① is that astronomers' understanding of the cosmos is changing so rapidly that some of ② which is accepted as correct today will be shown to be incorrect. I will correct myself ③ whenever I learn of changes in our body of knowledge." Virtually all the corrections I have provided over the years have been such details as the numbers of moons orbiting various planets and the details of the formation of new star systems. ④ What I am doing by making this announcement is putting the students on notice ⑤ not to take everything I have to say on cosmology as truth.

06

다음 (A), (B), (C)의 각 [ ] 안에서 어법에 맞는 표현으로 바르게 짝지어진 것은?

The word "drill" is considered bad teaching. In an educational environment, the phrase "drill and kill" (A) [is / are] used, meaning teachers can kill their students' motivation to learn through drilling skills. In fact, drilling itself is not as bad as originally thought. Even it can be useful when some students learn some things. First of all, drilling helps students (B) [focusing / to focus] on the structural or grammatical elements. Also, it can offer a way to measure what they've learned. Students easily check what they learn by drilling. Some teachers said that students are not good at some academic tasks, so they need to have some knowledge (C) [be / is] automatic. That is, they should be able to do something without thinking about it.

	(A)		(B)		(C)
①	is	-	focusing	-	is
②	is	-	to focus	-	be
③	are	-	focusing	-	is
④	are	-	to focus	-	be
⑤	is	-	to focus	-	is

Conjunctions

접속사

접속사 that, 동격의 that

It just implies that you don't have to lose sleep over the fact that it's never going to be completely done—because it isn't.

그것은 당신이 그것이 완벽하게 끝나지 않을 것이라는 사실에 대해 크게 걱정할 필요가 없다는 것을 암시하는데, 왜냐하면 그렇지 않을 것이기 때문이다.

그것은 암시한다 // 당신은 크게 걱정할 필요가 없다고 / 사실에 대해서 //
It just implies [that] you don't have to lose sleep over the fact
what (X)
implies의 목적어절을 이끄는 접속사 that

그것이 결코 완벽하게 끝나지 않을 것이라는 // 왜냐하면 그렇지 않을 것이기 때문이다
[that] it's never going to [be completely done]—because it isn't.
the fact의 동격절을 이끄는 접속사
be done : ~이 끝나다
be done –ing : ~을 끝내다
I'm done doing this job.
나는 이 일을 끝냈다.
의미상 never going to~가 생략됐다고 볼 수 있다.

Grammar Point

that의 성격

1. 지시형용사	That boy is my brother. 저 소년은 내 남동생이다.
2. 대명사	This year's fashion is quite different from that of last year. 올해 패션은 작년 패션과 아주 다르다.
3. 관계대명사	This magazine was the only thing that we were able to obtain. 이 잡지는 우리가 구할 수 있는 유일한 것이었다.
4. 관계부사	This building is the last place that they stayed. 이 건물은 그들이 머물렀던 마지막 장소이다.
5. 접속사	He thought that he could be the winner. 그는 승자가 될 수 있다고 생각했다.
6. 강조 용법	It was at the playground that Jack found his puppy. 잭이 그의 강아지를 찾은 장소가 바로 그 운동장이었다.

Words & Phrases

imply [implái] 암시하다, 의미하다

lose sleep over ~을 크게 걱정하다

indicate [indəkèit] 나타내다

facial expression (얼굴) 표정

Check-up

정답 및 해설 p.38

1. Experimental results indicated [that / what] each sign language almost always follows facial expression.

2. [That / What] we are worried about is that it is likely that the situation can become worse than ever before.

UNIT 160

as 구문

As you get older, your memory gets worse, but your wisdom and experience grows deeper.

나이를 먹음에 따라 기억력은 점차 나빠지지만, 지혜와 경험은 점점 더 깊어진다.

당신이 나이를 먹음에 따라 // 당신의 기억력은 / 점점 나빠진다 // 하지만 당신의 지혜와 /
As you get older, your memory gets worse, but your wisdom and

경험은 / 점점 더 깊어진다
experience grows deeper.

Grammar Point

1. '~할 때' (= when)
2. '~ 때문에' (= because)
3. ~ 함에 따라
4. '~만큼 …한' 〈as+형용사/부사+as〉 (동등 비교)
5. '~에도 불구하고' (= though)
   Little as he is, he can do it. 그는 작음에도 불구하고, 그것을 할 수 있다.
6. '~로서' (as+명사)
   I'll do my job as a teacher. 나는 교사로서 내 일을 할 것이다.
7. '~이지만', '~인데, 그것은' (문장이나 일부를 선행사로 받는 관계대명사)
   He was English, as I noticed from his speaking. 그는 영국인이었는데, 나는 그것을 그의 말투로 알았다.
8. as of/from '~으로 부터'
9. as to ~에 관하여

cf.) 〈get / turn / grow / go / become + 형용사/비교급〉 '~가 되다' / '점점 ~해지다'
As time passed, the audience got bored. 시간이 지남에 따라 관객은 지루해졌다.
As he talked, they grew angry. 그가 이야기를 할수록 그들은 화가 났다.
As you exercise more, you'll become thinner. 운동을 더 많이 할수록 더 날씬해질 것이다.

Words & Phrases

memory [méməri] 기억력

make a difference 차이를 만들다

a bunch of 한 다발의, 한 무리의

demonstrator [démənstrèitər] 시위자

Check-up

정답 및 해설 p.38

다음 문장을 읽고, 해석하시오.

1. It makes me happy, as a woman, to have been able to make a difference.

2. As he was walking down the street, he was met by a bunch of demonstrators.

EXERCISE

정답 및 해설 p.38

[01-10] 다음 중 어법상 가장 적절한 표현을 고르시오.

01 Jim, look at the house [that / whose] roof is covered with snow.

02 It was because of heavy snow [that / what] the flight was delayed.

03 Scholars seek to understand human history through studying both developments within societies and the way in [that / which] societies relate to each other.

04 The public opinion [which / that] the death penalty should be abolished will get stronger and stronger.

05 The definition of pronunciation highlights the fact [that / which] listeners' perceptions play a critical role.

06 [As simple / Simple as] it may seem, so far nobody has solved this problem.

07 All of you know the chances are slim [which / that] their loved ones survived the explosion aboard the British airplane.

08 기출응용 By increasing the frequency of an advertisement, advertisers increase the likelihood [that / which] products of the target market will be exposed to it.

09 기출응용 There is little evidence [that / what] the city's system of inspections makes any difference in air quality.

10 News came to me [that / what] Sujin won first prize in the English Speaking Contest.

ACTUAL TEST

정답 및 해설 p.38

01 다음 글의 밑줄 친 부분 중, 어법상 <u>어긋난</u> 것은?

In Texas years ago, people got most of all the oil from surface operations. At that time, someone came up with the idea ① <u>that</u> there might be more oil deeper down. ② <u>Following</u> his idea, people dug out the oil well five thousand feet deep. Surprisingly, a great gusher came out. Many of us usually operate on the surface. We are reluctant ③ <u>to going</u> deeper to discover our wonderful resources. In other words, we don't do our best to find a new field for our ability. When we spend a lot of time and effort, we get ④ <u>something greater</u> in return—a gusher. Have you ever dug deeply to be successful? There is a big difference between the successful and the unsuccessful. ⑤ <u>The deeper</u> you dig, the closer to you the gusher is.

02 다음 (A), (B), (C)의 각 [ ] 안에서 어법에 맞는 표현으로 바르게 짝지어진 것은?

It is said that people get tattooed or pierced to express their own personality. But according to recent research, there are other psychological factors. Researchers in Poland researched about 200 men and women, half of (A) [them / whom] were tattooed or pierced in other parts except their ears for body symmetry. Men with these decorations showed better body balance than those without, while there were no differences in women. Moreover, those who are less balanced (B) [not tending / did not tend] to have tattoos and piercings. This survey suggested the new theory (C) [which / that] people do bodily decorations not because they want to hide drawbacks in their appearance, but because only those with high biological quality can afford risky behavior—infection from getting stuck with needles.

	(A)		(B)		(C)
①	them	-	not tending	-	which
②	whom	-	not tending	-	which
③	whom	-	did not tend	-	which
④	them	-	did not tend	-	that
⑤	whom	-	did not tend	-	that

UNIT 161

because vs. because of

Because of years of restrictions on poaching, the wild deer population in Canada is higher than ever.

수년 간 밀렵을 제한한 덕분에 캐나다의 야생 사슴의 수가 여느 때보다 많아졌다.

때문에 / 밀렵에 대한 수년 간의 제한 /

Because of | years of restrictions on poaching,

Because (X) 뒤에 문장이 아닌 명사구가 왔으므로 Because of가 왔다.

캐나다의 야생 사슴의 수가 / 여느 때보다 많아졌다

the wild deer population in Canada is higher than ever.

Grammar Point

because vs. because of

because 다음에는 절(주어+동사)이 오고, because of 다음에는 명사(구)가 온다. because of 다음에 아무리 많은 단어가 오더라도 주어 · 동사가 없는 구가 와야 한다. 절이 오려면 접속사가 반드시 필요하다.

Because | I was sick in bed, I was absent from class.

나는 아파서 누워 있었기 때문에 수업에 결석했다.

⇒ 절〈주어+동사〉을 이끌기 위해서는 접속사 because가 와야 한다.

The consumer price index increased 0.9% last month because of | a rise in prices for industrial products.

공산품 가격의 상승으로 인해 지난달에 소비자 물가 지수가 0.9% 증가했다.

⇒ a rise ~ products는 길지만 명사구이므로 because of가 와야 한다.

Words & Phrases

restriction [ristríkʃən] 제한

poaching [póutʃiŋ] 밀렵

be absent from ~에 결석하다

consumer [kənsjúːmər] 소비자

industrial [indʌ́striəl] 공업의, 산업의

irrelevant [iréləvənt] 관계없는

diffuse [difjúːs] 확산되다

hygiene [háidʒi(ː)n] 위생

Check-up

정답 및 해설 p.38

1. It is often difficult to catch the main point that is being made because / because of the irrelevant details that speakers include.
2. HIV, the virus leading to AIDS, has diffused in a short time in the third world because of / because low education level and little sense of hygiene.

UNIT
162 despite vs. though

Whale hunting is still going on, despite the declaration of a stop on commercial whaling by the International Whaling Commission in 1990-91.

1990~1991년의 국제 포경 협약에 의한 상업적 고래잡이에 대한 중지 선언에도 불구하고 고래 사냥은 여전히 계속되고 있다.

고래 사냥은 / 여전히 계속되고 있다 / 선언에도 불구하고 /
Whale hunting is still going on, despite the declaration

though (X)

뒤에 the declaration이라는 명사가 오므로 despite가 왔다. of 이하는 명사를 수식하는 전치사구이다.

상업적 고래잡이에 대한 중지 /
of a stop on commercial whaling

국제 포경 협약에 의해서 / 1990~1991년에
by the International Whaling Commission in 1990-91.

Grammar Point

despite, in spite of vs. though, although

despite나 though 모두 '~임에도 불구하고'라는 양보의 의미를 지닌 어휘이다. 하지만, despite는 전치사로 뒤에 명사가 오며, though는 접속사로 뒤에 절이 온다. 특히 despite의 경우, 뒤에 긴 구절이 오더라도 despite 뒤에 온 명사를 수식하는 관계사절이나 분사구문일 수도 있으므로 주의하자.

길지만 that 이하는 the fact의 동격절이다.

Juliet and Jennifer are not identical twins, despite the fact that they were born on the same day.

줄리엣과 제니퍼는 같은 날 태어났음에도 불구하고 일란성 쌍둥이는 아니다.

cf.) 일부 접속사는 문맥이 분명한 경우 주어와 동사를 생략할 수 있다.
The eggplant is delicious when eaten baked. 가지는 구워먹으면 맛있다.
If cold, close the window. 추우면, 창문을 닫아라.

Words & Phrases

whale [weil] 고래

declaration [dèkləréiʃən] 선언

commercial [kəmə́ːrʃəl] 상업적인

mature [mətʃúə] 성숙하다

real estate brokerage 부동산 중개

Check-up

정답 및 해설 p.38

1. Although / Despite the fact that girls tend to mature faster than boys, my daughter is far behind most of her peers in every way.

2. Although / In spite of the best-known franchises are fast-food businesses, franchises are available in many industries, such as real estate brokerages and video rental.

EXERCISE

정답 및 해설 p.39

[01-10] 다음 중 어법상 가장 적절한 표현을 고르시오.

01 [Although / Despite] every nerve in her body warned her not to do it, she slowly pushed and opened the door.

02 기출응용 Therefore, color psychology, [although / despite] interesting, provides only broad generalizations in analyzing personality types.

03 [Despite / Although] Tom's request that publicity be avoided, his coworkers gave many interviews with the media.

04 [Because / Because of] their ability to store and release smell, some flowers attract insects to eat them.

05 We get along [because / because of] no one group has enough people to be in the majority and to dominate.

06 기출응용 The cattle, [despite / though] owned by Tony Sandowski, are considered to belong to the entire Sandowski family.

07 The reservation system, [although / despite] quite similar to the appointment system, is used when the client actually uses facilities related to the service.

08 The pub was small but warm and welcoming in part [because / because of] a crowd managed to squeeze their way inside last Sunday night.

09 기출응용 [Despite / Although] the increase of labor-saving devices ranging from microwave ovens to vacuum cleaners, modern humans seem to have less leisure time than their long-lost ancestors.

10 [Despite / Although] the potential of advanced technologies, such as computers, CD-Rom multimedia, and the Internet, some writers still claim that these technologies are not ideal for learning foreign languages.

01 기출응용 **다음 글의 밑줄 친 부분 중, 어법상 어긋난 것은?**

Sissi was not discouraged as a child by the boys who wouldn't let her ① play her favorite game. Eventually, she got her way on the streets of Salvador, Brazil, ② because of the soccer ball that the boys wanted to play with was ③ hers. Still, she often ran home with her ball after she grew frustrated with the negative attitudes the boys displayed. Sissi ④ had learned to play soccer by practicing with all kinds of objects that she found around the house. These included rolled-up socks and the heads of her dolls. Her father finally decided that she needed a soccer ball to keep her ⑤ from destroying her dolls.

02 **다음 (A), (B), (C)의 각 [ ] 안에서 어법에 맞는 표현으로 바르게 짝지어진 것은?**

Most of GE's business units were inefficient, keeping more inventory than (A) [needing / needed] in order to accomplish a desired level of product delivery. They often used simplified approaches such as ABC analysis to determine their safety stocks for independent demand items, which ignore supply-and-demand uncertainty or cost. The solution for this situation was to develop a periodic review system that used part availability targets and included as many uncertainties as possible. The system, (B) [although / despite] in principle similar to the *P* system is relatively easy to understand and uses complex equations to determine the inventory interval and variables. The complexity (C) [arises / arouses] from considering uncertainties in supply as well as demand in the determination of the safety stocks.

	(A)		(B)		(C)
①	needing	-	although	-	arises
②	needing	-	despite	-	arouses
③	needing	-	although	-	arouses
④	needed	-	although	-	arises
⑤	needed	-	despite	-	arises

UNIT 163

while vs. during

The most important factor in reducing the negative effects of divorce during the school years is parents' efforts to reduce their own conflicts.

학창 시절 동안 이혼의 부정적인 영향을 줄이는 가장 중요한 요인은 자신들의 다툼을 줄이려는 부모의 노력이다.

가장 중요한 요인은 / 이혼의 부정적인 영향을 줄이는 /
The most important factor in reducing the negative effects of divorce

학창 시절 동안 / 부모의 노력이다 / 줄이려는 /
during the school years is parents' efforts to reduce
while (X)

얼핏 보면 the school years is parents' ~ 로 연결되는 것 같지만 실제로는 the school years에서 끊기는 구절이다. 따라서 명사 앞에 during이 왔다.

그들의 다툼을
their own conflicts.

Grammar Point

while vs. during

while 다음에는 절이 오고, during 다음에는 명사가 온다. 접속사 뒤에 올 수 있는 것은 문장, 분사, 전치사구 등이다.

The researchers found that [while / during] the dry season some elephants ventured out of Samburu to eat tasty drops at a farm. 기출응용

연구원들은 건기 동안 일부 코끼리들이 농장의 맛있는 낙과를 먹으려고 위험을 무릅쓰고 삼부루 밖으로 나가는 것을 발견했다.

⇒ 뒤에 시간을 나타내는 명사가 나오므로 during이 옳다.

Words & Phrases

reduce [ridjú:s] 줄이다
divorce [divɔ́:rs] 이혼
conflict [kánflikt] 다툼, 분란
venture out of 위험을 무릅쓰고 ~의 밖으로 나가다
drastic [drǽstik] 급격한
victim [víktim] 희생자
creative [kriéitiv] 창의적인

Check-up

정답 및 해설 p.38

1. During / While the same period of drastic increases in the price of oil, industrial production in Japan, Sweden, and Germany became 40 percent more energy-efficient.
2. Those victims of education should receive training to develop creative talents while / during in school. 기출응용

UNIT 164

not A but B

The difference between a successful person and others is not a lack of knowledge but a lack of will.

성공한 사람과 그렇지 않은 사람들 사이의 차이점은 지식의 부족이 아니라 의지의 부족이다.

차이점은 / 성공한 사람과 다른 사람 사이에 /

The difference between a successful person and others is

지식의 부족이 아니라 / 의지의 부족이다

not a lack of knowledge but a lack of will.

Grammar Point

not A but B – 'A가 아니라 B다'

not A but B 용법은 'A가 아니라 B다'를 의미한다. 이때, not only A but also B 'A 뿐만 아니라 B 역시' 용법과 구별해야 한다. 특히 해석을 할 때 주의하지 않으면 전체적인 내용이 달라지게 된다.

Citizens in New York do not enjoy their city's awful traffic but see it as something that must be endured.

뉴욕의 시민들은 도시의 끔찍한 교통 체증을 즐기는 것이 아니라 참아야 하는 것으로 본다.

⇒ '뉴욕의 시민들이 끔찍한 교통 체증을 즐길 뿐만 아니라, 참아야 하는 것으로 본다'라고 해석하면 안 된다.

Words & Phrases

knowledge [nάlidʒ] 지식

will [wil] 의지

observe [əbzə́ːrv] 관찰하다

evaluate [ivǽljuèit] 평가하다

distraction [distrǽkʃən] 주의산만, 기분전환

at this point 지금

Check-up

정답 및 해설 p.39

1. Other people can affect our performance not by observing and evaluating us but creating / by creating distractions.
2. What matters to us at this point is not what to eat, but / and how to live.

EXERCISE

정답 및 해설 p.40

[01-10] **다음 중 어법상 가장 적절한 표현을 고르시오.**

01 [During / While] in the conference, she was introduced to experimental films that prompted her to break the stereotype of Asians in films.

02 [During / While] the last two weeks, Jenny's health has improved a lot, and her family feels relieved.

03 기출응용 [During / While] his visit to New York, Charles encountered an old friend from elementary school.

04 Karen was amazed to see that she had accomplished a 7% to 12% annual increase in sales [during / while] at her company.

05 [During / While] the semester that I taught Thomas, he began to work with an eighth-grade physics class on his portfolio.

06 You cannot buy your friends with money and jewelry [and / but] with your heart.

07 [During / While] in prison, she started writing short stories based on her own experiences.

08 Our purpose is not to do it for you [and / but] to teach you to do it for yourself.

09 When lateralization is over, the theory says, it finishes the critical period of life [during / while] which we can acquire native-speaker pronunciation in a language.

10 The government office has group activities that highlight the unique character and heritage [during / while] building working relationships among delegates.

정답 및 해설 p.40

01 다음 글의 밑줄 친 부분 중, 어법상 어긋난 것은?

Biotech is the most ① frequently chosen crop technology in human history. Supporters consider biotech as the only way to improve output ② during we escape the trends of a growing world population and finite farmland nourished by water resources. The industry claims that after ③ nearly 20 years of using genetically modified crops, there are no well-documented food-safety problems and no threat to biodiversity, since traditional cropland and biotech crops have ④ been shown to coexist peacefully. Some problems could arise, such as superweeds that have adapted features from herbicide-resistant genetically modified plants. But until now, biotech crops seem to ⑤ mostly benefit the environment, if only by reducing pesticide use by about 10%.

02 기출응용

다음 (A), (B), (C)의 각 [ ] 안에서 어법에 맞는 표현으로 바르게 짝지어진 것은?

Many people take numerous photos (A) [while / during] traveling or on vacation to preserve the experience for the future. But the role of photographer may actually detract from their delight in the present moment. I know a father who devoted himself earnestly to (B) [photograph / photographing] the birth of his first and only child. The photos were beautiful but, he lamented afterward he felt that he had missed out on the most important first moment of his son's life. Looking through the camera lens made him (C) [detach / detached] from the scene. He was just an observer, not an experiencer. Teach yourself to use your camera in a way that accepts your ongoing experiences, by truly looking at things and noticing what is beautiful and meaningful.

	(A)		(B)		(C)
①	while	-	photograph	-	detach
②	during	-	photograph	-	detached
③	while	-	photographing	-	detached
④	during	-	photographing	-	detach
⑤	while	-	photographing	-	detach

UNIT
165 if vs. as if vs. even if

It's easy to feel as if there are few things one person can do to save the planet, but this is far from the truth.

마치 이 행성을 지키기 위해 한 사람이 할 수 있는 일이 거의 없는 것처럼 느끼기 쉽지만, 이것은 전혀 사실이 아니다.

느끼기 쉽다 // 마치 거의 없는 것처럼 / 한 사람이 할 수 있는 일이 /

It's easy to [feel] [as if] there are few things [one person can do]

if (X)

as if 는 감각동사와 어울린다.

이 행성을 지키기 위해서 // 하지만 이것은 전혀 사실이 아니다

[to save the planet], but this is [far from] the truth.

전혀 ~이 아닌

Grammar Point

if vs. as if vs. even if

if는 조건문이나 가정법에 쓰고 '~한다면'으로 해석한다.

as if는 '마치 ~인 것처럼'이라는 뜻으로, 감각 동사(look, sound, feel)나 2문형 동사(be, seem), almost와 잘 어울린다.

even if는 '비록 ~ 일지라도'라는 뜻으로, 어떠한 일이 일어나더라도 다른 일이 여전히 진실일 것임을 강조할 때 쓴다.

It seemed [as if / if] all of them could take part in the party.

마치 그들 모두가 파티에 참석할 수 있을 것처럼 보인다.

⇒ 앞에 2문형 동사 seem이 왔고, 내용상 '마치 ~ 처럼'이 더 잘 어울리므로 as if가 정답이다.

We will still go on a picnic [as if / even if] it rains tomorrow.

내일 비가 올지라도 우리는 그래도 소풍을 갈 것이다.

⇒ 비가 오는 일이 발생하더라도 소풍을 갈 거라는 사실을 강조하는 문장이다. 따라서 '비록 ~일지라도'라는 뜻인 even if가 정답이다.

Words & Phrases

planet
[plǽnit]
행성

take part in
~에 참석하다

beneath
[biníːθ]
아래

surface
[sə́ːrfis]
표면

Check-up

정답 및 해설 p.40

1. Some things look [if / as if / even if] they had not been cared for deeply in a long time, but I know their beauty is still there beneath their worn surface.

2. He heard someone fall behind him, but he didn't turn and kept walking [if / as if / even if] he had heard nothing.

UNIT

166 if vs. unless

Such tragedies are clearly remarkable today and are sure to get worse unless steps are taken to limit population growth.

인구 성장을 제한하는 조치를 취하지 않는다면 그런 비극들은 오늘날 확실히 두드러지며 악화될 것이 분명하다.

그런 비극들은 / 확실히 두드러지다 / 오늘날 / 그리고 악화될 것이 분명하다 //

Such tragedies are clearly remarkable today and are sure to get worse

unless를 기점으로 두 문장 사이의 관계가 '~하지 않는다면'으로 이어져야 한다.

~하지 않는다면 / 조치가 / 취해지다 / 인구 성장을 제한하는

unless steps are taken to limit population growth.

if (X)

Grammar Point

if vs. unless

if는 '~한다면', unless는 '~하지 않는다면'을 의미한다. if로 연결될 경우 두 문장의 관계가 긍정적이지만, unless로 연결될 경우 두 문장의 관계는 부정적이게 된다. 따라서 해석을 통해 문제를 풀어야 한다.

[If / Unless] you have been in a cave for years, you have probably heard of this network system and its users.

수년 동안 동굴에서 살았던 것이 아니라면, 당신은 이 네트워크 시스템과 사용자들에 대해서 들어본 적이 있을 것이다.

⇒ 네트워크에 대해서 들어본 사람은 동굴에서 살지는 않았을 것이다. 따라서 unless가 적절하다.

Words & Phrases

tragedy [trǽdʒidi] 비극

remarkable [rimáːrkəbl] 두드러진

limit [límit] 제한하다

eclipse [iklíps] 가리다; 일식

Check-up

정답 및 해설 p.40

1. They should follow what he said as usual if / unless something unexpected happens.
2. IT industries like Apple, HP, and Google could be eclipsed by their foreign rivals, if / unless we, Americans, invest more money in technology and science.

EXERCISE

정답 및 해설 p.41

[01-10] 다음 중 어법상 가장 적절한 표현을 고르시오.

01 It seemed [if / as if] no one had ever built a structure like this before.

02 When he approached them, they continued to talk [if / as if] he weren't even there.

03 기출응용 A painting was not completed [if / unless] both of them said it was finished.

04 We both can understand and appreciate, [if / even if] we come from very different parts of the world.

05 [If / Even if] they leave us money in their wills, there is no way we ever will have the chances to get it.

06 The train is always on time, so you won't be late [if / unless] you miss your train.

07 The dark skies were threatening to pour down over the stadium, [as if / even if] they were going to ruin the event.

08 A teenage girl may eat nothing but a lettuce salad for lunch, [if / even if] she becomes hungry later, because that is what her friends are eating.

09 My next-door neighbor should not complain to me about my barking dog [if / unless] he wants to hear about his screeching cat.

10 기출응용 If something can be readily repaired, this lessens the chance that it'll end up in the landfill, and could easily save you money in the long run, [if / even if] it's initially more expensive.

ACTUAL TEST

정답 및 해설 p.41

01 다음 글의 밑줄 친 부분 중, 어법상 어긋난 것은?

Romania has declared war on obesity. The government is planning to introduce Europe's first fat tax—a levy on fast food, sweets, and sugary drinks. Junk-food sales in schools will also be banned. Other European countries seem impressed by this trail-blazing measure and will be watching the results keenly. But they shouldn't get their hopes up. Here, no meal is considered to be ① complete without meat. Food is considered tasteless ② if it is smothered in salt, while vegetables must be deep-fried or pan-fried. The standard cookbook, which has been required reading for generations of housewives, ③ is full of fatty horrors, some of ④ them bordering on the obscene. The Romanian government is well aware of the scale of this problem. Our eating habits may be a disgrace, but it will take more than a few taxes ⑤ to change them.

02 기출응용

다음 (A), (B), (C)의 각 [ ] 안에서 어법에 맞는 표현으로 바르게 짝지어진 것은?

I recently overheard a conversation between two students. One asked (A) [another / the other] if he had copied his essay from a website. After agreeing, they started to complain that since essays available online are in high demand, they cost too much. Nothing they said came close to (B) [acknowledge / acknowledging] the ethical issues about academic honesty. In the past, people who stole essays from others were punished, but now they are allowed to resubmit their work. It's certainly problematic to give cheaters a second chance. It looks (C) [even if / as if] the procedures exist to justify academic theft. There should be no excuses for it because it is not a mistake.

(A)		(B)		(C)
① another	-	acknowledge	-	even if
② the other	-	acknowledge	-	as if
③ another	-	acknowledge	-	as if
④ the other	-	acknowledging	-	as if
⑤ the other	-	acknowledging	-	even if

UNIT 167

if vs. whether (1)

Whether our team can arrive at the destination in time depends on the weather condition.

우리 팀이 제 시간에 목적지에 도착할지는 기상 상태에 달려 있다.

인지 아닌지 / 우리 팀이 / 도착할 수 있다 / 목적지에 / 제 시간에 / 달려 있다 /

Whether our team can arrive at the destination in time depends on

if (X)

'~인지 아닌지'라는 뜻으로 주절을 이끄는 whether가 왔다.

기상 상태에

the weather condition.

Grammar Point

if vs. whether

if와 whether는 '~인지 아닌지'의 의미를 가지는 접속사이다. whether는 주절, 보어절, 목적어절을 모두 이끌지만, if는 주절을 이끌지 않고, 보어절도 whether를 선호한다. 따라서 if가 문장의 맨 앞에 쓰였다면 '~라면'에 해당하는 조건문이나 가정문이지 '~인지 아닌지'의 의미가 아니다. if나 whether 중 선택하는 문제나 문장 앞에 존재하는 if에 밑줄이 쳐 있다면, if의 의미를 잘 확인해야 한다.

if	목적어절 주절 불가	whether	주절, 목적어절, 보어절

Words & Phrases

destination [dèstənéiʃən] 목적지, 도착지

in time 제 시간에

depend on ~에 달려 있다

recommend [rècəménd] 추천하다

Check-up

정답 및 해설 p.41

1. If / Whether our company can buy plane tickets for the customers is another problem.

2. If / Whether you are given the opportunity, would you recommend our product to others?

UNIT 168

if vs. whether (2)

During her time in France, she was apparently wrestling with the question of whether to give up her more independent life as a doctor.

그녀는 프랑스에 있는 동안 의사로서의 더 독립적인 삶을 포기할지 안 할지에 대한 문제로 분명 악전고투하고 있었다.

프랑스에 있는 그녀의 시간 동안 / 그녀는 / 분명 악전고투하고 있었다 /
During her time in France, she was apparently wrestling with

그 문제로 / 포기할지 안 할지에 대한 / 그녀의 더 독립적인 인생을 /
the question of whether to give up her more independent life

if to give up (X)

뒤에 to부정사가 나오므로 whether가 왔다.

의사로서
as a doctor.

Grammar Point

if vs. whether

if는 '~인지 아닌지'라는 뜻으로 쓰일 때 주절을 이끌지 못하는 것 이외에도 다른 제약이 있다. whether는 〈whether+to부정사〉, 〈whether or not〉, 〈전치사+whether〉의 형태로 쓰이지만, if는 이 구조에서 whether를 대신할 수 없다.

or not이 바로 뒤에 왔으므로 if로 바꿔 쓸 수 없다.

Few young people are completely free of food-related pressures from peers, whether or not these pressures are imposed intentionally. 기출응용

if or not (X)

이 압력이 의도적이든지 아니든지 간에 음식과 관련해서 또래들의 압력으로부터 완전히 자유로운 젊은이들은 거의 없다.

Words & Phrases

apparently [əpǽrəntli] 분명

wrestle with ~을 해결하려고 애쓰다

peer [piər] 동료, 친구

impose [impóuz] ~을 지우다, 부과하다

intentionally [inténʃənəli] 의도적으로, 고의로

burn out 소진하다, 다 타다

the authorities 관계 당국

Check-up 정답 및 해설 p.41

1. If / Whether their free time is filled with assignments and projects, kids will burn out quickly.

2. Eleanor couldn't decide if / whether or not to go to the authorities with the money and information.

EXERCISE

정답 및 해설 p.42

[01-10] 다음 중 어법상 가장 적절한 표현을 고르시오.

01 기출응용 His motivation for the long, solitary walk was to decide [if / whether] to get married.

02 Linda says that the question of [if / whether] innovation really can be acquired is an age-old debate.

03 This skill is familiar to the people of Botswana, [if / whether] or not they learn to read and write.

04 [If / Whether] Jameson visited Korea to promote his movie, I would be willing to watch it.

05 기출응용 [If / Whether] there is a real gender difference in math ability has long been debated.

06 기출응용 The television set would stare blankly into the living room [if / whether] someone somewhere were not transmitting images to it.

07 기출응용 The tension is due to physical contact, the lack of control, and the fear of [if / whether] it will tickle or hurt.

08 [Whether / If] you see someone getting robbed, you might look the other way since you don't want to be involved in any trouble.

09 [Whether / If] the person in need were one of your family members, could you possibly just pass by?

10 People could have become great artists and scientists [if / whether] their teachers or parents had focused on their creativity.

정답 및 해설 p.42

01 다음 글의 밑줄 친 부분 중, 어법상 어긋난 것은?

An aspect about human behavior is best presented with an experiment called the *ultimatum game*. The game is played like this: Two players ① are told that they are going to play a game and could get $200 if they win. Before starting to play, they learn how to play. The game begins with flipping a coin, ② which is used to allocate the players to the roles of players A and B. Player A's mission is to propose a division of the prize of $200 between himself and ③ the other player. After player A makes his proposal, player B determines ④ if to accept it or not. If he takes it, both players ⑤ are paid according to the proposal. If player B rejects the proposal, both players walk away with nothing. In either case, the game then ends.

02 다음 (A), (B), (C)의 각 [ ] 안에서 어법에 맞는 표현으로 바르게 짝지어진 것은?

We're constantly making decisions, ranging from what to eat for dinner each night to whom we should marry, not to mention all those flavors of ice cream. We base many of our decisions on (A) [if / whether] we think a particular preference will increase our well-being. Intuitively, we seem convinced that the more choices we have, the better off we'll ultimately be. But our world of unlimited opportunity imprisons us more than it makes us happy. In (B) [that / what] one psychologist calls "the paradox of choice," facing many possibilities leaves us stressed out and less satisfied with whatever we do decide. Having too many choices keeps us (C) [wonder / wondering] about all the opportunities missed.

	(A)		(B)		(C)
①	if	-	that	-	wonder
②	if	-	what	-	wonder
③	whether	-	that	-	wondering
④	whether	-	what	-	wondering
⑤	whether	-	what	-	wonder

UNIT
169 because vs. why

Amy got up and continued to perform without missing a beat. This is why she is truly deserving of the gold medal.

에이미는 일어나서 주저하지 않고 계속해서 연기를 했다. 이것이 그녀가 정말 금메달을 딸 만한 이유이다.

에이미는 일어나서 / 계속해서 연기를 했다 / 주저하지 않고 //

Amy got up and continued to perform without missing a beat.

금메달의 원인

why

이것이 / 이다 // 이유 / 그녀는 정말로 금메달을 받을 만하다

This is why she is truly deserving of the gold medal.

because (X)

연기의 결과

앞의 내용이 원인, 뒤에 나오는 것이 결과이므로
why가 와야 한다.

Grammar Point

because vs. why

because나 why를 고르는 문제의 경우 앞뒤 문장의 관계를 잘 살펴봐야 한다. 앞에 진술된 내용이 이유나 원인이면 why를, 앞의 내용이 결과에 해당하면 because를 선택한다.

결과 + because + 원인/이유 | 원인/이유 + why + 결과

disturbance는 휴대폰 금지의 결과이므로 because가 온다.

This disturbance was because recently the use of cell phones has been banned in certain places.

이 소란은 최근에 어떤 지역에서 휴대폰 사용이 금지되었기 때문에 일어났다.

Words & Phrases

perform
[pərfɔ́ːrm]
연기하다, 공연하다

without missing a beat
주저하지 않고

deserve
[dizə́ːrv]
~할 만하다

disturbance
[distə́ːrbəns]
혼란, 소란; 방해

despot
[déspət]
독재자, 폭군

Check-up

정답 및 해설 p.42

1. I believe that there is a place for students to play. That is because / why I have decided to hold a meeting to discuss this matter further.

2. Critical discussion disappears as internal opposition is removed. That is because / why the successes of despots have usually been followed by the silencing of opposition.

절+절

When she tried to rent Washington, D.C.'s Constitution Hall for a concert, her request was denied.

콘서트를 하려고 워싱턴 D.C.의 컨스티튜션 홀을 빌리려고 했을 때 그녀의 요청은 거절당했다.

그녀가 빌리려고 했을 때 / 워싱턴 D.C.의 컨스티튜션 홀을 /

When she tried to rent Washington, D.C.'s Constitution Hall

But she tried ~ (X)

절과 절의 연결이므로, 접속사인 when이 필요하다.
when 없이 She tried ~ 로 쓰인다면 틀리다.

콘서트를 위해 / 그녀의 요청은 / 거절당했다

for a concert, her request was denied.

Grammar Point

절(주어 + 동사) + 절(주어 + 동사)

절과 절 사이에는 연결사가 필요하다. 이 연결사에는 접속사, 관계사, 분사구문이 있고, 연결사 없이 〈절 + 절〉 구조로는 쓸 수 없다. 또한 접속사와 관계사는 하나의 절 안에 함께 나오지 못한다 .

[Just / Just as] the silver dollar and those strengthening words of hope were passed on to me and to the kind man before me, I will pass them on, too.

그 은화와 희망을 강화하는 그러한 말들이 나와 내 앞의 그 친절한 사람에게 전달된 것처럼 나도 그것들을 전달할 것이다.

⇒ 〈절+절〉 구조이고 부사인 Just는 절과 절을 연결하는 기능이 없으므로 접속사 as가 있는 Just as가 적절하다.

Words & Phrases

request [rikwést] 요청, 요구

deny [dinái] 거부하다, 부인하다

a couple of 몇 개의, 두서너 개의

incentive [inséntiv] 장려책, 우대책, 장려금

out of print 절판된

Check-up

정답 및 해설 p.42

1. There are a couple of incentives, among [them / which] flexible time is one of the most powerful.

2. Christie has written several books over the years, and most of [them / which] are presently out of print.

EXERCISE

정답 및 해설 p.43

[01-10] 다음 중 어법상 가장 적절한 표현을 고르시오.

01 Everybody loves a love story. That's [why / because] the poet Longfellow invented one to tell about the Pilgrims.

02 기출응용 The first eight expeditions to Everest were British, all of [them / which] attempted the mountain from the northern, Tibetan, side.

03 기출응용 I usually persist longer than most people would in a similar situation—which is [why / because] I often succeed where others have failed.

04 [They actually live / When they actually live] their lives, the significance of wealth drops to almost nothing in evaluating their relationships.

05 기출응용 Finding good prices for travel is so complicated. That is [because / why] airlines have complex formulas for inventory management so they can maximize profits by filling planes.

06 Consumers who have a loss of net income could require increased wages, [and / which] further makes production cost higher and is then passed on to consumers.

07 An eighteen-hole golf course uses about 1,000 tons of water a day for free, and [it / which] is the average amount needed for fifty households for one month.

08 Students are to be selected at the end of each year for the new first semester, [beginning / begins] in March.

09 [Put / Putting] a dish towel over the potatoes to make them warm and absorb steam so that they stay dry.

10 Police and firefighters are also rarely cast in a negative light on local TV news stations because reporters need the cooperation of law enforcement. That's [because / why] viewers see few, if any, stories about issues like radar traps, brutality, and police or firefighter mistakes.

ACTUAL TEST

정답 및 해설 p.43

01 다음 글의 밑줄 친 부분 중, 어법상 어긋난 것은?

Last year, the German government achieved the goal of creating dozens of jobs in youth career programs. This was the result of the government's policy to encourage many companies ① to recruit young workers. More and more young graduates ② are expected to get a job in the new fields. That is ③ because the private sector is expanding huge investments, while small and large businesses try to offer ④ many more opportunities to be employed. Especially, the government has a plan to introduce more welfare policies to guarantee the livelihood of young women. A wide variety of new rules and policies ⑤ cover welfare for the young are scheduled to begin this year as a result of legal revisions.

02 기출응용 다음 (A), (B), (C)의 각 [ ] 안에서 어법에 맞는 표현으로 바르게 짝지어진 것은?

Most people assume that the water in a bottle is cleaner and better for you than the water from your kitchen tap. However, what people do not realize (A) [is / are] that plastic water bottles themselves might be harmful to people. When water is stored in plastic containers, chemicals from the plastic can dissolve into the water. These chemicals have been linked to a number of different human health concerns, and many scientists and doctors advise people (B) [drinking / to drink] water from glass or stainless steel containers. This is (C) [why / because] these containers can safely hold water unlike plastic which contains chemicals. So next time you drink water, make sure what your bottle is made of.

(A)		(B)		(C)
① is	-	to drink	-	why
② is	-	to drink	-	because
③ is	-	drinking	-	because
④ are	-	drinking	-	why
⑤ are	-	drinking	-	because

REVIEW TEST

정답 및 해설 p.43

[01-05] 다음 문장 중 어법상 틀린 부분을 고쳐 쓰시오.

01 Despite Teresa was a superior student in high school, she is having serious problems in adjusting to collcgc lifc. .

02 Recently most advertisers have preferred young idols for their commercial models. That's why they can encourage their fans to buy the advertised products.

03 Research shows that after thinking about fast food, people were also more interested in time-saving products, and they read a paragraph faster although the fact that there was no time limit.

04 It was highly unlikely what he would meet such a lively and beautiful girl on his trip to Jamaica, but he did.

05 Jasmine works and eats around here, so she usually prints a lot of coupons that look good regardless of if or not she uses them.

[06-10] 다음 빈칸에 들어갈 알맞은 말을 보기에서 골라 알맞은 형태로 쓰시오.

보기	although	whether	because	despite	because of

06 The program can see __________ or not they were writing the truth by analyzing the physical characteristics of their handwriting.

07 This study noted that more exercise often made school performance better, __________ the time it took away from reading, writing and arithmetic.

08 기출응용 Some jerboas do not need to drink, __________ they get water from their food.

09 __________ recent progress in neuroscience and psychology, we have started to note the importance of emotional intelligence.

10 She wore a yellow dress to her senior prom __________ her favorite color was red.

FINAL CHECK

정답 및 해설 p.44

01 다음 글의 밑줄 친 부분 중, 어법상 <u>어긋난</u> 것은?

News media reported that some scientists found organic carbon elements from Mars, ① <u>which</u> would show the possibility of the existence of life on that planet. According to NASA, the investigation robot which landed on Mars discovered MCIO4. Scientists studied later the substance in the Atacama Desert, a place environmentally similar to Mars. The scientists heated the desert sand with MCIO4. Carbon dioxide and methyl chloride elements were extracted from the gas made by heating. This gas is the same as the gas ② <u>generated</u> when another lander heated the sand on Mars before. It was estimated that the new finding made a great advancement in discovering ③ <u>much</u> evidence for life on Mars. However, to confirm ④ <u>if</u> or not it is the real proof of life composing substances on Mars, scientists will launch another probe there. A research team said that determining whether the organic elements are the appropriate elements of Mars or the components of a meteorite from another planet ⑤ <u>was</u> not easy.

*perchlorate : 과염소산염

02 

기출응용

다음 (A), (B), (C)의 각 [ ] 안에서 어법에 맞는 표현으로 바르게 짝지어진 것은?

When something doesn't meet our expectations, many of (A) [us / whom] operate this assumption, "When in doubt, it must be someone else's fault." You can see this assumption in action almost everywhere you look—something is missing, so someone else must have moved it. This type of blaming-thinking has become extremely common in our culture. But in terms of personal happiness, you cannot be peaceful while at the same time (B) [blame / blaming] others. Blaming others takes an enormous amount of mental energy. It's a "drag-me-down" mind-set that creates stress and disease. Blaming makes you (C) [feel / to feel] powerless over your own life because your happiness is contingent on the actions and behaviors of others, which you can't control.

	(A)		(B)		(C)
①	us	-	blame	-	feel
②	us	-	blaming	-	feel
③	whom	-	blame	-	to feel
④	whom	-	blaming	-	feel
⑤	whom	-	blaming	-	to feel

03 기출응용

다음 글의 밑줄 친 부분 중, 어법상 어긋난 것은?

Contrary to popular belief, most octopuses are poor swimmers. For instance, they usually use their arms to crawl along the ocean bottom. However, they can squeeze through tiny holes ① even if they were moving from room to room through keyholes. A beak, the only hard part of their body, enables them ② to squeeze through very narrow gaps between underwater rocks. They can also bury ③ themselves in sand or mud. Some of them can even swim through the sand ④ sticking up an eye like a periscope in a submarine. Some spend their lives swimming in the ocean in shells that they build, and use them ⑤ almost like canoes.

04

다음 (A), (B), (C)의 각 [ ] 안에서 어법에 맞는 표현으로 바르게 짝지어진 것은?

Once you have finished exploring Taiwan's cultural sights and uncovering its natural beauty, culinary wonders await. Savor delicious local delicacies at (A) [alive / lively] night markets, indulge in spicy Sichuan flavors and Hakka specialties in hidden havens or (B) [experience / experiences] international fine dining at world-class hotels. Taiwan is truly a gourmand's paradise with taste sensations for every budget and preference. (C) [If / Whether] you relish its delicious local dishes, wonder at its cultural diversity, or escape to its mountains and jungles, your expectations are sure to be exceeded every time.

	(A)		(B)		(C)
①	alive	-	experience	-	If
②	alive	-	experiences	-	Whether
③	alive	-	experience	-	If
④	lively	-	experiences	-	Whether
⑤	lively	-	experience	-	Whether

Chapter XIV

05 다음 글의 밑줄 친 부분 중, 어법상 어긋난 것은?

For years we've been warned against spending too long talking on mobile phones ① <u>because</u> concerns that the radiation they emit could cause cancer. But scientists find there ② <u>is</u> precious little evidence for that, and it now seems electromagnetic radiation could benefit the brain, by ③ <u>protecting</u> it from Alzheimer's disease. They exposed three groups of mice—one with an Alzheimer's-like condition, the second genetically prone to develop it, and ④ <u>the other</u> group of normal mice—to the same electromagnetic field frequencies as are generated by mobile phones. They were looking for signs of mental deterioration, but after eight months all the mice performed better at memory tests than rodents that ⑤ <u>hadn't been</u> exposed to the electromagnetic field.

06 다음 (A), (B), (C)의 각 [ ] 안에서 어법에 맞는 표현으로 바르게 짝지어진 것은?

기출응용

Conditioning occurs indirectly, which adds to its impact on us. Let's say, for example, that you watch another person get an electric shock. Each time, a signal light comes on before the shock is delivered. (A) [If / Even if] you do not receive a shock yourself, you will soon develop an emotional response to the light. Children who learn to fear thunder by watching their parents react to it (B) [has / have] undergone similar conditioning. If horror movies can affect us, we might expect the emotions of parents, friends, and relatives to have even more impact. How, for instance, does a city child learn to fear snakes and respond emotionally to mere pictures of them? Being told that "snakes are dangerous" may not explain the child's emotional response. More likely, the child has observed others reacting (C) [fearful / fearfully] to the word snake or to snake images on television.

	(A)		(B)		(C)
①	If	-	has	-	fearful
②	If	-	have	-	fearfully
③	Even if	-	has	-	fearful
④	Even if	-	have	-	fearfully
⑤	Even if	-	have	-	fearful

Subjunctives

Chapter 15

가정법

UNIT
171 가정법 과거

If I won the lottery, I would give everyone enough money to buy whatever they want.

만약 내가 복권에 당첨된다면, 나는 모든 사람에게 그들이 원하는 무엇이든지 살 수 있는 충분한 돈을 줄 것이다.

만약 내가 복권에 당첨된다면 // 나는 줄 것이다 / 모든 사람에게 / 충분한 돈을 /

If I won the lottery, I would give everyone enough money

would have given (X)

현재 사실을 반대로 가정한 것이므로 if절에는 과거(won)가,
if절 밖에는 〈would+동사원형〉(would give)가 왔다.

살 수 있는 // 그들이 원하는 것은 무엇이든지

to buy whatever they want.

Grammar Point

가정법 과거

가정법 과거는 현재 사실에 대한 가정으로, 사실상 현재는 반대의 상황에 처해 있음을 의미한다. 형식은 if절 안의 시제는 과거(-ed)이고 주절의 시제는 〈would/could 등+동사원형〉을 사용한다. 단, if절에 be동사가 올 때에는 주어의 인칭이나 수에 상관 없이 were를 쓰지만, 구어체에서는 was도 가능하다.

if+주어+동사의 과거형, 주어+would/could 등+동사원형

If he felt ashamed of his cheating, he would not turn in his answer sheet.

만약 그가 자신의 부정을 부끄러워한다면, 답지를 내지 않을 텐데.

⇒ 현재 사실에 대한 반대를 가정한 것으로 if절 안에는 과거(felt)가, 주절에는 would turn이 왔다.

Words & Phrases

lottery [látəri] 복권

ashamed of ~을 부끄럽게 느끼다

answer sheet 답지

barren [bǽrən] 불모인

devoid of ~이 없는

Check-up

정답 및 해설 p.45

1. If our company offered to pay 3 times as much for that project, we could be / have been selected as a partner.
2. If it were / had been either farther away or closer to the Sun, the Earth might be a hot, dry, and barren planet devoid of life.

UNIT 172

가정법 과거완료

If it had been not for our courage, we would not have met the bank president in the conference.

만약 우리의 용기가 없었다면, 우리는 그 회의에서 은행장을 만나지 못했을 거야.

만약 우리의 용기가 없었다면 // 우리는 만나지 못했을 것이다 /

If it [had been] not for our courage, we [would not have met]

would not meet (X)

과거 사실에 대한 가정이므로 if절에는 과거완료(had been)가, if절 밖에는 would have p.p.가 왔다.

은행장을 / 그 회의에서

the bank president in the conference.

Words & Phrases

courage [kə́:ridʒ] 용기

conference [kɑ́nfərəns] 회의장

otherwise [ʌ́ðərwàiz] 그렇지 않으면

attempt [ətémpt] 시도하다

prepare [pripέər] 대비하다, 준비하다

casualty [kǽʒjuəlti] 사상자

Grammar Point

가정법 과거완료

가정법 과거완료는 과거 사실에 대한 가정으로, 사실상 과거의 상황에 반대되는 내용을 가지고 있다. if절 안의 시제가 과거완료(had p.p.)이고, 주절의 시제가 현재를 의미하지 않는다면 〈would / could 등+have p.p.〉를 사용한다.

if+주어+had p.p., 주어+would / could 등+have p.p.

If you had turned a light toward Mars that day, it would [reach / have reached] there in 186 seconds. 기출응용

만약 당신이 그날 화성 쪽으로 빛을 돌렸다면, 186초 후에 그곳에 도달했을 텐데.

⇒ If절 안에 had turned가 있고, 과거 사실에 대한 반대이므로 주절에는 would have reached가 와야 한다.

Check-up 정답 및 해설 p.45

1. I was a better and happier woman than I otherwise would have been if I [did not attempt / had not attempted] it.

2. If the government [prepared / had prepared] for the typhoon then, human casualties and injuries could have reduced.

EXERCISE

정답 및 해설 p.45

[01-10] 다음 중 어법상 가장 적절한 표현을 고르시오.

01 They have to be right. If they weren't right, they [would / will] not save their own lives.

02 If I had been sensible, it would [be / have been] a one-day story, not a two-day story.

03 If you had lived in the seventeenth century, would you [leave / have left] your country and come to America?

04 기출응용 If Clauss [haven't / hadn't] reacted so quickly and decisively, there would have been two drownings instead of one.

05 기출응용 He felt extremely fortunate—if he [fell / had fallen] differently, he might have broken his neck.

06 Without his courage 3 days ago, my 5-year-old son would [be / have been] hit by a car then.

07 If they had been understood at that time, the diseases from which people had suffered could [be / have been] easily dealt with.

08 If I had asked my father to go down to the schoolyard and play baseball with me, he would [say / had said] "Yes."

09 기출응용 If the experiment had been performed with people wearing only swimming trunks, they would [lose / have lost] no more than 10% of their body heat through their heads.

10 If she [tied / had tied] a rope with one end to the pillar and the other end to her car and drove away so that it bent down, the carpenter could then reach up and get the cat.

ACTUAL TEST

정답 및 해설 p.45

01 다음 글의 밑줄 친 부분 중, 어법상 어긋난 것은?

Many of people start their criticism with general praise ① followed by the word "but" and ending with a critical statement. For instance, in trying to change a child's unconcerned attitude toward studies, you might say, "I'm very proud of you, Tom, for raising your grade in math, but if you ② studied harder on your English, the grade would have been better." In this case, Tom might feel ③ encouraged until he heard the word "but." After hearing the word "but," he might wonder whether the praise is just lip service. Credibility would ④ be torn down, and you would not succeed in changing Tom's attitude. This could be easily solved by changing the word "but" to "and." "I'm really proud of you, Tom, for raising your grade in math, and by continuing the same sincere efforts on English, your English grade can be up with all the others." Now, Tom would accept the praise because there ⑤ was no follow-up of an inference of failure.

02 다음 (A), (B), (C)의 각 [ ] 안에서 어법에 맞는 표현으로 바르게 짝지어진 것은?

You have been renting your apartment for one year, and your landlady tells you that she is going to raise the rent $500 a month. One day, you run into (A) [another / the other] building tenant, Tina, in the hall. You tell her of your problem with the landlady. Tina gives you some advice. Later that week, you run into another tenant, Frank, who has heard about your situation from Tina. Frank says to you, "Listen, I know this is none of my business, but if I (B) [were / had been] you, I wouldn't take Tina's advice about housing issues. She was forced to leave her last apartment." Indeed, since Tina was evicted from her last apartment, it would appear as if what Frank says makes a lot of sense. But it does not. That is because Frank is not attacking Tina's advice; instead, he is simply attacking her advice with emotion. In fact, because she has dealt with a fairly serious housing issue, she might (C) [consider / be considered] a housing expert. Whether you like her or not is a separate matter from whether she has good advice or not. The credibility of advice should be based on freedom from your biases.

	(A)		(B)		(C)
①	another	-	were	-	consider
②	another	-	had been	-	consider
③	another	-	were	-	be considered
④	the other	-	had been	-	be considered
⑤	the other	-	were	-	consider

UNIT

173 혼합 가정법

If we had headed towards the back hill 2 hours ago, we could see the colorful cherry blossoms now.

만약 우리가 2시간 전에 뒷동산으로 향했다면, 우리는 지금 화려한 벚꽃을 볼 수 있을 텐데.

만약 우리가 향했다면 / 뒷동산으로 / 2시간 전에 //

If we [had headed] towards the back hill 2 hours ago,

if절의 시제가 had headed로 과거완료지만, 주절에 now가 있으므로 주절은 현재 상황의 반대이다. 따라서 could see가 왔다.

우리는 / 볼 수 있을 텐데 / 화려한 벚꽃을 / 지금

we [could see] the colorful cherry blossoms [now].

would have seen (X)

Grammar Point

혼합 가정법 – 가정법 과거완료 + 가정법 과거

if절의 시제가 had p.p.라면, 주절에는 would have p.p.가 온다. 하지만, 주절에 now 등 현재를 의미하는 말이 있을 경우 〈would/could 등+동사원형〉이 온다.

if+주어+had p.p., 주어+would/could 등+동사원형+now

If he had studied harder at school, James would [be / have been] working in a comfortable office now.

만약 학창시절에 열심히 공부했더라면, 제임스는 지금 편안한 사무실에서 일하고 있을 텐데.

⇒ if절에 과거완료인 had studied가 왔으나 주절에 now라는 현재를 나타내는 부사가 있으므로 주절은 〈would+동사원형〉을 써야 한다.

Words & Phrases

head towards
~로 향하다

back hill
뒷동산

cherry blossom
벚꽃

novel
[nάvəl]
소설; 새로운

translate
[trænsléit]
번역하다

Check-up

정답 및 해설 p.46

1. If his novels had not been translated then, we would not [enjoy / have enjoyed] reading them now.

2. If you had not listened to me, you could not [do / have done] the work now.

UNIT **174**

가정법 공식

If I were president, I would offer everybody a warm and strong house in which to live safely.

만약 내가 대통령이라면 모든 사람들에게 안전하게 살 수 있는 따뜻하고 튼튼한 집을 제공할 텐데.

만약 / 내가 / 대통령이라면 // 나는 / 제공할 텐데 / 모든 사람들에게 / 따뜻하고 튼튼한 집을 /

If I were president, I would offer everybody a warm and strong house

현재 사실의 반대를 가정하므로 if절의 시제는 과거(were),
주절에는 〈would+동사원형〉(would offer)가 왔다.

안전하게 살

in which to live safely.

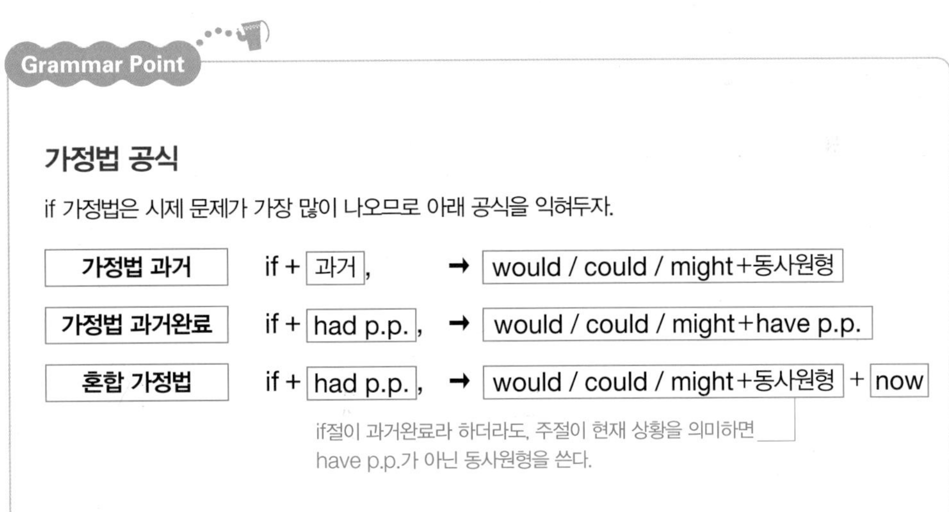

Grammar Point

가정법 공식

if 가정법은 시제 문제가 가장 많이 나오므로 아래 공식을 익혀두자.

가정법 과거	if + 과거,	→ would / could / might+동사원형
가정법 과거완료	if + had p.p.,	→ would / could / might+have p.p.
혼합 가정법	if + had p.p.,	→ would / could / might+동사원형 + now

if절이 과거완료라 하더라도, 주절이 현재 상황을 의미하면 have p.p.가 아닌 동사원형을 쓴다.

Words & Phrases

offer [ɔ́(ː)fər] 제공하다

go on a picnic 소풍을 가다

Check-up

정답 및 해설 p.46

1. Would you be more comfortable if we [change / changed] the date of the meeting?
2. We could [go / have gone] on a picnic to the zoo if it had been clear yesterday.

EXERCISE

정답 및 해설 p.46

[01-10] **다음 중 어법상 가장 적절한 표현을 고르시오.**

01 If I had proposed to her then, I [would be / would have been] to her now.

02 If this journey had occurred two weeks earlier, all this would [please / have pleased] their eyes now.

03 기출응용 You would [be / have been] treating your body with more consideration now if you had several small meals instead of a single big one.

04 기출응용 If the employee knew that individual rewards were possible, she would [be / have been] more likely to strive to outperform expectations.

05 If Jake had said so—not that he ever did—it would [be / have been] a lie.

06 If you had not committed such a foolish act then, you would [be / have been] happy now.

07 If the government had built more homes for the poor in the mid-2000s, the housing problems now in some parts of the country wouldn't [be / have been] so serious.

08 If she had eaten the sandwich one hour ago, she would not [be / have been] so hungry this time.

09 The report would not [be / have been] released last December if the new manager had not made it necessary to revise all conclusions drawn from the first research.

10 If Shawn Kent had not invented a man-made heart implant, the development of the mechanical heart wouldn't [be / have been] in use today.

ACTUAL TEST

정답 및 해설 p.47

01 다음 글의 밑줄 친 부분 중, 어법상 어긋난 것은?

Through socialization, humans learn the social roles of the family, school, peer, and society ① into which they are born and come to understand the social relations that surround them. For example, the ways a teacher and a student will interact ② is mostly referred as the roles of "teacher" and "student." Teachers learn what they should do in a college of education, and students learn ③ theirs in school or through the mass media. People come into a world of fairly stable pre-existing relations. If they had made the world, they ④ would not learn how to play assigned roles now. This is called a top-down system. However, this system is frequently confronted with challenges from people. By interacting with others, they negotiate with them. The negotiation process creates and re-creates ⑤ what we call social structure.

02  (A), (B), (C)의 각 [ ] 안에서 어법에 맞는 표현으로 바르게 짝지어진 것은?

On April 12, 1965, baseball changed the world of stadium architecture by opening the Harris County Domed Stadium in Houston. It became better (A) [knowing / known] to the world as the Houston Astrodome. It was the world's first enclosed and air-conditioned stadium for baseball. Before the domed stadium existed, baseball players in Houston had been playing outdoors in the mosquito-filled humidity and, sometimes, in extreme heat. If the domed stadium (B) [were not / had not been] built, major league baseball may not have survived in Houston, because passionate baseball players as well as professional players (C) [must / could not] have endured the uncomfortable weather.

	(A)		(B)		(C)
①	knowing	-	were not	-	must
②	known	-	were not	-	must
③	known	-	had not been	-	must
④	known	-	had not been	-	could not
⑤	knowing	-	had not been	-	could not

UNIT 175

if의 생략

Should she win her party's nomination, Hillary Clinton claims her stance on the issue will appeal even to voters who disagree with her.

힐러리 클린턴은 만약 그녀가 당 후보 지명에서 승리하면 그 쟁점에 대한 그녀의 입장은 심지어 그녀를 지지하지 않는 유권자의 흥미도 끌 것이라 주장한다.

민약 / 그녀가 / 승리한다면 / 당 후보 지명에서 // 힐러리 클린턴은 / 주장한다 //

Should she win her party's nomination, Hillary Clinton claims

if가 생략되면 should가 앞으로 나온다. 즉 주어와 should가 도치된다.

그 쟁점에 대한 그녀의 입장은 / 흥미를 끌 것이다 / 심지어 유권자에게도 //

her stance on the issue will appeal even to voters

그녀에게 동의하지 않는

who disagree with her.

Grammar Point

if의 생략

if절 안의 동사가 should, were, had일 경우 if를 생략하고 주어와 동사를 도치할 수 있다.
즉, should, were, had로 시작하는 문장은 if가 생략된 가정법 문장일 수 있다.

If she had

Had she bought the car, she would have wasted a lot of money.

만약 그녀가 그 차를 샀다면, 그녀는 많은 돈을 낭비했을 것이다.

If they were

Were they my son and daughter, I would be happy to talk with them.

그들이 내 아들과 딸이라면, 나는 그들과 기꺼이 이야기할 텐데.

If I should

Should I remarry, I would choose you as my fiancé.

내가 재혼한다면, 나는 내 약혼자로 당신을 선택할 것이다.

Words & Phrases

nomination [nɑ̀mənéiʃən] (후보자) 지명, 임명

stance [stæns] 입장, 태도

appeal [əpíːl] 흥미를 끌다, 마음에 들다

voter [vóutər] 투표자

disagree [dìsəgríː] 의견이 다르다

liquidity [likwídəti] (자산의) 유동성

shortage [ʃɔ́ːrtidʒ] 부족

disappointed [dìsəpɔ́intid] 실망한

Check-up

정답 및 해설 p.47

1. Had we known / We had known that TLC Co. was suffering from liquidity shortage, we would have not invested our money.

2. Should he fail / He should fail, his mother would be disappointed with the result.

UNIT

176 if의 대용

Supposing everyone lived until the age of 75.8 years, about one out of three would develop cancer in some parts of the body.

모든 사람이 75.8세까지 산다면 약 세 명 중 한 명꼴로 신체의 어떤 부위에 암이 생길 것이다.

모든 사람이 산다면 / 75.8세까지 //
Supposing everyone lived until the age of 75.8 years,

if 대신 supposing이 '~라면'의 뜻으로 쓰였다.

약 세 명 중 한 명꼴로 / 암이 생길 것이다 /
about one out of three would develop cancer

신체의 어떤 부위에
in some parts of the body.

Grammar Point

if의 대용

supposing (that), suppose (that), provided (that), providing (that), in case (that), on condition (that) 등은 '~라면'의 의미로 if를 대신해서 쓸 수 있다.

Provided that I can solve the present problem in the experiment, I will leave Seoul on June 1st.

그 실험에 존재하는 문제를 해결할 수 있으면 나는 6월 1일에 서울을 떠날 것이다.

In case you find the boy, please let us know at once.

그 소년을 발견하면 즉시 우리에게 알려 주세요.

Words & Phrases

cancer [kǽnsər] 암

at once 즉시

temperature [témpərətʃər] 온도

furnace [fə́:rnis] 화로, 난로

melt [melt] 녹다

iron [áiərn] 철; 다림질

Check-up 정답 및 해설 p.47

1. Supposing / Supposed that the temperature in the furnace is high enough, it will easily melt the iron.

2. Provide / Provided you use money wisely, it could give us a number of benefits.

EXERCISE

정답 및 해설 p.47

[01-10] 다음 중 어법상 가장 적절한 표현을 고르시오.

01 [He had / Had he] given me the keys to the car, I would have driven home and we would have avoided the accident.

02 [Two vehicles should meet / Should two vehicles meet], as often happens, it would be necessary for one to reverse to the nearest open space in order to let the other pass.

03 [Provided / Provide] we are defeated by the war against terrorism, our descendants cannot have a happy life like ours.

04 [She had / Had she] not died from the car crash, she would be attending college with me now.

05 [Suppose / Supposed] we had seen her at the amusement park yesterday, what would we have done at that time?

06 [Provided / Provide] enough time is given, our company will send all products by the end of this month.

07 [In case / In case of] I do not have any laundry detergent, I'll not be able to wash my clothes and dry them overnight.

08 [Had they / They had] known the snowstorm would be so heavy, the hikers would not have climbed that mountain without proper equipment.

09 [Only some sections of the wheel were / Were only some sections of the wheel] repaired, it would be unwise to use it.

10 [Were they / Had they been] able to choose for themselves, some of the most successful men would have selected professions quite different from those in which they made their fortunes.

ACTUAL TEST

정답 및 해설 p.48

01 다음 글의 밑줄 친 부분 중, 어법상 어긋난 것은?

We hear or see that business or political leaders are talking about several issues including their business deals on the golf course. They, like other players, spend ① much of their time on the course looking for capricious golf balls. But it's true that golf may help you ② make more personal connections. That's one reason to play. And it can be the 200th-most-important reason. More important reasons include spending time with friends, climbing the corporate ladder, gaining pleasure from the beautiful scenery surrounding you, and ③ talking a lot—perhaps you may spend more time talking than playing. Moreover, it's a game for a lifetime. You may have played football and basketball in high school. However, ④ were you 40 or 60 years old, could you be still kicking the ball or rebounding it? The most important reason to play, though, is that golf is addictive. After you enter the golf world, barely ⑤ you can imagine life without it.

02 다음 (A), (B), (C)의 각 [　] 안에서 어법에 맞는 표현으로 바르게 짝지어진 것은?

기출응용

Our experiences may consist partly of certain emotions we feel and partly of certain thoughts we think, but most of (A) [which / them] will be a cluster of sense impressions. The sense impressions of a spring day, for instance, will consist of seeing blue sky and white clouds, budding leaves and daffodils. Poets (B) [seek / seeking] to express the experience of a spring day, therefore, provide a selection of sense impressions. Similarly, to present a winter day, Shakespeare gives hanging "icicles," milk "frozen," and Marian's "red and raw" nose as well as the melancholy "Tu-whit, tu-who" of the owl in his poem, *Winter*. (C) [He had / Had he] not done so, he might have failed to evoke the emotions of a winter day that accompany these sensations. The poet's language, then, is more sensuous than ordinary language. It is richer in imagery.

	(A)		(B)		(C)
①	which	-	seek	-	He had
②	which	-	seek	-	Had he
③	them	-	seeking	-	Had he
④	them	-	seeking	-	He had
⑤	them	-	seek	-	He had

UNIT 177

wish+가정법

Kathleen enjoys riding horses, but I wish she had a less dangerous hobby.

캐슬린은 승마를 즐기는데, 나는 그녀가 덜 위험한 취미를 가졌으면 좋겠다.

캐슬린은 / 즐긴다 / 말을 타는 // 하지만 / 나는 바란다 // 그녀가 갖다 /

Kathleen enjoys riding horses, but I [wish] she [had]

현재 상황의 반대를 소망하는 내용이므로 wish가 오고 뒤에 과거(had)가 왔다.

덜 위험한 취미를

a less dangerous hobby.

Grammar Point

wish + 가정법

wish 가정법은 실현 불가능하거나 현재와 다른 상황을 원하는 경우, 또는 과거에 이루지 못한 일에 대한 아쉬움을 나타낼 때 사용하며, wish 뒤에는 직설법이 아닌 가정법 구문이 온다. wish와 시제가 동일할 경우에는 과거를, wish보다 먼저 발생한 사건일 경우는 과거완료를 쓴다.

It's raining. I [wish] it [would stop]. 비가 오고 있어. 멈추면 좋으련만.

wish가 나오고, 현재와 다른 상황을 바라는 것이므로 would stop이 온다.

Words & Phrases

weather [wéðər] 날씨

realize [rí(ː)əlàiz] 깨닫다, 실현하다

make a mistake 실수하다

at that time 그때

Check-up

정답 및 해설 p.48

1. I wish you [realize / realized] those mistakes that you made yesterday.
2. She wishes she [met / had met] me earlier than you at that time.

UNIT

178 as if 가정법

When they meet children in the amusement park, many parents treat them as if they were their own son and daughter.

많은 부모는 놀이공원에서 아이들을 보면, 마치 그들이 자신의 아들과 딸인 것처럼 대한다.

그들이 아이들을 만날 때 / 놀이공원에서 // 많은 부모들은 /

When they meet children in the amusement park, many parents

아이들을 대한다 // 마치 그들이 자신의 아들과 딸인 것처럼

treat them as if they were their own son and daughter.

are (X)

as if 안의 사건 발생 확률이 희박하기에 가정법 시제가 왔다.

Grammar Point

as if + 가정법

as if는 '마치 ~처럼'이라는 뜻이고, 실제로 그렇지 않은데 그런 것처럼 행동한다는 의미로 사용한다. as if 다음에 오는 시점이 주절의 시점과 동일할 경우 과거를, 주절보다 먼저 발생할 경우에는 과거완료를 쓴다. 단, 이때 as if 안의 사건은 사실일 확률이 거의 없다. 사실일 가능성이 있으면 가정법이 아닌 직설법을 사용한다.

While I listen to the tune, the whole scene comes before my eyes as if I [am / were] there.

내가 그 곡조를 듣는 동안, 전체 장면이 내가 마치 거기에 있는 듯 내 눈 앞에 펼쳐졌다.

⇒ 내가 지금 그 장소에 있는 것이 아니므로 가정법을 쓴다. 따라서 were가 정답이다.

Words & Phrases

amusement park
놀이공원

treat
[triːt]
대하다

tune
[tjuːn]
곡조

strange
[streindʒ]
이상한

Check-up 정답 및 해설 p.48

1. Everyone looked strange to Emerson as if he didn't meet / hadn't met them before.

2. Melinda looks as if she is / were a teacher. It seems that I heard she taught math in high school.

EXERCISE

정답 및 해설 p.48

[01-10] 다음 중 어법상 가장 적절한 표현을 고르시오.

01 I wish Kennedy [is / were] alive these days.

02 I wish you [looked / had looked] at me when I'm trying to talk to you.

03 I wish I [wrote down / had written down] Julie's phone number at the last conference.

04 The men were envious of their friends, wishing they [come / had come] with them on the trip to London.

05 Jim looked at me as if he [never saw / had never seen] me before, which made me a little bit embarrassed.

06 Catherine took a shower, washed away the mud, and went about her business as if nothing [happens / had happened].

07 기출응용 We anticipate the future as if we [find / found] it too slow in coming and we were trying to hurry it up.

08 Everybody loved your presentation because of the way you speak and keep people entertained. I wish mine [is / were] half as good.

09 I wish you [will / would] say something instead of just sitting and doing nothing.

10 My friends wish that they [studied / had studied] business and economics when they were in college.

ACTUAL TEST

정답 및 해설 p.49

01 기출응용

다음 글의 밑줄 친 부분 중 어법상 어긋난 것은?

A person trying to interpret a situation often looks at those around him to see ① how he should react. If everyone else is calm and indifferent, he will tend to remain so; if everyone else is reacting strongly, he is likely to become ② stimulating. However, occasionally the reactions of others can provide false information. For example, the studied nonchalance of patients in a dentist's waiting room doesn't show their inner anxiety well. ③ It is considered embarrassing to "lose your cool" in public. In a potentially severe situation, then, everyone will appear less concerned than he ④ is in fact. A crowd can thus force inaction on its members by implying that an event is not an emergency. Any individual in such a crowd fears that he may appear a fool if he behaves as if it ⑤ were serious.

*nonchalance : 무관심, 태연

02

다음 (A), (B), (C)의 각 [ ] 안에서 어법에 맞는 표현으로 바르게 짝지어진 것은?

The "politics" usually divides into two sections—ethics and politics. For Aristotle, ethics is social, and his politics is ethical. He didn't forget in his book *The Ethics* that the individual is essentially a member of society, (A) [or / nor] in his book *The Politics* that the happiness of the state is based on the happiness of its citizens. He's sure that the former phrase is different from the latter. In the beginning of *The Ethics*, he considers the happiness of the state as a greater and more perfect thing (B) [as / than] that of the individual. That is, he thought if we cannot achieve the former, the latter is to be endured. However, in the end of the book, he speaks as if the state (C) [is / were] just subordinate to individual life.

	(A)		(B)		(C)
①	or	-	as	-	is
②	nor	-	as	-	were
③	or	-	than	-	is
④	nor	-	than	-	were
⑤	or	-	than	-	were

UNIT 179

It is time+가정법

It's high time we thought about our future and took serious steps to preserve our environment.

미래에 대해서 생각하고 환경을 보존하기 위한 중대한 절차를 취할 시간이다.

~ 할 시간이다 // 우리가 / 미래에 대해서 생각하고 / 중대한 절차를 취할 /

It's high time we thought about our future and took serious steps

조치를 취해야 할 때인데 취하지 않았다는 뜻으로 〈It's high time+가정법 과거〉 구문이 왔다.

우리의 환경을 보존하기 위하여

to preserve our environment.

Grammar Point

It is time + 가정법

〈It is time+(that)+가정법 과거〉 구문은 '~할 때/시간이다'라는 뜻으로 ~할 때인데 하지 않았으므로 …하라는 화자의 소망이나 재촉을 포함한다.

It is about time those students [must / should] come inside and go directly to bed. It's too late.

그 학생들이 안으로 들어와서 바로 잠자리에 들어야 할 시간이야. 너무 늦었어.

⇒ It is time 가정법 구문으로 must가 아닌 should가 온다.

cf.) It's time to go to bed. 잠자리에 들 시간이다.
⇒ 단순히 잠자리에 들 시간이 됐음을 알려주는 문장으로, 화자의 감정이 포함되어 있지 않다.

Words & Phrases

serious [sí(:)əriəs] 중대한, 심각한

preserve [prizə́ːrv] 보호하다, 보존하다

geometry [dʒiɑ́mətri] 기하학

required subject 필수 과목

Check-up

정답 및 해설 p.49

1. It is time we [take / took] the geometry class as it is a required subject. This is my last semester.

2. It is high time my son [have / had] a haircut. His hair is too long.

UNIT
180 if any vs. if ever

It has fueled a political controversy about what measures, if any, should be taken to address the possible problem of climate change. 기출응용

그것이 기후 변화에 있어 발생 가능한 문제를 처리하기 위해 취할 조치가 만약 있다면 어떤 조치를 취해야 하는지에 대한 정치적 논쟁을 가열시켰다.

그것은 가열시켰다 / ~에 대한 정치적 논쟁을 // 어떤 조치가 /
It has fueled a political controversy about what measures,

앞의 명사(measures)를 수식해서
'~이 있다 해도'라는 의미이므로 if any가 왔다.

만약 있다면 / 취해져야 하는지 / 발생 가능한 문제를 처리하기 위하여 /
if any, should be taken to address the possible problem of
if ever (X)

기후 변화에 대한
climate change.

Grammar Point

if any vs. if ever

if any나 if ever는 강조하는 역할을 한다. if any는 명사를 강조하고, if ever는 동사를 강조한다.
if any는 '설사 있다 해도', '만약 있다면'이라는 뜻이고, if ever는 rarely나 seldom과 주로 함께 쓰여 '(만일 ~ 하더라도) 매우 드물게, (설사 하더라도) 좀처럼 ~하지 않는'는 '라는 뜻이다.

There were few, if any, women or Jews in leadership positions in the 1920s.
1920년대에 지도자 계층에는 여성과 유대인들은 (설사 있다 하더라도) 거의 없었다.

Now that they have a baby, they seldom, if ever, go out to eat.
이제 그들은 아기가 있어서, 좀처럼 외식을 하지 않는다.

cf.) if ever there was one 확실히, 틀림없이

Words & Phrases

fuel [fjú(:)əl] 가열시키다, 부채질하다

controversy [kántrəvə̀:rsi] 논쟁

address [ədrés] 처리하다, 대처하다, ~에 본격적으로 착수하다

position [pəzíʃən] 위치, 계층

thorough [θə́:rou] 철저한

slush fund 비자금

prosecution [prɑ̀səkjú:ʃən] 검찰

Check-up

정답 및 해설 p.49

1. We need to take a thorough look at the bank transactions that are linked to British Finance Center slush funds, if any / if ever, prosecution officials said.
2. A politician who is worthy of great respect is rarely, if any / if ever, fully neglected in his life time.

EXERCISE

정답 및 해설 p.49

[01-10] 다음 중 어법상 가장 적절한 표현을 고르시오.

01 기출응용 Now it's time they [turned / had turned] their eyes to the other side of the world.

02 Bring your gold and diamonds, if [any / ever], to the bank so we can put them in a safety deposit box.

03 It is high time that you [put / have put] your money where your mouth is.

04 There are few, if [any / ever], misunderstandings in his ideas about Korean history.

05 Jennifer seldom, if [any / ever], meets other boys without her brother.

06 It's time you [have / had] to study hard for the final test in the library. Why are you still here?

07 It is about time we [happen / happened] to have a meeting for the plan. We're behind schedule.

08 There is little, if [any / ever], similarity among Korean electronics companies.

09 Your cousin Russell is a cheap guy who seldom, if [any / ever], pays for a meal at a restaurant.

10 You're self-centered. It's high time you [realize / realized] that you're not the most important person in the world.

ACTUAL TEST

정답 및 해설 p.50

01 기출응용

다음 글의 밑줄 친 부분 중 어법상 어긋난 것은?

It's time that we ① talked about saving our Lake Culture Center. The plan of covering one side of the exterior of the center with huge artwork banners is getting underway. The banners will ② be created by the students from Sigmund Art College in the neighborhood. The idea of encouraging them by exhibiting their artworks ③ are fully understood. However, it has a strangely comical point. Spend $55 million on the design of the center, and then try to hide most of the new architecture behind banners. That's an obvious waste of money. The plan should be withdrawn immediately. Practically, it even makes ④ it difficult for those inside the building to see outside ⑤ clearly and vice versa.

02

다음 (A), (B), (C)의 각 [　　] 안에서 어법에 맞는 표현으로 바르게 짝지어진 것은?

Giving to and caring for children makes Mother more cognitive. How about Father? Research found it has the same effect on him. Experiments were done on father and bachelor mice, and father mice turned out to be better foragers and created more comfortable and less stressful condition. The study found there were more electric signals in father mice's brains than (A) [bachelor / bachelors']. Father mice also released more vasopressin, hormones related to caregiving behavior. In another study, when a monkey becomes a father, his brain structure becomes complex and dense with neurons, which (B) [make / makes] him more cognitive. These results are similar to those from experiments with mothers, but fathers are more important in that they aren't pregnant. Now it is time fathers (C) [care / cared] for children the same as mothers.

	(A)		(B)		(C)
①	bachelor	-	make	-	care
②	bachelor	-	make	-	cared
③	bachelors'	-	make	-	cared
④	bachelors'	-	makes	-	cared
⑤	bachelors'	-	makes	-	care

REVIEW TEST

정답 및 해설 p.50

[01-10] **다음 주어진 단어를 이용하여 문장을 완성하시오.**

01 The research suggests that if educators ______________ all of their students' senses, the children would not only learn better, but they would think better. (engage)

02 Nick and Tim both found out that they would have been better off by $5,000 if they ____________________ different actions then. (take)

03 If they had asked for my help, I ______________________ the police. (will, cooperate with)

04 기출응용 If you knew me well, you ____________________ that I am shameless enough to take all compliments at their face value and not to think that they might be mere flattery. (will, know)

05 If I ____________________ Peter Jackson, I could not have developed my passion for films and plays. (meet, not)

06 기출응용 Flash photography is not permitted inside museums unless permission ____________________ by the Public Affairs Office. (grant)

07 I wish I ______________________ busy last Sunday; I could have handled the problem together with you. (be, not)

08 Are you still working on the same question? Time is running out. It's time you ________ ________ another question. (move onto)

09 If Catherine had studied the problem carefully yesterday, she ______________________ any difficulty now. (will, not, find)

10 If she ______________________ for the last interview, we would have given her that position. (come in)

FINAL CHECK

정답 및 해설 p.50

01

다음 글의 밑줄 친 부분 중 어법상 어긋난 것은?

We have been talking of social science as if it ① is a single entity. That is hardly the case. Which, in fact, are the social sciences? One way to answer the question is to see ② what departments and disciplines universities group under this name. Social science divisions usually include departments of anthropology, economics, politics, and sociology. Why do they not ordinarily include schools of law, education, business, social service, and public administration as well, all of ③ which draw on the concepts and methods of the social sciences for their development? The reason is ④ that the main purpose of such schools is to train for professional work outside of the university, while the previously mentioned departments are more exclusively ⑤ dedicated to the pursuit of systematic knowledge of human society, an activity that usually goes on within the university.

02

다음 (A), (B), (C)의 각 [ ] 안에서 어법에 맞는 표현으로 바르게 짝지어진 것은?

A philosopher once said that it is most difficult to take the lead in the introduction of a new order of things. In fact, doing something new is scary. But from the time we are born, our growth as functioning human beings (A) [depend / depends] on how well we adapt to changes and new circumstances. If we did not overcome our fear of falling, we (B) [could never learn / could have never learned] to stand up. Many of us have the scars on our knees to prove that we persisted even to the point of physical injury in our desire to learn a new skill (C) [calling / called] bicycle riding. But what a thrill it was to feel the wind in our face when we mastered the art. We conquered the dread, and the feeling we got from it was truly great.

	(A)		(B)		(C)
①	depend	-	could have never learned	-	calling
②	depend	-	could have never learned	-	called
③	depends	-	could have never learned	-	called
④	depends	-	could never learn	-	calling
⑤	depends	-	could never learn	-	called

03 기출응용 다음 글의 밑줄 친 부분 중 어법상 어긋난 것은?

Despite the fact that the recording industry wants teenagers to download music from fee-based web sites, it does not understand that the high prices of downloading music amount to ① the same as buying a CD. Although the industry's production cost for CDs ② is low, their price for teenagers is too high at $20 each. If the prices ③ are lowered to a maximum of $10 each, maybe teens could afford to buy music from stores without bothering to download music illegally. Wishful thinking? No. The world's largest record company has reduced its ④ suggested retail price of CDs to $12.98 in October. You may find a $10 CD at discount chains. Rather than blaming those who illegally download music, the recording industry should extend a helping hand to ⑤ get them back on the right track.

04 다음 (A), (B), (C)의 각 [ ] 안에서 어법에 맞는 표현으로 바르게 짝지어진 것은?

With summer just around the corner, it's time that you (A) [went / go] to beach. Before jumping into the sea, you should choose the Tone Me Up treatment which involves Body Scrub and Elemis Visible Brilliance Facial. (B) [By getting / To get] rid of all the dead skin cells and invigorate your skin, you first get a gentle massage. Then the therapist applies the clay to your legs. You're then wrapped in foil and the clay softens and nourishes your skin. With your face scrubbed, cleansed, and massaged, it's time to remove the clay (C) [most / almost] like a peel mask. You feel relaxed, and your skin becomes noticeably softer and smoother. Now, you're ready to enjoy the summer!

	(A)		(B)		(C)
①	went	-	By getting	-	almost
②	went	-	To get	-	almost
③	went	-	To get	-	most
④	go	-	By getting	-	most
⑤	go	-	By getting	-	almost

05 다음 글의 밑줄 친 부분 중 어법상 어긋난 것은?

Eating nutritious foods and taking regular exercise will help keep you mentally and physically healthy. When the acid from some foods and drinks ① comes into contact with teeth, the tooth's hard enamel surface temporarily softens. Then when we brush our teeth afterwards, the enamel can be worn out more ② easily and become softer as time goes on, ③ which is known as acid erosion. There are some simple ways to help protect your teeth from this acid erosion. To avoid this situation, wait as long as possible before brushing your teeth after eating acidic foods because this period is ④ when the enamel is at its thinnest. Another is chewing gum. It can help to neutralize the acid since this stirs the production of saliva as if you ⑤ eat something.

06 기출응용 다음 (A), (B), (C)의 각 [ ] 안에서 어법에 맞는 표현으로 바르게 짝지어진 것은?

Have you ever wished you (A) [have / had] someone to give you a ride somewhere, or just give you a hand when you needed it? Many of us have friends, neighbors and family members who help us out, but they cannot always be there in times of need. In a Time Banking community, someone is always there for you. It is like having an extended family. Time Banking turns strangers into friends. Time Banking is simply about spending an hour (B) [done / doing] something for somebody in your community. That hour goes into the Time Bank as a Time Dollar. Then you have a Time Dollar (C) [spend / to spend] on having someone doing something for you. Time Banking has powerful effects on building community connections.

	(A)		(B)		(C)
①	have	-	done	-	spend
②	have	-	doing	-	to spend
③	had	-	doing	-	to spend
④	had	-	doing	-	spend
⑤	had	-	done	-	spend

Stress and Inversion

강조, 도치

UNIT 181

It ~ that 강조 구문 (1)

It was the greatest poet who Korea has ever produced that gave me his book of poetry.

나에게 그의 시집을 주었던 사람이 바로 한국이 배출한 가장 위대한 시인이었다.

바로 가장 위대한 시인이었다 // 한국이 지금까지 배출한 //

It was the greatest poet who Korea has ever produced that

앞의 명사를 수식한다.

나에게 그의 시집을 주었다

gave me his book of poetry.

Grammar Point

It ~ that 강조 용법

It ~ that 강조 용법 사이에 무언가 추가되어서 it과 that의 거리가 멀어진 경우, 해석에 주의해야 한다. 특히 관계대명사가 있는 경우에 조심하자.

관계사절의 첨가

It is the characters who lie, cheat, or hurt others that are routinely punished by the end of the story. 기출응용

이야기의 마지막에서 통상적으로 벌을 받는 사람이 바로 거짓말하고 속이고 남에게 상처를 입힌 등장인물이다.

삽입어구의 첨가

It is the combination of foods eaten, not the amount or kinds of food, that is the main focus of the popular "Fit for Life" diet.

그 유명한 Fit for Life 식단의 핵심은 바로 음식의 양이나 종류가 아니라, 섭취한 음식의 조합이다.

⇒ 강조 구문에서도 수 일치에 주의한다. the combination이 주어이므로 is가 왔다.

It was a wonderful theory of the human-relationship which was found by researchers in Chicago University that makes people surprised.

사람들을 놀라게 만드는 것이 바로 시카고 대학의 연구원들이 발견한 인간 관계에 대한 놀라운 이론이었다.

⇒ 수식어구가 두 개일 때 특히 주의하자. 이 문장에서는 전치사구와 관계사절이 나왔다.

Words & Phrases

poetry [póuitri] 시

cheat [tʃiːt] 속이다

routinely [ruːtíːnli] 통상적으로

punish [pʌ́niʃ] 처벌하다

combination [kɑ̀mbənéiʃən] 조합

skinny [skíni] 바싹 마른

catcall [kǽtkɔ̀ːl] 날카로운 휘파람; 고양이 울음 같은 야유

Check-up

정답 및 해설 p.51

1. It was a skinny kid with two straw hats that [was / were] fishing on a rocky shore on Jeju Island.

2. It [was / were] the students at Westside High School who threw eggs at the man and welcomed him with catcalls.

UNIT 182

It ~ that 강조 구문 (2)

It was Thomason Rogan who emerged in the annual shareholders' meeting as the white knight that could help us.

우리를 도울 수 있는 백기사로서 연례 주총에 나타난 사람이 바로 토마슨 로건이었다.

바로 토마슨 로건이었다 // 나타난 / 연례

It was Thomason Rogan who emerged in the annual

강조하는 대상이 사람이므로 that 대신 who가 왔다.

주주총회에 / 백기사로 // 우리를 도울 수 있는

shareholders' meeting as the white knight that could help us.

Grammar Point

It ~ that 강조 구문에서 that의 대용

It ~ that 강조 용법에서 that 대신에 who, which, when, where를 쓸 수 있다. 특히 뒤에 that이 나올 경우 사람, 사물, 장소 등 어떤 것을 강조하는 것인지 주의해서 해석해야 한다.

It was Sue who strongly insisted that Tim finish the project by June.

팀이 6월까지 프로젝트를 끝내야 된다고 강하게 주장한 사람은 바로 수였다.

⇒ 이 문장의 that은 It ~ that 강조의 that이 아니라 insisted의 목적어절을 이끄는 that이다.

It was yesterday when Tommy said that he wanted to enter SNU.

토미가 SNU에 입학하기를 원한다고 말한 게 바로 어제였다.

⇒ 이 문장의 that은 It ~ that 강조의 that이 아니라 said의 목적어절을 이끄는 that이다.

It was in the park where Tom lost his dog that he bought 4 days ago.

톰이 나흘 전에 산 강아지를 잃어버린 곳은 바로 그 공원이었다.

⇒ 이 문장의 that은 It ~ that 강조의 that이 아니라 his dog을 수식하는 목적격 관계대명사절을 이끄는 that이다.

Words & Phrases

emerge [imə́:rʤ] 나타나다

shareholder [ʃέərhòuldər] 주주

white knight 백기사(기업 매수의 위기에 있는 회사를 구제하기 위해 나선 개인이나 조직)

insist [insíst] 주장하다

harass [hǽrəs] 괴롭히다

antagonist [æntǽgənist] 적대자, 라이벌

refugee [rèfjuʤí:] 피난민

Check-up

정답 및 해설 p.51

다음 문장을 읽고, 해석하시오.

1. It is the character who harasses, hurts, bothers a hero in the story that is called an antagonist.
2. It was the president who suggested that our country should help African refugees to escape from the city.

EXERCISE

정답 및 해설 p.52

[01-10] 다음 중 어법상 가장 적절한 표현을 고르시오.

01 It's not just the people in Australia [that / where] look good.

02 [It / This] is not because of only wisdom that we grow mentally and spiritually but our irritating problems.

03 기출응용 [It / That] is our parents who have given us our sense of right and wrong, our understanding of love, and our knowledge of who we are.

04 It was at the amusement park [which / that] Catherine had her first date with her husband-to-be.

05 It was while he was studying in New York [where / that] he met Anderson for the second time.

06 기출응용 It is when the differences between sports and everyday life are recognized [that / which] people are able to open themselves up to new experiences in sports.

07 It was in the book you bought me last year [when / where] I read about his discovery.

08 It was between 1860 and 1868 [which / that] the modern newspaper was born.

09 [It / This] was not until the accident happened that James became aware of his foolishness.

10 It is the uses to which the device is put that [determine / determines] its value to society.

ACTUAL TEST

정답 및 해설 p.52

01 다음 글의 밑줄 친 부분 중, 어법상 어긋난 것은?

Commodity and metal stealing has become one of the specific problems across the nation. For example, drug users steal metal items, such as copper or aluminum pipes from buildings, and then sell ① them for scrap to gain money to buy drugs. And highways in Utah often become ② darker than usual at night because thieves repeatedly steal the wiring from the street lamps. The government pays tens of thousands of dollars to replace the stolen wiring. But the thief gets $100 or less through ③ sold the wiring. Also, construction materials and tools are frequent targets for theft, since ④ it was without any security that they're often found left in the construction sites. To prevent this situation, some states have passed laws asking metal dealers ⑤ to record identity information from people who sell them these metals.

02 다음 (A), (B), (C)의 각 [   ] 안에서 어법에 맞는 표현으로 바르게 짝지어진 것은?

One of the words which have been most devalued in our language (A) [is / are] love. We use it for anything—we love our family, we love our new i-Phone, we love soccer, Beatles, and being left alone. It (B) [thinks / is thought] that first we think, and then we find words to express our thoughts. In fact, the truth is quite the other way around. For instance, we do not love our family in the same way we love our sweethearts. We do not love God in any sense that we love the taste of pizza. We do not love our country in the way we love our pet. It is a manner of speaking (C) [that / what] makes these verbal distinctions. The words we use control what we think. It is why we usually take action by slogans rather than by the definite realities they embody.

	(A)		(B)		(C)
①	is	-	thinks	-	what
②	is	-	is thought	-	what
③	is	-	is thought	-	that
④	are	-	thinks	-	what
⑤	are	-	is thought	-	that

UNIT
183 It ~ that 강조 구문 (3)

It is only when our lovers are gone and we cannot meet them that we realize that we cannot forget them.

우리는 사랑하는 사람들이 떠나고 그들을 만날 수 없을 때 비로소 그들을 잊을 수 없음을 깨닫게 된다.

~했을 때야 비로소 ~하다 // 우리가 사랑하는 사람들이 떠난다 // 우리가 그들을 만날 수 없다 //
It is only when our lovers are gone and we cannot meet them
→ 강조 받는 부분

우리는 깨닫는다 // 우리가 그들을 잊을 수 없다
that we realize that we cannot forget them.
which, what (X)

Grammar Point

주의해야 할 It ~ that 강조 구문

It ~ that 강조 구문 사이에는 명사, 대명사, 부사뿐만 아니라 부사절도 들어갈 수 있다. It으로 시작하고 중간에 that이 보이는 문장은 강조 구문인 경우가 많으므로 해석에 주의한다. 'that절 이하가 바로 ~이다'라고 해석한다.

It was because he was ill that we had to return early.
우리가 일찍 돌아와야 했던 이유는 바로 그가 아팠기 때문이다.
⇒ because로 시작되는 접속사절이 It ~ that 강조 구문 사이에 들어간 형태의 문장이다.

It is the act of believing that is the starting force or generating action that leads great men and women to success. 기출응용
위대한 남녀를 성공으로 이끈 원동력이 바로 그 믿는 행위이다.
⇒ leads 앞에 that은 the starting force or generating action을 수식하는 절을 이끄는 주격 관계대명사이다. that이 두 번 나오는 구문에 주의하자.

Words & Phrases

generate [dʒénərèit] 일으키다
evidence [évidəns] 증거
relate [riléit] 관련시키다
trial [tráiəl] 재판

Check-up 정답 및 해설 p.52

1. It was because the letters came to James [that / who] we had to look for him.
2. It was the evidence related to this case [that / what] we needed for winning the trial.

UNIT 184

not until vs. not only

Not until the World Chess Organization asserted its control over international play in 1946 was the chess game well organized. 기출응용

1946년에 세계 체스 연맹이 국제 게임에 대한 통제권을 주장하면서 비로소 체스 게임이 잘 조직되었다.

세계 체스 연맹이 주장하면서 비로소 / 그것의 통제권을 /
Not until the World Chess Organization asserted its control
Not until did the World Chess Organization assert (X)

국제 게임에 대한 / 1946년에 // 체스 게임이 잘 조직되었다
over international play in 1946 was the chess game well organized.
the chess game was (X)

Grammar Point

not until vs. not only

〈It is not until ~ that …〉는 '~하고 나서야 비로소 …하다'라는 뜻이고, 강조를 위해 not until이 문장 앞으로 보내지면, not until이 없는 절이 도치된다. not only A but also B는 'A 뿐만 아니라 B도'라는 의미이며, not only가 있는 절(A)이 도치된다. 단, not until, not only 등의 부정어구가 문장의 앞에 위치하지 않으면 문장은 도치되지 않는다.

- **not until 도치 : not until이 없는 절(주절)을 도치**
  Not until the show began did my friends arrive.
  그 쇼가 시작되고 나서야 비로소 내 친구들이 도착했다.

- **not only 도치 : not only가 있는 절을 도치**
  Not only did the candle go out, but also all the windows were closed.
  촛불이 꺼졌을 뿐만 아니라, 모든 창문이 닫혔다.

Words & Phrases

organization [ɔ̀ːrgənizéiʃən] 협회, 조직, 단체

assert [əsə́ːrt] 주장하다, 단언하다

violate [váiəlèit] 위반하다

board [bɔːrd] 위원회

Check-up

정답 및 해설 p.52

1. Not until he crossed the finishline [he knew / did he know] he won the 100 meter race.

2. Not only [Jack violated / did Jack violate] the law, but also the board didn't stop his violation.

EXERCISE

정답 및 해설 p.53

[01-10] 다음 중 어법상 가장 적절한 표현을 고르시오.

01 It was not until she was forty-five [that / which] she started to write poems.

02 Not until he met his attorney [he began / did he begin] talking about what he witnessed at the park.

03 Not only [the employees of the factory want / do the employees of the factory want] a pay increase, but they also want reduced working hours.

04 Not until [she arrived / did she arrive] were we able to start the meeting and discuss the company's problems.

05 It was [not only / not until] we were married that I realized what kind of person he is.

06 Not until [a monkey is / is a monkey] several years old does it begin to show indications of independence from its mother.

07 기출응용 It is around these details [that / which] a conversation between adults and children starts.

08 Not until his thirtieth year [Beethoven composed / did Beethoven compose] his first symphony.

09 It was not until 2007 when [the lack of a national pension became / did the lack of a nation pension become] a hot issue between the young and the old.

10 기출응용 Not only [my pause gave / did my pause give] my students time to think about what I had said, but it also gave me time to think about what I was going to say.

정답 및 해설 p.53

01 기출응용

다음 글의 밑줄 친 부분 중, 어법상 어긋난 것은?

Many of common chemicals are so toxic ① that they have bad effects on mammals and other animals. For example, one class of chemicals, called alkyphenols, can interfere with hormone systems and growth. Alkyphenols are often found in shampoo. ② Another group of chemicals, called phthalates, which are widely used in vinyl flooring, are toxic to the reproductive system. Not only are these chemicals toxic, but also ③ do they not readily biodegrade. In other words, they will be on our planet for a very long time. Chemicals with a combination of these properties are commonly known as "Persistent Organic Pollutants," or POPs. The combined effect of POPs on our health and on the environment ④ is increasingly being studied and recognized. Some work ⑤ has been done to control the use of POPs, but only a handful of chemicals fall under current government controls.

*Persistent Organic Pollutants : 잔류성 유기오염물질

02

다음 (A), (B), (C)의 각 [ ] 안에서 어법에 맞는 표현으로 바르게 짝지어진 것은?

Even if Socrates did not work out accurate guidelines for its definition, he did make use of (A) [that / what] came to be known as the "Socratic method." To reach the true definition of some terms, Socrates would enter into conversation with someone who claimed to understand the term. He kept carefully probing and persistently questioning. Not until they finally arrived at a correct version (B) [Socrates would / would Socrates] elicit from his opponent all sorts of definitions and show their inadequacy and imperfection. Naturally, this approach was irritating and humiliating to those with whom he discussed that issue and (C) [whom / that] confidently thought they knew it all.

	(A)		(B)		(C)
①	that	-	Socrates would	-	whom
②	what	-	Socrates would	-	whom
③	that	-	would Socrates	-	that
④	what	-	would Socrates	-	that
⑤	what	-	would Socrates	-	whom

UNIT 185

부사구의 도치

Along with this interesting finding have scientists concluded that, due to their greater range of motion, flowers with long, thin stalks attract more insects. 기출응용

과학자들은 이 흥미로운 발견과 더불어 길고 가는 줄기를 가진 꽃이 움직임의 범위가 더 크기 때문에 더 많은 곤충들을 끌어들인다고 결론을 내렸다.

흥미로운 발견에 덧붙여 / 과학자들은 결론을 내렸다 //

Along with this interesting finding have scientists concluded that,

이 부분을 주어로 보고 has라고 하면 안 된다.

부사구 Along ~ finding이 앞에 나와서 주어인 scientists가 조동사 have 뒤로 도치되었고, 일반동사인 concluded는 주어 뒤에 위치했다.

그들의 더 큰 움직임의 범위 때문에 / 길고 가는 줄기를 가진 꽃들이 /

due to their greater range of motion, flowers with long, thin stalks

더 많은 곤충들을 끌어들인다

attract more insects.

Grammar Point

부사구/보어의 도치

부사구나 보어가 문장 맨 앞으로 오면 대부분 주어와 동사가 도치된다. 도치된 문장의 경우, 동사의 수 일치에 주의해야 한다. 앞에 있는 것은 부사구이므로 동사 뒤에 있는 주어의 수를 잘 확인해야 한다.

very long이라는 어구가 문장 맨 앞으로 나와서 주어와 동사가 도치되었다.

Very long was our conversation last night, but nobody was tired.

어젯밤에 우리의 대화는 매우 길었지만, 어느 누구도 피곤해하지 않았다.

Words & Phrases

along with
~에 덧붙여; ~과 함께

range
[reindʒ]
범위

stalk
[stɔːk]
줄기

attract
[ətrǽkt]
끌어들이다

encircle
[insə́ːrkl]
둘러싸다

Check-up

정답 및 해설 p.53

1. Among the movie stars at the Academy Awards was / were the lovely, blonde Marilyn Monroe.

2. Just outside the historic site is / are a castle encircled by stone walls and tall trees.

UNIT
186 so ~ that 구문의 도치

So fraught with political conflicts was the arrangement that the minister refused to attend key meetings called by the president.

그 협정이 너무 정치적 분쟁으로 가득해서 장관은 대통령이 소집한 중요한 회의의 참가를 거절했다.

너무 정치적 분쟁으로 가득해서 / 그 협정이 //
So fraught with political conflicts was the arrangement that

So ~ conflicts가 앞에 나와서 주어와 동사의 위치가 도치되었다.

장관은 거절했다 / 중요한 회의에 참가하는 것을 / 대통령에 의해 소집된
the minister refused to attend key meetings called by the president.

Grammar Point

so ~ that 구문의 도치

⟨so+형용사/부사+that+S+V⟩ '너무 ~ 해서 S가 V하다'
종종 ⟨so+형용사/부사⟩ 부분이 도치되어 앞으로 나오고 주어와 동사가 도치되는 경우가 있는데, 이 경우 동사 뒤에 나오는 것이 주어이므로 해석에 주의해야 한다.

The professor was so fat that he couldn't get through the door.

⇒ So fat was the professor that he couldn't get through the door.

그 교수는 너무 뚱뚱해서 그 문을 지나갈 수 없었다.

Words & Phrases

fraught with
~이 가득한, ~로 충만한

political
[pəlítikəl]
정치적인

arrangement
[əréindʒmənt]
협정; 조정, 배열

refuse
[rifjú:z]
거절하다

fall in love with somebody at first sight
첫눈에 ~와 사랑에 빠지다

pollution
[pəljú:ʃən]
오염

reduce
[ridjú:s]
줄이다

Check-up

정답 및 해설 p.53

1. So [beautiful is / is beautiful] the lady that I fell in love with her at first sight.
2. So great [the problem is / is the problem] of pollution that we should do something to reduce it.

EXERCISE

정답 및 해설 p.54

[01-10] 다음 중 어법상 가장 적절한 표현을 고르시오.

01 So little [has / have] the ways of life changed here that it is easy to imagine yourself back in the 15th century.

02 Under the sea, [you can see / can you see] a lot of fish and sea animals such as sea horses, turtles, jellyfish, etc.

03 So different [is / are] the world of sleep and the world of wakefulness that everyone is said to live in two worlds.

04 [So / Very] much will science have advanced that we will have robots in our bodies to monitor our condition on a daily basis.

05 In the SST Museum in LA [a collection is / is a collection] of medieval and Renaissance art works.

06 Next to the piano [a huge box was / was a huge box] with its lid open, also made of wood, containing a lot of musical scores.

07 On the couch [one hundred-dollar bill was / was one hundred-dollar bill].

08 Observing the local high school students [was / were] Detective John Smith, who thought one of them might have witnessed a crime.

09 So important [this element was / was this element] that some scientists used it as a subject of experimental study.

10 기출응용 I got off the bus and only then [I noticed / did I notice] that my wallet was stolen.

ACTUAL TEST

정답 및 해설 p.54

01 다음 글의 밑줄 친 부분 중, 어법상 어긋난 것은?

The American middle class has ① been divided into three new groups: an underclass out of favor with the growing economy; an overclass socially and economically stable to the rapid shift; and an anxious class, most of ② whom are employed but worried about their future. What categorizes them ③ is both the quality of their formal educations. Only in the 1990s did a college graduate earn 49% more than a high school graduate. Of course, that's a sizable difference, but it's ④ small enough for both people to reach the territory they would call middle class. In 2009, a male college graduate outearned his high school graduate counterpart by 95%. So great ⑤ the difference is that they no longer occupy common territory or share common prospects.

02 기출응용 다음 (A), (B), (C)의 각 [ ] 안에서 어법에 맞는 표현으로 바르게 짝지어진 것은?

The convention of communication between scientists (A) [is / are] formal and complicated. If new discoveries are to be taken seriously by other scientists, certain rigid criteria must be met. This means, before the new finding can be published and accepted, the experiment must be repeated and verified according to accepted procedures. Then, the finding is (B) [most / almost] always communicated through a formal scientific paper or a journal article. The most important new findings may appear in a journal of general interests to all scientists, such as *Science* or *Nature*. In either case, not until it has undergone the examination of the journal's editor and of two or three anonymous volunteer referees (C) [the article will / will the article] be published. This is one of the extensive safeguards of formal science.

	(A)		(B)		(C)
①	is	-	most	-	the article will
②	is	-	almost	-	will the article
③	is	-	almost	-	the article will
④	are	-	almost	-	will the article
⑤	are	-	most	-	the article will

UNIT 187

부정어구의 도치

Not only is Phil Grin's artwork technically sophisticated, but also it asks what our lives mean to us.

필 그린의 예술 작품은 기술적으로 정교할 뿐만 아니라 삶이 우리에게 있어 어떤 의미인지 묻는다.

~ 뿐만 아니라 / 필 그린의 예술 작품은 / 기술적으로 정교한 //
Not only | is | Phil Grin's artwork | technically sophisticated,

└ 부정어구 not only가 앞으로 와서 동사 is가 앞으로 나왔다.

또한 그것은 묻는다 // 우리의 삶이 우리에게 어떤 의미인지를
but also it asks what our lives mean to us.

Grammar Point

부정어구의 도치

부정어구가 문장 맨 앞으로 오면 주어와 동사가 도치된다. 일반동사일 경우 do동사가 앞으로 오고, be동사와 조동사의 경우는 주어와 be동사 또는 조동사의 위치만 바꾼다.

No sooner | had | I | heard a dog barking than I felt faint and took off as fast as my heels could carry me.

개가 짖는 걸 듣자마자, 나는 쓰러질 것 같았고, 할 수 있는 한 빨리 자리를 떴다.

⇒ No sooner가 앞으로 와서 주어인 I와 동사 had가 도치되었다. 완료 시제의 경우 have 동사가 앞으로 온다.

Not until I pass the examination | will | I | meet you.

나는 시험에 통과해야 비로소 너를 만날 것이다.

⇒ Not until ~ examination은 하나의 부정어구이므로 도치가 되어야 할 것은 주어인 I와 조동사 will이다.

cf.) 부정어구가 강조하기 위해 문두로 나간 경우에 도치가 일어나는 것이다. 이 문장의 No one 자체가 주어라고 볼 수 있으므로 도치가 일어나지 않는다.
No one knows the truth. 아무도 진실을 모른다.

Words & Phrases

artwork [ɑ́ːrtwə̀ːrk] 예술 작품

technically [téknikəli] 기술적으로

sophisticated [səfístəkèitid] 정교한

no sooner ~ than … ~하자마자 …한

faint [feint] 실신할 것 같은, 흐린

skyscraper [skáiskrèipər] 고층 빌딩

Check-up

정답 및 해설 p.54

1. Little [she realizes / does she realize] the danger she is in.

2. Nowhere but in America [doctors save / do doctors save] children, or newspapers print honest news.

UNIT
188 nor 도치

No government would try to rid risk taking of the system. Nor would we.

정부는 시스템에서 위험 부담을 없애려고 하지 않을 것이다. 우리도 그럴 것이다.

정부는 시도하지 않을 것이다 / 시스템에서 위험 부담을 없애려고 //
No government would try to rid risk-taking of the system.

우리도 않을 것이다
Nor would we.

Nor we would (X)

부정어인 Nor가 문장 맨 앞에 있으므로 주어 we와 조동사 would의 위치가 도치되었다.

Grammar Point

nor 도치

'~도 아니다'를 의미하는 nor가 문장 맨 앞에 나오면, 주어와 동사가 도치된다. 일반동사일 경우 do동사가 앞으로 오고, be동사와 조동사의 경우는 주어와 be동사 또는 조동사의 위치만 바꾼다.

He didn't have interest in his grades, nor [he sympathize / did he sympathize] with the competitive drive for good grades of some of his classmates.

그는 자신의 성적에 관심이 없었고, 좋은 성적을 얻으려는 몇몇 급우들의 경쟁심에도 공감하지 않았다.

⇒ 부정어인 nor가 앞에 있으므로 주어와 동사가 도치된다. 따라서 did he sympathize가 정답이다.

Words & Phrases

rid A of B
A에서 B를 없애다

risk-taking
[téikiŋ]
위험 부담

sympathize
[símpəθàiz]
공감하다, 동정하다

competitive drive
경쟁심

get on the phone
통화하다

ashamed
[əʃéimd]
부끄러운

Check-up

정답 및 해설 p.54

1. I haven't met him since the last conference, nor [I have / have I] got him on the phone.
2. Julian isn't ashamed to be an American, [or / nor] is he ashamed to wear the colors of his country.

EXERCISE

정답 및 해설 p.55

[01-10] 다음 중 어법상 가장 적절한 표현을 고르시오.

01 No sooner [I had / had I] seen him than I burst into tears.

02 Not [everyone is / is everyone] going to object to how this issue should be dealt with.

03 Not only [the dead have / have the dead] come back to life, they have become cannibals as well.

04 Not only does the vocabulary mean "moving quickly or rapidly," as in "She runs fast," but [it means / does it mean] "never moving at all," as in "The window is stuck fast."

05 A gentleman does not curse like a sailor, nor [he should / should he] be out drinking at 2 a.m.

06 기출응용 Rarely [a computer is / is a computer] more sensitive and accurate than a human in managing the same geographical or environmental factors.

07 Never at any other time, not even after the biggest promotion in my career, [have I felt / I have felt] such happiness for the birth of my daughter.

08 My neighborhood in Detroit is rather gloomy, and hardly [the atmosphere / is the atmosphere] conducive to peaceful thoughts.

09 기출응용 Remember that not only [curveballs are / are curveballs] the universe's way of keeping us awake—which is a gift in and of itself—but they are also its method of bringing us wonderful surprises.

10 기출응용 As you can see, he wrote back and not only did he apologize for the way I was treated, but also [he offered / did he offer] to let me trade in my car.

정답 및 해설 p.55

01 기출응용 다음 글의 밑줄 친 부분 중, 어법상 어긋난 것은?

New ideas or sudden realizations are ① almost always the product of the mind working unconsciously on a problem, using materials ② stored up through long study and conscious thought. The greater the storehouse of your knowledge and the wider its range, ③ the more creative you will be. The interactions of your diversified knowledge are so subtle and so sophisticated that their results cannot be predicted. New inventions are made through ④ creatively combining various types of knowledge. When Benjamin Franklin flew a kite into a storm to investigate the properties of electricity, he did not foresee the wonderful inventions that future students of his discoveries would produce—the washing machines, microwave ovens, or television sets. ⑤ Nor many of the inventors foresee them while they studied Franklin's work.

02 다음 (A), (B), (C)의 각 [ ] 안에서 어법에 맞는 표현으로 바르게 짝지어진 것은?

Activities such as treasure hunting and tomb raiding, grabbing gold from underground or underwater, or excavating graves that may be someone's sacred ancestors to become rich, are not what archaeologists do these days. (A) [Nor they / Nor do they] wear funny hats, carry whips or pistols, or fight off Nazis or international smugglers. The notion (B) [which / that] all archaeology is adventurous is groundless when you consider that there is much paperwork and boring laboratory processing involved with it. In fact, you do get the lure of the unknown; you never know what the excavation will uncover, (C) [if / even if] it's a cola bottle from the 1950s. Some archaeologists study how popular culture portrays the profession. Books and web sites point out the mistakes amid all the fun in the movies and even archaeology-related toys.

	(A)		(B)		(C)
①	Nor they	-	which	-	if
②	Nor they	-	that	-	even if
③	Nor do they	-	that	-	if
④	Nor do they	-	that	-	even if
⑤	Nor they	-	which	-	even if

UNIT 189

부정어가 포함된 부사구의 도치

Nature seems to hate sameness at least as much as vacuums because nowhere in the universe can you find identical entities.

자연은 적어도 공백만큼이나 동일함을 싫어하는 것 같은데, 왜냐하면 우주 어느 곳에서도 동일한 존재를 찾을 수 없기 때문이다.

자연은 / 동일함을 싫어하는 것 같다 / 적어도 공백만큼이나 //
Nature seems to hate sameness at least as much as vacuums

왜냐하면 / 당신은 우주 속 어느 곳에서도 찾을 수 없다 / 동일한 존재를
because [nowhere in the universe] [can you find] identical entities.

you can find (X)

앞에 부정어(nowhere)가 포함된 부사어구가 와서 주어와 동사가 도치되었다.

Words & Phrases

sameness [séimnis] 동일함

vacuum [vǽkjuəm] 공백; 진공

nowhere [nóuhwὲər] 어디에도 없다

identical [aidéntikəl] 동일한

entity [éntəti] 존재

pond [pɑnd] 연못

frontier [frʌntíər] 개척자

keenly [kíːnli] 강렬하게; 날카롭게, 예민하게

under no circumstances 어떠한 경우에도

Grammar Point

부정어가 포함된 부사구의 도치

not only, not until과 마찬가지로 부정어가 포함되어 있는 부사구가 문장 앞으로 나가게 되면 주어와 동사를 도치시켜 준다. 이때 도치 여부뿐 아니라 주어와 동사의 수 일치에도 신경을 써야 한다.

부정어인 not이 포함된 부사구 Not so far from Philips's lab이 문장 앞으로 나왔으므로 동사인 are가 주어인 a quiet ~ zone 앞으로 도치된다.

Not so far from Philips' lab [are] [a quiet public park and a small pond, located in a traffic-free zone].

차량 통행이 없는 곳에 위치한 조용한 공원과 작은 연못은 필립스의 연구소에서 멀지 않다.

Check-up

정답 및 해설 p.55

1. In no other heart [this frontier spirit was / was this frontier spirit] more keenly planted than in that of J.P Morgan as a youth.
2. Under no circumstances [the window must / must the window] be left open.

UNIT 190

간접의문문

The management still doesn't care what those workers think of the policy who have been fired as part of restructuring.

경영진은 구조 조정의 일환으로 해고 당한 그 직원들이 그 정책에 대해 어떻게 생각하는지 여전히 신경 쓰지 않는다.

경영진은 / 여전히 신경 쓰지 않는다 // 그 직원들이 어떻게 생각하는지 /
The management still doesn't care [what those workers think] of

what do those workers think (X)

의문사가 중간에 나오는 간접의문문이므로 〈의문사+주어+동사〉의 어순이 왔다.

those workers 수식

그 정책에 대해서 // 해고 당한 / 구조 조정의 일환으로써
the policy [who have been fired as part of restructuring].

Grammar Point

간접의문문의 어순

문장 중간에 의문문이 들어간 간접의문문은 〈의문사+주어+동사〉의 어순으로 일반적인 의문문처럼 〈동사+주어〉의 도치가 일어나지 않는다. 특히, 문장 자체가 의문문이더라도 의문사가 중간에 들어간다면, 그 문장도 역시 간접의문문으로 어순의 변화 없이 〈의문사+주어+동사〉로 쓴다.

Do you know [how Jack could finish / how could Jack finish] the project despite that turmoil?

어떻게 잭이 그런 소동에도 불구하고 프로젝트를 끝냈는지 아니?

⇒ 이 문장은 직접의문문이지만 중간에 의문사가 걸린 부분은 간접의문문이다. 따라서 〈의문사+주어+동사〉의 어순인 how Jack could finish가 정답이다.

Words & Phrases

management [mǽnidʒmənt] 경영진, 경영

policy [pɑ́lisi] 정책

fire [fáiər] 해고하다

restructuring [riːstrʌ́ktʃəriŋ] 구조 조정

turmoil [tə́ːrmɔil] 소동, 소란

further [fə́ːrðər] 더

unique [juːníːk] 독특한

Check-up

정답 및 해설 p.55

1. I wonder [what I can / what can I] do to take certain ideas even further with my own unique voice.
2. The sound of the woodwind can be made louder or softer depending on how much [wind is used / is wind used].

EXERCISE

정답 및 해설 p.56

[01-10] 다음 중 어법상 가장 적절한 표현을 고르시오.

01 I saw that I had lost not just my husband but my place — my way of life and [who I was / who was I].

02 기출응용 In one test, researchers asked the participants to predict how much [they could / could they] control over a certain task that was given for the test.

03 When Jim asked her [what she was / what was she] doing, she looked blue and then wrote down something.

04 Since he came here, not a single word [he has / has he] said.

05 기출응용 In their work, they are asking critical questions about [how the body is / how is the body] trained, disciplined, and manipulated in sports.

06 기출응용 In no way [Sports Fitness Advisor will / will Sports Fitness Advisor] be responsible for any injuries or problems that may occur due to use of this website or the advice contained within.

07 Under no circumstances [I would / would I] do such a mean thing that might sacrifice others' welfare.

08 In no place in the book [it says / does it say] that the ancient Japanese kingdom occupied Korean territory.

09 We hope this detective can see [who stole the golden ball / who the golden ball stole].

10 Before Noel visited her family, he wanted to know [what kinds of boys her brothers were / what kinds of boys were her brothers].

ACTUAL TEST

정답 및 해설 p.56

01 다음 글의 밑줄 친 부분 중, 어법상 어긋난 것은?

In a modern building on Bloomsbury Street is the Alexander Centre ① where *the Alexander Technique*, a way of working with the self-prevention of unhelpful or harmful habits, ② has been taught for more than twenty years. The goal of this exercise is to change ③ how we use the body in everyday activities. For sufferers of joint or muscular pain, it can improve posture and ease of movement. Recent research has found that with just 6 lessons it gives enduring benefits for those who suffer from chronic back pain. In a lesson, the teacher watches your posture and movement while ④ placed her hands on your body to get enough information about your body condition. It also teaches you to become more aware of your body, not just as a whole but the individual body parts and thus ⑤ to avoid bad physical habits.

02 

다음 (A), (B), (C)의 각 [ ] 안에서 어법에 맞는 표현으로 바르게 짝지어진 것은?

In America, there are many immigrants that came from different countries to succeed in the States. Because they suffer in lots of areas such as getting a job or (A) [try / trying] to speak English, they want their children to speak English, not only at school, but also at home to be more successful. Consequently, some of the second generation are lost in (B) [who they are / who are they] among different ethnic groups. Even more, they are ignoring their parents whose English is not fluent, which (C) [cause / causes] a communication breakdown within the family. Immigrant parents should teach them their ethnic language, so as not to be ignored by their children. Communicating with the shared language can also help their children understand their heritage.

	(A)		(B)		(C)
①	try	-	who are they	-	cause
②	try	-	who are they	-	causes
③	trying	-	who they are	-	causes
④	trying	-	who are they	-	causes
⑤	trying	-	who they are	-	cause

UNIT
191 so 도치 구문 (1)

The philosopher said that we all should be cheerful givers. My father felt more cheerful when he gave a quarter to one beggar. So did I.

철학자는 우리 모두는 기꺼이 주는 사람이 되어야 한다고 말했다. 우리 아버지는 거지에게 25센트를 주었을 때 기분이 더 좋아졌다. 나도 그랬다.

철학자가 말했다 // 우리 모두는 / 기꺼이 주는 사람이 되어야 한다 //
The philosopher said that we all should be cheerful givers.

나의 아버지께서는 / 기분이 더 좋아졌다 // 그가 25센트를 한 거지에게 주었을 때 //
My father felt more cheerful when he gave a quarter to one beggar.

나도 그랬다
So did I.

So I did. (X) So was I. (X)
so가 앞으로 나왔으므로 동사와 주어가 도치되고,
앞의 felt를 받으므로 did가 왔다.

Grammar Point

so 도치 구문

앞의 문장을 so 구문으로 받을 경우, so가 문장 앞으로 나가게 되는데, 이때 주어와 동사가 도치된다. 또한 동사는 앞 문장의 동사의 종류를 따른다.

"I'm very hungry. I will go to McDonald's."
"나 매우 배가 고파. 맥도날드에 갈 거야."

"So will I."
앞 문장의 동사의 종류를 따르므로 will이 왔고,
주어와 동사가 도치되었다.
"나도 갈 거야."

Words & Phrases

philosopher [filάsəfər] 철학자

cheerful [tʃíərfəl] 기꺼이 하는, 마음에서 우러나온; 기분이 좋은

quarter [kwɔ́:rtər] 25센트; 4분의 1

beggar [bégər] 거지

thesis [θí:sis] 논문

Check-up 정답 및 해설 p.56

1. "I didn't research enough data about my thesis. I need more time for that."
"[So do I / So I do]. I hope the professor will give me more time."
2. John was asked to fill out this form for the research on the street.
[So was I / So did I].

UNIT
192 so 도치 구문 (2)

It wasn't just the trees that were devastated—so were the lives of many Brazilians who depended on the rain forest.

황폐해지는 것은 단지 나무들만이 아니었다. 열대 우림에 의존하는 많은 브라질 사람들의 삶도 그러했다.

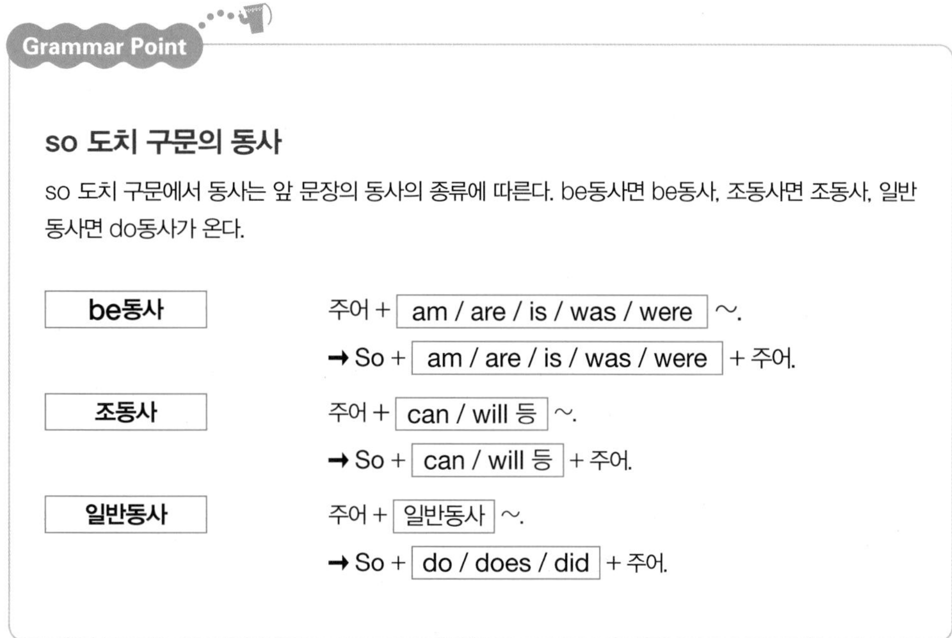
Grammar Point

so 도치 구문의 동사

so 도치 구문에서 동사는 앞 문장의 동사의 종류에 따른다. be동사면 be동사, 조동사면 조동사, 일반동사면 do동사가 온다.

be동사	주어 + am / are / is / was / were ~.
	→ So + am / are / is / was / were + 주어.
조동사	주어 + can / will 등 ~.
	→ So + can / will 등 + 주어.
일반동사	주어 + 일반동사 ~.
	→ So + do / does / did + 주어.

Words & Phrases

devastate [dévəstèit] 파괴하다

depend on ~에 의존하다

rain forest 열대 우림

pollute [pəljú:t] 오염시키다

Check-up

정답 및 해설 p.56

1. An increasing number of birds and fish are dying due to polluted water. So do / are our forests.
2. Robinson claimed that Tom had made a lot of mistakes. So did / had others.

EXERCISE

정답 및 해설 p.57

[01-10] 다음 중 어법상 가장 적절한 표현을 고르시오.

01 He was used to his bad condition, and so [did / were] my friends.

02 기출응용 Music is routinely recognized as beautiful. So [do / are] sounds, like the whispering of wind through pines or the gentle purring of a cat.

03 기출응용 So imprudent [we are / are we] that we wander in times which are not ours and do not think of the one that belongs to us.

04 기출응용 It completely depends on other products. [So do / So are] tape recorders, refrigerators, and thousands of other products that work only when combined with others.

05 The winner of this year's contest is Susan, whose daughter is so cute and smart and so [is / does] her son.

06 New Zealand relies heavily on income from tourism and the education industry, and so [Australia does / does Australia].

07 Seoul signed a contract with SKS Corp. to build a china museum in Youngsan, and so [was / did] Bucheon city.

08 His movies which were released last weekend used many spectacular special effects, and so [did / could] several of his other films.

09 When they entered the ring, Foreman would raise his hands with the fans and so [did / would] Tyson.

10 Jackson is too far from the mainstream in some respects, and so [does / is] his best friend, Charlie.

ACTUAL TEST

정답 및 해설 p.57

01 다음 글의 밑줄 친 부분 중, 어법상 어긋난 것은?

Greenhouse effect ① is usually considered the principal reason for global warming. However, it is a natural and essential process of our atmosphere, ② without which our planet would be uninhabitable. Most greenhouse gases allow radiation from the sun to pass through them while simultaneously ③ absorbing some radiation reflected by atmosphere layer, which controls the temperature on the surface of the earth. The problem is that human beings have made the situation worse. In the last decade, global icebergs have decreased, and so ④ permanent snow has. Due to industrial development, humankind has released more greenhouse gases than the earth can handle. That is ⑤ why greenhouse gases gained such notoriety.

02 기출응용

다음 (A), (B), (C)의 각 [ ] 안에서 어법에 맞는 표현으로 바르게 짝지어진 것은?

If you compare a walnut with some of the beautiful and exciting things (A) [that / what] grow on our planet, it does not seem to be a marvelous creation. It is common, rough, not particularly attractive, and certainly not of much value. Besides, it is small. Its growth is limited by the hard shell that surrounds it—the shell from which it never escapes during its lifetime. Of course, that is the wrong way to judge a walnut. Break one open and look inside. See (B) [how / however] the walnut has grown to fill every corner available to it. It had no say in the size or shape of that shell. However, given those limitations, it achieved its full growth. How lucky we will be if, like the walnut, we blossom and bloom in every aspect of the life that is given us. Take heart! If one nut can do it, so (C) [can / do] you.

(A)		(B)		(C)
① that	-	how	-	can
② what	-	how	-	do
③ what	-	however	-	can
④ that	-	however	-	do
⑤ that	-	however	-	can

UNIT 193

so 도치 vs. neither 도치

Glavine Brown didn't get enough votes to be reelected mayor, so his policies wouldn't be continued. Neither would the plan for the grand park.

글래빈 브라운은 시장으로 재선되는 데 충분한 득표를 얻지 못해서 그의 정책은 지속되지 않을 것이다. 또한 대공원을 위한 계획도 그렇지 못할 것이다.

글래빈 브라운은 / 충분한 득표를 얻지 못했다 / 시장으로 재선될 만큼 //
Glavine Brown didn't get enough votes to be reelected mayor,

그래서 그의 정책은 / 지속되지 않을 것이다 //
so his policies **wouldn't** be continued.

앞이 부정문이므로 so가 아닌 neither가 왔고,
Neither 뒤의 주어와 동사는 도치됐다.

또한 대공원을 위한 계획도 그렇지 못할 것이다
Neither would the plan for the grand park.
so (X)

Grammar Point

so 도치 구문 vs. neither 도치 구문

앞 문장이 긍정문이면 so 도치 구문으로 받고, 부정문이면 neither 도치 구문으로 받는다.

앞 문장이 부정문이므로 so가 아닌 neither가 온다.

Jacob **isn't** staying home, and **neither** **is** Martha.

동사가 isn't이므로 is로 받는다.

제이콥은 집에 없고, 마사도 그래.

Words & Phrases

reelect [rìːilékt] 재선하다

policy [pálisi] 정책

manufacture [mæ̀njəfǽktʃər] 생산하다

television station TV방송국

attractive [ətrǽktiv] 매력적인

purchase [pə́ːrtʃəs] 구매하다

Check-up

정답 및 해설 p.57

1. Suddenly, Jack could not name the company which manufactures his favorite fast food. [So / Neither] could I.
2. Most television stations structure their pricing to make it more attractive to purchase advertising. [So / Neither] do the other media.

UNIT 194

only가 포함된 어구의 도치

Only in 1967 did they find that air pollution in Europe caused acid rain to fall in Scandinavia.

1967년에서야 그들은 유럽의 대기 오염으로 인해 스칸디나비아에 산성비가 내렸다는 사실을 알아냈다.

바로 1967년에 / 그들은 발견했다 // 유럽의 대기 오염이 /

Only in 1967 did they find that air pollution in Europe

they found (X)

야기했다 / 산성비가 내리도록 / 스칸디나비아에

caused acid rain to fall in Scandinavia.

Grammar Point

〈only + 부사구〉 〈only + 절〉 – 도치

only가 들어간 부사구나 절이 문장의 맨 앞에 오면, 주어와 동사가 도치된다. 일반동사의 경우 do 동사가 일반동사 대신 앞으로 나온다. 도치되기 전 문장의 시제나 주어에 맞춰 do, does, did를 써 준다. 도치 후 주어 뒤에 오는 일반동사는 동사원형으로 써야 한다.

〈only + 부사구〉가 문장의 앞에 나와서 주어와 동사가 도치되었다. 이때 도치 전 문장의 동사가 일반동사의 과거이므로 did가 앞으로 나오고 주어 뒤의 동사는 accept가 된다.

Only then did he accept the fact that he should take his rival by the hand to stand together against the common enemy.

그때서야 그는 공동의 적에 대항하기 위해서 경쟁자와 손을 잡아야만 한다는 사실을 받아들이게 되었다.

Only when he found love for his family could he work hard.

그가 가족에 대한 사랑을 깨달았을 때 비로서 그는 열심히 일할 수 있었다.

⇒ only 안쪽에 절이 올 수도 있는데 only 안에 있는 절이 아니라 주절에서 도치가 일어나야 한다.

Words & Phrases

pollution [pəljú:ʃən] 오염

cause [kɔ:z] ~의 원인이 되다

acid [ǽsid] 산성의

take somebody by the hand ~와 손을 잡다

Check-up

정답 및 해설 p.57

1. Only before and after the match [you can / can you] interview the players on the field.

2. Only in Korea [young students give / do young students give] their seat to the old.

EXERCISE

정답 및 해설 p.58

[01-10] **다음 중 어법상 가장 적절한 표현을 고르시오.**

01 Neither [she could / could she] state that she danced better herself because that would obviously be untrue.

02 Only then [our ally joined / did our ally join], and we worked together to defeat our common enemy.

03 Only after his death [they were / were they] able to appreciate what he had done for their country.

04 기출응용 Only when he is willing to put forth an effort [a life of value is / is a life of value] possible.

05 Human beings change with the passing of time, and [so / neither] does nature including animals and plants.

06 Because the computer didn't work, I couldn't do anything, and [so / neither] could my colleagues.

07 Only on Saturday and Sunday [do / does] Catherine get a chance to go to the movies with her friends.

08 Only when the patient is stable [we can / can we] start operating on her.

09 The Liverpool team can't fight each other with just eight players, and [so / neither] can the Chelsea team.

10 You can advise him against it, but the choice will be John's, and [so / neither] will the consequences.

ACTUAL TEST

정답 및 해설 p.58

01 기출응용

다음 글의 밑줄 친 부분 중, 어법상 어긋난 것은?

If someone were to say "Life is a cup of coffee," it is unlikely that you would have heard this expression before. But its novelty forces you ① to think about its meaning. The vehicle used, a cup of coffee, is a common object of everyday life and therefore easily perceivable as a source for thinking about that life. The metaphor compels you to start ② thinking of life in terms of the kinds of physical, social, and other attributes that are ③ associated with a cup of coffee. For this metaphor to gain currency, however, it must capture the fancy of many other people for a period of time. Only then ④ its novelty will have become worn out and the basis for a new conceptual metaphor: *life is a drinking substance*. After that, expressions such as "life is a cup of tea, life is a bottle of beer, life is a glass of milk," ⑤ become similarly understandable as offering different perspectives on life.

02 기출응용

다음 (A), (B), (C)의 각 [ ] 안에서 어법에 맞는 표현으로 바르게 짝지어진 것은?

"Hey," Jonathan said, his voice causing two small birds to take flight. The woman did not acknowledge him at all but continued to sketch. (A) [Frowning / Frowned], he said a little louder, "Hey, lady." Again she did not acknowledge him, and Jonathan began to wonder whether she might be deaf. Purposefully, he walked up to the woman with every intention of telling her to leave his backyard. She did not even look up at him until he was standing within a couple of feet of her. Only then (B) [she looked / did she look] up. For a moment, Jonathan was struck by the most amazing green eyes he had ever seen. He opened his mouth, but instead of the sharp order he had intended to bark, he asked quietly, "Who are you?" The woman smiled and he felt (C) [as if / even if] she lit up the world around her.

	(A)		(B)		(C)
①	Frowning	-	she looked	-	as if
②	Frowned	-	she looked	-	even if
③	Frowned	-	did she look	-	even if
④	Frowned	-	did she look	-	as if
⑤	Frowning	-	did she look	-	as if

정답 및 해설 p.58

[01-05] 다음 문장 중 어법상 틀린 부분을 고쳐 쓰시오.

01 You and Catherine may have a future together, but you should not presume it, nor you should put your social life on hold waiting for her.

02 The researchers discovered that not only both sets of pigs were exposed to the same behavioral symptoms but the behaviors seemed to be associated with antibody deposits in brain areas.

03 Not only we were surprised at the fragments of huge sculptures, but we also found that the mound is man-made.

04 When trying to understand why do many people have difficulty living within their means, we tend to blame factors such as high interest rates.

05 Even at an extremely young age and before the development of language, among objects children can spontaneously discriminate.

[06-10] 다음 주어진 단어를 사용하여 문장을 완성하시오. (단, 필요하면 형태를 바꾸시오.)

06 Not only ____________________ high, but also many of them discovered they really liked math. (their math grades, were)

07 Although the cognitive benefits of manipulating toys and dolls are well known, only for the past decade ____________________ uncovering a link between more vigorous physical activity and intellect in children. (scientist, have begun)

08 Not until the last second ____________________ who the goalkeeper was—his teacher! (Jameson, noticed)

09 Little ____________________ that this meeting was going to lead to marriage with Jane, my fellow student. (I, dreamed)

10 Not until we have developed this medicine ____________________ free from terrible pain. (patients, can, be)

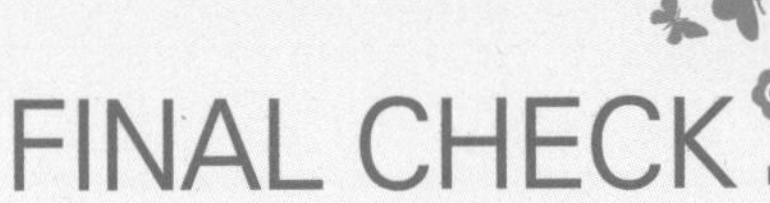

FINAL CHECK

정답 및 해설 p.59

01 다음 글의 밑줄 친 부분 중, 어법상 어긋난 것은?

Located in one of the enclosed shopping arcades ① is a new and exciting cafe that features street foods of East Asia. The second-floor cafe is situated in ② what is now the P.E. District and the fun begins with the colorful sign at street level. The bright yellow and white, neon-outlined letters stand out from the red, pink and yellow backlit panels. A curry-colored wall ③ leading to the elevator is highlighted with Asian masks which will reappear in a mural upstairs. Inside, the cafe is bright and energetic—a playful melange of vibrant colors and textures. The first impression the visitor has ④ been of the high industrial ceiling filled with a giant light of luminous forms. The bar area is highlighted by the many suspended and unusual light forms that make the surroundings ⑤ more modern.

02 

다음 (A), (B), (C)의 각 [ ] 안에서 어법에 맞는 표현으로 바르게 짝지어진 것은?

Newton was the first to point out that light is colorless, and that consequently color has to (A) [occur / be occurred] inside our brains. He wrote, "The light waves themselves are not colored." Since his time, we have learned that light waves are characterized by different frequencies of vibration. When they (B) [enter / enter into] the eye of an observer, they set off a chain of neurochemical events, the end product of which is an internal mental image that we call color. The essential point here is: What we perceive as color is not made up of color. Red as (C) [an apple may / may an apple] appear, its atoms are not themselves red.

	(A)		(B)		(C)
①	occur	-	enter	-	an apple may
②	occur	-	enter	-	may an apple
③	occur	-	enter into	-	may an apple
④	occurred	-	enter	-	may an apple
⑤	occurred	-	enter into	-	an apple may

03 다음 글의 밑줄 친 부분 중, 어법상 어긋난 것은?

The character of people's personal work environments ① makes a big difference in their performance in profound and surprising ways. The arrangement of desks, the level of natural light, and the noise in your office are major predictors of your comfort, your contentment, and especially your productivity. Employees perform best when they are encouraged to decorate their surroundings as they see fit, with small plants or photographs of their children—② whatever makes them feel most comfortable. Not only ③ office design determines whether people's necks are painful or not, but it affects how much they achieve and their job satisfaction. Rarely ④ do employers consider these psychological sides, but they should. That is ⑤ because paying more attention to workspace design can build up employees' well-being and productivity at minimal cost.

04 다음 (A), (B), (C)의 각 [ ] 안에서 어법에 맞는 표현으로 바르게 짝지어진 것은?

(A) [What / Whatever] we are shopping for, it is not primarily a brand we are choosing, but a culture, or rather the people associated with that culture. Whether what you wear torn jeans or like to recite poetry, by doing so you make a statement of (B) [belonging / being belonged] to a group of people. Who we believe we are is a result of the choices we make about who we want to be like, and we subsequently demonstrate this desired likeness to others in various and often subtle ways. Artificial as this process is, this is what becomes our 'identity,' an identity grounded on all the superficial differences we distinguish between ourselves and others. This, after all, is what we are shopping for: self-identity, knowledge of (C) [who are we / who we are].

	(A)		(B)		(C)
①	What	-	belonging	-	who are we
②	Whatever	-	belonging	-	who we are
③	What	-	being belonged	-	who are we
④	Whatever	-	belonging	-	who are we
⑤	Whatever	-	being belonged	-	who we are

Chapter XVI

05 기출응용

다음 글의 밑줄 친 부분 중, 어법상 어긋난 것은?

It is through the use of sound ① which composers describe their private world. Making such a description concrete and detailed ② requires not just inspiration but certain practical tools and skills. ③ Whatever style of music you write, you need to understand dynamics and speed, the uses of harmony and rhythm. You also need to know the range and capabilities of instruments, the possibilities of the human voice, and the problems of acoustics. You need to be able to devise a blueprint that communicates to your musicians what it is you want to hear. A young composer ④ taking a shortcut in this technical training in his rush to play the role of a composer will dry up very fast. If you ⑤ learn the proper techniques someday, then the passion, if it is genuine, will come through.

06

다음 (A), (B), (C)의 각 [ ] 안에서 어법에 맞는 표현으로 바르게 짝지어진 것은?

Neanderthals are our closest known relatives on the evolutionary tree. They lived in Europe and Asia approximately 130,000 years ago. But about 30,000 years ago, they disappeared. What happened to them? Scientists recently recovered DNA from Neanderthal fossils and compared it with (A) [modern humans / that of modern humans]. They found that certain gene adaptations unique to us might (B) [give / have given] an evolutionary advantage in cognitive functions such as communication, social skills, and perceptual sensitivity. Ironically, mutations or overexpression of these same genes are sometimes associated with autism and down syndrome. But never (C) [Neanderthals disappeared / did Neanderthals disappear] completely. The genetic evidence shows that humans mixed with Neanderthals sometime after they emigrated from Africa. As much as 4% of your DNA may come from a distant Neanderthal ancestor.

	(A)		(B)		(C)
①	modern humans	-	give	-	Neanderthals disappeared
②	modern humans	-	have given	-	did Neanderthals disappear
③	that of modern humans	-	give	-	Neanderthals disappeared
④	that of modern humans	-	have given	-	did Neanderthals disappear
⑤	that of modern humans	-	have given	-	Neanderthals disappeared

Parallel structures

병렬 구조

UNIT **195**

병렬 구조

This behavior will lead only to anger, irritation and therefore, further unhappiness.

이러한 행동은 오직 분노와 짜증을 유발해서 그래서 더 큰 불행을 유발할 것이다.

이러한 행동은 / 오직 분노와 짜증을 유발할 것이다 / 그래서 /
This behavior will lead only to [anger], [irritation], and therefore,

명사, 명사, and 명사로 병렬 구조가 된다.

더 큰 불행을
further [unhappiness].

unhappy (X)

Words & Phrases

behavior [bihéivjər] 행동

irritation [ìritéiʃən] 짜증, 화

therefore [ðέərfɔ̀:r] 그래서

analyze [ǽnəlàiz] 분석하다

abandon [əbǽndən] 버리다

culprit [kʌlprit] 범인

archaeological [ὰ:rkiəlάdʒikəl] 고고학의

astronomical [æ̀strənάmikəl] 천문학의

Grammar Point

병렬 구조

〈A, B, and C〉와 〈A, B, or C〉의 병렬 구조에서, A, B, C의 품사가 같아야 한다. 이때 형태만으로는 병렬 구조를 이루는 대상을 찾기 어려운 경우가 많이 있으므로 해석으로 병렬 구조를 이루는 대상을 잘 찾아야 한다.

We should [analyze] the samples from the body abandoned in the field and [help] to search for the culprit.

helped (X)

우리는 들판에 버려진 시체로부터 샘플을 분석해야 하고, 범인을 찾도록 도와주어야 한다.

⇒ 병렬 구조를 이루는 것은 abandoned가 아니라 analyze이므로 (should) help가 되어야 한다.

Check-up

정답 및 해설 p.60

1. Other popular working vacations include going on digs at archaeological sites or [participate / participating] in community development.
2. The ancient Aztecs of Central America possessed great architectural, astronomical, and [mathematics / mathematical] knowledge.

UNIT 196

비교급의 병렬 구조

The physical structure of a chimpanzee's brain and central nervous system is surprisingly like that of humans.

침팬지의 두뇌와 중앙 신경계의 물리적 구조는 놀라울 정도로 인간의 것과 같다.

물리적 구조 / 침팬지의 두뇌와
The physical structure of a chimpanzee's brain and

비교 대상이 chimpanzee가 아니라 The physical structure이므로 humans가 아닌 that of humans가 왔다.

중앙 신경계의 / 놀라울 정도로 같다 / 인간의 그것과
central nervous system is surprisingly like that of humans.

Grammar Point

비교급의 병렬 구조

비교급에서 비교 대상은 그 성격과 문법적 특성이 동일해야 한다. 위 문장에서 비교 대상은 '침팬지의 물리적 구조' 와 '인간의 물리적 구조'이지 '인간' 그 자체가 아니다. 따라서 that of humans 대신 humans을 쓰면 틀리게 된다. 우리말로는 humans라고 해도 이상하지 않기 때문에 주의해야 한다.

Prices of these products this year are higher those last year. (O)
Prices of these products this year are higher than last year. (X)
이 상품들의 올해의 가격은 작년보다 비싸다.

⇒ 비교 대상은 올해의 가격과 작년의 가격이다.

The climate of Korea is very similar to that of Japan. (O)
The climate of Korea is very similar to Japan. (X)
한국의 날씨는 일본의 날씨와 비슷하다.

⇒ 비교 대상은 한국의 날씨와 일본의 날씨이다.

Words & Phrases

physical [fízikəl] 물리적인, 신체적인
central [séntrəl] 중심의
nervous [nə́:rvəs] 신경계의
surprisingly [sərpráiziŋli] 놀라울 정도로
elementary [èləméntəri] 초등의
exceed [iksí:d] 넘다, 초월하다

Check-up 정답 및 해설 p.60

1. The proportion of males who tend to select a job with considering 'past experience' is lower than that / those of females.
2. Even at the elementary school level, especially in cities like Seoul, the number of girl students greatly exceeds boy students / that of boy students.

EXERCISE

정답 및 해설 p.60

[01-10] 다음 중 어법상 가장 적절한 표현을 고르시오.

01 Mercury's velocity is much greater than [the Earth / the Earth's].

02 Most of these early ones could not support heavy weights or [endure / endured] strong current.

03 Should the wishes of the victim's family be more important than [the victim / those of the victim]?

04 기출응용 They are putting the information into memory when they circle, underline, or [mark / marking] it in some way.

05 It offers you the choice of taking a break on deck, watching a movie, having a drink, watching wonderful scenery, and [reaches / reaching] the next destination.

06 기출응용 In Argentina, the ratio of the transgenic seed cost to the cost of the conventional one was higher than [the other countries / that of the other countries].

07 기출응용 Some users take advantage of this privilege by sending spam mail, using e-mail to abuse people, and [hack / hacking] into government and corporate systems.

08 기출응용 Farmers often protected the stored seeds from insects or animals by sealing them in clay pots or [buried / burying] them in baskets covered with ash.

09 This trend was found to be the same across all food types, with adults enjoying vegetables if they had been fed a lot of greens as a child, or [enjoyed / enjoying] mostly meat if meat had been their main childhood consumption.

10 A woman who had done a lot of physical labor at home might actually enjoy going to work and [to sit / sitting] down for a while, allowing her brain to work and her back to relax.

ACTUAL TEST

정답 및 해설 p.61

01 기출응용

다음 글의 밑줄 친 부분 중, 어법상 어긋난 것은?

"A long, long, long time ago..."—so begins every Korean fairy tale. The repetition not only contributes to ① create a stable, calm tone for the narrative but also reflects the "triple repetition" rule for Korean tales. The final repetition of "long" can sometimes ② be substituted with something like "back when tigers smoked pipes," but it should never be omitted altogether. The rule of threes ③ does not apply only to the beginning sentence but also ④ to the different elements throughout the story. For instance, in *Kongjui and Patjui*, the Korean version of the Cinderella story, Kongjui's stepmother orders her to complete three impossible chores. And in the tale of *Sister Sun and Brother Moon*, three helpers each take turns rescuing the poor brother and sister from the tiger's tormenting. Less than three ⑤ is always too few; more than three is like too much frosting on a cake.

02

다음 (A), (B), (C)의 각 [ ] 안에서 어법에 맞는 표현으로 바르게 짝지어진 것은?

Planting bulbs is simple. But before you start, make sure that you choose a suitable pot. If you choose to use a shallow pot, then it makes your work much easier. The two most important things that you should know about planting a bulb (A) [is / are] to set the bulb at the correct depth, and make sure you place the bulb right side up in the hole. Here are several tips for planting them in your garden. Begin with a few reliable, (B) [wide / widely] available varieties, such as tulips, hyacinths, and daffodils. You can plant bulbs in the fall just before the ground freezes. Place each bulb in a hole three times as deep as the bulb is tall and (C) [give / gives] them a good watering to help the roots to grow.

	(A)		(B)		(C)
①	is	-	wide	-	give
②	are	-	widely	-	gives
③	is	-	widely	-	gives
④	are	-	wide	-	gives
⑤	are	-	widely	-	give

UNIT 197

동사의 병렬 구조

Have you ever observed water on the road where there is nothing and mistaken it for real water?

당신은 실제로는 아무것도 없는데 길 위에서 물을 보고 그것을 진짜 물로 착각한 적이 있나요?

당신은 본 적이 있나요 / 길 위에 물을 / 아무것도 없다 /

Have you ever observed water on the road where there is nothing

앞의 동사가 have observed의 완료형이므로 뒤에 and로 연결된 동사도 have가 생략된 mistaken이 되어야 한다.

그리고 그것을 진짜 물로 착각한 적이 있나요

and mistaken it for real water?

mistook, mistake (X)

Grammar Point

동사의 병렬 구조

동사가 병렬 구조로 연결되어 있을 때, 시제와 수 일치, 능동태와 수동태 여부를 살펴봐야 한다.
〈A and B〉는 병렬 구조이므로 A와 B의 문법적 형태는 동일해야 한다.

Market managers take charge of assessing the market's various needs and making strategies that will satisfy those needs.

시장 관리자들은 시장의 다양한 요구를 평가하고 그러한 요구를 충족시킬 전략을 만드는 데 책임이 있다.

⇒ 전치사 of 다음에 동명사 assessing이 나왔으므로 and로 연결된 동사도 동명사 making이 되어야 한다.

Words & Phrases

observe [əbzə́ːrv] 보다, 관찰하다

mistake [mistéik] 착각하다

take charge of ~의 책임이 있다

assess [əsés] 평가하다

needs [niːdz] 요구

inadequate [inǽdəkwit] 부족한, 불충분한

Check-up

정답 및 해설 p.61

1. This has the entirely unintended result of making the food supply inadequate and lowers / lowering the standard of life in some parts of the world.
2. You need to inspire yourself because there is nobody to force you to complete your project, make your schedule, or get / to get up on time.

UNIT 198

from A to B의 병렬 구조

They claim that all kids go from having primarily just psychological and physical characters to having a biological one right around age six.

그들은 모든 아이들이 겨우 처음으로 정신적, 육체적 특성을 가지기 시작해서 바로 6세 경에 생물학적 특징을 가지는 것으로 진행된다고 주장한다.

그들은 주장한다 // 모든 아이들은 진행된다 / 겨우 처음에 가지는 것에서부터 /
They claim that all kids go **from having** primarily just

from A to B 구문이므로 to는 전치사이다.
따라서 동명사 having이 온다.

정신적, 육체적 특징을 / 생물학적 특징을 가지는 것으로 /
psychological and physical characters **to having** a biological one

to have (X)

바로 6세 경에
right around age six.

Grammar Point

from A to B의 병렬 구조

〈from A to B〉의 병렬 구조에서 A와 B의 문법적 형태는 동일해야 한다. 특히 A와 B 사이의 거리가 멀 경우, 다른 것과 혼동해서 병렬 구조의 원칙을 깨지 않도록 조심한다. 특히 to를 to부정사로 혼동하는 경우가 많은데 여기서 to는 전치사이다. 따라서 to 뒤에 동사가 올 경우 동명사가 와야 한다.

An electronic nose can be used for a variety of detections, from sniffing for drugs to [detect / detecting] explosives at various places.

전자 코는 마약 냄새를 맡는 것에서부터 다양한 장소의 폭발물 탐지에 이르는 여러 가지 탐지에 사용될 수 있다.

⇒ 〈from A to B〉 구조로, sniffing과 병렬 구조이므로 detecting이 온다.

Words & Phrases

primarily [práimerəli] 최초로; 우선적으로

biological [bàiəládʒikəl] 생물학적인

electronic [ilektránik] 전기적인, 전자의

sniff [snif] 킁킁거리며 냄새를 맡다

detect [ditékt] 발견하다, 탐지하다

explosive [iksplóusiv] 폭발물; 폭발성의

Check-up 정답 및 해설 p.61

1. Several African governments are considering policies related to preserving the environment; from prohibiting poaching in the forest to [dispatch / dispatching] police officers there.

2. I'm emotionally exhausted from taking care of to [be / being] supportive of my mother.

EXERCISE

정답 및 해설 p.61

[01-10] **다음 중 어법상 가장 적절한 표현을 고르시오.**

01 The students in Mr. Constantine's class were having fun and [learned / learning] at the same time.

02 기출응용 At the Metro, you have to open the doors yourself by pushing a button, depressing a lever or [slide / sliding] them.

03 기출응용 As a reviewer, you analyze the book for how it tells a story and [evaluate / evaluates] the quality of writing and organization.

04 기출응용 You'll spend little time testing assumptions, challenging the rules, asking what-if question, or just [play / playing] around with the problem.

05 기출응용 Because some societies actually did go from foraging to [farm / farming], you may be inclined to think that every society should.

06 Brains and computers both have the capacity to check their environment and [respond / responding] with various reactions to handle their surroundings.

07 You should develop it by making more and more specific, narrowing down your subject, and [say / saying] exactly what you mean.

08 기출응용 The DNA extracted from these bits of whale skin not only identifies the individuals in the group, but also [reveal / reveals] their relationships to each other.

09 As soon as they start reading, they underline key points, take notes in the margins, and [highlight / highlights] key words or phrases with their own personal code of symbols.

10 We were happily looking forward to seeing our friends, gossiping about some of them, listening to music on the car radio and [hummed / humming] old-style tunes.

정답 및 해설 p.62

01 기출응용

다음 글의 밑줄 친 부분 중, 어법상 어긋난 것은?

Because our busy schedules are hard to work around, many families have trouble ① finding time to eat dinner together. But we need to be aware of the importance of family meals. Scientists ② have found interesting benefits to such meals. According to them, if they eat with family members an average of five to seven times weekly, the family comes to have several benefits from reducing eating disorders ③ to develop children's language. One more thing to say is ④ that vegetables are certainly important for their health, and children eat more of them ⑤ when dining with their families. Like most people, you probably have a busy schedule. Nevertheless, family dinners are clearly well worth the time.

02

다음 (A), (B), (C)의 각 [ ] 안에서 어법에 맞는 표현으로 바르게 짝지어진 것은?

Scientists started watching men and women be funny, in addition to (A) [research / researching] what people considered funny. According to the research, interesting patterns appeared. The literature prior to the 1990s focused on joke appreciation. This was an artificial situation where researchers presented subjects with jokes and then documented their reactions. Experiments began looking at producing humor, asking subjects to come up with jokes or (B) [study / studying] how people make one another laugh in the real world. This showed them a much more accurate explanation about what was happening. They found that women sought a mate who could amuse them twice as often as they return the favor, whereas men offered humor about a third more than they required it. These results indicate (C) [that / what] both men and women approach humor from different angles.

(A)		(B)		(C)
① research	-	study	-	that
② researching	-	study	-	what
③ research	-	studying	-	what
④ researching	-	studying	-	what
⑤ researching	-	studying	-	that

이중 부정 금지

These tough tasks have caused some students to feel alienated and not to do anything.

이 힘든 과업이 일부 학생들에게 소외감을 느끼게 하고 어떠한 것도 하지 못하게 만들었다.

이러한 힘든 과업이 / 일부 학생들이 ~하게 했다 /
These tough tasks have caused some students

소외감을 느끼도록 / 그리고 어떠한 것도 하지 못하도록
to feel alienated and not to do anything.

nothing (X)

앞에 부정어구 not이 존재하므로 anything 대신 부정어 nothing을 사용할 수 없다.

Grammar Point

이중 부정 금지

영어에서는 한 문장 내에서 부정을 나타내는 어구를 동시에 사용하지 않는다. 두 개의 부정어가 함께 쓰이면 강한 긍정을 나타낸다.

Without any knowledge of the law related to construction, Mrs. Yan [can / cannot] hardly give the correct and accurate answers.

건축과 관련된 법에 대한 이해 없이, 얀 여사는 올바르고 정확한 대답을 할 수 없다.

⇒ 뒤에 부정어 hardly가 있으므로 의미상 부정인 cannot은 올 수 없다. 따라서 can이 정답이다.

Words & Phrases

cause A to B
A가 B하도록 유발하다

alienated
[élijənéitid]
소외된

hardly
[há:rdli]
거의 ~하지 않다

investigator
[invéstəgèitər]
조사관

untamed
[ʌntéimd]
야생의

Check-up

정답 및 해설 p.62

1. The investigators don't think the storm had anything / nothing to do with the camera's movement.

2. Methods of training untamed horses have / haven't hardly changed at all in the last 10 centuries.

전치사구 vs. to부정사구

By using this oil paint, art designers were able to express the light glowing on furniture or on people's skins. 기출응용

예술가들은 이 유성 물감을 사용함으로써 가구나 사람들의 피부에 반짝이는 빛을 표현할 수 있었다.

이 유성 물감을 사용함으로써 / 예술가들은 / 빛을 표현할 수 있었다 //

[By using] this oil paint, art designers were able to express [the light]

To use (X) — 내용상 To use(사용하기 위하여)보다는 By using(사용함으로써)가 더 자연스럽다.

가구나 사람들의 피부에서 반짝이는

[glowing on furniture or on people's skins].

the light를 수식하는 분사구문

Grammar Point

전치사구 vs. to부정사구

문두에 전치사구가 나오느냐 to부정사구가 나오느냐에 따라 문장의 의미가 달라지므로, 문장의 전반적인 내용 이해를 위해 전치사구와 to부정사구 중에 고르는 문제가 자주 출제 된다. 부분적 의미뿐만 아니라 전체적인 글의 흐름을 이해해야 정답을 유추해 낼 수 있다.

[In approaching / To approach] the last stage, we need to set up this year's vacation schedule.

마지막 시기에 다가갈 때 우리는 올해의 휴가 계획을 세울 필요가 있다.

⇒ 내용상 '마지막 시기에 다가가기 위해서'보다는 '마지막 시기에 다가갈 때'가 자연스러우므로, In approaching이 적절하다.

Words & Phrases

express [ikspréс] 표현하다

glow [glou] 빛나다

approach [əpróutʃ] 접근하다, 다가가다

temporarily [tèmpərέ(:)rəli] 일시적으로

drastically [drǽstikəli] 극적으로, 대폭, 과감하게

archaeologist [ɑːrkiɑ́ːlədʒist] 고고학자

Check-up

정답 및 해설 p.62

1. [By living / To live] temporarily with Jacob's friends and drastically cutting their leisure expenses, they hoped to save enough money to buy a modest house in 3 years. 기출응용

2. [To find / By finding] these ruins, many archaeologists these days depend heavily on systematic research and a diversity of high-technology instruments and techniques.

EXERCISE

정답 및 해설 p.62

[01-10] 다음 중 어법상 가장 적절한 표현을 고르시오.

01 Trips allow some companions to feel that they do not belong to any groups [any / no] more.

02 Amie couldn't see [anything / nothing] at all of its shape or size—only two shining eyes.

03 [To copy / By copying] her boss's voice, she managed to access the system and get the necessary information.

04 Many pictures are not about [anything / nothing], but just pretty patterns.

05 [To pass / By passing] the qualification exam, you can get the opportunity to take the test for entering the university of California.

06 Jameson and his colleagues didn't think the storm had [anything / nothing] to do with the robot movement, because it was 1,500 feet below sea level.

07 I [can / cannot] hardly pick up a magazine nowadays in a library because someone always borrows it prior to me.

08 Although talking with him may not be pleasant, nothing will change [if / unless] you don't do it.

09 I firmly told my son that if he keeps misbehaving, I will not take him on my shopping excursions [any / no] more.

10 It hurts James so much to accept the fact that his son has died and now, he doesn't have [anywhere / nowhere] to go.

ACTUAL TEST

정답 및 해설 p.63

01 다음 글의 밑줄 친 부분 중, 어법상 어긋난 것은?

Astrology has ① been considered one field of popular culture, not scientific or academic. That is, no one in the academic world ② didn't take it seriously. However, some researchers in Britain are trying to shift this situation. Scholars at the University of Cambridge have started a study called *The Critical Study of Astrology*. They're trying to require the ③ introduction of university-level courses to study the role of astrology in science, history, and religion. But most academics ④ are skeptical of this trend. "Astrology belongs to just the same category as fairies," says David Mackay of the University of Southampton. He thinks that universities should invest their money, time, and effort on ⑤ other, more important matters.

02 기출응용

다음 (A), (B), (C)의 각 [ ] 안에서 어법에 맞는 표현으로 바르게 짝지어진 것은?

Sometimes all a good cheese needs to keep it (A) [going / from going] bad is a sympathetic ear. Researchers in France have come up with an ultrasonic sensor that will listen to cheese as it matures and warn cheese makers of defects. Cheese makers have to downgrade up to one-fifth of their produce (B) [because / because of] undetected faults. If the new device works well, that problem could be reduced. The technique involves sending a low frequency ultrasonic signal through the cheese to a sensor at the other side. (C) [To measure / By measuring] the change in the speed and size of the emerging signal, the moisture and porosity of the cheese can be mapped.

*porosity : 물질의 내부에 작은 구멍이 많은 성질

	(A)		(B)		(C)
①	going	-	because	-	To measure
②	from going	-	because	-	To measure
③	going	-	because of	-	By measuring
④	from going	-	because of	-	By measuring
⑤	from going	-	because of	-	To measure

UNIT

201 like vs. unlike

Unlike other pollutants that are left in the air only for days or weeks, carbon dioxide and methane will remain there for 1,000 years.

대기 중에 고작 며칠이나 몇 주 동안 남아 있는 다른 오염 물질과는 달리, 이산화탄소와 메탄은 대기 중에 천 년 동안 남아 있을 것이다.

다른 오염 물질과는 달리 // 대기 중에 남아있다 / 고작 며칠이니 몇 주 동안 //

Unlike other pollutants that are left in the air only for days or weeks,

Like (X)
주절과 내용이 정반대이므로
Unlike가 온다.

이산화탄소와 메탄은 / 남아 있을 것이다 / 그곳에 / 천 년 동안

carbon dioxide and methane will remain there for ten 1,000 years.

Words & Phrases

pollutant [pəlúːtənt] 오염물질

carbon [káːrbən] 탄소

cop [kɔp] 경찰관

clone [kloun] 복제품

boring [bɔ́ːriŋ] 지루한

fascinating [fǽsənéitiŋ] 매혹적인, 황홀한

tension [ténʃən] 긴장

wormhole [wəːrmhoul] 웜홀 (우주의 시간과 공간의 벽에 뚫린 구멍)

like vs. unlike

like는 '~와 같이', '~처럼'이라는 뜻이고, unlike는 '~와 달리'라는 뜻이다. 비교하는 대상의 유사성이나 대조성에 따라 like와 unlike를 선택한다.

[Like / Unlike] cop drama clones and boring sitcoms, reality TV offers exciting and fascinating human stories.

수사 드라마의 아류 작품이나 지루한 시트콤과는 달리 리얼리티 TV는 흥미롭고 매혹적인 사람의 이야기를 제공한다.

⇒ 앞의 boring은 주절의 exciting과는 어울리지 않으므로, 반대를 나타내는 unlike가 옳다.

Check-up

정답 및 해설 p.63

1. Like / Unlike these situations where one could feel worried, test anxiety can bring about a stomachache or a tension headache.

2. Like / Unlike a black hole, providing one-way travel to nowhere, a wormhole could play a role such as not only an entrance but also an exit.

동사+대명사+전치사

When he couldn't see or find sheet music, Jamie simply wrote it down through listening to performance.

악보를 볼 수 없거나 찾을 수 없었을 때, 제이미는 그저 연주를 듣고 받아 적었다.

그가 악보를 보거나 찾을 수 없었을 때 // 제이미는 단순하게 /
When he couldn't see or find sheet music, Jamie simply

그것을 받아 적었다 / 연주를 듣고
wrote it down through listening to performance.

wrote down it (X)
it이 대명사이므로 wrote와 down 사이에 와야 한다.

Grammar Point

동사 + 대명사 + 전치사

두 단어 이상으로 이루어진 동사구의 구조는 〈동사+전치사〉와 〈동사+부사〉의 두 가지이다. 동사와 함께 쓰이는 것이 전치사인지 부사인지에 따라 목적어의 위치가 달라질 수 있다.

write down (부사) vs. listen to (전치사)	
write down his address (O)	listen to his address (O)
write his address down (O)	listen his address to (X)
write down it (X)	listen to it (O)
write it down (O)	listen it to (X)

〈동사+부사〉 목적어로 대명사가 올 경우 무조건 동사와 부사 사이에 위치해야 한다. 단, 명사는 부사 앞, 뒤 어디에든 올 수 있다.
〈동사+전치사〉 동사와 전치사 사이에 목적어가 오지 않는다. 즉, 동사와 전치사는 분리해서 쓰지 않는다.

Words & Phrases

sheet music
악보

write down
받아 적다

performance
[pərfɔ́ːrməns]
연주, 공연

pick up
~을 도중에서 태우다, 마중 나가다

Check-up

정답 및 해설 p.63

1. Because I'm going to Seoul Station, I'll [pick them up / pick up them] there.
2. I was lying on the bed, and Jack [called me up / called up me] and said that Susie had not attended the class.

EXERCISE

정답 및 해설 p.63

[01-10] 다음 중 어법상 가장 적절한 표현을 고르시오.

01 They have to make a hole in the asteroid and [blow it up / blow up it] with nuclear weapons.

02 [Like / Unlike] other Asian countries, not a single foreign company can hire its employees freely in North Korea.

03 I need to go to the airport on business, so I can [pick them up / pick up them] for free.

04 기출응용 Without shedding a tear or showing alarm, Amy would [push up herself / push herself up] and try again.

05 [Like / Unlike] humans, almost all monkeys can use a kind of tool and cooperate with others in order to deal with problems.

06 기출응용 [Like / Unlike] tears that flow when you chop onions, tears with laughter are unusually rich in protein-based hormones that are released when you're stressed.

07 기출응용 Note taking is dependent on one's ability to maintain attention, understand what is being said, and hold it in working memory long enough to [write down it / write it down].

08 [Like / Unlike] most parts of New England where heavy rain is expected today, it will be clear and bright in Boston.

09 When its neighboring country asked for financial aid, the government [cut it down / cut down it].

10 [Like / Unlike] most teens in Japan, Mitsuki does not like playing video games or using high-tech toys.

ACTUAL TEST

정답 및 해설 p.64

01 기출응용 **다음 글의 밑줄 친 부분 중, 어법상 어긋난 것은?**

You might think that vampires only come out at night or during Halloween. Well, guess what? They are everywhere, working 24 hours a day, ① using energy at your house. Vampire energy, also called standby power, ② refers to the electric power consumed by home electronic devices even when they are turned off or ③ not being used. You think you have ④ turned off them, but they are still running. The wasted standby power of household electronic devices is typically very small, but the sum of all such devices within the household ⑤ becomes significant. TVs, VCRs, DVD players, computers, microwaves, coffee machines, etc. are the everyday secret users of vampire energy.

02 **다음 (A), (B), (C)의 각 [ ] 안에서 어법에 맞는 표현으로 바르게 짝지어진 것은?**

Children can show several acts of real life roles through play in a variety of ways. Play gives them a chance of reversing the role they usually have in real life. For instance, a timid child may become a lion or a tiger. In the game, the shy (A) [take / takes] on the general character of these animals—becoming fearless, aggressive, and self-sufficient. He or she can run and jump toward playmates, who scatters in pretending to be frightened. Through the game, the child becomes strong and brave rather than timid. Play also gives children an opportunity to release impulses that might be unacceptable in other situations. A child can kick a ball in frustration or play at "cops and robbers," activities (B) [which / in which] aggression and conflict are acceptable and feelings may be manifested without fear of adult censure (C) [like / unlike] the real life.

	(A)		(B)		(C)
①	take	-	which	-	like
②	take	-	in which	-	unlike
③	take	-	in which	-	like
④	takes	-	in which	-	like
⑤	takes	-	which	-	unlike

UNIT 203

명령문, or 구문 / be sure to[of] 구문

Say all you have to say in the fewest possible words, or your reader will be sure to skip them.

-*John Ruskin*

당신이 말해야 하는 모든 것을 가능한 최소한의 어휘로 말해라. 그렇지 않으면 여러분의 독자는 분명 그것을 지나칠 것이다.

모든 것을 말하라 // 당신이 말해야 하다 / 가능한 최소한의 어휘로 //

Say all you have to say in the fewest possible words,

그렇지 않으면 당신의 독자는 / 분명 그것들을 지나칠 것이다

or your reader will be sure to skip them.

and (X)

Grammar Point

명령문, or 구문

명령문 +	, and ~ 해라, 그러면 ~ 할 것이다 Get up early, and you will succeed. 일찍 일어나라, 그러면 성공할 것이다.
	, or ~ 해라, 그렇지 않으면 ~ 할 것이다. Get up early, or you will be late. 일찍 일어나라, 그렇지 않으면 늦을 것이다.

be sure to 구문

- **be sure to : 확실히 ~ 하다 (화자나 타인의 확신)**

  He is sure to succeed in his plan. 그는 그의 계획을 성공할거야.

  = I am sure of his success in his plan. 나는 그가 자신의 계획을 성공할거라고 확신해.

- **be sure of : ~을 확신하다 (주어의 확신)**

  He is sure of his success. 그는 자신의 성공을 확신한다.

Words & Phrases

skip
[skip]
지나치다, 건너뛰다

tissue
[tíʃuː]
조직

figure out
~을 알아내다

Check-up

정답 및 해설 p.64

1. Hand in your paper by the deadline, and / or you may get a D grade from the professor.

2. Compare the patterns discovered in cancer cells with those in normal tissue, and / or you come to figure out the difference.

명령문 vs. 분사구문 vs. to부정사 구문

Make sure to bring chocolate to room temperature before eating it. 기출응용

초콜릿을 먹기 전에 반드시 상온에 두어라.

확실히 해라 / 초콜릿을 가져오는 것을 / 상온으로 //

Make sure to bring chocolate to room temperature

making / to make (X)

하나의 문장에는 하나의 동사가 오는 것이 원칙이다.
문장인데 뒤에 본동사가 없으므로 명령문의 형태인 동사원형이 되야 한다.

먹기 전에

before eating it.

Words & Phrases

make sure
~을 확실히 하다

room temperature
실내 온도

antique
[æntíːk]
골동품의, 고풍의, 고미술의

separate
[sépərit]
분리하다

valuable
[vǽljuəbl]
가치 있는

worthless
[wə́ːrθlis]
가치 없는

mixture
[míkstʃər]
혼합물

stir
[stəːr]
휘젓다, 섞다

Grammar Point

명령문 vs. 분사구문 vs. to부정사 구문

동사가 문장의 처음에 위치할 경우 그 형태에 주의하자. 명령문의 동사원형과 동명사, 분사, to부정사 중 고르는 문제가 자주 출제된다. 해결책은 뒤에 본동사가 존재하느냐를 살펴보는 것이다. 본동사가 있다면, 문장 처음에 위치하는 동사원형은 답이 아니다.

[Call / Calling] an antique dealer to help you separate the valuable from the worthless junk. 기출응용

당신이 가치 있는 것과 가치 없는 쓰레기를 구별하는 것을 돕도록 골동품 상인에게 전화해라.

⇒ 뒤에 본동사가 없으므로 문장의 형태는 명령문이어야 한다. 따라서 Call이 정답이 된다. separate은 〈help+목적어+동사원형〉 구조에 해당하므로 본동사가 아니다.

Check-up

정답 및 해설 p.64

1. Add some flour to the mixture and stir / stirring it until it becomes thick.
2. Before you have a garage sale, check / checking what you should not put on sale.

EXERCISE

정답 및 해설 p.64

[01-10] 다음 중 어법상 가장 적절한 표현을 고르시오.

01 To help you concentrate, [make / making] a question for yourself and skim for the answer.

02 If you are seated in a bulkhead row and have enough room, [lean / leaning] your upper body on your things.

03 [Discover / To discover] your self-concept, consider how you might answer the question "What kind of person am I?"

04 기출응용 [Use / By using] computers, we surf the websites and exchange e-mails with our friends.

05 기출응용 [Make / Making] such a description concrete and detailed requires not just inspiration but certain practical tools and skills.

06 [Read / Reading] the first sentence or paragraph quite carefully, and it will give you several ideas of what the writer is going to say.

07 기출응용 [Making / Make] sure to bring rice cake to room temperature before eating, as frozen pieces of rice cake always strike me as rather hard and tasteless.

08 [Begin / Beginning] by visiting your local coin shop and check out some of the coins to know whether the grade you expect coincides with their real grade.

09 While you're at the table, [making / make] a courtesy purchase of some inexpensive coin to show your appreciation for the help.

10 We are now entering one of the greatest museums in Europe, so please [be / being] careful not to touch any of the precious works of art.

ACTUAL TEST

정답 및 해설 p.65

01 다음 글의 밑줄 친 부분 중, 어법상 어긋난 것은?

One study shows that immersing yourself in a language in a country ① where it's spoken is the surest and quickest way to pick it up. Presently, several immersion schools are marketing ② themselves to busy professionals by providing super-intensive mini-language courses. For examples, at Paris Educational Community in France, time-crunched students can attend an intensive language program for a weekend. But for a good foundation in a foreign language, experts say at least four weeks ③ is optimal. Speaking like a local doesn't happen by osmosis. You have to make a concerted effort to break away, especially in the time of connectedness. It ④ is recommended to choose a program in a small town where you're less likely to encounter distractions. Once you become fluent in another language, use and practice it regularly, ⑤ and you will lose it.

*osmosis : 조금씩 스며듦

02 

(A), (B), (C)의 각 [ ] 안에서 어법에 맞는 표현으로 바르게 짝지어진 것은?

Parents are sometimes surprised when their children's grammar starts getting worse. When young children begin using sentences, their grammar is reasonably correct. For example, a child (A) [using / used] the word "mice" might start saying "mouses," (B) [if / even if] she had never heard anyone else make that mistake. As they get a little older, the same children start making more mistakes. If you see this pattern of mistakes in your own child, don't worry. Child development specialists say it's actually a good sign. (C) [By making / To make] these mistakes, children are showing a deeper understanding of grammar.

	(A)		(B)		(C)
①	using	-	if	-	By making
②	using	-	even if	-	To make
③	using	-	even if	-	By making
④	used	-	if	-	By making
⑤	used	-	if	-	To make

REVIEW TEST

정답 및 해설 p.65

[01-05] **다음 문장 중 어법상 틀린 부분을 고쳐 쓰시오.**

01 The value of the original results not only from its unique but from its being the source of many reproductions.

02 New eateries look for publicity offer free meals to people such as Shan and Kim, who are frequent reviewers.

03 Like most other young singers, his fans are not limited to a certain age group; they range from 7-year-olds to old ladies.

04 Americans are sometimes surprised to learn that the market of China is seen to be more open than America.

05 This device lets users understand speech a in noisy atmosphere, without needing to lip-read, and even hearing a lecture in many cases.

[06-10] **다음 주어진 단어를 알맞은 형태로 바꿔 문장을 완성하시오.**

06 The brain region plays a critical role in learning new information, forming spatial memories and __________ short-term memories as long-term ones. (store)

07 This not only creates the use of improved technology for the coach but also __________ a sport-science attitude among the athletes. (make)

08 The research team concluded that making kids move around more can sharpen intelligence, enhance creativity and planning skills, and __________ math and reading performance. (improve)

09 Our office can deal with a variety of problems; from finding lost cat or dog to __________ love letters. (deliver)

10 A human is even more capable of operating those tools correctly and __________ them in proper and useful positions. (place)

FINAL CHECK

정답 및 해설 p.65

01 기출응용 **다음 글의 밑줄 친 부분 중 어법상 어긋난 것은?**

Who says that learning has to happen in a classroom? Or take time away from work? Well, it doesn't have to. In fact, research shows you learn more when you apply ① <u>that</u> you are learning to your own work. We all have memories of attending classes, sitting through a lengthy lecture, taking copious notes, and then ② <u>returning</u> to work only to put the notes on a bookshelf and never look at them again. Not only ③ <u>did we waste</u> precious time, but we really didn't develop professionally, ④ <u>either</u>. Wouldn't it be better to immediately apply new skills or information ⑤ <u>to</u> what you are doing in your day-to-day life? Wouldn't it be great if you could actually learn and grow from your professional development endeavors?

02 **(A), (B), (C)의 각 [ ] 안에서 어법에 맞는 표현으로 바르게 짝지어진 것은?**

Guessing the meaning of unknown words from context can be listed as both a strategy and a skill in reading texts. When readers first meet this concept and practice (A) [how / what] to use context to catch the meaning of unfamiliar vocabulary, they are using several strategies. The use of the strategies (B) [is / are] completely conscious while they learn and practice. As the capacity to guess unknown words from context becomes automatic, the readers can move from using a conscious strategy to (C) [utilize / utilizing] an unconscious skill. The use of the skill takes place outside the direct consciousness of the reader. In other words, the objective for explicit strategy instruction is to move readers from conscious control of reading strategies to unconscious use of reading skills.

	(A)		(B)		(C)
①	how	-	is	-	utilize
②	what	-	is	-	utilizing
③	how	-	is	-	utilizing
④	what	-	are	-	utilize
⑤	how	-	are	-	utilize

03 다음 글의 밑줄 친 부분 중, 어법상 <u>어긋난</u> 것은?

The Kims Group is the leading source of ① <u>analysis</u> on international business and world affairs. Our mission is various, from delivering newspapers and magazines ② <u>to hold</u> several conferences. ③ <u>What</u> ties us together is the objectivity of our opinion, the originality of our insight and our advocacy of economic and political freedom around the world. We are establishing a new business to create online fairs, ④ <u>bringing</u> sponsors and delegates together within fields that are relevant to our audience, such as business education. We have a record of success with similar events and perceive significant commercial opportunities in using technology to extend and improve our current offering. We plan to launch this business soon and are in the process of building an ambitious and dynamic team to help us ⑤ <u>realize</u> our commercial ambition.

04 (A), (B), (C)의 각 [ ] 안에서 어법에 맞는 표현으로 바르게 짝지어진 것은?

Assertive behavior involves standing up for your rights and (A) [expresses / expressing] your thoughts and feelings in a direct, appropriate way that does not violate the rights of others. People who exhibit assertive behavior are able to handle conflict situations with ease and assurance (B) [during / while] maintaining good interpersonal relations. In contrast, aggressive behavior involves expressing your thoughts and feelings and defending your rights in a way that openly violates the rights of others. Those exhibiting aggressive behavior seem to believe that the rights of others must be subservient to (C) [them / theirs]. Thus, they have a difficult time maintaining good interpersonal relations. They are likely to interrupt, talk fast and ignore others to maintain control.

	(A)		(B)		(C)
①	expressing	-	while	-	theirs
②	expressing	-	while	-	them
③	expressing	-	during	-	theirs
④	expresses	-	while	-	them
⑤	expresses	-	during	-	them

05  **다음 글의 밑줄 친 부분 중, 어법상 어긋난 것은?**

Baseball players often place a weighted ring around their bat before ① taking their warmup swings. They say repeatedly swinging a heavier bat makes the unweighted bat feel lighter in comparison. The primary principle ② underlying this effect is known as perceptual contrast. Simply put, the characteristics of objects are perceived in comparison to others. If you ③ are asked to pick up a ten-pound weight in a gymnasium, it will appear lighter if you had first picked up a twenty-pound weight and ④ heavy if you had first picked up a five-pound weight. Nothing has actually changed about the ten-pound weight except your perception of it. This psychological process holds for ⑤ almost any type of judgment you could make. In every case the perceptual process is the same: Prior experience colors perception.

06 **(A), (B), (C)의 각 [ ] 안에서 어법에 맞는 표현으로 바르게 짝지어진 것은?**

(A) [If / Whether] you want to know why your child ends every sentence on an "interrogative upbeat," talks about going to high school and is more likely to dial 911 in an emergency than 999, (B) [take / takes] a look at the television schedules. Britain used to be the global leader in children's TV but in the past decade, US imports have taken over. As research revealed this week, spending on children's TV has fallen by 48% since 2003, while original British programming has dropped from 1,900 hours a year to just 900. In part, this is a result of the ban on advertising junk food during children's broadcasting. Ad revenues—already hit by the proliferation of new channels—have plummeted, and the big commercial channels have stopped (C) [making / to make] new programs. Only the BBC is still commissioning, and at a paltry rate given the lack of competition.

	(A)		(B)		(C)
①	If	-	take	-	making
②	If	-	takes	-	to make
③	If	-	takes	-	making
④	Whether	-	take	-	to make
⑤	Whether	-	takes	-	making

MEMO

MEMO

MEMO

MEMO

구문을 알면 독해가 저절로!

구문 독해

204개의
핵심 구문을 통한
직독직해
완전정복!

204

BOOK 2

김상근 지음

SENTENCE STRUCTURE
+READING

정답 및 해설

NEXUS Edu

구문을 알면 독해가 저절로!

구문 독해

204개의
핵심 구문을 통한
직독직해
완전정복!

204

BOOK 2

SENTENCE STRUCTURE
+READING

정답 및 해설

김상근 지음

NEXUS Edu

chapter

10 관계사

UNIT 099~100

Check-up P. 8~9

099 **1.** who **2.** who 100 **1.** whom **2.** whom

099

1. 선행사가 Many people로 사람임

지구상의 이 지역에 사는 다수의 사람들은 추운 날씨의 시작으로 다시 걱정하게 될 것 같다.

2. a craftsman을 선행사로 받는 주격 관계대명사 필요

우리 가족은 우리가 여러 해 동안 소중히 여겨온 가구를 만든 장인 제리 스미스의 작업실로 여행을 떠났다.

100

1. 전치사 to의 목적어가 되는 목적격 관계대명사 필요

그런 역할들은 개인과 그 또는 그녀와 이야기하고 있는 사람 간의 관계와 밀접하게 연관되어 있다.

2. 전치사 on의 목적어가 되는 목적격 관계대명사 필요

분노한 시민 한 명은 심지어 사무실에 전화를 걸어 그가 복수하고 싶은 몇몇 이라크 사람들을 어디에서 찾을 수 있는지 물었다.

EXERCISE P. 10

01 who 02 whom 03 whom 04 whom 05 whoever
06 who 07 who 08 who 09 who 10 who

01 선행사가 a toll booth attendant로 사람임

잭은 아버지를 떠오르게 하는 요금 정산소 직원을 보았다.

02 전치사 with의 목적어가 되는 목적격 관계대명사 필요

그는 총명하고, 마음만 먹으면 학교에서 잘 해낼 수 있다. 그리고 그에게는 함께 있으면 즐거운 친구들이 있다.

03 전치사 with의 목적어가 되는 목적격 관계대명사가 필요

나는 당신이 그 기술들을 가장 잘 선보일 기회를 지녔던 그런 교사들에게 추천서를 요청하도록 권장합니다.

04 전치사 with의 목적어가 되는 목적격 관계대명사가 필요

동창회는 결속감을 느끼는 학생들에게 돈을 대출해 줄 수 있고, 대출한 학생들은 일 년에 4번 자신을 지원해 주는 사람들로부터 정보 갱신을 요청 받는다.

05 전치사 to가 왔지만, could gain의 주어가 되는 주격 관계대명사가 필요

16세기에는 상황이 매우 달랐다. 향신료는 그것을 얻을 수 있는 누구에게나 부와 권력을 가져다 주는 인기 있는 보물이었다.

06 선행사가 an acquaintance로 사람, ~ I was certain who was going ~ 인데, 관계대명사가 선행사 가까이에 있기 위해 I was certain 앞으로 나감

나는 거짓말을 할 거라고 확신하는 지인의 뉴스 인터뷰를 보았다.

07 선행사가 patients로 사람임

그 진료소의 좋은 점은 더 오래 있고 싶어하는 환자들에게 그렇게 하는 것이 허용된다는 점이다.

08 선행사 those는 '사람들'을 의미

많이, 불규칙적인 식사를 하는 사람은 규칙적으로 더 적게 먹는 사람들보다 더 살찌고 혈액 내 지방 수치가 더 높은 경향이 있다.

09 선행사가 your sister로 사람, in the picture가 삽입되어 선행사와 관계대명사 사이가 멀어졌고, ~ I heard who was pretty ~에서 관계대명사가 선행사 가까이 있기 위해 I heard 앞으로 나감

나는 사진 속에서 꽤 예쁘다고 들었던 너의 여동생을 찾을 수 없다.

10 the actress가 선행사, ~ my sister claims who has attracted ~에서 관계대명사가 선행사 가까이 있기 위해 my sister claims 앞으로 나감

이 사람이 내 여동생이 자기 친구를 유혹했다고 주장한 여배우다.

ACTUAL TEST P. 11

01 ⑤ 02 ⑤

01 ⑤ the people이 선행사이므로 which가 아니라 who가 돼야 함 ① no baseball gloves가 주어, were가 동사 ② '~으로 여겨졌다', disabled는 목적격 보어 ③ my son이 주어, was가 동사 ④ '내가 느끼는 것', 선행사를 포함하는 관계대명사

어린 시절, 친구들이 야구팀 선수를 선택할 때면 나는 항상 제외됐다. 그 시절에는 나와 같은 왼손잡이를 위한 야구 글러브가 없었다. 나는 다른 때는 정상이었지만 야구 시합을 할 때마다 장애가 있는 사람 취급을 당했다. 역시 왼손잡이인 내 아들은 다행히도 왼손잡이용 글러브가 발명된 후에 태어났다. 그래서 그 아이는 야구를 하고 싶을 때 내가 느꼈던 감정을 느낄 필요가 없다. 장애 상황을 줄여 줄 수 있는 다른 다양한 발명품들이 있다. 안경 덕분에 나는 살아가면서 무력감을 피할 수 있다. 휠체어는 걷지 못하는 사람들의 이동성을 향상시킬 수 있다.

leave out 빼다 **disabled** 장애가 있는 **reduce** 줄이다 **powerless** 무기력한 **mobility** 이동성

02 (A) to부정사의 부정은 to 앞에 not을 붙여야 하므로 not to have가 적절 (B) one이 주어이므로 was가 적절 (C) someone이 선행사이므로 who가 적절

피터의 할머니는 잠시 쉬고는 천천히 대답했다. "너도 알다시피 때로는 치밀하게 계획하지 않는 것이 최선일 때가 있단다. 나는 네 할아버지와 처음 뉴욕에 갔던 때를 기억한단다. 우리는 매일 박물관이나 콘서트 장에 갔었지. 축제와 야구경기도 봤어. 우리는 맛있는 음식도 먹고, 재미있는 사람들도 많이 만났단다. 하지만 그 여행에서 얻은 가장 멋진 기억 중 하나는 정말 예상치 못했던 거란다." 할머니는 다시 잠시 멈추신 후 말씀하셨다. "우리는 특히 유명한 작품을 보러 간 거였어. 그런데 어느 날 기분 전환 겸 동물원에 갔었어. 그리고 거기서 나에게 엄청난 영향을 준 누군가를 만났단다. 그의 이름은 존 아담스야." 그녀는 계속했다. "그는 고릴라야. 매우 하얀 털과 핑크색 피부를 가진 특별한 알비노 고릴라란다."

pause 쉬다 **unexpected** 예상치 못한 **have a great effect on** ~에 큰 영향을 미치다

UNIT 101~102

Check-up P. 12~13

101 **1.** whose **2.** whose **102** **1.** which **2.** who

101

1. truths' meaning를 의미하므로 truths'를 대신하는 소유격 관계대명사가 필요

다음날까지 그 의미를 알 수 없는 많은 진실이 있다.

2. a mouse's age를 의미하므로 a mouse's를 대신하는 소유격 관계대명사 필요

60이나 70세의 인간과 같은 나이의 쥐를 이용한 실험에서 과학자들은 그 쥐들에게 다양한 곡물을 먹였다.

102

1. 선행사인 a main body는 기관을 의미하므로 which가 적절

우리는 조사를 시작할 수 있는 주요 기관으로 경찰을 승인할 것이다.

2. workers가 선행사이므로 who가 적절

사람들의 지지 때문에 오늘부터 파업에 참가하는 근로자의 수가 급격히 증가할 것이다.

EXERCISE

P. 14

01 which 02 whose 03 whom 04 whose 05 which
06 whose 07 whose 08 whose 09 whom 10 whose

01 12 cargo containers가 선행사, held의 주어가 되는 주격 관계대명사 필요

1992년 1월 10일, 거친 바다를 통해 이동하던 배 한 척이 12개의 화물 콘테이너를 잃어버렸는데, 그 중 하나는 28,800개의 물에 뜨는 목욕용 장난감을 싣고 있었다.

02 Mike's stage name을 의미하므로 Mike's에 해당하는 소유격 관계대명사 필요

마이크의 예명은 "시각장애인 마이크"였는데, 그가 매년 15만 불 정도를 벌기까지는 많은 시간이 걸리지 않았다.

03 전치사 with의 목적어가 되는 목적격 관계대명사 필요

우리와 대화하는 사람은 그의 말이 경청되고 있다고 생각될 때, 우리 곁에서 더욱 편안함을 느낄 것이다.

04 title of TV animation을 의미하므로 소유격 관계대명사 필요

제임스와 카터는 제목이 '톰과 제리'인 TV 만화를 따서 '톰과 제리'라고 불린다.

05 would enable의 주어가 되는 주격 관계대명사가 필요

꿈은 적절히 해석될 때 우리가 미래를 예상할 수 있게 해주는 예언적 의사소통으로 간주됐다.

06 a famous filmmaker's work을 의미하므로 a famous filmmaker's에 해당하는 소유격 관계대명사 필요

웬디는 매우 칭송 받는 '조이 럭 클럽'처럼 미국 내에서 동양 사람으로 사는 것의 복잡성을 다룬 작품으로 유명한 감독이었다.

07 people's diets를 의미하므로 소유격 관계대명사 필요

주된 연구는 최근에 바나나, 토마토, 오렌지 같이 칼륨이 풍부한 음식으로 구성된 식사를 하는 사람은 뇌졸중 발생의 위험이 3분의 1로 줄어들 수도 있다는 것을 발견했다.

08 child athletes' and performers' parents라는 의미이므로 소유격 관계대명사 필요

우리는 부모의 야망으로 인해 삶을 망친 어린 운동선수들이나 연주자들을 찾기 위해 오늘 신문에서 주요 뉴스들을 보기만 하면 된다.

09 선행사가 many parents ~ young people로 사람

청중은 많은 부모와 몇몇 젊은이들로 구성되어 있었는데, 나는 그 중 대부분을 알았다.

10 pupils' families를 의미하므로 pupils'를 대신하는 소유격 관계대명사 필요

듀크 대학의 부유한 졸업생들은 이미 약 350억 달러의 장학금을 지원하고 있는데, 이는 고등 교육에서 가장 일반적인 장학 프로그램 중 하나를 지원하는 것으로 가족이 5만 달러 이하의 소득을 가지고 있는 학생들에게는 전액 장학금을 약속하고 있다.

ACTUAL TEST

P. 15

01 ① 02 ②

01 ① high school students가 선행사이므로 which가 아니라 who가 돼야 함 ② 수업이 제공되는 것이므로 수동태 ③ every class가 주어, has가 동사 ④ '늦어도' ⑤ not ~ any 전체 부정

샌프란시스코 시사이드 대학은 다시 한번 영어 실력을 향상하는 데 관심이 있는 전 세계의 고등학생을 대상으로 2주 간의 겨울 영어 캠프를 열게 됨을 자랑스럽게 생각합니다. 기초에서 고급까지 5단계의 반이 있습니다. 학생들은 도착 즉시 테스트를 받고, 자신의 영어 실력에 적절한 단계에 배치됩니다. 모든 반은 최대 15명의 학생으로 구성됩니다. 교실에서는 교사가 조언과 도움을 제공하는 동시에 학생과의 상호 작용에 초점이 맞춰집니다. 만약 여러분이 입학이 승인 된 후에 캠프를 취소하려면, 늦어도 11월 30일까지는 지불한 모든 비용이 환불될 것입니다. 만약 11월 30일 후에 철회한다면, 유감스럽게도 저희는 요금을 환불해 드릴 수 없습니다.

advanced 고급의 appropriate 적절한 interaction 상호 작용 withdraw 취소하다 fee 요금

02 (A) 문장이 오므로 접속사 although가 적절 (B) the blue-eyed black lemur's habitat를 의미하므로 whose가 적절 (C) 수치가 줄어든다고 믿는 것이 아니라 믿어지는 것이므로 are believed가 적절

630종의 영장류가 있고, 그중 한 종은 70억에 가까운 인구와 함께 잘 지내고 있지만, 300종 이상은 멸종 위기에 있다. 지난 주 한 그룹의 동물 학자들은 가장 위험에 처해있는 25종의 이름을 대면서 원숭이와 고등 유인원, 긴팔원숭이와 물론 인간을 포함하는 생물학적 목인 영장류의 위험을 강조하고자 했다. 그 목록은 마다가스카르에서 5개의 종, 아프리카에서는 6개의 종, 아시아에서는 11개의 종, 중앙아메리카와 남아메리카에서는 3개의 종으로 구성되어 있다. 이것들은 마다가스카르가 서식지이고, 화전농으로 인해서 멸종되고 있는 파란 눈 검정 여우원숭이에서 수마트라 오랑우탄까지 이른다. 가장 희귀한 영장류 중 하나인 하얀 여우 원숭이, 비단 시파카의 수는 100마리 정도로 줄어들고 있다고 믿어진다.

primate 영장류 threaten 위협하다 extinction 멸종 zoologist 동물학자 ape 원숭이 species 종 comprise 포함하다 habitat 서식지 slash-and-burn agriculture 화전 농업

UNIT 103~104

Check-up P. 16~17

103 **1.** which **2.** which **104** **1.** who **2.** that

103-

1. 앞 문장 전체가 선행사이므로 which가 적절

주디는 젊은 시절 열심히 일했고, 이는 그녀가 자신의 회사를 설립하는 것으로 이어졌다.

2. 앞 문장 전체가 선행사이므로 which가 적절

이런 종류의 역설은 시간 여행자가 과거를 바꾸려고 노력할 때 생기는데 이것은 명백히 불가능한 일이다.

104

1. thinks의 주어가 되는 주격 관계대명사 필요

제임스는 아마도 내가 그에게 적대감을 가지고 있다고 생각하는 유일한 사람일 것이다.

2. was의 주어가 되는 주격 관계대명사가 필요

해리스버그는 많은 광부들이 넘쳐났던 마지막 마을이었다.

EXERCISE P. 18

01 which **02** that **03** which **04** that **05** that
06 which **07** which **08** that **09** which **10** which

01 앞 문장 전체가 선행사이므로 which가 적절

당신은 많은 다양한 방식으로 다른 나라의 문화와 관습을 배울 수 있는데, 아마 그것이 당신에게는 새로울지도 모른다.

02 the only one을 선행사로 받는 관계대명사 필요, one은 사물

인쇄 산업이 에어컨의 발명으로 혜택을 받은 유일한 산업은 아니다.

03 앞 문장 전체가 선행사이므로 which가 적절

에스트로겐은 스트레스 호르몬인 코티졸의 수치를 올릴 수 있고, 이는 여성들의 우울증의 비율이 더 높은 것을 설명하는 데 도움을 준다.

04 The very technology를 선행사 받는 관계대명사 필요

대중 사회로부터 우리를 자유롭게 해 줄거라 여겨졌던 바로 그 기술이 정보 고속도로인 만큼 유리 어항이기도 하다는 것이 드러났다.

05 뒤에 완전한 문장이 오므로 관계부사 why를 대신하는 관계부사 that이 적절

우리가 반복적으로 같은 실수를 하는 이유는 연상이 사고의 고리 속에 있는 사이에서 형성되며, 연상이 사용될 때마다 더 확고해지기 때문이다.

06 앞 문장 전체가 선행사이므로 which가 적절

당신은 3주 치의 임대료에 해당하는 담보 비용을 지불해야만 하는데, 이는 이 지역 주택 임대에서 일반적인 관례이다.

07 앞 문장 전체가 선행사이므로 which가 적절

잭의 부인은 매우 똑똑한데, 이것이 그의 대단한 자부심의 원천이었다.

08 선행사가 사람(the girl)과 사물(the dog)이므로 that이 적절

함께 뛰고 있는 소녀와 개를 봐. 아주 빨라.

09 앞 문장 전체가 선행사이므로 which가 적절

학생 중 한 명이 계속 웃었고 그것이 스미스 선생님을 심각하게 언짢게 했다.

10 앞 문장 전체가 선행사이므로 which가 적절

절연 처리는 전기적 충격으로부터 기본적인 보호를 해 주는데, 이는 사람들이 안전하게 일하도록 해준다.

ACTUAL TEST P. 19

01 ③ **02** ③

01 ③ 뒤에 완전한 문장이 왔고 the first floor를 선행사로 받으므로 관계대명사 which가 아니라 관계부사 where가 돼야 함
① 앞 문장을 선행사로 받은 which가 주어, makes가 동사
② 일반동사 has를 강조 ④ '~라고 불리는' ⑤ On the fifth floor가 문두로 나와 주어와 동사가 도치된 구문

타이베이는 관광객들에게 많은 전통적인 절로 유명한데, 이것으로 타이베이가 현대적인 건축물로 널리 알려지지 못했다. 하지만, 타이베이는 508미터에 달하는 매우 인상적인 L 모양의 타이베이 101 몰을 가지고 있는데, 이 건물은 세계에서 가장 높은 건물 중 하나이다. 최근에 그 빌딩은 타이베이의 발전과 정체성, 그리고 비전의 상징이 되고 있다. 여러분은 지하에서 그랜드 마켓을 볼 수 있다. 그리고 붐비는 쇼핑몰이 시작되는 1층으로 올라가며, 시티 스퀘어라고 불리는 4층은 중앙 광장에 테이블을 갖춘 커피숍을 제공한다. 5층에서는 전망대로 가는 엘리베이터 티켓을 살 수 있다. 그것은 세계에서 가장 빠른 것 중 하나이며, 여러분은 건물의 꼭대기로 바로 올라간다. 500미터 아래에 풍경은 도시의 조명으로 오렌지 핑크 빛이 난다. 심지어 해가 진 이후에 여전히 저녁 하늘보다 더 어두운 타이베이 주변 산의 윤곽을 볼 수 있다.

architecture 건축물 progress 진보 identity 정체성 square 광장 deck 갑판 in no time at all 바로 outline 윤곽

02 (A) 뒤에 복수 명사가 오므로 other가 적절 (B) 앞 문장을 선행사로 받는 which가 주어이므로 helps가 적절 (C) Theories가 주어이므로 are가 적절

하프는 넓은 음역의 소리를 갖고 있기 때문에 그 진동을 다른 악기보다 우리 몸에 더 잘 전달한다. 연구는 하프의 진동이 인체 기관을 자극하고, 이는 질병과 싸우려는 인체의 본능에 도움을 준다는 것을 보여준다. 물리 치료사인 사라 제이 윌리엄스는 신경 근육의 장애가 있는 많은 사람들이 하프로부터 실제로 도움을 받는 것을 발견했다. 하프의 효과에 대한 이론들은 새로운 것이 아니다. 전통적으로 그리스 신이나 천사들의 악기로 불린 하프는 오랫동안 서구 문화에서 치료의 도구였다.

vibration 진동 stimulate 자극하다 instinct 본능 disorder 질병 neuromuscular 신경 근육의 cure 치료 theory 이론

UNIT 105~106

Check-up P. 20~21

105 **1.** that **2.** what **106** **1.** in which **2.** for which

105

1. images가 선행사, remembered의 목적어가 되는 목적격 관계대명사 필요

내가 여러 해 전에 다녔던 학교로 돌아갔을 때 나의 머리는 어린 시절로 부터 기억해낸 장면들로 흘러 넘쳤다.

2. 선행사가 없고, influences의 주어가 없는 불완전한 문장이므로 what이 적절

최근의 식품 연구 프로그램은 정확히 무엇이 성인들의 음식 선택에 영향을 주는지에 대해 놀라운 소식을 대중들에게 알려주었다.

106

1. 뒤 문장이 완전한 문장이므로 〈전치사+관계대명사〉가 적절

네덜란드 화가 렘브란트는 성인의 책상에 걸려있는 안경을 포함하여 성 히에로니무스의 초상화를 그렸다.

2. 뒤 문장이 완전한 문장이므로 〈전치사+관계대명사〉가 적절

내가 뜻을 찾아야만 하는 속담은 다음과 같다: 유리로 된 집에 사는 사람들은 돌을 던져서는 안 된다(역지사지).

EXERCISE P. 22

01 of which **02** into which **03** in which **04** what **05** in which **06** through which **07** on which **08** in which **09** what **10** what

01 뒤에 완전한 문장이 왔으므로 of which가 적절

만약 당신이 자랑스럽지 않은 어떤 방식으로 행동했다면, 우리는 실망했을 것이다.

02 뒤에 완전한 문장이 왔으므로 into which가 적절

그녀는 그 결과물을 붙이거나 새로운 아이디어를 적어 넣을 수 있는 커다란 스케치북을 가지고 있었다.

03 뒤에 완전한 문장이 왔으므로 in which가 적절

사람들은 약간 다른 점이 있는데, 그런 면에서 자신들의 전통을 자랑스러워 하도록 격려 받는다.

04 선행사가 없고 pleases의 주어가 없으므로 what이 적절

당신이 그것을 어떻게 정의하든 아름다움은 시각적인 것을 훨씬 초월하여 다른 감각이나 우리 마음도 기쁘게 하는 것까지 포함한다.

05 뒤에 완전한 문장이 왔으므로 in which가 적절

지능 차이는 보통 평균 남성의 키가 대부분의 여성보다 더 크다고 하는 성인 신장의 격차보다 훨씬 더 좁다.

06 뒤에 완전한 문장이 왔으므로 through which가 적절

사전은 용기를 사람이 반감, 적대감, 경멸을 유발할 수 있는 행동의 정당한 과정을 추구할 수 있도록 하는 가치라고 정의한다.

07 뒤에 완전한 문장이 왔으므로 on which가 적절

테이블이나 소파가 하나도 없었다. 우리가 그릴 위에 한 줄로 배열된 핫도그처럼 그 위에 누어야 하는, 무릎 높이의 리놀리움으로 깐 단들로 채워진 두 개의 서랍만 있을 뿐이었다.

08 뒤에 완전한 문장이 왔으므로 in which가 적절

완벽한 하수도망이 부족한 이웃에서 널리 사용되는 이 컨테이너는 얕게 묻힌 탱크를 담고 있는데 그 안에서 박테리아는 가정집 하수구에서 나오는 고형 폐기물을 분해한다.

09 called의 목적어가 없고, 선행사가 없으므로 what이 적절, conditional reflexes는 목적격 보어

그는 침 흘리기처럼 특정한 이전의 경험에 의해서 조건적으로 발생하는 자신이 '조건 반사'라고 칭한 것의 확립과 소멸에 대한 기본적인 법칙을 설립했다.

10 doing의 목적어가 없고, 선행사가 없으므로 선행사를 포함하는 관계대명사 what이 적절

그녀의 친구들 대부분은 그녀가 미친 듯 행동하기 시작했다고 생각했지만, 그녀가 정말 한 일은 자신의 인생을 위해서 싸웠던 것이다.

ACTUAL TEST P. 23

01 ③ **02** ④

01 ③ 뒤에 완전한 문장이 왔으므로 which가 아닌 at which가 돼야 함 ① 의문사 의문문이므로 동사, 주어의 어순 ② the products and services를 수식하는 분사, '나라에서 생산된 서비스와 상품' ④ the time, money and work를 수식하는 분사, '필요한 시간, 돈, 노동' ⑤ Wage or price increases를 수식하는 분사의 부정형

왜 국가들이 그들의 생산성을 늘리고 싶어 하는지 아는가? 그렇다면, 국가의 생산성은 무엇이며 어떻게 우리가 국가의 생산성을 측정할 수 있을까? 국가적인 수준에서, 생산성은 전형적으로 노동 단위 당 생산성의 달러 가치로 측정된다. 생산성은 특히 그것들을 생산하기 위해 필요한 시간, 돈, 노동과 관련하여 한 국가에서 생산되는 서비스와 상품의 질, 물건이 생산되는 비율, 생산된 양에 의존한다. 국가 생산성은 중요한데, 그것이 한 나라의 생활 수준에 대한 주요한 결정 인자이기 때문이다. 만약 근로 시간 당 총 수익 가치가 증가한다면, 국가는 전체적으로 높은 수입 수준에서 이득을 보는데, 근로자 임금은 인력의 생산성에 의존하기 때문이다. 반면에, 생산성이 감소하는 것은 생활 수준을 낮춘다. 생산성 증가가 동반되지 않은 임금이나 가격 상승은 생활 수준의 실질적인 상승 대신에 인플레이션의 압박을 야기한다.

productivity 생산성 **gauge** 측정하다 **generate** 일으키다 **determinant** 결정자 **yield** 총수익 **accompany** 동반하다 **inflationary** 인플레의

02 (A) 뒤에 완전한 문장이 왔으므로 about which가 적절 (B) 뒤에 원인이 나오므로 because가 적절 (C) 뒤에 진목적어인 to 부정사가 나오므로 가목적어 it이 있는 makes it이 적절

좋아하는 작가가 있었는데 후에 당신이 알지 못하는 다른 이름으로 책을 쓴 것을 알게 된 적이 있나요? 필명은 한 가지 장르 이상의 글을 쓰는 작가들에게 절대적으로 필요한 것이다. 이것은 한 유형의 책에 대한 독자가 그들이 좋아하는 작가가 쓴 완전히 다른 소설을 고름으로써 실망할 수도 있기 때문이다. 그러나 하나의 장르나 아

주 비슷한 장르의 글을 쓰는 작가에게는 필명이 실제로 해로울 수 있다. 필명은 독자가 작가를 찾는 것을 훨씬 더 어렵게 만든다. 만약 작가가 글을 쓰는 장르들이 미스터리나 스릴러와 같이 서로를 보완한다면, 필명을 사용하는 것은 작가가 잠재적 독자 수의 절반을 잃게 할 뿐이다.

necessity 필수품 complement 보완하다 assume 취하다, 가지다 potential 잠재적인 readership 독자 수

UNIT 107~108

Check-up P. 24~25

107 **1.** which **2.** which 108 **1.** which **2.** whom

107

1. 관계대명사 that은 계속적 용법으로 쓸 수 없음

신랑은 보통 턱시도를 입는데, 턱시도는 일반적으로 결혼식 날을 위해서만 대여된다.

2. 관계대명사 that은 계속적 용법으로 쓸 수 없음

여기에 배심원제를 도입하려는 계획을 진행해 온 위원회의 위원들은 월요일에 그 계획에 만장일치로 동의했다.

108

1. 관계대명사 that은 전치사 바로 뒤에 올 수 없음

사람들은 흰개미가 사는 집을 몇 개 지었다.

2. 관계대명사 that은 전치사 바로 뒤에 올 수 없음

아동 학대는 가족이나 친척, 아버지의 친구 등과 같이 피해자와 가까운 사람에 의해서 행해진다.

EXERCISE P. 26

01 that 02 which 03 which 04 what 05 that
06 that 07 that 08 which 09 that 10 which

01 '~라는 점에서'

많은 학자들이 그 상황에서 그들의 전제가 잘못된 실험에 근거를 두고 있다는 점에서 그것은 잘못되었다는 결론을 내렸다.

02 앞에 전치사 on이 있으므로 관계대명사 that은 올 수 없음

WBC 분자 생물학자가 유전자 이식 실험을 할 때 의존하는 두 종류의 바이러스 중 하나이다.

03 앞 문장이 선행사이므로 which가 적절

동쪽으로 영국은 북해에 접해 있는데, 그것은 서서히 물로 가득 채워지고 있는 오래된 저지대일 뿐이다.

04 앞에 전치사 of가 있으므로 that은 올 수 없고 선행사와 belongs의 주어가 없으므로 what이 적절

이 표현은 모든 사람에게 속해 있는 것에 특정한 표시를 하거나 외형을 훼손해야 한다고 느끼는 공공 기물 파손자에 대한 일반 대중의 거부 의사를 나타낸다.

05 '~라는 점에서'

영국의 도시화는 노동자들을 생산성이 낮은 분야에서 생산성이 높은 일이 있는 공장으로 보냈다는 점에서 국가 경제를 개선시켰다.

06 many buildings가 선행사, 관계대명사절이 후치 된 문장

최초의 고층빌딩이 지어진 지 정확히 40년 만에, 100층 높이로 솟은 건물들이 많이 세워졌다.

07 a country가 선행사, 앞에 나온 콤마는 삽입구를 표시해 주는 콤마이므로 계속적 용법과는 관계 없음

내 친구 중 한 명은 뛰어난 과학 기술로 유명한 '떠오르는 태양의 땅'이라고 불리는 나라 사람이다.

08 관계대명사 that은 전치사 바로 뒤에 올 수 없음

그 회사는 우리가 자랑스러워할 만한 거대한 쇼핑센터를 건립했다.

09 '~라는 점에서'

제니는 그 편지가 잭의 부정 행위의 증거가 될 수도 있다는 점에서 그것을 찢고 태워버렸다.

10 관계대명사 that은 전치사 바로 뒤에 올 수 없음

마을을 대표하는 모든 씨족은 의식에 사용되는 가면과 다른 신성한 물건을 사용하지 않을 때 보관하는 건물을 소유하고 있다.

ACTUAL TEST P. 27

01 ④ 02 ②

01 ④ 계속적 용법이므로 that이 아닌 which가 돼야 함 ① keep의 목적어가 되는 선행사를 포함한 관계대명사 ② has를 강조, every company가 주어로 3인칭 단수 ③ a company가 주어, has가 동사 ⑤ 뒤에 나오는 내용은 앞의 결과임

우리가 두 번째로 염두에 두어야 할 것은 첫 번째 것보다 더 복잡하다. 그것은 회사가 목표에 도달하기 위해서 추구하는 전략, 전술과 관련이 있다. 평범한 회사가 첫 번째로 생각하는 것이 바로 생존이다. 물론 모든 회사가 그런 목표를 가지는 것은 아니다. 예를 들어 과제를 수행하고 그 활동을 끝내도록 만들어진 회사는 마감 시간 직후에 생존 목적이 생긴다. 예상했다시피, 그들 중 대부분은 그것을 해낼 수도 있다. 이것은 만약 회사는 적절한 이익 증가를 보장하고 생존에 가장 큰 위협이 되는 지출을 줄여 준다면 회사는 내부적 혹은 외부적 활동을 한다. 한 활동에서 생긴 수익을 발표하는 것은 회사가 다음 생존을 위해 또 다른 수익 모델을 찾도록 격려할 수 있다. 그것이 바로 회사가 새로운 시장을 개척하려고 투쟁하는 이유이다.

keep in mind 명심하다 strategy 전략 tactic 전술
cut down 줄이다 revenue 수익 struggle 투쟁하다

02 (A) all the wild plants and animals가 주어이므로 were가 적절 (B) why ~ gradual이 주어이므로 동사 is가 적절 (C) 앞에 콤마가 있는 계속적 용법이므로 which가 적절

초기 식량 생산에서부터 식량을 생산하는 방식은 점진적으로 발전했다. 모든 필요한 기술이 짧은 시간 안에 이루어진 것은 아니며, 결국 특정한 장소에서 길들여진 모든 야생 식물과 동물이 동시에 길들여진 것은 아니다. 수렵과 채집 생활 방식에서도 완전히 야생에 식량을 의존하는 것에서 야생 음식이 거의 없는 식사로 되는 데 수천 년의 시간이 걸렸다. 이러한 변화가 점진적이었던 이유는 식량 생산 시스템이 시간과 노력을 할당하는 방법을 축적한 결과로 진화했기 때문이다. 수렵하는 동물과 마찬가지로 수렵하는 사람은 유한한 시간과 에너지를 가지고 있고, 그들은 시간과 에너지를 다양한

방식으로 소비할 수 있다. 인간과 동물 수렵자들은 무의식적으로라도 계속해서 노력, 즉 할당 판단을 하고 있다. 그들은 처음에는 좋아하는 음식이나 높은 대가를 주는 것에 집중한다. 만약 이러한 것들을 획득할 수 없다면, 그들은 덜 선호하는 음식으로 관심을 돌린다.

gatherer 수집자 domesticated 길들어진 transition 변화 gradual 점차적인 accumulation 축적 allocate 할당하다 forage 수렵 생활하다 finite 유한한 payoff 대가

UNIT 109~110

Check-up P. 28~29

109 **1.** what **2.** that **110** **1.** what **2.** which

109

1. 선행사가 없고, 뒤에 was의 보어가 없는 불완전한 문장이 나오므로 what이 적절

비록 여러 번 설명을 들었음에도 불구하고, 그는 여전히 무엇이 문제인지 알 수가 없었다.

2. 뒤에 완전한 문장이 나오므로 보어절을 이끄는 접속사가 적절

가장 널리 받아들여지는 설명은 O.K.가 원래는 1840년대의 뉴욕의 정치 단체인 Old Kinderhook Club을 의미한다는 것이다.

110

1. 선행사가 없고, caused의 주어가 없는 불완전한 문장이 나오므로 what이 적절

그 비행기 충돌에서 생존자는 없었고, 경찰에 따르면 여전히 그 충돌의 원인이 무엇인지에 대한 어떤 설명도 없다고 한다.

2. 뒤에 오는 문장이 완전하므로 〈전치사+which〉가 적합

그 도시를 유명하게 만든 그 지역의 전통 음식들을 맛볼 수 있는 기회가 있을 것이다.

EXERCISE P. 30

01 which **02** that **03** which **04** that **05** what
06 what **07** what **08** that **09** that **10** what

01 앞에 선행사가 있으므로 which가 적절

나는 잘 알려진 텔레비전 프로그램의 이야기보다 더 나은 슬프고 기쁜 이야기를 들었다.

02 완전한 문장인 explaining의 목적어절을 이끄는 접속사 필요

나는 그녀와 열쇠를 교환했고, 내가 그녀의 차를 수업이 끝난 후에 집에 가져다 놓겠다고 말하면서 내 차로 운전해서 집에 가라고 했다.

03 앞 문장을 선행사로 받는 계속적 용법의 관계대명사 필요

코를 심하게 고는 사람 옆에서 자는 사람은 한 시간에 열 번 이상 깨고, 이것은 그들의 수면 질과 양을 심각하게 감소시킨다.

04 완전한 문장인 보어절을 이끄는 접속사 필요

제조업과 서비스업의 중요한 하나의 차이점은 서비스업은 불확실한 수요를 완화하기 위해 재고를 만들 수 없다는 점이다.

05 선행사가 없고, were의 주어가 없으므로 what이 적절, 'the website claimed what were favorite choices ~'라는 문장에서 관계대명사가 동사(select)와 가까이 있기 위해 앞으로 나옴

그들은 인기 순위가 매겨진 사람들은 웹사이트가 인기 있는 것이라고 주장하는 것을 선택할 가능성이 더 많다는 것을 발견했다.

06 선행사가 없고, is의 주어가 없으므로 what이 적절

새와 바람에 의해서 이동하는 삼나무의 씨앗은 지금의 잉글랜드의 북쪽 가장 끝에서 러시아까지 수천 마일을 이동했다.

07 선행사가 없고, like의 목적어가 없으므로 what이 적절

아마도 채팅하는 사람들이 온라인 상의 교제에 있어서 가장 좋은 점은 그들이 싫어하는 누군가로부터 원하는 않는 접근을 막을 수 있다는 점일 것이다.

08 the reading이 선행사이므로 that이 적절

즐거움을 위한 독서는 네가 연구를 위해서 하는 독서와는 다르다.

09 완전한 문장인 show의 목적어절을 이끄는 접속사 that 필요

뉴욕 대학의 연구원들에 따르면 비용이 덜 드는 곳보다 비용이 더 많이 드는 지역과 기관이 더 많은 실험과 서비스, 중환자 입원 치료를 제공한다.

10 선행사가 없고, 전치사 about의 목적어가 없으므로 what이 적절

이 프로그램은 학생들이 그들이 무엇에 열정이 있는지 찾도록 도와주며, 스스로 그것을 실용적으로 적용시키는 법을 배우도록 고안되었다.

ACTUAL TEST P. 31

01 ③ **02** ④

01 ③ 뒤에 완전한 문장이 나오므로 what이 아니라 that이 돼야 함 ① '매우' ② 상금을 받는 것 ④ 교수가 베낀 것이 과거의 일, 학생이 논문을 쓴 것은 그 이전 ⑤ 화자의 의지

덴마 나오키 박사는 지난 10년 동안 교육부에서 매우 존경 받는 교수였다. 그는 많은 논문을 출간했고, 학생들로부터 항상 놀랄 만한 교수 평가를 받았다. 몇 개월 전, 그는 그가 썼던 논문으로 상을 탔다. 그는 몇 천 달러의 상금도 받았고, 그가 최근에 쓴 경제 관련 글은 한 저널에 기재되었다. 현재 대학 관계자는 덴마 박사가 학생이 박사 학위 논문으로 쓴 글에서 그대로 다섯 단락을 베꼈다는 사실을 발견했다. 덴마 박사는 그 학생의 자료를 인용한 데 대한 출처를 명시하지 않았다. 그는 사과했고 다시는 이와 같은 일이 벌어지지 않을 것을 약속했다.

respected 존경 받는 remarkable 놀랄만한 evaluation 평가 thesis 논문

02 (A) 선행사가 없고, wear의 목적어가 없는 불완전한 문장이 왔으므로 what이 적절 (B) 부정문이므로 either가 적절 (C) 사람들을 고려해서 만들어야 하므로 taking이 적절, anyone이 목적어

학생들이 학교에서 입을 수 있는 것에 몇 가지 제한이 필요하다. 복장 규정이 없다면, 학생들은 공격적이고 부적절하며 주의를 분산시키며 위협적인 어떤 옷도 입을 수 있다. 마약이나 술, 담배를 장려하는 공격적인 문구나 그림이 있는 옷은 허용되어서는 안 된다. 인종이나 성에 대해 공격적인 그림이나 슬로건도 역시 금지되어야 한다.

주의를 분산시키는 그림이나 글이 있는 옷 때문에 학생들은 학생이 여기(학교)에 있는 이유인 공부에 집중하지 못한다. 학생이나 교사를 위협하는 메시지나 글, 그림이 있는 옷은 착용해서는 안 된다. 복장 규정이 없는 학교에 있는 것은 매우 해롭다. 학교에서 공부하고 일하는 사람들을 고려해서 복장 규정이 만들어져야 한다.

offensive 공격적인 distracting 주의를 분산시키는

UNIT 111~112

Check-up P. 32~33

111	**1.** Whatever	**2.** Whatever
112	**1.** whom	**2.** which

111

1. What은 부사절을 이끌 수 없음

당신의 성이 무엇이든, 우리는 당신의 조상과 그들의 직업을 알 수 있다.

2. What은 부사절을 이끌 수 없음

둘 사이의 다음 토론이 무엇이든, 그들의 목적에 있어서는 명백하게 중요한 문제이다.

112

1. 문장 두 개가 연결되므로 whom이 적절

5백 명의 군중이 기차를 맞이했는데, 그들 중 일부는 3시간 넘게 기다리고 있었다.

2. 문장 두 개가 연결되므로 which가 적절

그는 첼시에서 80경기에 출전해서 7골을 득점했고, 그 골 모두는 마지막 시즌에 넣었다.

EXERCISE P. 34

01 Whoever **02** which **03** them **04** which **05** them **06** which **07** whoever **08** whom **09** which **10** neglect of which

01 선행사가 없으므로 선행사를 포함하는 관계대명사가 필요

이 나라를 통치하고픈 사람은 누구든지 선거에서 이기기 위해서 다른 인종 집단들에게 호소해야만 한다.

02 접속사가 없으므로 which가 적절

비와 녹은 눈은 수십 개의 호수로 흘러들어 가며, 그중 4개는 현지인들에 의해 신성시 되고 있다.

03 접속사 and가 있으므로 them이 적절

강당은 학생들이 꽉 차서 너무 붐볐고, 그들 중 일부는 바닥에 앉아야만 했다.

04 접속사가 없으므로 which가 적절

논리는 폭넓고 잘 정의된 일련의 규칙과 지침을 가지는데, 그중 상당수는 모두 너무 쉬워서 무심코 위반한다.

05 접속사 while이 있으므로 them이 적절

세상에는 부유하게 되고, 권력을 가지는 방법이 많이 있지만, 그들 중 일부는 사람을 파멸 직전에 이르게 할 수 있다.

06 접속사가 없으므로 which가 적절

혈액 내에 더 증가된 코티졸의 수치는 부정적인 효과를 가지며, 그중 하나는 복부 지방을 늘리는 것이다.

07 선행사가 없으므로 선행사를 포함하는 관계대명사가 필요

지식 자체가 권력인 현대 사회에서, 우리는 정보를 잘 얻을 것 같은 사람은 누구든지 인생에서 성공할 것 같다.

08 접속사가 없으므로 whom이 적절

논쟁이 되는 등급 매기기 서비스는 많은 동전 딜러와 수집가의 존중을 받고 있으며, 그중 일부는 맹목적으로 받아들여 진다.

09 접속사가 없으므로 which가 적절

만약 현 정부가 보험이 없는 수백 만의 사람들을 위해서 보험금을 지원하는 것을 도우려면 노인 의료 보험 비용을 위해 상당한 비축금을 찾아내야 할 것인데 적어도 그중 일부는 과도한 치료를 줄이는 것에서 나와야 한다.

10 접속사가 없으므로 neglect of which가 적절

똑같이 중요한 다른 고려사항들이 있는데, 그것을 무시하면 나중에 좌절하게 될 수도 있다.

ACTUAL TEST P. 35

01 ③ **02** ③

01 ③ 접속사가 없으므로 them이 아니라 which가 돼야 함, buys의 목적어가 되는 목적격 관계대명사 필요 ① '더 가깝게' ② by의 목적어 ④ cash가 주어, was가 동사 ⑤ 완전한 문장을 이끄는 how 의문사

창고업과 유통업에 있어서 배송비와 시장에의 근접성은 매우 중요하다. 창고가 가까이 있다면, 많은 회사들은 재고를 고객에 보다 가깝게 유지할 수 있으며, 그래서 홍보 판매와 배송 시간을 줄이게 된다. 예를 들어 텍사스에 있는 딕시 웍스는 재고를 전국에 있는 32개의 창고에 분산함으로써 가정용 의료 용품의 유통에 있어서 경쟁력을 얻었다. 딕시는 병원용 침대와 휠체어, 그리고 다른 환자 용품을 고객에게 파는 중간 상인에게 판매하는데, 그 용품 중 일부는 그 회사가 다른 회사로부터 구매한 것이다. 이전에 상인들은 3주 정도 배송을 기다려야 했는데, 이는 많은 현금이 넘쳐 나는 재고에 묶여 있다는 것을 의미했다. 딕시의 새로운 유통망과 함께 상인들은 한 개의 회사로부터 당일 배송을 받는다. 딕시의 위치 전략은 적절한 배달이 어떻게 경쟁력이 될 수 있는지를 보여주고 있다.

warehousing 창고업 distribution 분배 proximity 근접성 inventory 재고 decentralize 분산시키다 surplus 잉여

02 (A) 자동사이므로 belongs가 적절 (B) 접속사가 없으므로 which가 적절 (C) 언어가 사람들에 의해 말해지는 것이므로 spoken by가 적절

맬러개시는 아프리카의 남동쪽 해안에서 떨어진 곳에 위치한 섬나라인 마다가스카르에서 쓰이는 언어이다. 1500만의 사용자들은 그 나라 거의 전체 인구를 포함한다. 맬러개시는 아프리카 어족 중 하나에 속한다고 보는 것이 논리적일 것이다. 하지만, 그렇지 않다. 사실 그것은 오스트로네시아 어족 중 하나이고, 그 어족의 나머지 언어는 동쪽으로 수천 킬로미터 떨어진 동남아시아에서 주로 쓰인다. 맬러개시는 동남아시아 보르네오섬에 사는 다야크 족 사람들에 의

해 사용되는 언어 중 한 그룹과 가장 밀접하게 연관이 있다.

virtually 사실상 assume 추정하다 family 어족(語族)

UNIT 113~114

Check-up P. 36

113 **1.** who **2.** that 114 **1.** where **2.** where

113

1. 선행사는 15 states가 아니라 students이므로 who가 적절

그 연구는 2007 ~ 2008년과 2009 ~ 2010년 사이에 1학년에서 3학년에 재학 중이었던 학생들의 학업 수행을 분석한다.

2. the graceful ~ the river가 선행사이므로 that이 적절

나는 어린 시절부터 기억했던 우아한 곡선들, 나무가 우거진 고지, 강을 따라 반사된 모습에 대한 기대로 탑승하면서 몹시 설레었다.

114

1. 뒤에 완전한 문장이 왔으므로 where가 적절

영아돌연사증후군은 아이와 부모가 같은 침대에서 자는 문화에서는 덜 흔하고, 이는 잠자는 위치가 중요할 수도 있다는 것을 암시한다.

2. 뒤에 완전한 문장이 왔으므로 where가 적절

킴은 다음 달에 열리는 세계 선수권 대회의 금메달을 목표로 하고 있는데 이 대회는 그녀가 이기고 싶어 하는 대회 중 하나이다.

EXERCISE P. 38

01 which **02** which **03** why **04** where **05** where
06 where **07** where **08** where **09** who **10** where

01 전치사 in의 목적어가 되는 관계대명사 which가 적절

칼이 꽂혀 있는 그 장소에 한 어린 소년이 나타났다.

02 앞에 전치사가 있으므로 관계대명사 which가 적절

한순간 닐슨은 남극 대륙은 영혼을 쓸 수 있는 백지 상태라고 썼다.

03 뒤에 완전한 문장이 오므로 관계부사 why가 적절

즐거운 독서가 당신의 영어 실력을 향상시키는 데 아주 효과적인 방법이라는 것에는 세 가지 주된 이유가 있다.

04 뒤에 완전한 문장이 오므로 관계부사 where가 적절

선인의 군대는 위의 군대를 좁은 길로 꾀어 내어 후퇴했는데, 그곳에서 그들은 매복하고 있다가 위의 군대를 공격했다.

05 뒤에 완전한 문장이 오므로 관계부사 where가 적절

젊은이다운 낙관주의와 한때 불가능했던 꿈이 실현되는 미래를 상상하는 기대의 순간이다.

06 뒤에 완전한 문장이 오므로 관계부사 where가 적절

그들에게 있어 노인들이 기술을 연습할 수 있는 무도회를 준비하는 것은 쉬운 일이 아니다.

07 뒤에 완전한 문장이 오므로 관계부사 where가 적절

글을 읽고 쓸 줄 아는 사람들이 거의 대부분인 인도 남부의 주 케랄라에서는 유아 사망률이 개발 도상국 중에서 가장 낮다.

08 뒤에 완전한 문장이 오므로 관계부사 where가 적절

방문객들은 랄프 로렌의 직물로 치장된 260개의 손님방과 옛 아이리쉬 스타일의 재즈를 듣게 될 Piano Bar 식당을 보게 될 것입니다.

09 선행사인 the English는 영국인을 지칭하고, gave의 주어가 없으므로 주격 관계대명사가 적절

1762년에 이 섬은 영국인에 의해 점령되었는데, 그들은 그 다음 해에 파리 조약에 의해 프랑스인에게 섬을 반환했다.

10 뒤에 완전한 문장이 오므로 관계부사 where가 적절

우리는 열대 지방의 집약농업에 대한 전망을 낙관할 수 없는데, 현재 기술로서는 열대지방의 토양에서 집약농업을 지속하지 못할 것이다.

ACTUAL TEST P. 39

01 ⑤ **02** ①

01 ⑤ 뒤에 완전한 문장이 오므로 which가 아니라 where가 적절 ① 병렬 구조로 앞의 that절과 연결, think의 목적어절을 이끎 ② 〈as+형용사+a+명사〉의 어순 ③ '영감을 받다, 고무되다' ④ 주어는 동명사 doing이므로 단수

정치인들은 분명한 목적의식을 가진다. 정치적 지도자가 전체로서의 사회의 복지를 찾고, 그들이 효율과 공평의 최적의 조화를 목표로 하고 있다고 생각하는 것은 좋다. 이 말은 우리에게 좋아 보이지만, 사실적이지는 않다. 이기심은 다른 사람들과 마찬가지로 정치적인 사람들에게 강력한 동기이다. 어떤 정치인들은 재선되기를 원하는 마음에 의해 고무되고, 그와 같은 일을 하는 것이 자신을 지지하는 유권자들에게 자신들이 영향력을 강화할 때 국가적 이익을 기꺼이 희생시키고자 한다. 다른 정치인들은 단순한 탐욕에 동기를 가지게 된다. 만약 당신이 이러한 사실을 의심한다면 가난한 나라들을 살펴봐야 하는데, 정부 관리들의 부패는 경제 성장의 공통된 장애물이다.

welfare 복지 optimal 최적의 equity 공평 inspire 고무하다 sacrifice 희생하다 motivate 동기화하다 corruption 부패

02 (A) A new job opportunity가 선행사이므로 what은 올 수 없음 (B) 뒤에 부사가 오므로 however가 적절 (C) 2문형 동사 felt 다음에 오므로 형용사 wonderful이 적절

연봉 4만 달러에 흥미로운 일을 만족스럽게 하고 있는 한 여성을 상상해 보자. 그녀에게 연봉 6만 달러를 제공하는 새로운 취업 기회가 생겼다. 그녀는 직업을 바꿨지만, 유감스럽게도 6개월 후에 그 새 회사는 파산했다. 이전 회사는 그녀가 다시 돌아와서 행복하다. 사실 너무 행복해서 그녀의 연봉을 4만 5천 달러로 인상해 주었다. 그녀가 이 연봉 인상에 행복할까? 연봉 인상처럼 느껴지기나 할까? 대답은 아마도 '아니다'일 것이다. 아무리 잠시 동안 받았다 할지라도 연봉 6만 달러는 새로운 기준선을 그녀에게 설정해 주었고 그래서 그보다 더 적은 것은 손해로 여겨지는 것이다. 비록 6개월 전만 하더라도 연봉 4만 달러에서 4만 5천 달러로의 인상은 정말 멋진 것이었겠지만 지금은 6만 달러에서 4만 5천 달러로 삭감된 것처럼 느껴지는 것이다. 한때 충분히 좋았고 그보다 심지어 훨씬 더 좋았던 것이 이제 더 이상 좋지 않다.

contentedly 만족스럽게 arise 발생하다 switch 바꾸다 establish 설립하다 baseline 토대

UNIT 115~116

Check-up P. 40~41

115 **1.** them **2.** which **116** **1.** that **2.** which

115

1. 접속사 and가 있으므로 them이 적절

그 시스템은 너무 복잡하고 너무 많은 회사와 관련되어 있으며, 그 중 중 일부는 하청을 받는다고 한다.

2. 접속사가 없으므로 which가 적절

더 많은 질문이 있을 것 같은데 그 중 70%는 여기 있는 사람들이 대답할 수 있을지도 모른다.

116

1. voices가 선행사이고, belonged의 주어가 되는 주격 관계대명사가 필요. he believed that belonged to ~라는 문장에서 관계대명사가 선행사 가까이 위치하기 위해 앞으로 나옴

1425년, 13세의 나이에 마틴은 그가 믿기에 초기 기독교 성자들의 목소리라고 생각되는 소리를 들었다고 주장했다.

2. 앞에 선행사 the cost가 있으므로 what은 올 수 없음

그는 자신이 생각하기에 5달러쯤 될 것 같은 비용을 지불하지 않았다.

EXERCISE

P. 42

01 who 02 which 03 whom 04 them 05 that
06 them 07 which 08 which 09 them 10 which

01 is의 주어가 되는 주격 관계대명사가 필요. as you know는 삽입구

아시다시피 잭은 자격이 없는 소년 중 한 사람일 뿐이에요.

02 is의 주어가 되는 주격 관계대명사가 필요. ~ I think which is ~에서 관계대명사가 선행사 가까이 있기 위해 앞으로 나옴

내 생각에 다음 주에 개최될 예정이었던 세미나가 다음 달 말까지 연기되었다.

03 접속사가 없으므로 whom이 적절

맥은 20여 개국에 지점이 있고, 10만 명의 직원이 있는데, 그들 대부분은 주요 대도시권 밖에서 살고 있다.

04 접속사 and가 있으므로 them이 적절

준비된 주제에 관해 아무것도 모르던 두 남자는 요점 없는 미사여구만 잔뜩 늘어놓았다.

05 was의 주어가 되는 주격 관계대명사가 필요. ~ he though that was ~에서 관계대명사가 선행사 가까이 있기 위해 앞으로 나옴

그가 거대한 흰 고래라고 생각한 하얀색 덩어리를 누가 봤나요?

06 접속사 and가 있으므로 them이 적절

우리의 과거에 대한 이해는 대개 글로 남겨진 기록에 근거를 두고 있으며, 모든 기록은 많은 전문가들에 의해서 해석되어야만 한다.

07 접속사가 없으므로 which가 적절

포터 여사는 작은 곰과 개를 만들기 시작했으며, 그중 곰은 미국에서 큰 성공을 거두었다.

08 접속사가 없으므로 which가 적절

나는 '타잔', '지구의 중심에서'와 같은 공상 과학 소설을 읽었는데, 그것은 모두 에드거 라이스에 의해 쓰였다.

09 접속사 and가 있으므로 them이 적절

유머와 사랑 외에도 그 뮤지컬은 다른 주제를 제공하는데 그중 하나는 자기 내면의 목소리에 귀를 기울이는 것이다.

10 접속사가 없으므로 which가 적절

세계보건기구는 작년에 약 10만 명을 사망으로 이끈 710만 건의 사건이 발생했다고 발표했는데, 그중 대부분은 저개발국에서 발생했다.

ACTUAL TEST

P. 43

01 ⑤ 02 ④

01 ⑤ 접속사가 없으므로 it이 아니라 문장을 연결해 주는 which가 돼야 함 ① make의 목적격 보어 ② 의미를 잃어버리게 될 수도 있다는 뜻 ③ because of+명사(구) ④ much of the original script가 주어, is가 동사

대부분의 감독들은 오늘날의 사회에 더욱 적합하게 만들기 위해서 원본에 적어도 몇 가지 변화를 만드는 것을 선택할지도 모른다. 이것은 원본의 의미 중 일부를 잃을 수도 있다는 것을 의미하는 반면, 마지막 결과물은 현대 관객에게 친숙하지 않은 그러한 요소의 생략 때문에 더 효과적일 수 있다. 하지만, 이러한 것은 감독들에게 자신의 해석을 극에 부여할 더 많은 범위를 제공하는데, 그것은 원래 의도한 의미와 효과를 왜곡할 수 있다. 비록 파올로 파졸리니의 오이디푸스 왕 안에 원본 스크립트의 상당 부분이 보존되어 있다고 하더라도 많은 변화가 이루어졌는데, 그것은 원본의 의미를 바꾸고 감독 자신의 경험에 특별한 의미를 추가하였다.

omission 생략 **intended** 의도된 **distort** 왜곡하다 **interpretation** 해석 **script** 원고 **preserve** 보존하다

02 (A) social scientific practice가 선행사이고, 뒤에 완전한 문장이 오므로 관계부사 where가 적절 (B) the positive instances가 선행사이므로 that이 적절 (C) 접속사가 없으므로 which가 적절

증거가 사용되는 사회과학 연구의 수행에서도 때때로 그것은 적합한 과학적 검증을 위해 올바르게 사용되지 않는다. 사회과학에 있어 많은 경우, 증거는 오직 특정한 이론을 증명하기 위하여, 즉 그것을 뒷받침하는 긍정적인 사례를 찾기 위하여 이용된다. 그러나 이것들은 알아내기 쉬우며 사회과학에서 널리 알려진 딜레마로 이끄는데, 두 상충되는 이론이 있을 때, 각각의 이론들은 자신을 지지하는 긍정적인 실증적 증거를 주장하지만 각각은 반대의 결과를 낸다는 것이다. 그것들 사이에서 우리는 어떻게 결정해야 하는가? 여기서 증거의 과학적인 이용이 도움이 될 것이다. 과학에 대한 독특한 점은 부정적인 사례를 찾는다는 것인데, 즉 이론을 증명하는 것 대신 거짓임을 입증하는 방법을 찾는 것이다. 과학적인 검증의 진짜 힘은 긍정적인 것이 아니라 부정적인 것이다. 검증은 그저 우리의 이론을 확증해 주는 것이 아니라 그 증거와 일치하지 않는 것을 제거하게 해준다.

bankroll 자금을 지원하다 sip 홀짝 마시다 swap 교환하다 suspicious 의심스러운 freak 변종 courtesy 예의 bon-mot 농담

REVIEW TEST P. 44

01 which → where 02 whom → whose 03 which → where 04 what → that 05 them → which 06 them 07 what 08 where 09 whose 10 which

01 which 뒤에 완전한 문장이 왔으므로 which가 아니라 관계대명사가 the specific circumstance를 선행사로 받는 관계부사가 필요

남자가 여자에게 말을 거는 특정한 상황에서 남자들이 그들의 파트너보다 10% 덜 웃었다.

02 the guy's 1988 book이라는 의미로 whom이 아니라 소유격을 대신하는 소유격 관계대명사가 필요

스티븐 호킹은 '시간의 역사'라는 1988년에 쓰여진 역사상 가장 읽혀지지 않은 베스트셀러라고 판명된 책의 저자이다.

03 which 뒤에 완전한 절이 왔으므로 which가 아니라 Vietnam을 선행사로 받는 관계부사 필요

그것은 베트남에서는 비교적 새롭고 젊음을 지향하는 현상으로, 나라가 중앙계획에서 자본주의로 변해감에 따라 소비지상주의는 비로소 시작되었고, 성장하기 시작했다.

04 what 뒤에 나오는 문장이 완전하므로 what이 아니라 보어절을 이끄는 접속사 that이 필요

추론의 공통적 특성은 그것은 직접적으로 알려져 있지 않은 문제들에 대한 진술이라는 것이다.

05 접속사가 없으므로 them이 아니라 which가 적절

그 연구팀은 영국 학생들에게 독일어 문장 모음 읽기를 부탁했는데, 그 문장 중 일부는 양쪽 언어에서 비슷해 보이고 같은 의미를 지니고 있는 단어들을 포함하고 있었다.

06 접속사 If가 있으므로 them이 적절

만약 내가 50명의 학생들에게 로마제국이 멸망한 이유에 대해 5장 분량의 에세이를 써오라고 한다면, 그들 중 대부분은 궁극적으로 국력의 약화를 이끈 경제적, 사회적 원인의 결합이라고 말할 것이다.

07 class는 선행사가 아니므로 관계대명사 what이 적절

맨체스터 유나이티드의 선수는 국제 무대에서 그의 마지막 토너먼트가 될 경기에서 그의 탁월함을 보여주었다.

08 뒤에 완전한 문장이 나오므로 관계부사가 적절

사람들은 아이들이 편안하고 안전하다는 느끼는 즐겁고 보호적인 환경을 만들기 위해 최선을 다한다.

09 answers of the inquires라는 의미이므로 소유격을 대신하는 소유격 관계대명사가 필요

그 교수는 질문을 했는데, 그 질문의 대답은 처음 그룹이 따뜻하고, 두 번째 그룹은 차갑다는 그들의 추측이 사실임을 확인해 주었다.

10 20 installations를 선행사로 받으면서 can be called의 주어가 되는 주격 관계대명사 필요. in archeological terms는 삽입구

발굴을 통해 최소한 20개의 설치 미술품들이 존재한다는 것을 발견했는데, 그 발견물은 고고학적 관점에서 신전이라 부를 수 있는 것이다.

FINAL CHECK P. 45~47

01 ④ 02 ④ 03 ② 04 ⑤ 05 ④ 06 ⑤

01 ④ 주어가 없는 불완전한 문장이 오므로 that이 아니라 what이 돼야 함 ① '멸종된 이유' ② 매머드가 사냥된 것 ③ 앞 문장을 선행사로 받는 계속적 용법의 관계대명사 ⑤ 사역동사 make의 목적격 보어

한 연구는 왜 매머드가 2만 1천 년 전에 멸종되었는지 밝혔다. 지금까지 사람들은 코끼리의 친척인 매머드가 사냥되었기 때문에 멸종되었다고 믿어왔다. 영국의 더럼 대학에서 주도한 연구에 따르면, 그들은 풀이 부족했는데, 이는 지구 온난화로 인해 발생되었다. 지구가 더워지면서 매머드는 풀을 뜯을 땅을 잃어버렸다. 이 연구는 매머드에게 발생했던 것이 오늘날 풀을 먹는 동물인 다수의 초식동물에게 발생할 수 있다고 경고했다. "중요한 환경 변화와 서식지의 상실은 코끼리 같은 몸집이 큰 동물의 멸종을 야기할 수 있습니다. 게다가 이런 상황은 악화되고 있습니다. 인간이 경작지를 확장하기 위해서 숲을 개발하는 동안 우리는 대형 초식 동물들이 비슷한 운명을 겪게 만들고 있습니다. 인간이 야기한 서식지 변화는 환경적 재앙이 될 수 있습니다"라고 연구원 중 한 명이 말했다.

mammoth 매머드 extinct 멸종된 herbivore 초식동물 habitat 서식지 cropland 경지

02 (A) 앞에 선행사(the light)가 오므로 that이 적절 (B) most of the material이 주어이므로 is가 적절 (C) 가장 일반적인 방법이라는 뜻으로 The most가 적절

과학자들은 우리가 볼 수 있는 빛으로 우주를 알게 된다. 빛은 전파, 엑스선, 감마선 발산의 형태이다. 하지만, 빛나지 않는 물질이 있다면 어떨까? 어떻게 우리는 그것이 있다는 것을 알게 될까? 그런 물질은 암흑 물질이라고 부르며, 현재 천문학자들은 우주에 있는 대부분의 물질은 이 물질로 이루어져 있다고 생각한다. 이 물질은 우리가 그것을 직접적으로 관찰할 충분한 빛을 발산하지 않는 물질이다. 그러나 간접적으로 이 물질을 발견할 수 있는 다양한 방법이 있다. 가장 일반적인 방법은 암흑 물질은 빛과 광원 모두에 대해서 중력을 가지고 있다는 사실과 연관된다. 이것은 우리가 암흑 물질이 얼마나 무거운지를 측정할 수 있게 한다.

radio wave 전파 emission 발산 glow 빛나다 sufficient 충분한 detect 발견하다 gravitational pull 중력

03 ② 선행사가 없고, wear의 목적어가 없는 불완전한 문장이 왔으므로 that이 아니라 what이 돼야 함 ① 전치사 for의 목적어 ③ All we have to do가 주어, is가 동사 ④ '교복이 없다면' ⑤ find의 목적격 보어로 형용사(구)가 옴

우리 학생들은 시행착오를 통해 배울 기회를 충분히 제공받고 있지 않다. 이것이 내가 교복에 반대하는 이유 중 하나다. 우리는 선택을 전혀 하지 않기 때문에, 입을 옷을 고르는 데 실수를 하지 않는다. 우리가 해야 할 일은 매일 똑같은 교복을 입는 것뿐이다. 교복이 없다면 우리는 선택을 해야만 할 것이다. 그러면 가끔 우리는 우리의 선택이 잘못되었거나 장소에 어울리지 않는다는 것을 알게 될 것이다. 우리는 그것을 통해 배울 것이다. 교복은 우리에게서 실수를 통해 배울 수 있는 소중한 기회를 빼앗았다.

trial and error 시행착오 out of place 장소에 어울리지 않는 deprive A of B B에게서 A를 빼앗다

04 (A) 역할이라는 측면에서 고려되는 것이므로 be considered가 적절 (B) 〈as+부사/형용사의 원급+as〉 구문이므로 far가 적절 (C) 전치사의 목적어가 되는 관계대명사 which가 적절

두뇌는 생존 도구이고, 두뇌의 다양한 능력인 이성, 직관, 인지, 감정은 각 유기체가 생존하도록 돕는 역할을 한다는 측면에서 고려되어야 하는 기술이다. 신체의 다른 모든 기관과 마찬가지로 두뇌는 진화 과정에 의해 형성되어 왔다. 진화의 각 단계에서 두뇌는 우리 조상이 환경을 이용하고 적절한 행동을 취할 수 있는 능력을 누릴 수 있도록 하기 위한 자연 도태에 의해서 만들어졌다. 여기서 핵심 단어는 바로 행동이다. 두뇌의 기본적인 디자인은 신체적인 면을 추구한다. 즉, 식량을 찾고 자신과 가족을 위한 안식처를 찾고 번식에 성공하며, 가족을 보호하고, 친구를 사귀고 좋은 지위를 얻고, 가능한 멀리 환경을 통제하는 것을 말이다. 두뇌는 철학적인 고찰, 정신적인 명상, 재정적인 처리나 경제 시험을 보는 것을 위해서 만들어지지 않았다. 다시 말해서, 두뇌는 지금 원래의 목적이 아니었던 다양한 기능을 수행하고 있다.

intuition 직감 perception 인지 in terms of ~의 측면에서 organism 유기체 evolutionary 진화적인 bless 축복하다 reproduction 번식 philosophic 철학적인 speculation 고찰 contemplation 명상

05 ④ 뒤에 완전한 문장이 오며 선행사가 시간이므로 which가 아니라 when이 돼야 함 ① 〈the 비교급, the 비교급〉 구문 ② 전치사 about에 걸리는 동명사 ③ 〈one of the 복수 명사〉 구문 ⑤ 명령문

불행히도 은퇴 예금은 최근의 경제 변동성에 면역력이 없습니다. 여러분의 은퇴가 점점 다가올수록, 여러분은 당연히 주식 시장의 하락에 의해 타격을 받을 당신의 투자에 대해서 더 걱정하게 됩니다. 이런 때에, 사람들은 더 많은 보장과, 적은 위험 부담, 기본적으로 돈에 대한 안전한 피난처를 찾고 있습니다. 우리 회사에서는 연금이 여전히 여러분의 은퇴를 보호할 최고의 방법 중 하나라고 믿습니다. 예를 들어, 낙관론자들은 우리가 위험에 대한 당신의 욕구에 따라 투자할 장소에 대한 선택을 제공할 것이라는 사실을 선호합니다. 명백히 여러분의 특정한 계획의 가치는 변동을 거듭할 것이고, 여러분이 원금을 되찾지 못하는 시기도 있을 수 있습니다. 염려되고 걱정되는 분들이 보장 옵션이 있는 우리 펀드에 끌린다면, 당신의 돈을 우리에게 투자하세요. 당신은 최소한 원금은 돌려받고 적은 수수료를 부담하게 될 것을 확신할 수 있습니다.

immune 면역의 volatility 변동성 guarantee 보장하다 haven 피난처 pension 연금 appetite 욕구 fluctuate 변동을 거듭하다 gravitate 끌리다

06 (A) '사람들이 어떻게 텔레비전에 반응하는지를' determine의 목적어절을 이끄는 how가 적절 (B) 대명사는 동사와 부사 사이에 오므로 turning it off가 적절 (C) 선행사가 없고 뒤에 주어가 없는 불완전한 문장이 오므로 what이 적절

텔레비전이 사람의 뇌 속에서 고유한 반응을 활성화시키는 것은 확실하다. 이런 반응으로 인해 특별히 건강에 해로운 것은 없지만, 문제의 소지가 있다. 사람들이 텔레비전에 대해 생리학적으로 그리고 행동학적으로 어떻게 반응하는지 밝히기 위해 연구들이 수행되어져 왔다. 이러한 연구들은 텔레비전을 시청하는 동안 사람들이 느긋해지고 수동적이고 경계심을 덜 느낀다는 것을 보여준다. 이런 느긋해진 느낌은 텔레비전이 꺼지는 순간 곧 사라진다. 그러나 수동적인 느낌과 긴장감이 약해진 정도는 그대로 지속된다. 이것이 바로 어떤 행동에 중독되게 만드는 것이다. 그것은 끊기도 어렵고, 사람들의 삶을 지배한다. 이러한 정의는 텔레비전 시청자들에게도 적용되는 것 같다. 그와 같이 텔레비전을 켜는 행동은 편안함이라는 긍정적인 느낌으로 인해 긍정적으로 강화되지만, 텔레비전을 끄는 것은 불쾌한데 그것은 다른 부정적인 느낌은 지속되는데 반해 편안함의 느낌은 없어지기 때문이다.

intrinsic 고유한 physiologically 생리학적으로 behaviorally 행동학적으로 alert 경계하는 passivity 수동성 diminish 약해지다 persist 지속하다

chapter 11 분사구문

UNIT 117~118

Check-up P. 50

117	**1.** crossing	**2.** Examining
118	**1.** painted	**2.** Watched

117

1. 내(I)가 길을 건너는 것이므로 능동

학교로 가는 도중에 길을 건너는 동안, 나는 사고를 당했다.

2. 그들(they)이 검사하는 것이므로 능동

주의 깊게 표면을 검사한 후, 그들은 품질에 대한 실망감을 나타냈다.

118

1. 그 집(the house)이 색칠이 되는 것이므로 수동

그 집은 다양한 색들로 밝게 칠해져서 많은 이목을 끌었다.

2. 그런 사건(a happening)이 관찰되는 것이므로 수동

다양한 각도에서 보면, 여기의 그런 사건은 빠르게 감기는 비디오와 비슷할 것이다.

EXERCISE P. 52

01 exporting **02** interested **03** giving
04 photographed **05** remind **06** Following
07 imposed **08** needed **09** promoted **10** Found

01 인도가 수출을 하는 것이므로 능동

인도는 두 번째로 큰 차 생산국인데, 매년 4억 파운드를 수출한다.

02 학생들이 흥미를 느끼는 것이므로 수동

그 자리에 관심이 있는 학생들은 급우들에게 말할 것이다.

03 판매 촉진 목적으로 가스 마일리지나 수리 교환권을 주는 것이므로 능동, 뒤에 본동사 would be가 나옴

차의 가스 마일리지나 수리 교환권을 주는 광고는 구매자들에게 더 중요하다.

04 얼굴의 사진이 찍히는 것이므로 수동

그것이 영화 배우들이 자신의 얼굴 중 이쪽이 사진 찍히는 것을 선호하는 이유이다.

05 주어 없이 문장이 성립되어야 하므로 명령문이 적질

만약 당신의 라이벌이 잘 할 때 위협을 느낀다면, 당신 스스로에게 당신의 강인함과 성공을 연상하도록 해라.

06 문장을 연결하는 접속사가 없으므로 분사가 적절

산업적 관심이 2차 세계대전 이후 디자인으로 옮겨질 때 시작된 쇠락 기간 후, 케빈의 회사는 이제 창조적인 건축의 목표로 성공했다.

07 업무 제약이 부과하는 것이 아니라 부과되는 것이므로 수동

직원 스케줄에 부과된 업무 제약은 직원 채용 계획이 제공하는 자질과 자격 요건이다.

08 시간이 필요한 것이 아니라 시간을 필요로 하는 것이므로 수동

강의들의 전체적인 스케줄은 지금 단 세 시간 안에 만들어질 수 있으며 이는 교수 선호도의 갈등을 해결하기 위해서 필요한 시간을 포함한다.

09 무역이 촉진하는 것이 아니라 촉진되는 것이므로 수동

현재 물 다음 두 번째로 가장 일반적인 음료인 차의 소비는 영국의 동인도회사가 촉진했던 무역을 19세기에 시작하면서 아시아에서 다른 나라로 확장되었다.

10 제보아가 발견하는 것이 아니라 발견되는 것이므로 수동

아프리카와 아시아 모두의 다양한 서식지에서 발견된 제보아는 밝은 모래색과 짙은 모래색 털로 구별되는 조그마한 설치류이다.

ACTUAL TEST

P. 53

01 ① **02** ③

01 ① 본동사가 없으므로 being이 아니라 is가 돼야 함 ② book을 받는 one ③ to let ~을 진목적어로 받는 가목적어 it ④ To let이 이끄는 to부정사구가 주어, is가 동사 ⑤ 〈when it comes to -ing〉 '~에 대해서'

'짧은' 혹은 '쉬운'이라는 생각은 무엇을 읽을지를 선택하는데 있어 사용되는 일반적인 기준 중 하나이지만, 어떤 사람들은 이 생각이 게으름을 의미한다고 생각한다. 그들은 짧거나 쉬운 책은 좋은 책이 아니라고 생각한다. 하지만, 이것은 학생들이 책을 읽는 것을 멀리하게 할 수 있다. 예를 들어, 많은 학생이 학교로 가는 버스 안에서 읽을 수 있도록 일부러 짧은 책을 선택한다. 학생들은 그런 것이 책 선택 과정의 일부가 되는 것을 당연시 한다. 특별한 의미 부여 없이 책을 책으로 여기는 것은 일반 독자들에게 그리 복잡한 것이 아니다. 만약 누군가가 책 선택에 있어서 책의 페이지 수를 강요한다면, 이는 학생들의 독서하려는 의욕을 꺾을 수 있다.

purposely 고의로 **take A for granted** A를 당연시 여기다 **impose** 강요하다 **discourage** 의욕을 꺾다

02 (A) A primary source가 주어이므로 is가 적절 (B) 해가 입히는 것이 아니라 입혀지는 것이므로 수동인 done이 적절 (C) 선행사가 없고 is의 주어가 없으므로 What이 적절

환경 문제의 근본적인 원인은 깨끗한 공기와 맑은 강, 다른 환경 자원들이 사유재가 아니라 공공재라는 점이다. 만약에 네가 양을 기르고 있고 당신과 당신의 이웃은 방목을 위해 공통으로 땅을 공유한다고 가정해 보자. 소득을 늘리기 위해 당신은 더 많은 양을 길러 그 땅에서 풀을 뜯게 하고 싶을 것이다. 만약 그렇게 한다면 양들이 지나치게 많이 풀을 뜯어 먹게 되어 땅을 훼손시킬 수도 있지만 양을 그만큼 더 키움으로써 그 이익은 다 취하면서, 공유지에 가해진 훼손에 대한 비용은 일부만 부담하게 될 것이다. 그러므로 당신은 기존의 양떼 무리에 양을 하나 추가하고 아마도 또 추가할 것이다. 하지만 공유지를 사용하는 모든 이들은 그와 똑같은 계산을 하고, 자기만의 이익을 위하여 양떼의 수를 늘리게 된다. 결국에는 풀을 지나치게 뜯게 함으로써 공유지를 파괴할 만큼 문제가 심각해진다. 아리스토텔레스의 말을 빌면, "가장 많은 사람이 공유하는 것은 가장 적은 관심을 받는다."

goods 물건 **graze** 풀을 뜯어먹다, 방목하다 **property** 자산 **calculation** 계산 **self-interest** 이기심 **herd** 무리

UNIT 119~120

Check-up P. 54~55

119 **1.** There being **2.** Tom Clancy writing

120 **1.** 배리 그레이저는 행복했음에도 불구하고 하퍼 섬을 여행하면서 또 다른 모험을 찾으려고 노력했다.

2. 그레이 박사는 유능한 의사였기 때문에 환자를 치료하고 심각한 병을 다루는 데 실패한 적이 없다.

119

1. 주어가 다르므로 분사구문에 주어 필요

마을에 버스가 다니지 않으므로, 우리는 한 시간 동안 학교로 걸어가야만 했다.

2. 주어가 다르므로 분사구문에 주어 필요

탐 클랜시가 수필 형식으로 그의 소설을 쓰기 때문에 그의 많은 작품은 많은 독자들을 끌어당긴다.

EXERCISE

P. 56

01 The royal family having **02** needed **03** speaking **04** Judging **05** Considering **06** Being written **07** being very rich **08** It being **09** Informed **10** There being

01 주어가 다르므로 분사 구문에 주어 필요

왕족이 도착해서 그들을 위해 마련된 자리에 착석했을 때 개회식이 시작되었다.

02 if 다음에 being이 생략된 분사구문

출구 쪽 열에 앉은 사람들은 여분의 다리를 놓아둘 공간이 있지만 필요한 경우 비상구를 열어야 하는 책임 또한 있다.

03 strictly speaking '엄격하게 말하자면'

단호하게 말하면 당신은 규칙을 어겼지만 우리는 당신이 실수를 만회할 수 있는 기회를 한 번 더 주기로 결정했다.

04 judging from '~로 판단하건대'

토니가 어울리는 친구들의 행동으로 판단하건대, 그는 틀림없이 문제에 직면하게 될 것이다.

05 considering '~을 고려하면'

약한 소비 의욕을 감안할 때, 정부는 경제를 되살리기 위해 더 적극적인 조치를 취하는 것 밖에 선택의 여지가 없다는 것을 안다.

06 분사구문의 수동형

쉬운 영어로 쓰여 있어서 이 책은 아이들이 읽기가 쉽다.

07 주절과 주어가 다를 경우 being은 생략하지 않음

그는 부자이면서 은퇴하기 때문에 줄리는 그와 결혼하고 싶어 한다.

08 주절과 주어가 다르므로 분사구문에 주어 필요

어제 날씨가 좋았기 때문에 우리는 소풍을 가서 아이들과 즐거운 시간을 보냈다.

09 컴퓨터 수리 기사에게 알려진 것이므로 수동, being이 생략됨

즉시 연락을 했기 때문에 컴퓨터 수리 기사가 오늘 저녁까지 잃어버리고 손상된 데이터를 복구할 것이다.

10 there be 구문, 주절의 주어와 다르므로 There being이 적절

신의 존재에 옹호하거나 반박할만한 명확한 증거가 없으므로, 과학은 무엇이 옳은지 판단할 수 없다.

ACTUAL TEST

P. 57

01 ⑤ 02 ③

01 ⑤ 뒤의 내용이 원인에 해당하므로 why가 아니라 because가 돼야 함 ① your bare feet을 의미 ② '조개껍질로 장식된', castle을 수식하는 분사 ③ 주절과 주어가 다른 분사구문 ④ '비록 ~일지라도'

당신이 해변에 있고 파도가 부서지는 소리를 듣는다고 상상해 보라. 그 파도는 당신의 맨발까지 다가오고, 바닷물이 바다로 물러날 때 맨발 아래 있는 모래를 가져가려고 한다. 해변가 집의 투명한 유리창은 파란 하늘의 구름들을 비추고 있다. 당신 앞쪽에서는 소년과 소녀들이 모래밭에서 밝은 색 노란 바구니와 빨간 삽을 이용해서 조개껍질로 장식된 모래성을 만들면서 놀고 있다. 하늘색 바다 너머로 저녁 하늘은 오렌지색으로 타오르고, 당신은 해가 지는 모습에 시선을 돌린다. 인류의 반은 바다 근처에서 살고 있다. 내가 비록 바다에서는 멀리 살지만, 바다는 내가 방문하고 싶고 그림을 그리고 싶은 장소 중 하나이다. 많은 화가들이 바다를 그리고자 하는 정신적이며, 신비롭게 매혹적이고 강렬한 욕구를 가지고 있다. 아마도 그것은 우리 자신의 몸이 거의 물로 이뤄져 있기 때문일지도 모른다. 이유가 무엇이든, 수채화 물감은 바다를 그리려고 만들어졌다.

bare feet 맨발 retreat 물러나다 transparent 투명한 blaze 타오르다 mankind 인류 stare 응시하다 enchanting 매혹적인 compelling 강렬한

02 (A) 내가 신이 나는 것이므로 excited가 적절 (B) 일부 팬들이 말하는 것이므로 commenting이 적절 (C) 승자가 잊혀지는 것이므로 are forgotten이 적절

1972년 12살이었을 때, 나는 경기장으로 야구를 보러 갈 수 있어서 흥분했다. 주당 6일을 열심히 일하셨던 아버지는 하루 휴가를 내셨고, 나를 경기에 데리고 가셨다. 우리가 경기장에 도착했을 때, 왼쪽 외야석 가까이에 있는 옆문이 장비를 가지러 가기 위해서 열려 있었다. 수많은 팬들이 그 문으로 뛰어 들어갔고, 일부는 큰 목소리로 공짜 게임에 대해 말했다. 우리가 공짜 게임을 즐길 수 있다고 생각하면서 나는 그쪽에 합류하려고 했다. 하지만, 아버지는 우리가 그래서는 안 된다고 하셨고 우리는 표를 사기 위해 계속 줄을 섰다. 경기장에서의 동작과 게임의 승자는 곧 잊혀졌지만, 다정하고 절제력 있는 아버지로부터 받은 정직함에 대한 무언의 메시지는 잊혀지지 않는다.

comment 이러쿵 저러쿵 말하다 disciplined 절제력이 있는

UNIT 121~122

Check-up

P. 58~59

121 **1.** making **2.** opening 122 **1.** spoken **2.** covering

121

1. 네(you)가 몸의 힘이 빠지도록 만드는 것이므로 능동

충격을 받으면 몸의 힘을 빼면서 숨을 깊게 쉬어야 한다.

2. 에어컨이 거주 가능성을 열어준 것이므로 능동

에어컨이 찌는 듯한 남부지방과 사막이 있는 남서부지방의 거주 가능성을 열어주면서 미국인의 사는 지역에 영향을 미쳤다.

122

1. 언어가 말하여지는 것이므로 수동

영어는 전 세계적으로 사용되는 제1언어이다.

2. 화산재가 도시를 덮은 것이므로 능동

화산의 분출로 재가 일주일 동안 계속해서 떨어졌고, 위대한 도시 폼페이를 완전히 뒤덮었다.

EXERCISE

P. 60

01 offered 02 designed 03 taking 04 carried
05 pointing 06 leading 07 meaning
08 contaminating 09 revolving 10 causing, causing

01 휴대 전화 장치가 제공되는 것이므로 수동

저가 정책으로 내놓는 대부분의 휴대 전화 장치들은 아주 기본적이거나 상대적으로 가격이 싸다.

02 새로운 법안이 고안된 것이므로 수동

그의 통솔 아래, 그 나라는 인종적 평등을 촉진하기 위해서 만들어진 새로운 법을 통과시켰다.

03 부모가 휴직하는 것이므로 능동

휴직하는 부모는 세 달 동안 100% 상환을 받을 자격이 있다.

04 관행(practice)이 의사에 의해 행해지는 것이므로 수동

지지자들은 그것은 많은 의사들에 의해서 이미 수행된 그 관행을 단지 합법화하는 것일 뿐이라고 한다.

05 결과가 방법을 제시하는 것이므로 능동

이 결과는 콜레라의 확산에 있어서 물의 역할을 증명해서 그 병을 예방할 수 있는 방법을 제시한다.

06 초기 경험이 특별한 결과로 이끄는 것이므로 능동

초기 경험은 지속적으로 세포 내 유전자의 화학적 성질과 기능을

변화시키며 행동에 있어서 특별한 결과를 가져 온다.

07 'cor'가 심장을 의미하는 것이므로 능동

만약 'courage'가 '심장'을 의미하는 라틴어 'cor'로부터 파생되었다는 것을 기억한다면 그 단어는 추가적인 의미를 가지게 된다.

08 소녀의 태도가 다른 학생들에게 나쁜 영향을 끼치는 것이므로 능동

영어 수업 시간에 새로 온 소녀의 태도가 매우 안 좋았고 다른 학생들에게 나쁜 영향을 끼쳤다.

09 아홉 개의 행성이 별 주위를 도는 것이므로 능동

우리 지구는 우리가 태양이라고 부르는 별 주위를 도는 아홉 개의 행성 중 하나이다.

10 허리케인이 큰 피해를 입히고, 사망에 이르게 하는 것이므로 능동

허리케인이 미국 남부 해안을 강타했고 엄청난 피해와 수백 명의 사망자를 야기했다.

ACTUAL TEST

P. 61

01 ⑤ 02 ③

01 ⑤ end up이라는 본동사가 있으므로 분사가 되어야 하는데 you가 yourself에게 말하는 것이므로 told가 아니라 telling이 돼야 함 ① 현재진행 ② '끝난(=finished)'이라는 뜻의 형용사 ③ '너무 많은 것을 요구하는'이라는 뜻의 형용사 ④ 사정이 무엇이든 관계없다는 뜻, 의문사, It doesn't matter.+What are the circumstances?

감정적으로 음식을 먹는 사람들은 여러 다양한 방법으로 그들의 문제를 나타낸다. 많은 사람들에게 있어 감정적인 식사의 고전적인 징후는 야식이다. 야식을 먹는 사람은 종종 그들이 하루 종일 겪은 긴장이나 감정적 혼란에 대응하여 먹고 있다. 지루함과 외로움 또한 낮의 분주함이 끝나고 밤이 앞에 펼쳐질 때 표면으로 나타날 가능성이 더 높다. 때때로 감정적인 식사는 특정한 상황에 대한 반응이기도 하다. 당신은 직장에서 기분 나쁜 하루를 보냈다. 아이들은 너무 요구가 많아서 당신은 완전히 지쳤다. 당신과 당신의 중요한 타인이 싸우고 있다. 상황이 어떤지는 중요하지 않으며 마지막 결과는 100번 중 99번이 결국 손에 한 사발의 감자튀김이나 한 봉지의 쿠키를 들고 소파 위에 앉아서 이것이 진정할 수 있는 유일한 방법이라고 스스로에게 말하는 것이다.

manifest 나타내다 **in response to** ~에 대응하여 **throughout** 내내 **boredom** 지루함 **come to the surface** 표면으로 나타나다 **demanding** 요구가 많은

02 (A) 고립된 사람이 사는 것이므로 능동인 living이 적절 (B) no가 나오므로 almost가 적절 (C) 5문형 목적어 자리에는 to부정사가 오지 못하므로 using이 적절

전기가 핵발전소에서 생성되므로 프랑스에서 우라늄은 자원이다. 그러나 이리안 자야의 외진 고원에서 홀로 살아가는 사람에게 우라늄은 자원이 아니다. 이와 유사하게 도시에 사는 여덟 살짜리 소년에게 자전거는 자원이지만 이리안 자야에 사는 고지대 사람에게는 자전거는 거의 쓸모가 없을 것이다. 개울을 가로지르고 우뚝 솟은 산들을 넘는, 날카로운 바위가 있는 가파르고 좁은 산길로 인해 자전거 사용이 불가능하다. 잔 나뭇가지들은 남아프리카의 부시족에게는 자원이다. 하지만 그것들은 전 세계 대부분의 도시 사람들에게는 거의 소용이 없다. 그들에게 이런 잔 가지는 쓸모가 없다.

power plant 발전소 **remote** 떨어진 **steep** 가파른 **trail** 산길 **creek** 개울 **urbanize** 도시화하다

UNIT 123~124

Check-up

P. 62~63

123	**1.** taking	**2.** coming
124	**1.** surprising	**2.** surprised

123

1. 규칙이 발효되는 것이므로 능동

5개월 내로 새로운 규칙이 발효되면서 리그에서 영어를 하지 못하는 선수들에 대한 걱정이 높아지고 있다.

2. 밤이 되는 것이므로 능동

어두운 밤이 되면서 찬바람이 불고 비가 내리기 시작했다.

124

1. 잘 지내려고 노력하지 않는 것이 놀라움을 느끼게 만드는 것이므로 능동

놀라운 것은 도시의 주민들 대부분은 서로 잘 지내려고 노력하지 않는다는 것이다.

2. 선생님이 놀라움을 느끼는 것이므로 수동

너의 선생님은 네가 이 문제에 대한 계산을 얼마나 빠르게 할 수 있는지에 놀랐을지도 모른다.

EXERCISE

P. 64

01 eased 02 exhausted 03 surprising 04 satisfied
05 Irritated by 06 displeased 07 embarrassing
08 pleasing 09 coming 10 amazing

01 with 분사구문, 내 등이 담겨지는 것이므로 수동

내가 가장 좋아하는 흔들의자에 내 등을 천천히 담그고, 거기에서 발을 천천히 들면 나는 천국에 있는 것 같은 기분이다.

02 그의 상대편이 지침을 느끼는 것이므로 수동

그의 전략은 그의 상대편이 펀치를 날리는 것에 지칠 때까지 로프에 기대는 것이다.

03 경험이 놀라움을 느끼게 만드는 것이므로 능동

특히 만약 당신이 빠른 속도로 움직이고 있다면, 그것은 매우 놀라운 경험이 될 수 있다.

04 학생이 만족감을 느끼는 것이므로 수동

우리 학생 거의 모두는 우리 강의의 질이 개선되었다는 사실 때문에 꽤 만족한다.

05 학생들이 언짢음을 느끼는 것이므로 수동

학생들은 학교에서 교복을 입으라고 요구하는 전통에 화가 나서 이의를 제기하기로 결정했다.

06 주피터가 불쾌감을 느끼는 것이므로 수동

주피터는 매우 화가 났는데, 왜냐하면 그는 인류를 사랑했으므로 자신이 약속한 것 때문에 그 부탁을 거절할 수가 없었다.

07 상황이 당황스럽게 느끼도록 만드는 것이므로 능동

"솔직히 이런 종류의 상황은 당황스럽습니다."라고 뉴욕 경찰서의 20년 경력을 가진 베테랑인 케빈 월슨 중위가 말했다.

08 경험이 즐거움을 느끼게 만드는 것이므로 능동

나는 내가 굉장히 말이 많은 사람 옆에 앉아있음을 알아차렸다. 나는 사람을 만나는 것을 즐기기 때문에 이것은 종종 나에게는 즐거운 경험이다.

09 with 분사구문, 밤이 되는 것이므로 능동

밤이 되면서, 우리는 흡혈귀에 대한 두려움으로 떨기 시작했다.

10 process가 놀라움을 느끼게 만드는 것이므로 능동

지난 10년 동안, 한국의 암 연구와 치료에 놀라운 발전이 있었다.

ACTUAL TEST

P. 65

01 ④ 02 ⑤

01 ④ with 분사구문, this가 피부 탄력의 손실을 유발하는 것이므로 triggered가 아니라 triggering이 돼야 함 ① 주어는 those이고, who chew gum은 앞의 those를 수식, are가 동사 ② 주어는 many of his patients로 복수, have가 동사 ③ cause의 목적격 보어 ⑤ 앞의 on에 걸리는 동명사

만약 당신이 습관적으로 껌을 씹는다면 조심해야 한다. 일부 성형외과 의사는 껌을 씹는 사람들은 입 주변에 주름이 발생하기 쉽다고 한다. 네브라스카 대학의 칼 켄트 박사에 따르면 껌을 씹어온 많은 환자들은 입 주변에 일정 형태의 주름이 있다고 한다. 그는 껌이 주름을 어느 정도 유발한다고 밝혔다. 비록 아직 어떠한 연구도 껌을 씹는 것과 주름과의 관계를 연관시키지 않았지만, 일부 블로거들은 껌을 씹는 것은 사람들이 턱 관절을 무리하게 사용하도록 한다고 말한다. 사실 껌을 씹는 것은 피부의 탄력성을 제거하는 동시에 근육이 과도한 활동을 하도록 하며, 잠재적으로 피부 안에 있는 보완 조직을 붕괴시킬 수 있다. 하지만, 껌을 씹는 것에도 좋은 점은 있다. 독일의 한 연구는 껌을 씹는 것은 집중하는 행위와 스트레스 감소에 중요하고 긍정적인 효과를 가진다고 밝혔다.

cosmetic surgeon 성형외과 의사 wrinkle 주름 indicate 가리키다 overuse 남용하다 tissue 조직 trigger 촉발하다

02 (A) help는 목적격 보어로 (to) 동사원형을 취하므로 to track이 적절 (B) 숫자에 대해서 평상시에 잘 모르고 있다는 내용이므로 without이 와야 함 (C) they가 놀라운 감정을 느끼게 되는 것이므로 surprised가 적절

우리의 삶은 숫자와 얽혀 있다. 우리는 숫자를 생일이나 기념일 같은 중요한 사건을 나타내거나 혹은 사회 보장 번호 같은 신분 증명의 수단으로 사용한다. 또한 숫자는 서열을 매기거나 비교의 방법으로 사용된다. 대부분의 학생들은 평균 68점이 나오는 수학 시험보다 평균 98점이 나오는 수학 시험을 더 선호한다. 게다가, 숫자는 경제 상황을 파악하기도 하고 스포츠 점수를 기록하는 데 도움을 주기도 한다. 심지어 그것들은 우리의 키, 몸무게, 허리 사이즈를 말해 주기도 한다. 대부분의 학생들은 숫자가 지닌 진정한 중요성을 알지 못한 채 숫자를 삶의 일부로 받아들인다. 그러나 그들은 자신들이 숫자에 얼마나 의존하고 있는지 깨달을 때 놀랄 것이다.

interwoven with ~와 뒤섞인 anniversary 기념일 means 수단 social security number 사회 보장 번호

UNIT 125~126

Check-up

P. 66~67

125 **1.** Not knowing **2.** Never accepting

126 **1.** attended **2.** including

125

1. 분사를 부정하는 부정어(not)는 분사 앞에 위치

어찌할 바를 몰라서, 그녀는 그에게 동전을 건네며 "싱싱한 빨간 장미 한 송이를 사고 싶으세요?"라고 걱정스럽게 물었다.

2. 분사를 부정하는 부정어(never)는 분사 앞에 위치

그녀가 말하는 것을 절대로 받아들이지 않기에, 난 그녀가 자기 친구들을 위해서 자신을 희생할 거라고 생각한다.

126

1. 주어(the children)의 동사가 없으므로 attended가 적절

컨퍼런스에서 아이들은 박물관 견학을 하고 다른 아이들의 발표를 들으면서 교육적인 강좌들도 들었다.

2. 문장의 본동사(expect)가 이미 나왔으므로 분사가 적절

나는 은행 이사회에 의한 그 보고서가 임금이 위험 부담에 어떻게 영향을 미치는 가를 포함하여 효과적인 위험 관리에 대해 추천해 주기를 기대한다.

EXERCISE

P. 68

01 not known 02 regarded 03 have 04 alienating 05 asking 06 acted 07 watching 08 focusing 09 working 10 Compared

01 분사구문의 부정어는 분사 앞에 위치

비록 유명한 작곡가로서 알려지지 않았지만 그는 많은 곡을 썼다.

02 본동사(is)가 있으므로 분사가 와야 함

알버트 아인슈타인 이후로 위대한 우주 사상가로 널리 여겨지는 캠브리지 대학의 물리학자는 그야말로 우주에 대한 완벽한 이해를 하려고 시도하고 있다.

03 주어(Many areas)의 동사가 없으므로 have가 적절

지난 10년 동안 성 평등을 추구해온 다수의 지역이 마침내 성 평등을 얻었다.

04 접속사가 없으므로 분사구문이 적절

곧 그는 중독자가 되었고, 마약이 그의 인생을 삼켜버렸고, 그리고 가족과 친구, 학교로부터 그를 멀어지게 만들었다.

05 문장의 본동사는 is이므로 명사를 수식하는 분사구문이 적절

도움을 요청하는 학생은 23세로 예일대에서 신경 생물학을 전공하고 있고, 예일 동문회에 대출을 신청하고 있다.

06 본동사는 make로 뒤에 오는 동사는 분사 형태가 적절

확실히 부모들은 화면에서의 폭력과 장난감 총을 가지고 연기하는 폭력을 차별한다.

07 독자들이 공연을 보는 것이므로 능동, they might have가 experience를 수식, the experience와 they 사이에 목적격 관계대명사 생략

상상력이 풍부한 독자들은 무대 위의 공연을 보면서 그들이 가지고 있을 지도 모르는 경험에 대해서 적어도 모방은 할 수 있다.

08 자동차 회사들이 집중하는 것이므로 능동

연료 전지가 선택 가능한 자동차 엔진이 되었을 때, 내부 연소 엔진의 효율성을 늘리는 데 집중한 자동차 회사들은 스스로가 뒤처져 있음을 깨닫게 될 지도 모른다.

09 접속사가 없으므로 분사구문이 필요, 애슐리가 일을 하는 것이므로 능동

애슐리는 밤늦게까지 일하면서 맛있는 쿠키와 함께 커피 몇 잔을 마셨다.

10 접속사가 없으므로 분사구문이 필요

서울에서의 삶과 비교했을 때, 여기에서의 삶은 여러 가지 면에서 불편하다.

ACTUAL TEST

P. 69

01 ③ **02** ④

01 ③ 본동사 is가 있으므로 is communicated가 아니라 being communicated가 돼야 함, 메시지가 전달된다는 뜻 ① 〈형용사+enough〉 어순 ② viewers를 선행사로 받는 주격 관계대명사 ④ '~임에 틀림없다' ⑤ captures를 수식하는 부사

광고주들은 어떤 상품이 급속도로 성장하거나 가장 많이 팔릴 때 우리에게 알리고 싶어 하는데 왜냐하면 그들은 그 상품이 좋다는 사실을 직접적으로 우리에게 설득할 필요가 없기 때문이다. 그들은 많은 다른 사람들 역시 그렇게 생각한다고 말하기만 하면 되고 이는 충분한 증거가 되는 것 같다. 자선 모금을 위한 텔레비전 방송 제작자들은 기부를 이미 약속한 시청자들의 명단을 끊임없이 보여 주는 데 과도한 시간을 쏟아 붇는다. 망설이고 있는 사람들에게 전해지는 메시지는 분명하다. 즉, "기부하겠다고 결정했던 모든 사람들을 보아라. 이는 올바른 일임에 틀림없다."는 것이다. 판매원들은 그 상품을 구매했던 무수히 많은 사람들의 수를 통해 상품 판매를 강조하도록 교육 받는다. 판매와 동기 부여 전문가인 로버트 카벳은 수습 판매원들을 위한 그의 조언 속에서 이 원리를 멋지게 표현하고 있다. "사람들은 우리가 제공할 수 있는 어떠한 증거보다도 다른 사람의 행동에 의해 더 쉽게 설득된다."

convince 설득하다 proof 보증된 charity 자선단체 telethon 장시간 텔레비전 모금 활동 devote 헌신하다 excessive 초과하는 pledge 약속하다 contribution 기부 hesitater 망설이는 사람 trainee 수습 직원

02 (A) a festival이 선행사이므로 which가 적절 (B) 본동사가 없으므로 are가 필요 (C) the religious ideas가 주어이므로 were가 적절

모든 일반적인 그리스 비극은 디오니소스를 기리는 축제인 디오니소스제를 위해서 쓰여졌는데, 이 축제는 비극과 풍자극, 희극공연으로 가득한 4일로 기려진다. 이것은 연극들이 명확한 종교적인 목적, 즉 신 디오니소스를 기리고 숭배하는 목적이 있다는 것을 의미한다. 시인은 종종 '사람들의 스승'이라고 여겨졌고, 그리스 비극의 성공은 종교적 지도자로서의 역할을 해낸 시인의 성공에 기반을 둔다. 이것은 그리스 비극에서 발견되는 일반적인 주제가 보통은 신과 사람과의 관계와 신의 힘과 신적인 정의의 관계처럼 종교적이거나 도덕적이라는 것을 의미한다. 또한 시인들이 가르쳤던 종교적인 사상은 대다수의 현재 종교에서 발견되는 것과는 다르다는 것을 알아채는 것은 중요하다.

in honor of ~을 기리는 theatrical 극장의 satire 풍자의 imply 의미하다 worship 숭배하다 moral 도덕의 divine 신성의

REVIEW TEST

P. 70

01 resulted → resulting **02** scanned → scanning **03** communicated → communicating **04** using → used **05** having → have **06** Known **07** confused **08** Using **09** climbing **10** packed

01 동사 result는 자동사로 수동형이 될 수 없음

그의 과학 논문에 따르면 지속적인 백색잡음으로 인한 스트레스는 스트레스를 유발하는 코티솔 호르몬의 배출을 유도할 수 있다고 한다.

02 주어(Jerry LeVias)와 동사(needed)가 존재하고, 제리 레비아스가 살펴보는 것이므로 scanned가 아니라 scanning이 돼야 함

제리 레비아스는 지지자들과 반대자들의 무리를 유심히 살펴봤고 선거일에 누가 그를 뽑을지를 알아야 했다.

03 침팬지가 다른 침팬지들과 의사소통을 하는 것이므로 능동

대부분의 침팬지들은 다른 친구들과 의사소통을 할 때 주로 오른손을 사용한다.

04 독특한 방법이 보전을 위해 사용되는 것이므로 수동

신전의 보존을 위해 사용된 독특한 방식은 이 놀라운 신전이 살아남은 정말 중요한 비결이다.

05 주어인 Statements의 본동사가 없으므로 having이 아니라 have가 되어야 함

알코올 중독을 겪었던 일부 사람들이 안전하게 통제된 음주를 할 수 있다는 주장은 격렬한 논쟁을 불러 일으켰다.

06 known as '~로 알려진'

쿠폰 세대로 알려진 젊은이들은 중국 경제에서 비즈니스가 이루어지는 방식을 바꾸고 있다.

07 목적격 보어, 그녀가 혼란스러운 감정을 느끼는 것이므로 수동

크리스틴은 열 두 개의 바늘에 꽂힌 채 방 안에 혼자 누워있다는 생각에 스스로 당혹스러워하고 있음을 깨달았다.

08 딜런과 그의 동료들이 새로운 종류의 기구를 사용하는 것이므로 능동

딜런과 그의 동료들은 새로운 종류의 광학 이미지 장치를 사용해서 신경 세포들이 전극으로 자극을 받았을 때 그것들을 관찰했다.

09 학생들이 사다리를 올라가는 것이므로 능동

사다리를 오르는 학생들은 그들의 진행 과정을 확인하기 위해서 반복적으로 위아래를 쳐다보았다.

10 parachute가 싸여지는 것이므로 수동

스카이다이버는 단단히 싸여진 낙하산을 매고 공중을 가르며 떨어지기 시작한다.

FINAL CHECK

P. 71~73

01 ③ 02 ④ 03 ④ 04 ② 05 ⑤ 06 ④

01 ③ 앞에 본동사(ends)가 있으므로 are가 아니라 being이 돼야 함 ① 과거에서 현재까지 이어지는 내용, Since는 현재완료와 어울리는 시간 부사구 ② '~이 있다' ④ 앞에 '이기지 못했다'라는 내용이 나오고 뒤에 '이겼다'라는 내용이 오므로 대립을 나타내는 접속사가 옴 ⑤ 문두에 나온 suppose는 '가령 ~ 라고 하자'로 해석됨

나는 대학에서 토론과 논쟁을 가르쳤다. 그 때부터 나는 수천 번에 달하는 논쟁의 결과를 듣고, 비난하고, 참여하고, 지켜봐 왔다. 그 결과, 논쟁에서 이기는 유일한 방법이 있으며 그것은 바로 논쟁에서 벗어나는 것이라는 결론에 도달했다. 십중팔구 논쟁은 결국 논쟁에 참가한 사람들 자신이 절대적으로 옳다는 생각을 더욱 확신시키며 끝나게 된다. 비록 당신이 논쟁에서 이긴다 하더라도 당신은 이길 수 없다. 왜일까? 당신이 다른 사람에게 승리했다고 가정해보자. 당신은 기분이 좋을 것이다. 그러나 패배한 사람은 어떨까? 당신은 그의 자존심에 상처를 주었다. 그는 당신의 승리에 화가 날 것이다.

argumentation 논쟁 **criticize** 비판하다 **contestant** 참가자 **triumph** 승리

02 (A) if가 생략된 조건문이므로 주어와 동사가 도치된 Should your Ultra Grinder가 적절 (B) 앞쪽에 문장의 본동사가 존재하여 본동사가 또 나올 수가 없으므로 found가 적절 (C) 앞에 선행사 any product가 나오므로 that이 적절

당신의 초강력 후추 갈이는 정상적으로 사용하고 작동하던 중 제품이나 기능에 있어서 결점이 생기면 원래 소유자에게 구입한 날짜로부터 1년 동안의 보증 기간이 제공됩니다. 만약 당신의 초강력 후추 갈이가 구매일로부터 1년 안에 결점이 발견된다면, 문제가 생긴 부품이나 제품을 본사에 설명과 함께 보내주세요. 이런 보증 정책 하에 함께 우리 회사는 제조 과정에서의 잘못 때문에 결점이 발견된 어떤 부분이라도 수리하거나 교체할 것입니다. 이 보증 기간은 오직 개인적 용도에만 관련되며, 상업적 이용이나 대여로 사용되는 제품에는 해당되지 않습니다.

warrant 보증하다 **defect** 결점 **workmanship** 기능 **defective** 결함 있는 **manufacturer** 제조업자 **extend** 관련시키다

03 ④ 그들의 작품이 출간되는 것이므로 publishing이 아니라 published가 돼야 함 ① '약간' ② 서평 숙제가 학생들에게 주어지는 것으로 능동 ③ the winners가 주어, receive가 동사 ⑤ 강조 구문으로 앞에 있는 명사를 강조

당신이 동기를 가지도록 할 수 있는 것은 바로 서평이다. 간단한 요약문과 평범한 보고서와는 약간 다른 형태인 서평은 학생들에게 특별 과제로 주어지거나 학교 신문을 위해서 부여될 수 있다. 교사들은 학교가 매년 서평 콘테스트를 하도록 장려할 수 있다. 일부 기관은 일종의 작문대회를 개최한다. 그들은 자신들의 학생 작품을 제출한 교사들을 초청한다. 대회의 승자는 보통 책을 받고 교사 신문에 자신의 작품이 게재되는 만족감을 얻는다. 서평은 대중적인 읽기를 위해 쓰였기 때문에, 그것은 보고서를 교사 학생간의 상호관계의 장에서 책 읽기 공동체 자체로 옮길 수 있다. 이것은 학생간의 구술 보고서와 같은 후속 활동이 될 수 있다.

assignment 과제 **institute** 기관 **composition** 구성, 작문 **follow-up** 후속의

04 (A) 미리가 놓여 있는 것이고 시제가 과거이므로, 자동사 lie의 과거형인 lay가 적절, lie-lay-lain '~이 놓여 있다, 눕다' (B) 큰 전쟁용 곤봉이 마련되는 것이므로 수동 (C) 고고학자들이 황금 접시를 들어올리는 것이므로 능동

페루의 고대 피라미드 안쪽 깊숙한 곳에서, 한 여성 고고학자가 연약 지반의 직사각형의 작은 땅을 발견했는데 그것은 무덤이 있다는 명백한 표시였다. 그녀는 신성한 장소를 조사하고 있었다. 몇 주간 조심스럽게 땅을 판 후 그녀는 고대의 먼지 사이로 안을 들여다 보았다. 미라가 그녀 앞에 누워 있었다. 그녀가 몇 겹으로 싸여진 천을 벗겨 냈을 때, 수백 개의 보물들이 발견되었는데 금, 번쩍이는 왕관, 그리고 대게 가장 위대한 전사들을 위해 마련해 두는 거대한 전쟁용 곤봉이 포함되어 있었다. 그러나 그녀가 미라의 얼굴을 덮고 있는 황금 접시를 올렸을 때, 고고학자는 이제까지 중 가장 놀라운 것을 발견했다. 미라는 왕이나 남자 전사가 아니었다. 그것은 젊은 여자였다. 미라는 온 몸에 신비로운 문신을 하고 있었다!

archaeologist 고고학자 **patch** 땅 **soft clay** 연약 지반 **telltale** 숨길 수 없는 **sacred** 신성한 **mummy** 미라 **unwrap** 풀다 **bundle** 싸다 **warrior** 전사 **tattoo** 문신

05 ⑤ 본동사(turns)는 앞에 있고, 형사가 가장 흔한 회피를 이용하는 것이므로 능동 ① 주어는 investigating이므로 단수 ② 뒤에 전치사가 나오므로 동명사가 아닌 명사가 옴 ③ 〈be reluctant to 동사원형〉 구문 '~하기를 꺼리다' ④ 선행사가 없고 뒤에 주어가 없는 문장이 오므로 what이 옴

화이트칼라 범죄를 조사하는 것은 어떤 범죄보다도 비용이 더 든다. 절도를 조사하는 것은 목격자를 인터뷰하고 시간이 걸리지 않는 조서를 작성하는 것을 포함한다. 하지만, 작은 회사의 단순한 뇌물 사건을 조사하는 것조차도 더 많은 작업뿐만 아니라 더 많은 시간이 걸린다. 절도의 경우와 마찬가지로 당연히 회사의 소유주와 모든 목격자를 조사한다. 하지만, 경찰은 모든 관련된 재정자료를 복사하고 완전한 분석도 해야 한다. 경찰서장은 모든 사건을 처리할 제한된 수의 형사들이 있는데, 보통 이러한 장기적인 돈과 관련된 사건에 한 명의 형사를 배치하는 것을 꺼리게 된다. 하지만, 알다시피 이 상황에서 가장 빈번하게 일어나는 일은 법 집행에서 가장 흔한 회피인 "이건 민사사건 같은데요."라고 말하면서 형사가 사건을 맡는 것을 간단히 거절하는 것이다.

witness 목격하다 **time-consuming** 시간이 걸리는 **bribe** 뇌물 **duplicate** 사본 **allot** 할당하다 **detective** 형사 **enforcement** 집행

06 (A) get은 〈get+p.p.〉의 형태로 수동의 의미를 지니고, 소비자들이 과일을 제공 받는 것이므로 offered가 적절 (B) 추상적 의미이므로 widely가 적절 (C) 앞의 throwing과 병렬 구조

소비자들이 일 년 내내 모든 계절의 과일을 제공 받게 되면서 제철 과일의 개념이 사라지기 시작하고 있다. 이에 대해 누구에게 고마워해야 할까? 냉동고와 진보된 포장기술이다. 이 최신 기술 덕분에 소매업자들은 갓 익은 과일의 맛과 향기 그리고 신선함을 확보하여

연중 내내 이를 소비자들에게 가져다 주고 있다. 소비자들에게 이는 상큼한 기쁨이다. 이런 냉동 포장 과일은 우리의 과거를 잊게 해 주는데, 그 시절에 우리는 제철에 수확되는 과일만 먹을 수 있었다. 업계 전문가들은, 지구 기후 변화가 제철 과일 수확에 영향을 주거나 피해를 줌에 따라, 냉동 과일이 점점 더 인기를 얻고 널리 소비될 것이라고 말한다. 게다가, 건강에 대한 높은 인식이 냉동 과일의 인기에 기여하고 있는데 사람들은 정크 푸드를 버리고 대신 냉동 건강 식품으로 관심을 돌리고 있다.

seasonal fruit 제철과일 **retailer** 소매업자 **fruity** 달콤한

chapter 12 동명사

UNIT 127~128

Check-up P. 76~77

127	**1.** expressing	**2.** production
128	**1.** reaching	**2.** understanding

127

1. 뒤에 목적어가 나오므로 동명사가 적절

우리는 음악에 대한 우리의 취향이 우리의 개성을 표현하는 정말 좋은 방법이라는 것을 믿는 경향이 있다.

2. 뒤에 전치사가 나오므로 명사가 적절

올해 국가는 엄청난 성공을 거두었고, 동해의 최초 연안 가스전에서 액화 천연 가스 생산을 시작했다.

128

1. 전치사 다음에 나오므로 동명사가 적절

문자메시지가 있으면, 당신은 전화로 연락하지 않고도 모든 대화를 할 수 있다.

2. 전치사 다음에 나오므로 동명사가 적절

그것은 종양이 세포층에서 어떻게 기능을 하는지 이해하고, 오직 문제를 발생시키는 세포만을 목표로 하는 스마트 폭탄처럼 작용하는 약을 개발하는 것에 관한 것이다.

EXERCISE P. 78

01 having **02** marking **03** the success **04** an analysis **05** the arrival **06** executing **07** creating **08** the creation **09** being **10** attempting

01 전치사 like의 목적어이므로 동명사가 적절

일이란 결혼이나 배우자를 얻는 것과 같다.

02 전치사 by의 목적어이므로 동명사가 적절

그 학급은 그리고 나서 투표 용지에 그들의 선택을 표시함으로써 투표할 것이다.

03 뒤에 전치사 of가 나오므로 명사가 적절

당신은 더 효과적으로 경기하며, 네가 속한 팀의 승리에 공헌할 수 있다.

04 뒤에 of가 나오므로 명사가 적절

금융 시장의 분석을 위한 출발점으로서, 우리는 이번 회의에서 핵심 변수들을 논의한다.

05 뒤에 of가 나오므로 명사가 적절

품질 관리 부서는 2주 전 주문했던 새로운 장치들의 도착을 초조하게 기다리고 있다.

06 전치사 by 뒤에 오며, 목적어를 가지므로 동명사가 적절

그들이 깨닫지 못하는 것은 주 정부가 범죄자를 사형에 처함으로써 자신들이 처벌하기를 원하는 범죄 행동을 처리한다는 것이다.

07 전치사 without 뒤에 오며, 목적어를 가지므로 동명사가 적절

우리는 어떤 골칫거리도 일으키지 않고 이처럼 민감한 문제를 해결하기 위하여 특별한 재능 있는 선생님을 필요로 합니다.

08 전치사 to뒤에 오며 뒤에 of가 따라오므로 명사가 적절

그 실비를 하기에 앞서, 건물 내의 공기를 점검할 필요가 있었다.

09 전치사 about이 나오므로 동명사가 와야 함

데이비드 베컴이 지난 여름 뉴욕 대학에서 미국의 다른 지역에 다문화 사회의 모델이 되는 뉴욕에 대해서 말할 때, 몇 가지 의문들이 제기되었다.

10 뒤에 목적어(to colonize~)가 나오므로 동명사가 적절

몇 명의 황제가 그것의 식민지화를 시도했음에도 불구하고 페트라(요르단 서남부의 고대 도시)는 로마가 점령했던 기원후 100년 정도까지 대체로 나바테아 사람 손에 남아 있었다.

ACTUAL TEST P. 79

01 ⑤ **02** ③

01 ⑤ 뒤에 목적어가 나오므로 production이 아니라 동명사 producing이 와야 함 ① '매우' ② 뒤에 문장이 오므로 접속사 Although가 옴 ③ '거의' ④ 병렬 구조로 claimed의 목적어절을 이끄는 접속사 that

20세기 초 미국에서의 자동 피아노의 소개는 매우 호된 비판이 뒤따랐다. 자동 피아노는 두루마리 악보에 저장된 지시에 따라 기계적으로 음악을 생산했다. 비록 피아노 생산자나 악보 발행인과 같은 지지자들은 이것이 거의 전세계적인 음악 교육을 이끌 것이라고 생각했지만, 많은 음악 선생님들과 음악가, 작곡가들은 그것에 반대했다. 반대자들은 자동 피아노는 음악적 해석 없이 소리만 베끼고 기계 도구가 음악의 표현을 수학 체계로 반감시킨다고 주장했다. 이러한 이유로 기계화된 음악은 영혼도 즐거움도 열정도 없이 그저 반복적으로 생산해냄으로써 아름다움의 이상을 감소시키고, 자동 피아노의 도입으로 인해 아마추어 연주가들이 사라지게 될 것이라고 믿었다.

accompany 동반하다 **fairly** 매우 **proponent** 지지자 **composer** 작곡가 **lessen** 줄이다

02 (A) 뒤에 명사구가 오므로 despite가 적절 (B) 접속사 and가 있으므로 them이 적절 (C) 뒤에 of가 오므로 adoption이 적절

정부 보조금 지원이 끊겨서 이제 상업적이 된 최근의 중국 매체는 한때 금지되었던 분야에 들어섰다. 하지만 왕성해진 활동과 적어도 소수의 개방된 출판물들의 신뢰성에도 불구하고 비밀 매체는 사라질 기미가 보이지 않고 있으며, 그중 일부는 새로운 사업을 하고 있다. 즉 건전한 정보는 잘 팔린다는 사업 말이다. 중국의 신속한 인터넷 채택은 완전히 새로운 보도 장르를 위해 풍부한 내용까지 제공하고 있다. 그리고 중국의 지도사들은 그것을 받아들이고 있는 것으로 보인다.

retraction 철회 subsidy 보조금 stray into 들어서다
reliability 신뢰 furnish 제공하다 abundant 풍부한

UNIT 129~130

Check-up P. 80~81

129	**1.** checking	**2.** throwing
130	**1.** not leaving	**2.** not revealing

129

1. quit은 동명사를 목적어로 취함

토미는 상품 검사하는 일을 그만두고, 다른 일을 찾으려 시도했다.

2. practice는 동명사를 목적어로 취함

학생들은 그들의 시험지를 바구니에 던지는 연습을 하는 것을 좋아했다.

130

1. 동명사의 부정어는 동명사 앞에 위치

폭우가 왔음에도 불구하고 당신이 나를 떠나지 않은 것에 감사한다.

2. 동명사의 부정어는 동명사 앞에 위치

그 부서는 이 시스템의 효율성에 대한 연구 결과를 밝히지 않아서 비난을 받았다.

EXERCISE P. 82

01 smoking **02** feeling **03** smoking **04** submitting
05 creating **06** not going **07** eating **08** paying
09 keeping **10** sharpening

01 give up은 동명사를 목적어로 취함

벤이 지적했던 것처럼, 금연은 세상에서 가장 쉬운 일이다.

02 enjoy는 동명사를 목적어로 취함

이런 분주함을 느끼기를 즐기는 사람들은 더 가치 있는 일을 미뤄놓고 하지 않음으로써 종종 스릴을 찾는 사람들이다.

03 quit은 동명사를 목적어로 취함

만약 여자들이 그들의 프로게스테론 수치가 높은 날에 시작한다면 금연에 성공할 가능성이 더 높다.

04 consider는 동명사를 목적어로 취함

만약 당신이 희귀한 동전을 가지고 있다면, 당신은 언제 그것을 등급매기는 서비스에 제출하겠는가?

05 suggest는 동명사를 목적어로 취함

일부 전문가들은 일부 딜러들의 어떤 고안된 지리적인 지역을 제한하는 방식을 사용해서 보다 공평한 경쟁의 장을 만들 것을 제안했다.

06 동명사의 부정은 부정어를 동명사 앞에 둠

그는 오늘 학교에 가지 않는 것을 고려했지만, 엄마에 의해서 묵살당했다.

07 keep은 동명사를 목적어로 취함

판다는 깨어있는 대부분의 시간을 먹는데 사용하며, 일 년 내내 끊임없이 먹는다.

08 avoid는 동명사를 목적어로 취함

홉킨스는 겨우 1천 달러의 벌금을 내는 것을 피하고자 불법적인 정보를 사용했고, 체포 당하게 되었다.

09 전치사 like의 목적어이므로 동명사가 적절

솔직히 말하자면, 나는 더 이상 너와의 관계를 유지하고 싶지 않다.

10 연필이 깎여야 되는 것이므로 수동이 되어야 하는데, need 다음에 동명사는 수동을 의미하므로 sharpening이 적절

만약 글쓰기에서 시간을 낭비하고 싶지 않다면, 연필은 뾰족하게 깎여 있어야 한다.

ACTUAL TEST P. 83

01 ③ **02** ②

01 ③ which에 대한 본동사가 없으므로 involving이 아니라 involved가 돼야 함 ① delay는 동명사를 목적어로 취함 ② 주절의 동사가 suggest지만 that절의 내용에 당위성이 없으므로 원형이 오지 않음 ④ has를 강조, 주어는 a man이므로 단수 ⑤ '~해야만', Only if가 앞으로 나와서 주절의 주어(the addition risk)와 동사(dies out)가 도치됨, does가 주어 앞으로 나오고 주어 뒤에 동사원형이 옴

아이를 가지는 것을 미루는 여자들은 자폐증을 가진 아이를 가질 위험이 증가하고 있을 지도 모른다. 1990년대 캘리포니아에서 이루어진 모든 출산에 대한 조사는 그 위험이 엄마의 나이가 5년 늘어날 때 마다 18% 정도 증가한다고 밝혔으며, 여성의 나이가 마흔이 될 때 그녀는 20대 후반의 여자들보다 자폐아를 낳을 확률이 50% 정도 높고, 25세 미만의 여자보다는 77%나 높을 것으로 예상된다. 자폐증을 가진 1만 2천 명의 아이들과 5백만 명 가량의 통제 집단을 포함한 그 연구는 아버지의 나이 또한 하나의 변수라고 밝혔다. 40대의 남자는 자폐아를 가질 위험이 증가한다. 엄마의 나이가 30세가 넘어야만 부가적인 위험도가 사라진다.

autism 자폐증 maternal 어머니의 autistic 자폐의 paternal 아버지의

02 (A) 뒤에 완전한 문장이 오므로 at which가 적절 (B) 동명사의 부정은 앞에 not을 붙임 (C) 주어는 how가 이끄는 절이므로 단수 취급하여 is가 적절

당신의 심장 박동은 신체의 컨디션과 기온, 생활 속 스트레스 수준 등에 영향을 받는다. 당신의 심장이 펌프하는 비율은 너무 많은 요인에 달려 있어서, 당신이 훈련이나 경쟁을 할 때에는 심장 박동수를 모르는 편이 낫다. 심장 박동 모니터는 유효하고 유용한 도구가 될 수 있다. 운동선수들은 그것과 함께 훈련해왔고 확실히 이것은 많은 운동선수들의 신체단련 수준을 개선해왔다. 하지만, 심장 박동

은 퍼즐의 조그마한 조각일 뿐이다. 당신의 심장이 얼마나 빨리 뛰는가는 자극에 대한 반응이다. 당신의 심장 박동을 차의 분당 회전수 눈금판과 비슷하다고 생각해 봐라. 당신이 가속 페달을 밟으면 밟을수록 분당 회전수는 올라간다.

valid 유효한 fitness 신체 단련 stimulus 자극

UNIT 131~132

P. 84~85

131 **1.** my **2.** his

132 **1.** having finished **2.** having investigated

131

1. 동명사의 의미상의 주어이므로 소유격이 옴

제가 창문을 열어도 될까요?

2. 동명사의 의미상의 주어이므로 소유격이 옴

그의 아버지에 따르면 그가 미대에 가는 것은 그가 얼마나 말을 안 듣는지를 보여 주는 또 다른 예일 뿐이다.

132

1. 프로젝트를 끝낸 것은 과거의 일이므로 완료형을 사용

당신과 당신의 팀이 한 달 전에 이 일을 끝냈을 수 있었던 비결이다.

2. 조사한 것은 과거의 일이므로 완료형을 사용

위원회가 어제 그 사건들을 조사한 것이 이번 스캔들을 해결하는 데 중요한 역할을 할 지도 모른다.

EXERCISE

P. 86

01 Our 02 having embezzled 03 having been 04 having made 05 having never spoken 06 her 07 his 08 having cheated 09 having secured 10 having helped

01 writing은 동명사이므로 의미상 주어인 소유격 our가 적절

독서가 집중력을 촉진시키는 반면 글쓰기는 이해력을 증진시키고 기억력을 지켜준다.

02 횡령한 것은 과거의 일이므로 동명사의 시제는 완료형이 적절

경영자는 많은 돈을 횡령했다고 의심받고 있다.

03 작년에 벌어진 일로 과거이므로 동명사의 완료형이 적절

로빈은 그의 아들을 자랑스러워 하는데 토니가 작년 권투 챔피언이 되었기 때문이다.

04 지난 회의에서 하지 못한 것을 의미하므로 동명사의 완료형이 적절

지난 회의에서 수입차 판매량 개선에 관한 제안을 하지 못해서 죄송합니다.

05 과거부터 지금까지 한번도 하지 않았다는 의미로 완료형이 적절

지금까지 한번도 사람들 앞에서 연설을 해본 적이 없어서 주장 톰슨은 매우 긴장해 있다.

06 동명사의 의미상 주어이므로 소유격이 적절

미국 중앙정보부는 그녀가 스파이임을 확신했기 때문에 그들은 명백한 증거를 찾기 위해서 그녀의 집을 수색했다.

07 동명사의 의미상 주어이므로 소유격이 적절

나는 지금 축구팀에 그가 합류해서 경기를 하는 것을 고려 중이다.

08 지난 기말고사의 일이므로 동명사의 시제는 완료형이 적절

주디는 지난 기말고사에서 부정행위 한 것을 강력히 부인했다.

09 이미 벌어진 과거의 사건을 의미하므로 동명사의 완료형이 적절

레온이 여기 대기업과의 계약을 상당수 성사시켰기 때문에 부사장으로 승진하는 것이 예상된다.

10 과거에 도와준 것이므로 과거를 의미하는 동명사의 완료형이 적절

그의 룸메이트들은 그가 매우 바빴음에도 불구하고 그냥 그들을 도와준 것에 대해서 고마워한다.

ACTUAL TEST

P. 87

01 ⑤ 02 ⑤

01 ⑤ 학생들이 듣고 말을 하는 것이므로 listened and spoken이 아니라 listening and speaking이 돼야 함 ① Students가 주어, are가 동사 ② 인지하는 것을 실패하는 것보다 단어를 배운 것이 먼저 일어난 일 ③ take place '~이 발생하다, 일어나다', 자동사 ④ missing은 '잃어버린'을 의미하는 형용사

학생들은 종종 고립된 개개의 단어의 발음을 배우고, 연결된 발화에서는 발음을 인지할 수 없다. 고립된 형태로 단어를 학습했기 때문에 모음이나 마지막 자음에서 변화가 일어나거나 소리가 함께 사라질 때, 학생들은 발화 상에서 그것들을 인지하지 못한다. 자신이 말할 때 학생들은 그러한 것들을 결합하기 보다는 분리시키는 경향이 있다. 그들은 또한 각각의 음절을 과장되게 발음하는 경향이 있으며, 짧거나 축약의 형태로, 강세를 받지 않는 음절을 줄이지 않는 경향이 있다. 원어민의 말을 더 잘 이해하기 위해서 학생들은 듣고 말할 때 단어들이 다른 것들과 함께 있을 때 어떻게 다르게 소리 나는지 좀 더 집중할 필요가 있다.

utterance 발화 vowel 모음 consonant 자음 syllable 음절 compress 압축하다

02 (A) 동명사를 수식하므로 부사 regularly가 적절 (B) make는 5문형 동사로 목적어가 to부정사인 경우 가목적어 it을 쓰고, 진목적어 to부정사를 뒤로 보내므로 making it이 적절 (C) 동명사의 의미상의 주어로 소유격인 their가 적절

과학자들은 정기적으로 하이힐을 신는 여성들이 신발을 벗을 때 더 큰 근육통을 받는다는 사실을 발견했다. 이것이 그들의 근육이 쉴 시간을 가지지 못하고 긴 시간 동안 너무 심하게 늘어나 있었기 때문이다. 보리스 존슨 박사에 따르면, 여성이 신발을 벗을 때 발을 쭉 뻗는 것이 더 힘들었다. 그는 여성들에게 고통을 줄이기 위해서 간단한 스트레칭 운동을 하라고 권했다. "만약 당신이 발 끝으로 서 있고 당신의 발꿈치를 위아래로 들썩거리는 것을 반복하면, 조직을 늘이게 될 것이고 이는 하이힐 없이 걷는 것을 더 쉽게 해줄 겁니다."라고 말했다. 그는 여성들에게 하이힐을 신지 말라고는 하지 않았지만 그들에게 좀 더 자주 굽이 낮은 신발을 신으라고 조언했다.

"패션은 불편하도록 의도된 것이고, 연구에서 어떤 여성들도 그들의 하이힐을 포기하려고 하지 않았어요."라고 말했다.

overstretch 지나치게 늘이다 recommend 추천하다 relieve 완화하다 intend 의도하다

UNIT 133~134

Check-up P. 88~89

133 **1.** talking **2.** knowing **134** **1.** taking **2.** hitting

133

1. could not help -ing '~하지 않을 수 없다'

목격자는 지난 토요일 그가 본 것에 대해서 말하지 않을 수 없었다.

2. be worth -ing '~할 만한 가치가 있다'

많은 아마도 상당한 수의 베네수엘라 사람들은 현재 그 정책에 반대하고 있다는 사실을 알만한 가치가 있다.

134

1. in addition to -ing '~와 더불어'

비타민제를 복용하는 것과 더불어, 마늘과 브로콜리, 콜리플라워를 많이 먹어야 한다.

2. come close to -ing '거의 ~할 뻔하다'

나는 너무 서두르다가 길을 건너고 있는 해명을 거의 칠 뻔 했다.

EXERCISE P. 90

01 using **02** buying **03** declining **04** saving **05** catching **06** trying **07** improving **08** store **09** looking **10** stabilizing

01 be accustomed to -ing '~하는 데 익숙하다'

만약 당신이 포크와 칼을 사용하는 데 익숙하다면, 젓가락을 사용하는 게 어려울 수 있다.

02 when it comes to -ing '~에 관한 한'

옷을 사는데 있어서, 쇼핑객들은 선택들에 압도감을 느낄 수 있다.

03 thanks to -ing '~덕택에'

다른 사람들은 주택 가격의 하락 때문에 집에 남겨둔 자산이 없다.

04 be worth -ing '~가 가치 있다'

보호할 만한 가치가 있는 일부 유산들은 어떻게 그들이 보이는 것뿐만 아니라 그들이 무엇을 의미하는지도 중요하다.

05 from A to B 'A에서 B까지'

그것은 서둘러 보트, 오두막, 텐트를 만드는 것부터 낚싯줄 없이 낚시하는 것까지 모든 상황을 포함한다.

06 be busy -ing '~하느라 바쁘다'

현대인들은 대개 행복한 삶을 즐기려고 점점 더 많은 활동을 점점 더 짧은 시간에 맞추느라 바쁘다.

07 be committed to -ing '~에 전념하다'

그들이 너무 신체적 능력과 그 분야에서의 기술을 향상시키는데 너무 몰두한 나머지 그들이 근육 형성 약을 복용할 때 젊은 선수들은 일탈적이게 된다.

08 칩이 저장에 이용됨

이 칩은 카드 소유자의 신분을 명확하게 확인할 수 있는 정보를 저장하는 데 사용된다.

09 아이를 돌보는 데 익숙함

에이미는 세 명의 여동생이 있어서 어린 아이를 돌보는 데 익숙하다.

10 pay attention to -ing '~에 주의를 기울이다'

나라를 안정시키고 삶의 질을 개선하는 네 좀 더 주의를 기울일 때였다.

ACTUAL TEST P. 91

01 ③ **02** ④

01 ③ in addition to에서 to는 전치사이므로 plant가 아니라 planting이 돼야 함 ① 완전한 문장을 이끄는 관계부사 ② '~만큼' ④ '치료하는 데 이용되다' ⑤ 농부들이 코를 잡고 개꽃을 뽑아낸 것보다 조니가 지나간 일이 먼저 일어난 일

우리는 조니 애플시드의 이야기가 친숙한데, 그는 1840년대에 미국의 국경 지대를 여행했다. 초기의 개척자들이 모든 나무를 잘라낸 땅에 다시 숲을 조성하기 위해 그는 사과 씨앗 자루를 가지고 다니면서 그가 간 곳마다 그것을 심었다. 하지만 그는 자연 환경 보호론자인 만큼 악의 없는 오염자인 것 같다. 사과 씨앗을 심는 것과 더불어, 조니는 다니는 길목마다 그것이 말라리아의 치료에 이용될 수 있다고 믿으며 개꽃이라고 불리는 잡초를 심었다. 그러나 그가 틀렸다. 개꽃에 대해서는 두 가지만이 분명하다. 그것은 다른 모든 잡초들처럼 널리 퍼지며, 악취가 아주 심하다. 그래서 조니가 지나간 후 몇 년 동안 화가 난 농부들은 그들의 코를 잡고 필사적으로 개꽃을 뽑아내고 있었다.

frontier 국경지역 pioneer 개척자 sack 자루 polluter 오염자 conservationist 환경 보호론자 wander 거닐다 desperately 필사적으로 root out 뿌리를 뽑다

02 (A) 뒤에 완전한 문장이 오므로 way를 수식하는 관계부사 that (B) 그들이 환경을 위태롭게 하는 것이므로 능동 (C) 뒤에 목적어가 나오므로 performing이 적절

호아 다 실바는 가장 유명한 환경 운동가 중 한 명이다. 그는 1954년 아마존 지역에서 수 세대 동안 고무나무에서 고무를 경작해왔던 가난한 브라질 가족에서 태어났다. 그들은 열대 우림을 사랑했고, 그 자원을 사람들이 파괴하지 않는 방식으로 이용해왔다. 하지만, 소농장주들과 광산 회사들은 1억 8천만 년이나 된 아마존의 열대 우림을 파괴하기 시작했다. 그들은 수십만 그루의 나무를 자르고 불태웠고 그곳에 사는 사람들의 삶의 환경을 위협했다. 다 실바는 이러한 위험한 행위를 실행하는 것에 반대하기 위하여 평범한 근로자들로 조직된 운동을 전개했다. 다 실바의 노력이 다른 나라의 사람들이 지구의 숲과 숲의 원주민들을 보호하도록 이끌었기 때문에 이 운동은 결국 다른 지역으로 퍼져 나갔다.

rancher 목장주 mining 광산 resident 거주민

UNIT 135~136

Check-up P. 92~93

135 **1.** means **2.** doesn't
136 **1.** studying **2.** settling

135

1. Fighting이 이끄는 동명사구가 주어

암만큼 다양한 질병의 무리와 싸우는 것은 분자 수준에서 우선적으로 적을 구별할 수 있음을 의미한다.

2. Stamping이 이끄는 동명사구가 주어

포괄적인 진단인 "종양"으로 누군가의 병을 낙인 찍는 것은 치료하는 과정에 도움이 되지 않는다.

136

1. 5문형의 목적어 자리이므로 to부정사는 올 수 없음

학생들은 교실에서 스스로 영어회화를 공부하는 것이 어렵다고 생각했다.

2. 5문형의 목적어 자리이므로 to부정사는 올 수 없음

린의 증언은 이 사건이 쉽게 해결되도록 만들었고, 마침내 우리는 진범을 잡았다.

EXERCISE P. 94

01 surviving 02 living 03 breathing 04 seems
05 enhances 06 is 07 watching 08 is 09 is 10 is

01 5문형의 목적어 자리이므로 to부정사는 올 수 없음

엑토는 규모가 더 작은 무리에서는 살아남기가 더욱 힘들다 것을 발견했다.

02 5문형의 목적어 자리이므로 to부정사는 올 수 없음

히말라야에 사는 사람들은 이곳에서 사는 것을 즐겁게 만들어 주는 일 년 내내 온화한 날씨를 즐긴다.

03 5문형의 목적어 자리이므로 to부정사는 올 수 없음

이것은 기도를 넓힐 수 있는데, 이는 숨을 가쁘게 하고, 호흡을 어렵게 만든다.

04 Watching이 이끄는 동명사구가 주어

이 프로그램을 보는 것은 어린 학생들에게 영어로 말하고 이야기하는 것에 동기를 부여하고 향상시키는 것 같다.

05 Setting이 이끄는 동명사구가 주어

긍정적이고 우호적인 작업 환경을 만드는 것은 생산성을 향상시키는데 사람들은 그런 환경에서 흥이 나기 때문이다.

06 Taking이 이끄는 동명사구가 주어

인터넷이 제공해야만 하는 모든 자원을 이용하는 것은 모든 종류의 작업을 능률적으로 하도록 돕는 가장 영리한 방법이다.

07 5문형의 목적어 자리이므로 to부정사는 올 수 없음

대중으로부터 우리를 분리시키기 위해서 만들어진 기술은 우리의 행동을 감시하는 것을 가능케 한다.

08 Comparing이 이끄는 동명사구가 주어

다른 학생과 우리 자신을 비교하는 것은 자연스럽고, 고무적이 될 수 있지만, 특히 우리가 스스로에게 너그럽지 않은 경우 너무 많은 비교는 시기심을 유발할 수 있다.

09 '그래픽을 사용하고 그것의 출처를 표시하는 것'이 별개의 행위가 아니라 하나의 행위이므로 단수 취급

도표를 사용하고 출처를 표시하는 것이 권장되며, 프레젠테이션이나 웹 페이지, 신문, 블로그나 기사에서 그렇게 해주시기 바랍니다.

10 Making이 이끄는 동명사구가 주어

낮은 생계비용 때문에, 아시아에서 빚을 지지 않고 사는 것이 유럽에서보다 더 쉽다.

ACTUAL TEST P. 95

01 ③ 02 ②

01 ③ using이 이끄는 동명사구가 주어이므로 increase가 아니라 increases가 돼야 함 ① words or phrases를 선행사로 받는 주격 관계대명사 ② this가 행해진다는 의미의 done ④ 사역동사(make)의 목적격 보어로 사용된 동사원형(view) ⑤ 명령문

시각적 회귀란 당신이 이미 읽은 단어나 어구들을 계속해서 되돌아가서 읽는 것이다. 예를 들면 다음과 같을 것이다. 그... 그 개는.... 그 개는 먹었다.... 그 개는 뼈를 먹었다. 불행하게도 이것은 당신의 독서 속도를 대가로 치르면서 행해지는 것이다. 이것은 독서하는 동안 손짓을 사용하여 곧 극복될 수 있다. 손짓을 사용하는 것은 독서 속도를 늦추는 몇 가지 습관을 극복하는 데 도움을 줄 뿐만 아니라 당신의 눈이 글을 더 잘 보도록 함으로써 독서의 속도를 빠르게 증가시켜 줄 수 있고, 손가락을 줄의 시작 부분에 놓고, 오른쪽 끝 부분으로 빠르게 움직이면서 독서 속도를 증가시키기 위한 간단한 조치를 취해 보아라.

at the expense of ~을 희생하여 overcome 극복하다

02 (A) 5문형의 목적어 자리에 to부정사는 올 수 없으므로 absorbing이 적절 (B) keeping이 이끄는 동명사구가 주어이므로 is가 적절 (C) 뒤에 오는 문장이 완전하므로 관계부사 where가 적절

일부 사람들은 종종 그들이 좋아하는 만큼 체육관에 가지만, 이런 것은 그들의 건강을 위해서는 그렇게 좋지는 않다. 새로운 연구는 우리 중 약 20% 정도는 산소 흡수를 어렵게 하는 유전자를 가지고 있으며, 그러므로 이는 심장병과 다른 질병을 멀리하는 것을 생각하는 한 유산소 운동을 거의 쓸모 없게 만든다는 사실을 밝혀냈다. 이 연구에 따르면, 과학자들은 500명의 지원자들에게 5개월의 에어로빅 운동 프로그램을 제시했다. 연구 말미에 실험대상자 대부분은 산소가 필요한 근육으로 가는 산소의 능력을 측정하는 그들의 VO2 max(최대 산소 소모량)에서 상당한 하락을 보여주었는데, 그들의 유전자가 그러한 행위를 막았기 때문이다. 이들은 조깅했던 것을 잊어야만 하고, 건강하고 균형 잡힌 식단을 먹는 것 같은 삶의 방식에 변화를 주어 그들의 심장을 건강하게 유지하는 것을 목표로 삼아야 한다.

gene 유전자 render (어떤 상태가 되도록) 만들다 all but 거의 measure 측정하다

UNIT 137~138

Check-up P. 96~97

137 **1.** Immediately **2.** safely
138 **1.** finding **2.** finding

137

1. 동명사 drinking을 수식하므로 부사가 와야 함

갈증을 느낄 때 즉각 물을 마시는 것은 심한 기침을 유발할 수 있다.

2. 동명사 releasing을 수식하므로 부사가 와야 함

그는 꿈이 욕구를 안전하게 발산하는 방식이라고 생각했다.

138

1. have a trouble -ing '~하는 데 어려움이 있다'

우리는 모형 비행기를 만드는 취미를 가진 사람들을 찾는 데 많은 어려움을 겪었다.

2. have a difficulty -ing '~하는 데 어려움이 있다'

전액이 현금으로 주어졌기 때문에 검사들은 그 돈이 어떻게 쓰였는지 알아내는 데 어려움을 겪어왔다.

EXERCISE P. 98

01 Actively 02 organizing 03 negatively 04 finding
05 subsequently 06 sorting 07 carefully 08 careful
09 actively 10 Successfully

01 동명사 practicing을 수식하므로 부사가 적절

일정하게 감사 표현을 적극적으로 하는 것은 당신에게 계속적으로 가장 좋은 가능성을 열어 줄 것이다.

02 have difficulty -ing '~하는 데 어려움을 겪다'

그들 중 한 명은 일을 조직하는 데 어려움을 겪을 수 있으며, 동료와의 직접적인 관계를 잃게 될지도 모른다.

03 동명사 affecting을 수식하므로 부사가 적절

쌀은 외형이나 맛에 부정적으로 영향을 미치지 않고는 질이 높아지는 것이 어렵다고 밝혀졌다.

04 have trouble -ing '~하는 데 어려움을 겪다'

그것을 하는 사람들은 그들이 대학 등록금을 내는 데 사용할 수 있는 주택 담보 대출을 흔쾌히 해주는 은행을 찾는 데 어려움을 겪을 수 있다.

05 동명사 generating을 수식하므로 부사가 적절

그 작가는 나중에 약에 내성이 있는 박테리아를 만들지 않고 위험한 미생물을 제거하는 방법을 발견하는 데 주로 관심이 있다.

06 have a hard time -ing '~하는 데 어려움을 겪다'

구조팀은 충돌 희생자 중에서 영어 이름을 분류하는 데 어려움을 겪었다.

07 동명사 plotting을 수식하므로 부사가 적절

주디는 주의를 기울이며 계획을 구상하여 곤란한 상황에서 결국 벗어났다.

08 동명사 plotting을 수식하나, 목적어가 없는 동명사이고 동명사 앞에서 수식하므로 형용사인 careful이 적절

사무엘은 주의 깊게 구성된 스토리로 유명한 프랑스 작가이다.

09 동명사 promoting을 수식하므로 부사가 적절

마케팅 부서원들은 새로운 상품들을 적극적으로 홍보하는 것을 고려해야 한다.

10 동명사 managing을 수식하므로 부사가 적절

성공적으로 재정 자원을 관리하는 것은 새롭고 확장되는 분야에 있어서 중요하다.

ACTUAL TEST P. 99

01 ① 02 ④

01 ① 동명사를 수식하므로 rapid가 아니라 rapidly가 돼야 함 ② 〈despite+동명사구〉 ③ 2008을 선행사로 받는 계속적 용법의 관계부사 ④ 사고가 산만한 운전 탓으로 돌려지는 것으로 수동, attribute A to B 'A를 B의 탓으로 돌리다' attribute는 뒤에 목적어가 없으면 수동형이 돼야 함 ⑤ drivers를 수식

한 연구에 따르면 전화를 하거나 문자메시지를 보내서 주의가 분산된 운전자들이 2001년부터 2007년 사이에 미국에서 대략 1만 6천 명의 사람을 사망하게 했다고 한다. 이러한 결과는 문자량의 급증이 미국 내에서의 수천 건의 다른 도로 사고를 유발했다는 것을 시사했다. 이 기간 동안 문자량은 백만 건에서 1억1천만 건으로 몇 백 센트나 증가했다. 이 연구는 비록 핸즈프리 장치를 사용함에도 불구하고 단지 전화기에 전화하는 것만으로도 운전자를 산만하게 할 수 있음을 밝혀냈다. 또한 이메일 서비스를 제공하는 스마트폰과 다른 전자기기들은 새로운 차원의 문제를 일으킬 수 있다. 스마트 폰의 판매가 증가하기 시작한 2008년에 대략 6건의 치명적인 자동차 사고 중 한 건은 문자메시지를 보내면서 주의가 산만해진 운전자 때문에 발생했다. 산만해진 운전자 때문에 발생한 사고로 5,870명의 사람들이 사망했음이 밝혀졌다. 이런 상황 때문에 30개 주는 운전 중 문자를 금지했고, 일부 도시와 주는 전화기를 사용하는 운전자에게 핸즈프리 장치를 요구한다.

surge 치솟다 distract 산만하게 하다 attributed to A A탓으로 돌리다

02 (A) 앞에서 제시된 두려움의 이유가 다음 문장에 나오므로 원인을 나타내는 because가 적절 (B) have a tough time -ing '~하는 데 어려움을 겪다' (C) people's fears를 의미하므로 소유격을 대신하는 소유대명사가 적절

어떤 두려움은 어린 시절에는 정상적인 것이다. 두려움이 불확실한 감정에 대한 자연스러운 반응이고 아이들은 경험하는 많은 것들에 익숙하지 않기 때문이다. 어린 아이들은 종종 어둠, 혼자 있는 것, 낯선 사람, 괴물 또는 다른 무서운 상상 속의 생물체에 대한 두려움을 가진다. 학교를 다닐 시기의 아이들은 폭풍이 몰아치거나 처음으로 집 밖에서 잘 때 무서워할지 모른다. 대부분의 아이들은 어른들의 도움을 받으며 성장하고 배움에 따라, 천천히 이러한 두려움을 정복하고 두려움을 느끼지 않을 정도로 성장한다. 어떤 아이들은 두려움에 더 예민해서 그것을 극복하는데 힘든 시간을 보낼 것이다. 두려움이 예상되는 나이를 넘어서 지속될 때, 그것은 그 사람이 과도하게 두려워하거나, 걱정하고, 또는 불안해 한다는 신호일 수 있다. 두려움이 너무 심하거나 오랫동안 지속되는 사람들은 그것을 극복하기 위해 도움과 힘이 필요할 지도 모른다.

sleep-over 외박 conquer 정복하다 outgrow ~보다 커지다

REVIEW TEST P. 100

01 listen → listening 02 excessive → excessively
03 offer → offers 04 to consider → considering
05 are → is 06 reflecting 07 assessment
08 looking 09 their 10 receiving

01 as oppose to -ing '~와 대조적으로'

그의 연구는 또한 사람들이 들을 때와는 대조적으로 말할 때 더 많이 웃는 경향이 있다는 것을 보여 주었다.

02 동명사 exercising을 수식하므로 부사가 와야 함

이 연구는 과도하게 운동하는 쥐와 비만인 쥐는 각각 신체적인 활동에 대한 보상과 음식에 대한 보상에 덜 민감할 지도 모른다는 점을 시사한다.

03 viewing이 이끄는 동명사구가 주어이므로 offer가 아니라 offers가 적절

이러한 의견들은 최소한 비극을 보는 것은 카타르시스를 위한 기회를 제공한다는 것을 주시했던 아리스토텔레스까지 거슬러 올라갔다.

04 be worth -ing '~할 만한 가치가 있다'

세심하게 관리된 음주는 특히 금주 프로그램이 반복적으로 실패해 왔던 환자들에게 특히 고려할 만한 가치가 있다.

05 동명사구는 부정형이라도 단수 취급하므로 are가 아니라 is가 돼야 함

십대들이 점점 더 복잡한 일상 생활을 다루기 때문에 그들은 더 어린 아이들이나 나이가 많은 성인들보다 더 많은 수면이 필요하며, 몇 달 동안 충분한 수면을 취하지 못하는 것은 문제가 된다.

06 전치사 of의 목적어 자리이고 it이라는 목적어를 취하므로 동명사가 와야 함

온실 가스는 열을 우주로 반사시키는 대신 열을 흡수해서 대기 중에 남아있게 하는 것으로 알려져 있다.

07 뒤에 of가 오므로 동명사가 아닌 명사형이 적절

과학은 정확성과 우리 눈으로 인식한 것에 대한 평가를 향상하기 위해서 판단 절차를 알려줄 수도 있고 그래야만 한다.

08 It is no use -ing '~해도 소용없다'

모험이나 부를 찾는 것은 소용없는데, 왜냐하면 그들은 벌써 그들의 삶에 만족감을 느꼈기 때문이다.

09 동명사의 의미상의 주어는 소유격 사용

나는 그들이 증가하는 인구를 먹이기 위해 더 많은 식량을 생산하기 위해서 점점 더 많은 숲을 벌채하리란 것을 확신한다.

10 be used to -ing '~에 익숙해지다'

수십 년 동안, 그녀는 유럽의 지도자들에게서 왕족의 대우를 받는 것에 익숙해졌다.

FINAL CHECK P. 101~103

01 ③ 02 ④ 03 ② 04 ① 05 ② 06 ④

01 ③ 동명사의 부정은 동명사 앞에 부정어를 붙이는 것이므로 living not there가 아니라 not living there가 돼야 함 ① its가 a room을 의미 ② 전치사 about의 목적어 자리 ④ with 분사구문, peel off '벗겨지다', 페인트가 벗겨지는 것이므로 능동 ⑤ 내가 알아챈 과거보다 찢어진 것이 먼저 일어난 일

나는 드레이크 호텔에 방 하나를 잡았는데 쾌적한 호텔에 쾌적한 방이었다. 작지만 편안했으며 전화기와 작은 컬러 텔레비전이 있었고 독립된 욕실이 있었다. 내가 새로운 곳에 있다는 것이 매우 기쁘고 기대감이 가득했다. 심늘을 던져 놓고 마을을 둘러보러 나갔다. 얼마 지나지 않아 내가 그곳에 살고 있지 않다는 것에 감사를 느끼게 되었다. 그곳은 내 기대와 완전히 반대였다. 호텔은 선적 사무실들과 창고들이 있는 어두운 지역에 위치해 있었다. 또한 은행 두 개, 칠이 벗겨져 가고 있는 매우 큰 경찰서, 그리고 앞에 한 줄로 공중전화 박스가 있는 비바람을 맞은 우체국이 있었다. 공중전화기 박스에 있는 전화번호부는 낡고 불에 타 있었으며, 쇠줄에 매달려 있는 것을 발견했다.

dump 내버리다 warehouse 창고 peel off 벗기다

02 (A) 뒤에 목적어가 나오므로 동명사 analyzing이 적절 (B) suggest의 that절이지만 당위성이 없으므로 were가 적절 (C) 비교하는 대상은 과거의 새와 현재의 새의 구조이므로 those of modern birds가 적절

공룡은 어떤 색일까? 진실은 누구도 알지 못한다는 것이다. 하지만, 현재 화석을 연구하는 사람들은 어떤 화석에 보존된 색조를 분석하는 방법을 찾았으며, 그들의 발견으로 일부 공룡이 회색도 아니고, 비늘도 없고 오히려 화려하게 다채롭다는 것을 알게 되었다. 예를 들어 올해 초 시노사우로테릭스는 오렌지와 하얀색으로 된 줄무늬 꼬리를 가지고 있음을 드러냈다. 그리고 현재 연구원들은 처음으로 완벽한 공룡인 안키오리니스 헉슬리의 색을 공개했으며, 이 공룡이 날개와 다리에 끝이 검은 하얀색 깃털과 심지어 붉은 갈색 모히칸 스타일의 머리털을 가지고 굉장한 모습을 지녔다는 증거를 발견했다. 전체적으로, 이 공룡은 커다란 이국적인 새처럼 보였다. 이 연구에서 화석 연구원들은 미세 수준의 색조 구조를 연구하기 위해 전자 현미경을 사용했다. 그 구조를 현대의 새의 구조와 비교함으로써 과학자들은 안키오리니스가 살아있을 때처럼 보이도록 완성할 수 있었다.

pigment 색조 fossil 화석 scaly 비늘 모양의
uncover 폭로하다 exotic 이국적인 electron 전자

03 ② 뒤에 목적어가 나오므로 동명사 destructing이나 destruction of가 와야 함 ① introduce는 타동사, 감염된 식물이 연못에 넣어지는 것이므로 수동 ③ 뒤에 나오는 affected를 수식하므로 부사, introduce A into B 'A를 B에 넣다' ④ 주어는 leaves와 growth로 복수, yellowing leaves를 동명사구가 아닌 '노랗게 되는 나뭇잎'으로 봐야 함 ⑤ choose, wash와 병렬 구조

균핵병은 가장 파괴적인 수상식물 질병이다. 그 질병은 감염된 식물이 연못에 들어가면서 퍼지게 된다. 전문가에 따르면 감염된 식물은 제거하는 방법 밖에는 없다. 이것은 안 좋게 들리지만 많은 수상 식물들은 저항력이 있으며, 감염에도 거의 영향을 받지 않지만, 민감한 수상 식물들은 심각하게 영향을 받는다. 끝이 결국 썩는 것뿐 아니라 여름에 노랗게 되는 잎과 성장하지 않는 것은 이 질병의 지표들이다. 만약 이러한 일이 발생한다면, 다른 종을 사서 키워라. 만약 여러분이 취미로 수상식물을 수집한다면, 그것을 보호하기 위해서

아주 작은 식물을 사고, 흙을 씻어내고 곰팡이 제거제 중 한 종류에 푹 담가라.

waterplant 수상식물 infect 감염시키다 expert 전문가 resistant 저항력이 있는 susceptible 민감한 indicator 지표 fungicide 곰팡이 제거제

04 (A) 가리키는 것은 a bike lane이므로 단수 (B) 동명사의 부정은 부정어가 앞에 옴 (C) 분사구문 having it이 streets를 수식하고 streets가 주어이므로 provide가 적절, think와 streets 사이에 think의 목적어절을 이끄는 접속사 생략

자전거 전용 도로는 몇 가지 이점들이 있다. 첫째, 이것은 질서정연한 교통 흐름을 촉진시키고, 자가용 운전자와 자전거 타는 사람들의 예측가능성을 증가시키는 것을 도울 수 있다. 둘째, 이것은 도로에서 자전거 타는 사람들의 스트레스를 감소시켜 주고, 자전거 타는 사람들도 도로를 사용할 권리가 있다는 것을 자가용 운전자들에게 알려준다. 게다가, 이것이 갖추어진 도로를 이용하는 자전거 타는 사람들은 인도를 덜 이용하게 될 것이며, 교통의 흐름도 덜 저해하게 될 것이다. 또한 자전거 타는 사람들이 교통의 흐름을 방해하지 않기 때문에, 자가용 운전자와 자전거 타는 사람들이 그들의 목적지로 좀 더 빠르게 갈 수 있다. 마지막으로, 여러 연구들은 자전거 타는 사람이 더 편안함을 느끼고, 자전거 도로가 갖춰 진 길이 그들에게 더 나은 서비스를 제공한다고 생각한다는 것을 발견했다.

orderly 규칙적인 predictability 예측 가능성 signal 신호를 보내다

05 ② raising이 이끄는 동명사구가 주어이므로 come이 아니라 comes가 돼야 함 ① 동사 fall을 수식하는 부사 ③ 앞의 내용에 대한 원인이 뒤에 나오므로 because가 옴 ④ 주어는 the number이므로 단수 ⑤ 선행사가 없고 뒤에 do의 목적어가 없으므로 what이 옴

만약 갑자기 한 정유소에서 휘발유 가격을 10% 정도 올린다면, 판매량은 상당히 떨어질 것이고, 수익에 큰 손해를 볼 것이다. 가격이나 비용을 올리는 것은 이익을 주기보다는 해를 끼친다. 반면에 물의 경우는 상황이 바뀐다. 만약 물을 공급하는 회사가 수돗물의 가격을 10% 심지어 20%까지 올린다면, 판매량에 있어서 약간의 하락만 있을 것이다. 이것은 회사의 수가 시장 구조를 결정하며 가격과 생산에 큰 영향을 끼치기 때문이다. 소비자는 낮은 가격에 가스를 공급하는 다른 정유소로 옮길 수 있다. 하지만, 수돗물 회사는 단 하나뿐이다. 대부분의 소비자들이 할 수 있는 것은 높은 가격 상승에 대해서 불평하는 것이다. 즉, 휘발유 시장과 수돗물 시장의 차이는 가격 결정권을 통제한다.

06 (A) 뒤에 of가 오므로 production이 적절 (B) 뒤에 완전한 문장이 오므로 after which가 적절 (C) '똑같이'라는 의미이므로 alike가 적절

성 호르몬의 생산은 생애의 흐름에 따라서 변동한다. 호르몬의 양은 날마다 다르며 심지어 시간마다 다르다. 호르몬 생산은 보통 유아기와 아동기 초기에 급증하기 시작하며, 사춘기의 시작을 알리는 십대 때 왕성해진다. 성호르몬의 양은 10대 후반부터 폐경기가 시작되는 50대 초 중반까지 점차 떨어지게 되는데 여성들은 에스트로겐 생성이 급격히 감소하는 폐경기에 접어들고, 남성들은 많은 의사들이 갱년기라 부르는, 테스토스테론의 생산량이 급격한 하락으로써 나타나는 상태에 들어선다. 남성과 여성 모두에게서 똑같이 과학자들은 고령 시기의 고갈된 호르몬 수치를 기억력 상실, 인지적 능력 감소, 심지어 급격한 우울증과도 연결시킨다.

fluctuate 변동하다 infancy 유아기 spike 급증 invigorate 활성화하다, 활력을 주다 puberty 사춘기 menopause 폐경기 deplete 고갈하다

chapter 13 to부정사

UNIT 139~140

Check-up P. 105~107

139 **1.** of **2.** for
140 **1.** for younger children **2.** her

139

1. 형용사가 칭찬의 의미로 쓰였으므로 of가 적절

당신이 나에게 이 동네를 보여주다니 친절하군요.

2. 형용사가 칭찬이나 비판의 의미가 아니므로 for가 적절

의사가 되기 위해서 그가 의과 대학 입학 자격 고사를 통과하는 것은 당연하다.

140

1. to부정사의 의미상 주어이므로 younger children 앞에 for를 붙임

국내 교육가들에 따르면, 어린 아이들이 뛰어난 영어 구사력을 습득하는 것이 훨씬 쉽다.

2. enables의 목적어

그녀는 두 나라에서의 경기 경험 덕분에 다른 탁구 스타일에 대한 날카로운 비교를 할 수 있다.

EXERCISE P. 108

01 for **02** for **03** for **04** for **05** for researchers
06 for students **07** for **08** for **09** for **10** him

01 형용사가 칭찬이나 비판의 의미가 아니므로 for가 적절

게다가, 주류 학자들은 여성들이 이 분야들을 공부하는 것이 적절하다고 생각하지 않았다.

02 형용사가 칭찬이나 비판의 의미가 아니므로 for가 적절

당신이 메이저 리그에서 제의한 제안을 받아들이게 되어 기뻤다.

03 형용사가 칭찬이나 비판의 의미가 아니므로 for가 적절

정부가 온라인 상의 외국어 서비스 예산을 늘릴 시점이다.

04 형용사가 칭찬이나 비판의 의미가 아니므로 for가 적절

그들은 아이들이 노래하고 춤추는 것을 보는 것이 매우 즐거웠다.

05 to live and study의 의미상 주어이므로 for가 필요

이 정거장에는 두 개의 작업 공간이 있고, 모든 장치와 연구원들이 일상생활을 하고 연구하는데 필요한 생명 유지 시스템과 장치들이 있다.

06 to learn의 의미상 주어이므로 for를 사용

그 원리는 문맥에서 소리를 제시하고 학생들이 발화의 연결된 흐름 속에서 소리를 배울 수 있는 기회를 제공하는 것이다.

07 형용사가 칭찬이나 비판의 의미가 아니므로 for가 적절

다른 이들에게 베푸는 가치를 배우게 되기 때문에 젊은이들이 의무적인 지역 봉사 프로그램을 위한 제안을 지지하는 것이 중요하다.

08 형용사가 칭찬이나 비판의 의미가 아니므로 for가 적절

기술이 발전함에 따라, 사업가들이 멀리 떨어진 곳에서 기업을 경영하는 것이 가능해졌다.

09 형용사가 칭찬이나 비판의 의미가 아니므로 for가 적절

아이들이 성냥을 가지고 노는 이것은 위험하다. 그러니까 성냥을 아이들에게서 멀리 치워라.

10 〈It takes 사람 시간 to부정사〉 = 〈It takes 시간 for 사람 to부정사〉 '누가 ~하는 데 시간이 걸리다'

그가 KTX를 타고 그의 목적지에 도착하는 데 2시간이 걸린다.

ACTUAL TEST

P. 109

01 ③ 02 ②

01 ③ 〈want+목적어+목적격 보어〉의 구조이므로 for your ideas가 아니라 your ideas가 돼야 함 ① kid를 수식하는 현재분사 ② brain을 선행사로 받는 계속적 용법의 주격 관계대명사 ④ '~할 때마다' ⑤ letting이 이끄는 동명사구가 주어, is가 동사

주유소에서 일하는 아이라면 누구나 가득 찬 연료 통에 연료를 더 넣을 수 없다는 것을 안다. 연료를 더 넣게 되면, 연료는 바닥으로 튄다. 마찬가지로 여러분의 말을 듣는 사람의 머릿속은 항상 그 사람의 생각과 걱정, 그리고 열정으로 가득 차 있다. 자신의 생각으로 가득 찬 듣는 사람 뇌에 당신 생각을 집어넣으면, 오염된 혼합물을 얻게 되고 그 다음에는 엎질러질 것이다. 여러분의 생각이 청자의 연료 통(뇌리)으로 흘러 들어가기를 바란다면, 우선 그 연료 통을 완전히 비워라. 감정이 실린 문제에 대해 얘기를 할 때마다, 끼어들기 전에 화자가 말을 마칠 수 있게 해라. 꼭 말을 해야 한다면 열까지 세라. 아주 긴 시간인 것 같지만, 화가 난 화자에게 말을 다 하도록 하는 것이 여러분의 차례가 되었을 때 그 사람이 여러분의 말을 듣게 하는 유일한 방법이다.

splash 튀기다 notion 생각 eternity 영원

02 (A) The number가 주어이므로 is가 적절 (B) 미국인의 수가 증가하는 것이므로 능동, 자동사인 rising이 적절 (C) 뒤에 to부정사가 나오며, 다시 주어와 동사가 나오므로 to부정사의 의미상 주어인 For people이 적절

비록 미국 고등학교 졸업생 중 30%가 대학에 들어간다 하더라도 최근에 대학 교정들을 지배하는 것은 고등학교 졸업생이 아니다. 다양한 연령대의 성인들이 새로운 직업 기술뿐만 아니라 자기 계발을 위해서 대학으로 돌아가고 있다. 예를 들어, 미국 대학생 20%는 35세 이상이다. 다수의 대학에서 50세 이상인 학생 수는 60만 명에 가깝다. 우리는 학사 학위를 가지고 있는 미국인의 수가 증가하는 것에서 교육의 가치에 대한 미국인의 신념을 알 수 있다. 대학은 부자와 재능 있는 사람에게만 이용할 수 있는 장소는 아니다. 모두에게 열려있다. 대학 수준의 업무를 처리하기 위한 사람들을 위해 많은 대학들은 경영학, 경제학, 마케팅과 관련된 추가 수업들을 제공한다.

dominate 주도하다 bachelor's degree 학사학위 available 이용할 수 있는 involved in ~와 관련된

UNIT 141~142

Check-up

P. 110~111

141 **1.** in order not to impede **2.** not to destroy
142 **1.** have finished **2.** have seen

141

1. to부정사의 부정어는 to부정사 앞에 위치

그의 부모들은 찰스를 방해하지 않기 위해 조용히 걸으려고 노력했다.

2. to부정사의 부정어는 to부정사 앞에 위치

그 지역의 많은 거주민들은 해안 마을들에게 연안의 숲을 파괴하지 말 것을 설득하려고 노력하고 있다.

142

1. 보고서를 끝낸 것이 과거의 일이므로 완료형이 적절

그는 어젯밤에 보고서를 끝내서 기쁘다.

2. 우주선을 본 것이 주장하는 것보다 과거의 일이므로 완료형이 적절

런던의 한 여인은 그 쇼가 TV를 통해 전국적으로 방송되고 있을 때, 골더스 그린 위를 날아다니는 우주 비행선을 보았다고 주장한다.

EXERCISE

P. 112

01 to have found **02** to have fed **03** not to allow **04** not to leave **05** to have thought **06** not to dread **07** not to return **08** to have been made **09** to have fallen **10** to have discovered

01 과거의 사건을 표현하므로 〈to have p.p.〉를 사용

지난 달에 그렇게 좋은 직장을 구했다니 너는 참 운이 좋구나.

02 과거의 사건을 표현하므로 〈to have p.p.〉를 사용

예수님께서 겨우 두 마리의 물고기와 다섯 덩이의 빵을 가지고 5천 명의 사람을 먹이셨다고 한다.

03 to부정사의 부정은 to부정사 앞에 not을 붙임

장군은 적군에게 귀항을 허용하지 않기로 결심했다.

04 to부정사의 부정은 to부정사 앞에 not을 붙임

그의 동생은 잭에게 차량 절도가 많으니까 차를 잠그지 않은 채로 두지 말라고 경고했다.

05 과거의 사건을 표현하므로 〈to have p.p.〉를 사용

그녀는 국제 회의를 준비하는 데 있어 적임자이기 때문에 당신은 왜 전에 아무도 그녀를 생각하지 않았던 것으로 보이는지 궁금해 할지도 모른다.

06 to부정사의 부정은 to부정사 앞에 not을 붙임

현명한 사람들은 두려워하지 않고 대신 문제들과 그것들을 해결할 기회를 기꺼이 받아들이는 법을 배운다.

07 to부정사의 부정은 to부정사 앞에 not을 붙임

노조원들이 고용주가 그들의 요구 사항 중 일부 혹은 전부에 대해 받아들일 때까지 일터에 돌아가지 않기로 결정할 때 파업이 발생한다.

08 과거의 사건을 표현하므로 〈to have p.p.〉를 사용

사람들은 초기의 지도가 기원전 7천 년에 현재 터키인 고대 도시에서 만들어졌다고 생각한다.

09 과거의 사건을 표현하므로 〈to have p.p.〉를 사용

중국에서 황제가 그림을 그리는 것은 드물지 않지만 휘종은 그것을 너무 진지하게 생각했고, 사람들은 북송 왕조가 그 때문에 망했다고 생각한다.

10 과거의 파티에서 배우자를 발견한 것이므로 완료형이 적절

파티에서 제임스를 만난 밀러 씨는 완벽한 배우자를 발견한 것 같다.

ACTUAL TEST

P. 113

01 ① **02** ③

01 ① 과거의 내용이므로 originate가 아니라 have originated가 돼야 함 ② 〈be made of〉 '~로 구성되다' ③ as는 전치사이므로 동명사가 옴. ④ 추상적 개념의 '널리'이므로 widely가 옴 ⑤ 〈there+be동사〉 '~이 있다'

사람들은 요요가 2,500년 전 중국에서 기원되었다고 생각한다. 탐험가들은 심지어 고대 이집트 신전에서 요요의 그림을 발견하기도 했다. 그때는 물론 그것이 플라스틱은 아니었지만 나무나 진흙으로 만들어졌고, "discs"라고 불렸다. 오늘 날 우리는 요요를 아이들의 장난감이라고 생각한지만 1700년대 후반에 프랑스의 왕은 유리나 상아로 만든 요요인 'Emigrette'을 가지고 놀았다. 요요가 미국에 소개되었을 때 널리 인기가 있었는데, 특히 어린이들에게 인기가 있었다. 미국 모든 길모퉁이와 모든 집에 요요가 있었던 것 같다. 정말 많은 어른들이 계속해서 요요를 가지고 놀았다.

02 (A) 과거의 사건을 의미하므로 〈to have p.p.〉가 적절 (B) 뒤에 완전한 문장이 오므로 〈전치사+관계사〉가 적절 (C) 무기가 만드는 것이 아니라 만들어지는 것이므로 수동

에너지의 광선을 이용하는 꿈은 사실 새로운 것이 아니다. 광선을 실제 무기로 사용한다는 개념은 인류 역사와 옛 영화들 속에서 드러나 있다. 기원전 214년에 아르키메데스는 태양 광선을 적함의 돛에 초점을 맞춘 대형 태양 광선 반사기 포대를 만든 것으로 알려진다. 광선 총은 1889년에 H.G. 웰스의 고전 '우주전쟁'과 같은 공상 과학 소설의 장면에 갑자기 등장하는데, 그 소설에서 화성에서 온 외계인들이 열 에너지 빔을 쏘아서 도시 전체를 황폐화시킨다. 제2차 세계 대전 동안 나치는 다양한 형태의 광선총에 대한 실험을 하였다. 집중된 광선으로 만들어진 무기들은 레이저를 특징으로 한 첫 할리우드 영화인 제임스 본드의 영화 골드핑거와 함께 대중의 상상 속으로 들어가게 되었다.

employ 이용하다 **reflector** 반사경 **burst onto** 갑자기 나오다 **devastate** 파괴하다

UNIT 143~144

Check-up

P. 114~115

143 **1.** It **2.** There
144 **1.** finds it hard **2.** find

143

1. To know 이하가 진주어이므로 가주어 it 필요

내가 아주 많은 아이들을 숙련되고 교육받은 성인이 되도록 도와줄 수 있다는 것을 알게 되어 굉장히 만족스럽다.

2. 〈there+be동사〉 '~이 있다', to help 이하는 an important person을 수식하는 형용사 역할

우리가 그 도서관을 건설하는 것을 시작하기 전에 계약서에 서명을 해야만 하는 중요한 사람이 있다.

144

1. 5문형으로 목적어인 to부정사가 뒤로 갔으므로, 가목적어 it이 필요

세계는 지금 정치적이고 경제적인 선택과 더불어 집단 노령화에 직면하는 것이 어렵다는 것을 발견한다.

2. find의 목적어가 되는 관계대명사 what이 앞에 있으므로 가목적어가 필요 없음

만약 당신이 충분히 웃지 않는다면, 당신이 재미있다고 생각되는 것을 찾아서 스스로 가능한 많이 그것에 노출시켜라.

EXERCISE

P. 116

01 there **02** to pay **03** to get **04** that
05 took it **06** It **07** found it **08** It **09** make it
10 understanding

01 〈there+be동사〉 '~이 있다', to be had는 food를 수식

그 개는 먹을 수 있는 음식이 있다는 것을 알지만, 어느 컵에 음식이 있는지는 모른다.

02 진주어 자리이므로 to부정사가 적절

유일하게 시간만이 브랜드의 이름을 위해 추가 비용을 지불하는 것이 정말로 가치 있는 일인지 여부를 말해줄 것이다.

03 5문형의 진목적어 자리이므로 to부정사가 적절

하지만 휴식 시간의 부족은 당신의 학습에서 최대한의 것을 얻는 것을 더 어렵게 만든다.

04 진주어 자리이므로 that이 적절

대학은 '전인적 학생'을 길러낼 수 있는 포괄적인 교육을 제공하는 것이 권장된다.

05 〈take it for granted that〉 '~하는 건 당연하다'

예전에 그들은 우리가 가게에서 많은 시간을 보내야만 한다는 것을 당연히 생각했다.

06 that절이 진주어이므로 가주어인 it이 나옴

그녀가 회의에 나오지 않음으로써 자기 자신을 이상한 존재로 만들어버린 것이 불가사의 했다.

07 뒤에 진목적어인 to have~ 가 있으므로 가목적어 it이 필요

포터 부인은 그녀의 방에서 자녀들과 식사를 하는 것이 기운을 북돋아 준다는 사실을 알게 되었다.

08 뒤에 진주어인 to부정사가 나오므로 가주어인 it이 필요

심지어 아이들조차 총을 사용하는 것이 가능하며, 따라서 총기규제는 더욱 엄격해져야 한다.

09 뒤에 진목적어인 to be ~ 가 나오므로 가목적어가 필요

오늘 발표된 학교 조사에 대한 새로운 계획은 있는 그대로의 성적 결과에 집중하도록 함으로써 학교가 좋은 것으로 분류되기 어렵게 만들 것이다.

10 5문형의 목적어로 to부정사는 오지 못함

그녀의 분명한 설명은 무슨 일이 일어나고 있는지 훨씬 더 쉽게 이해하도록 했다.

ACTUAL TEST

P. 117

01 ③ **02** ⑤

01 ③ 5문형 구문이고 뒤에 진목적어인 to부정사가 나오므로 most important가 아니라 it most important가 돼야 함 ① 과거를 의미하며 자동사이므로 능동태가 옴 ② 그가 짜증나는 감정을 느끼게 되는 것이므로 수동 ④ '~이든지' ⑤ 진주어 절을 이끄는 접속사

그는 25년도 더 전에 발생했던 것 전부를 설명하고 있지만, 그 기억은 아직도 그를 짜증나게 하고 있다. 그 시점에서 그는 학교로 되돌아가기 위해서 돈을 버는 게 가장 중요하다는 사실을 깨달았다. 그는 매일 도시로 기꺼이 갔고 단지 다시 학생이 되기 위해서 그가 해야만 하는 일은 무엇이든지 했지만, 학교 당국은 그에게 어떠한 것도 해줄 의향이 없었다. 그때가 바로 그가 고등 교육 없이 그가 바라는 것을 할 수 있다고 결심한 시기였다. 설사 그가 학위 없이는 할 수 없다고 하더라도, 그가 더 이상 그것을 하지 않을 거라는 것이 충분히 그를 불쾌하게 했다. 그래서 그는 학교를 그만 두었다.

02 (A) 주어는 동명사 keeping이므로 단수 (B) 뒤에 나오는 to arrange를 받는 가주어 필요(C) do를 수식하므로 부사가 필요

어떤 대학은 학생들에게 언제 그들이 지도 교수를 만나고, 무엇이 논의되었으며, 다음 과정으로 무엇이 합의되었는지를 기록하라고 요구한다. 박사 학위 같은 고등 연구 프로그램에서 이런 기록을 최신으로 유지하는 것은 한 단계에서 다음 단계로의 발전을 위한 필요조건이다. 당신의 지도 교수를 정기적으로 보는 것은 당신의 논문이 가능한 최고의 상태를 유지한다는 사실을 확신하는 최선의 방법 중 하나이다. 하지만, 당신은 얼마나 많은 학생들이 당신의 지도 교수를 가능하면 적게 보려고 하는지에 놀라게 될 것이다. 만약 당신이 오랜 기간 동안 보지 못했다면, 당신의 지도 교수가 아마도 당신을 보기를 원할지라도 그런 만남을 만드는 것은 보통 당신에게 달려 있다. 당신이 논의할 거리가 있을 때마다 가능한 한정기적으로 지도 교수를 만나야 한다.

supervisor 지도 교수 **up to date** 최신의 **requirement** 필요조건 **progression** 발전 **dissertation** 학위 논문

UNIT 145~146

Check-up

P. 118~119

145 **1.** make it possible **2.** it
146 **1.** made possible **2.** make it possible

145

1. make의 진목적어는 to buy~, 가목적어 it이 필요

그 시스템은 신뢰를 가지고 상품을 구매하는 것을 가능하도록 만드는 데 도움을 주고 있다.

2. find의 진목적어는 to take~, 가목적어 it이 필요

당신은 이른 아침에 달라스에 있는 화이트 록 호수 주변을 산책을 하는 것이 굉장히 좋다는 것을 깨달을 것이다.

146

1. 진목적어가 to부정사나 that절이 아니므로 가목적어 불필요

기술에서의 진보는 나중에 심각한 문제를 유발할 수 있는 상태의 초기 진단을 가능케 했다.

2. 진목적어가 to부정사이므로 가목적어 it이 필요

당신은 엄청난 창조적 에너지를 최고와 최선의 꿈을 이루는 데 집중하는 것이 가능하게 만들 것이다.

EXERCISE

P. 120

01 make it **02** possible **03** found **04** make it more expensive **05** make it possible **06** find it **07** unbelievable **08** it desirable **09** it impressive **10** possible

01 made의 진목적어는 to walk이므로 가목적어 it이 필요

나의 새 운동화는 물집이 생기게 했고, 그것들은 걷는 것을 문제로 만들었다.

02 뒤에 진목적어 구문(to부정사나 that절)이 보이지 않으므로 가목적어는 오지 않음

수소 연소 엔진의 마지막 개발품은 운전 습관에서의 변화를 가능케 한다.

03 목적어와 목적격 보어가 도치된 문장이므로 가목적어는 불필요

마우이는 줄리엣과 로미오가 죽는 장면이 약간 이상하다고 생각했다.

04 make의 진목적어는 to be, 가목적어가 필요하므로 it이 옴

그들은 결국 대학을 오래 지탱하게 만들고 대학에 다니는 것을 더 비싸게 만드는 일을 하게 될 것이다.

05 5문형의 진목적어인 to부정사가 나오므로 가목적어 it이 필요

당신은 우리가 학생에게 무료 교육 제공을 지속하는 것이 가능하도록 도와주었다.

06 5문형의 진목적어인 to부정사가 나오므로 가목적어 it이 필요

아이치고 너는 항상 운동을 잘 한다. 하지만, 팀의 일원이 되는 것은 어렵다.

07 단순히 목적어가 길어서 목적어와 목적격 보어가 도치된 것이므로 필요하지 않음

마을 사람들 대부분은 벽에서 작고 아름다운 꽃이 피어난 것이 믿을 수 없다고 생각했다.

08 consider는 5문형 동사이며, 뒤에 진목적어 구문인 to request가 나오므로 가목적어 it이 필요

정책 입안자들은 보통 여성들이 그들의 남편들에게 육아 업무를 나누자고 요구하는 것은 바람직하다고 생각한다.

09 동사 believe는 5문형 동사로 뒤에 진목적어 구문인 to concentrate가 나오므로 가목적어 필요

톰은 그녀가 그러한 상황 속에서 연구에 완전히 집중한다는 것은 인상적이라고 생각했다.

10 5문형이나 뒤에 진목적어인 to부정사나 that절이 보이지 않으므로 가목적어 it은 필요하지 않음

이번 재난은 허리케인과 급속한 도시화와의 관계에 대한 그의 연구를 가능하게 만들었다.

ACTUAL TEST

P. 121

01 ③ **2** ③

01 ③ 5문형이며 뒤에 진목적어인 to understand가 나오므로 make easier가 아니라 make it easier가 돼야 함 ① to use 이하를 진목적어로 받는 가주어 ② 수단을 의미하는 〈by -ing〉 ④ 〈have difficulty -ing〉 '~하는 데 어려움이 있다' ⑤ your ideas를 의미

주제를 고른 이후에, 당신은 프레젠테이션의 본문을 구성하는 것을 시작할 수 있다. 기본적으로, 당신은 주제를 몇 가지 중요한 사항들로 나눠가면서 본문을 발전시킨다. 그러고 나서 당신은 각각의 중요한 사항을 예나 설명, 사실, 세부 사항 등과 같은 구체적인 정보로 뒷받침한다. 당신의 주제를 발전시키는 동안, 두 가지에서 다섯 가지의 중요한 사항을 사용하는 것은 중요하다. 중요 사항의 수를 제한함으로써, 당신은 청취자들이 당신이 제시한 정보를 이해하고 기억하는 것을 쉽게 만들 것이다. 만약 당신이 다섯 가지 이상의 중요 사항을 사용한다면, 당신의 청취자들은 당신의 생각들을 이해하는 것을 어려워할 것이다. 많은 주제들은 보통 몇 가지 중요한 사항으로 나누어진다. 장점, 단점, 원인, 결과, 해결, 이유 등과 같은 것들 말이다. 하지만, 다른 경우에는 당신의 생각을 두 가지나 다섯 가지 중요한 사항으로 구성하기 위해서 당신의 생각을 가려내는데 약간의 시간을 써야 할 필요가 있을 것이다.

construct 구성하다 **fundamentally** 근본적으로 **break down** 나누다 **divide A into B** A를 B로 나누다

02 (A) 5문형으로 뒤에 진목적어인 that절이 나오므로 make it evident가 적절 (B) 강아지 탐사원과 침팬지 탐사원이 모집되는 것이므로 were recruited가 적절 (C) 주어가 creatures로 복수이므로 become이 적절

우주 여행과 로켓 여행이 인간에게 안전한지 확인하기 위한 테스트 파일럿의 역할을 수행하기 위해 동물들은 사람보다 먼저 우주에 갔다. 1950년대는 우주에서 생물체에 어떤 일이 일어날지 아무도 알지 못했다. 과학자들은 우주에 인간을 보내기 전에 가능한 많은 정보를 원했다. 그래서 '강아지 탐사원'과 '침팬지 탐사원'이 최초의 진정한 우주 개척자로 모집되었다. 우주에 보내진 최초의 동물은 1957년에 스푸트니크 2호에 승선한 라이카라는 소련의 개였다. 1959년에 미 항공 우주국은 침팬지들을 우주로 보냈다. 한 침팬지는 비행을 위해 훈련을 받는 데 1년을 보냈다. 오늘날 벌에서 황소개구리, 해파리에 이르는 생명체들은 수습 우주비행사가 되고, 그래서 우주 비행사들은 그들의 행동과 무중력 상태의 효과를 연구할 수 있다.

evident 분명한 **recruit** 모집하다

UNIT 147~148

Check-up

P. 122~123

147 **1.** to make **2.** to stop
148 **1.** is to find **2.** is to use

147

1. '계획을 세우는 것'이라는 뜻의 보어 필요

당신이 부인을 위해서 할 수 있는 가장 중요한 것은 그녀가 정말로 원하는 결혼 기념일을 위해 계획을 세우는 것이다.

2. '~해야 한다'는 의미의 be to 용법

당신은 금연을 해야 한다. 그렇지 않다면, 당신은 폐암에 걸릴 지도 모른다.

148

1. One more thing이 find 할 수 없으므로 주격 보어 자리

당신이 해야 하는 또 한 가지는 당신의 여생을 함께 견뎌 낼 진정한 짝을 찾는 것이다.

2. Golub's goal이 uses 할 수 없으므로 주격 보어 자리

골럽의 목표는 암을 표현형이 아닌 유전자형으로 분류할 수 있는 치료를 사용하는 것이다.

EXERCISE

P. 124

01 is to buy **02** is to have **03** be to earn **04** is to copy and paste **05** is to participate **06** is to exercise and run **07** is to gaze **08** is to assume **09** is to search **10** is to watch

01 The best way가 buys 할 수 없으므로 주격 보어 자리

성공적으로 보이는 가장 좋은 방법은 비싼 차와 좋은 집을 사는 것이다.

02 One of the membership conditions가 has 할 수 없으므로 주격 보어 자리

이 클럽의 회원 조건 중 하나는 천만 달러 이상의 자산을 가져야 한다는 것이다.

03 Kevin's first goal이 earn 할 수 없으므로 주격 보어 자리

케빈의 인생 첫 번째 목표는 트레이시와 결혼하기 전 10만 달러를 버는 것이다.

04 The worst way가 copies and pastes 할 수 없으므로 주격 보어 자리

숙제를 하는 가장 최악의 방법은 인터넷에서 필요한 정보를 복사하고 가져다 붙이는 것이다.

05 주어인 one way는 participates라는 행위를 하지 못하므로 주격 보어 형태인 is to participate가 적절

축구를 즐기는 한 가지 방법은 다른 동료들과 함께 운동장에서 실제 게임에 참가하는 것이다.

06 주어인 the lifestyle change가 exercises and runs이라는 행위를 하지 못하므로 주격 보어인 is to exercise and run이 적절

살을 빼기 위한 해야 하는 생활의 변화는 규칙적으로 운동하고 달리는 것이다.

07 주어인 the best advice는 gazes라는 행위를 하지 못하므로 주격 보어인 is to gaze가 적절

청취자가 여러분의 프레젠테이션에 집중하도록 만들기 위한 가장 좋은 조언은 그들과 소통할 때 그들의 눈을 쳐다보라는 것이다.

08 주어인 one common mistake는 assumes이라는 행위를 하지 못하므로 주격 보어인 is to assume이 적절

학생들이 하는 일반적인 실수는 다른 사람들도 같다고 추정하는 것이다.

09 주어인 the next thing은 searchos라는 행위를 하지 못하므로 주격 보어인 is to search가 적절

여러분이 다음에 해야 할 것은 사전에서 모르는 단어를 찾는 것이다.

10 주어인 what절이 watches라는 행위를 할 수 없으므로 주격 보어인 to watch가 적절

우리가 오늘 해야 할 일은 브라질 요리의 기본적인 원료와 피자에서 소시지에 이르는 모든 것을 제공하는 유럽식 전통 요리의 다채로운 결합물을 지켜보는 것이다.

ACTUAL TEST

P. 125

01 ⑤ **02** ③

01 ⑤ 주어가 This tiny tinker이므로 have가 아니라 has가 돼야 함 ① 주어인 The surest way는 do라는 행위를 하지 못하므로 주격 보어인 is to do가 옴 ② lashes, cuts와 병렬 구조 ③ 문장을 연결하는 분사구문 ④ instead of '~대신에'

더욱 건강하고 행복하게 보내는 확실한 방법은 일을 덜 하는 것이다. 6명의 영국 사람 중 1명은 일주일에 60시간 이상 일하고 있으며, 이는 심장 마비이나 뇌졸중에 걸릴 확률을 상당히 늘리고 있다. 하지만 요즘 사람들은 줄이는 새로운 방법을 찾고 있다. 2년 전 유타주의 주지사는 온실가스 방출을 줄이고, 혼잡함을 줄이며, 근로자를 더 행복하게 하려는 간단한 정책을 우연히 발견했다. 주 정부 건물의 난방과 조명 비용을 줄이는 방법을 찾으면서, 그는 주 정부 근로자의 근로 시간을 바꾸는 법을 통과시키기로 결정했다. 주 5일 9시에서 5시까지 대신에 그들은 주 4일 8시에서 6시까지 일하며, 모든 사람들은 금요일을 쉬게 되었다. 이러한 하루 일정에 대한 작은 수정은 놀라운 이득을 가져왔다. 근로자의 82%가 그들은 새로운 일정을 좋아하며, 병가는 줄어들고 효율성은 증가한다고 말한다. 좋은 인생은 멀리 있는 것이 아니다. 단지 약간의 상상력을 필요로 할 뿐이다.

stroke 뇌졸중 **stumble across** 우연히 발견하다 **lash** 묶다 **congestion** 혼잡 **take off** 쉬다 **tinker** 수정

02 (A) The first step이 determines라는 행위를 하는 것이 아니므로 is to determine이 적절 (B) 주어는 rapid changes로 복수이므로 are가 적절 (C) '어떤 기술과 학위가 필요한지 발견해야 한다'라는 의미이므로 which가 적절

요즘 직업 탐색에는 체계적인 노력이 필요하다. 그 첫 단계는 어떤 종류의 직업을 원하는지를 결정하고 거기에 필요한 올바른 교육을 받는 것이다. 기술과 과학의 급속한 발달은 최근까지 존재하지 않았던 많은 직업을 만들어 내고 있다. 그런 직업들 중 하나가 당신에게 딱 맞는 것일 수도 있으므로 그것들에 대하여 아는 것은 중요하다. 새로운 직종으로 가장 빠르게 성장하는 분야는 의료 서비스와 컴퓨터 공학이다. 이런 분야의 직업들은 대개 특정 기술을 요구해서 당신은 정확히 어떤 기술과 학위가 필요한지를 알아낼 필요가 있다.

systematic 체계적인 **profession** 직업

UNIT 149~150

Check-up

P. 126~127

149 **1.** to worry **2.** to reveal
150 **1.** surfing **2.** placing

149

1. afford는 to부정사를 목적어로 취하는 동사

우리는 중요한 문제가 되지 않을 수도 있는 어떤 것에 대해서 걱정할만한 여유가 없다.

2. refuse은 to부정사를 목적어로 취하는 동사

정부 관리들은 뉴타운과 관련된 프로젝트의 더 세부적인 사항을 밝히는 것을 거절했다.

150

1. prefer surfing ~ to reading 구조

아이들은 도서관에 가는 것을 즐기지 않고, 다양한 책을 읽기보다는 인터넷 서핑을 하는 것을 선호하는 것 같다.

2. continue는 to부정사와 동명사 모두를 목적어로 취하는 동사

그들은 신문에 광고를 내는 것을 계속하도록 다른 네티즌들이 회사에 압력을 가하는 것을 막았다.

EXERCISE

P. 128

01 to pay **02** visiting **03** to take **04** to hire **05** to focus **06** to ride **07** enhancing **08** using **09** to challenge **10** to change

01 cannot afford to부정사 '~할 여유가 없다'

출판사는 초과근무 수당을 지급할 여유가 없다.

02 consider는 동명사를 목적어로 취하는 동사

그녀는 대학 도서관이나 서점을 방문하는 것을 고려치 않는다.

03 fail은 to부정사를 목적어로 취하는 동사

그들은 그들 주위의 모든 것이었던 행복의 잠재적 원천을 즐기는 것에 실패했다.

04 can afford to부정사 '~할 여유가 있다'

미국 내에서 조합 임금은 매우 높아져서, 몇몇 회사는 미국인 근로자를 고용할 여유가 없다.

05 fail은 to부정사를 목적어로 취하는 동사

이 에세이는 특정한 측면에 집중하는 것과 그 주제의 요점을 잡는 것에 실패했다.

06 refuse는 to부정사를 목적어로 취하는 동사

흑인들은 인종 차별 정책이 철폐되기 전까지 버스에 타는 걸 거부했고, 그들의 캠페인은 성공했다.

07 suggest는 동명사를 목적어로 취하는 동사

작업 라인이 좀 더 효율적으로 일하도록 격려하기 위해서, 연구소는 기계의 질을 향상시키는 것을 제안했다.

08 discontinue는 동명사를 목적어로 취하는 동사

만약 당신이 휘발유 비용을 줄이고자 한다면, 즉시 그것을 사용하는 것을 멈추고 새로운 것을 시도해 봐라.

09 decide는 to부정사를 목적어로 취하는 동사

숀은 19살 때까지 부모님과 살다가, 스스로 도전하고 도시로 올 것을 결심했다.

10 refuse는 to부정사를 목적어로 취하는 동사

몇몇 다른 부서들은 표적 시장을 바꾸는 것을 거부했다.

ACTUAL TEST

P. 129

01 ⑤ 02 ④

01 ⑤ 〈contribute to -ing〉 '~에 공헌하다, 기여하다'이므로 retreat이 아니라 retreating이 돼야 함 ① 〈one of 한정사+복수 명사〉 구문 ② begin은 목적어로 to부정사와 동명사 모두를 취함 ③ in itself '그 자체로' ④ 앞 문장을 선행사로 받는 계속적 용법의 관계대명사

과학자인 콜와 폴리에 의하면 사바나 지역의 지나친 방목은 호수가 줄어드는 가장 큰 요인 중의 하나이다. "기후가 건조해지면서 방목하는 가축을 먹여 살리던 초목이 사라지기 시작했습니다. 초목은 특히 반 건조 지역에서 기후 양상을 결정하는 데 큰 영향을 끼칩니다."라고 폴리가 말했다. "초원이 사라지면 그 자체만으로 더욱 건조한 기후가 됩니다." 콜은 이런 상황을 '도미노 효과'라고 말했다. 지나친 방목은 초목을 감소시키며 그럼으로써 수분을 대기 중으로 재순환시키는 생태계의 능력을 저하시킨다. 그것은 몬순지역을 줄어들게 하는 데 기여한다. 계속되는 가뭄 상태로 인해 관개 수로를 위한 호수물의 사용이 크게 증가하게 되었고 반면 사하라 사막은 점차 남쪽으로 확장되고 있다.

shrink 줄어들다 vegetation 초목 livestock 가축 ecosystem 생태계 consequent 계속되는 drought 가뭄 trigger 유발하다 irrigation 관개 수로

02 (A) 콤마가 앞에 있으며 선행사인 less stress와 less hostility가 있으므로 which가 정답 (B) 동사 fail은 to부정사를 목적어로 취함 (C) 동명사의 부정은 앞에 부정어를 붙임

연구에 따르면, 용서를 해본 경험이 많은 유럽계 미국인들일수록 심장 질병에 치명적인 스트레스와 적대감을 덜 경험하게 된다. 자신에게 나쁜 짓을 한 사람을 용서하는 상상을 하는 유럽계 미국인들은 그들의 심장 혈관과 근육, 신경계에 즉각적인 개선을 보인다. 심지어 엄청난 상실을 경험한 사람들조차 용서를 할 때 심리나 감정적으로 더 좋아짐을 느낀다고 보고한다. 반면 용서하는 것에 실패한 유럽계 미국인들은 심장 혈관 관련 질병이나 암과 같은 질병에 걸릴 확률이 높아진다. 자신에게 잘못한 사람들을 용서하지 않는 것을 상상하는 유럽계 미국인들은 혈압이나 근육 긴장, 면역 체계에 부정적인 변화를 보여준다. 요약하자면, 용서라는 것은 우리 신체에 긍정적인 영향을 미치게 된다.

hostility 적대감 fatal 치명적인 offender 나쁜 짓을 하는 사람 incidence 발생 tension 긴장 immune 면역의

UNIT 151~152

Check-up

P. 130~131

151 **1.** to lock **2.** giving

152 **1.** breathing **2.** to drink

151

1. 문을 잠그지 않았으므로 to부정사가 적절

잭 바우어는 디자인 맵을 잃어버려서 비난을 받았는데 왜냐하면 그가 어제 사무실 문을 잠그는 것을 잊었기 때문이다.

2. 명함을 준 것을 잊어버린 것이므로 동명사가 적절

영업 사원은 나에게 자신의 명함을 주었던 것을 잊어버리고 다시 명함을 줬다.

152

1. 숨 쉬는 것을 멈춘다는 내용이므로 동명사가 적절

마침내 심바는 숨 쉬는 것을 멈췄다. 눈에 눈물을 머금은 채 의사는, "당신에게 그의 죽음을 말하게 되어 유감스럽다"라고 말했다.

2. 목이 마르므로 물을 마시기 위해서 하던 일을 멈춰야 함

제이미는 갈증이 나서 물 한 병을 마시기 위해서 하던 일을 멈췄다.

EXERCISE

P. 132

01 moving 02 to lock 03 taking 04 developing
05 to inform 06 talking and listening 07 reading
08 visiting 09 to talk 10 to bring

01 '움직임을 멈추다'가 되어야 하므로 동명사가 적절

무언가에 놀라게 될 때, 당신의 내장은 움직임을 멈추며 모든 소화와 관련된 모든 활동은 중단된다.

02 집에 돌아간다는 것은 아직 문을 잠그지 않았다는 것을 의미

나는 문을 잠그는 것을 잊어서 지금 집으로 돌아가야 한다.

03 카페인 섭취를 멈추는 것이므로 taking이 적절

다른 약처럼 중독성이 있지는 않지만, 일단 당신이 정기적으로 커피를 마시는 사람이라면 카페인을 끊는 것은 어렵다.

04 '발달시키는 것을' 멈추는 것이므로 developing이 적절

물고기는 그들의 눈을 발달시키는 것을 멈췄는데, 그들은 아주 어두

운 물속에서 살아서 더 이상 눈을 사용할 필요가 없기 때문이다.

05 회사에서 해고되었음을 알리는 내용이므로 '유감스럽다'를 의미하는 regret to가 되어야 함

우리는 당신의 자리가 없어졌음을 알려드려 유감스럽습니다. 오늘 5시 정각 이전에 책상을 비워주십시오.

06 부부가 소원해지는 이유가 나오므로 '대화를 멈추다'를 의미하는 〈stop -ing〉가 적합

부부들이 서로 대화하고 듣는 것을 멈출 때, 그들의 관계는 소원해진다.

07 '망을 보기 위해서'는 '잡지를 읽는 것'을 멈춰야 함

그 경찰관은 용의자들을 감시하기 위해서 잡지를 읽는 것을 멈췄다.

08 야스쿠니 신사 참배를 그만두라는 내용이므로 〈stop -ing〉 구문을 사용

그 뉴스는 한국의 외무부 장관이 일본 수상의 야스쿠니 신사 방문을 그만 둘 것을 요구하기 위해 그를 서울에서 만날 계획이라고 보도했다.

09 엘렌이 지나가는 것을 봤다는 것은 그녀와 이야기하고 있지 않다는 것을 의미함

아담이 엘렌이 은행을 지나가는 것을 보았을 때, 그는 그녀와 다시 얘기하기 위해서 멈췄다.

10 가져오지 않았으므로 to bring을 사용

그를 위한 추천서를 가져오는 것을 잊었네요. 다시 사무실로 되돌아가야만 해요.

ACTUAL TEST

P. 133

01 ② 02 ③

01 ② 야구를 했던 것을 기억하는 것이므로 to play가 아니라 playing 돼야 함 ① '비교해서' ③ 〈too+형용사+to부정사〉 '너무 ~해서 ~할 수 없다' ④ 〈stop+동명사〉 '~하던 것을 멈추다' ⑤ 〈try+to부정사〉 '~하려고 노력하다'

오늘날의 학생들을 비교할 때, 나는 집에서 많은 것을 할 수 있었고 밖에서 놀 수 있는 충분한 시간 또한 있었다고 생각한다. 숙제를 하는 데는 두 시간 이상 걸리지 않았다. 나는 거의 매일 오후 내내 학교 운동장에서 친구들과 야구를 했던 것을 기억한다. 하지만 나의 아들은 읽기 지문이 그가 읽기에는 너무 어렵고 찾아봐야 하는 모르는 단어가 많아서 숙제를 하는 데 너무 많은 시간을 보내야 한다고 불평한다. 아들은 "숙제를 그만할 수 있게 학창 시절이 빨리 지나갔으면 좋겠어요."라고 말한다. 나는 아들이 안됐고, 그가 학창 시절을 즐기도록 노력하기를 바란다. 나의 학창 시절을 돌아보면, 나는 자유와 즐거움의 세계에서 살았다.

passage 구절 look up (사전에서 정보를) 찾다 look back on 과거를 돌아보다

02 (A) 주어는 the number이므로 단수 (B) '나무 자르는 것을 멈추다' (C) '이용되다'보다는 '~였었다'가 더 자연스러우므로 used가 적절

내가 사는 마을은 벌목에 바탕을 두고 있다. 1980년대에는 많은 일자리와 돈이 있었다. 우리 마을은 활기로 가득 찼었다. 그러나 1992년경에는 우리가 벌목하는 나무의 수가 급격하게 줄어들었다. 왜? 점박이 부엉이가 발견되었고, 그 동물에만 관심이 있는 사람들이 우리 일을 그만 두게 했기 때문이다. 그들은 회사는 나무를 자르는 것을 그만 두어야 한다고 정부를 설득했다. 결과적으로 3만개 이상의 일자리가 사라졌다. 사람들은 식탁에 올릴 음식조차 구하기 힘들다. 우리 마을은 예전 크기의 3분의 1로 작아졌다. 내가 점박이 부엉이를 싫어해서가 아니다. 그러나 부엉이를 구하는 것이 사람들을 해치고 있다. 몇 마리의 부엉이와 성실하게 일하는 수천 명의 사람들 중 무엇이 더 중요한가?

log 벌채하다 drastically 극적으로 convince 설득하다

UNIT 153~154

Check-up

P. 134~135

153 **1.** to refrigerate **2.** to turn

154 **1.** to wear **2.** to create

153

1. 냉장 보관을 안 했으므로 to부정사가 옴

손님들은 도착했고, 와인은 따뜻했다. 또 다시 나는 와인을 냉장고에 넣는 것을 잊어버렸던 것이다.

2. 전화기를 제출하지 않았으므로 to부정사가 옴

보도에 따르면 학생들은 시험 도중에 휴대폰이 켜져 있는 것이 발각되면 시험 전에 휴대폰을 제출하는 것을 잊어버렸다고 말했다.

154

1. advise는 to부정사를 목적격 보어로 쓰는 동사

경찰은 사냥철에는 등산객들이 밝고 화려한 색상의 옷을 입을 것을 조언하고 있다.

2. urge는 to부정사를 목적격 보어로 쓰는 동사

그는 호박을 사는 사람들에게 이번 핼러윈에 그들 스스로 동물원을 만들어보면 어떻겠냐고 권한다

EXERCISE

P. 136

01 to give 02 to have 03 to avoid 04 to submit
05 to accept 06 to get 07 donating 08 to move
09 to apply 10 visiting

01 하지 않은 행동이므로 to부정사가 적절

이 선생님이 그들에게 숙제를 내주는 것을 잊어서 학생들은 안도했다.

02 allow는 목적격 보어로 to부정사를 취함

그는 영국의 영화 제작 스타일은 모든 사람들이 의견을 가지는 것을 허용한다는 것을 발견했다.

03 enable은 목적격 보어로 to부정사를 취함

이러한 전달은 공간적으로 분리된 곤충들이 서로를 피하도록 하는 것을 가능케 하며, 그래서 그들은 의도하지 않게 같은 식물에서 경쟁하지 않는다.

04 안 한 행동이므로 to부정사가 적절

짐은 역사 과목을 낙제했는데, 그는 로마에 대한 마지막 보고서를 내는 것을 깜박했기 때문이다.

05 urge는 목적격 보어로 to부정사를 취함

그녀의 오랜 친구 벤은 내 아들이 케이크를 받도록 재촉했는데 그것은 내 아들이 견디기 힘들 정도였다.

06 안 한 행동이므로 to부정사가 옴

머리카락이 자연스럽게 길게 자라도록 하려면, 머리카락 끝이 상한 것을 없애기 위해서 당신의 머리카락을 매 6~8주마다 자르는 것을 기억해라.

07 again이라는 부사로 보아 이미 발생한 일을 되풀이하는 것

재스민은 지난 달 고아원에 3백만 원을 기부했던 것을 잊었기 때문에, 또 다시 고아원에 3백만 원을 기부했다.

08 permit은 목적격 보어로 to부정사를 취함

컴퓨터의 마우스는 컴퓨터를 사용하는 사람이 비디오 화면상의 커서를 움직이는 것을 가능하게 한다.

09 forbid는 목적격 보어로 to부정사를 취함

그 진술에 따르면 아마도 최악의 행동은 단지 경제적인 문제로 인해 학생이 꿈꾸는 학교에 지원하는 것을 금지하는 것이다.

10 이미 벌어진 일이므로 동명사가 적절

그 아이들은 당신과 좋은 시간을 보냈다. 그들은 이 놀이공원을 방문했던 것을 절대 잊지 않을 것이다.

ACTUAL TEST

P. 137

01 ③ **02** ③

01 ③ force는 목적격 보어로 to부정사를 취하는 동사이므로 get up이 아니라 to get up이 돼야 함 ① sound 뒤에 명사가 올 경우 like가 와야 함 ② afflicts의 주어가 되는 주격 관계대명사 ④ regulates의 주어가 되는 주격 관계대명사 ⑤ news는 단수 취급

그것은 한번에 며칠 동안 잠을 자는 아름다운 소녀에 대한 동화처럼 들린다. 하지만, 클레인 레빈 증후군으로 알려진 희귀병인 잠자는 숲 속의 공주병에 걸린 사람에게는 그녀를 깨워 줄 왕자님이 없는데, 그 병은 전 세계적으로 천 명 가량의 환자가 있다. 환자들은 오랜 기간 동안 보통의 잠 패턴을 가지고 있고, 그러다 그들은 수 일이나 수 주 동안 잠을 자게 된다. 한 소녀는 가장 길게 13일 동안 잤다. 이 긴 낮잠을 자는 동안, 그녀의 부모는 그녀를 강제로 일어나도록 했다. 만약 그렇지 않았더라면 그녀는 이 세상에 없었을 것이다. 클레인 레빈 증후군은 여전히 의사들도 잘 이해하지 못하고 있다. 일부는 유전적이라고 하며, 다른 이들은 자가 면역 체계의 붕괴라고 한다. 대부분은 그 질병을 잠과 식욕을 조절하는 두뇌의 일부인 시상하부의 기능 고장과 연결시킨다. 좋은 소식은 성인이 되면 그러한 증상은 약해지며, 그러는 동안 증상은 약으로 완화될 수 있다는 것이다.

afflict 괴롭히다 **bout** 한바탕 **prolong** 늘리다 **hereditary** 유전성의 **malfunction** 고장 **alleviate** 완화하다

02 (A) become은 2문형 동사로 뒤에 형용사 보어를 취함 (B) encourage는 목적격 보어로 to부정사를 취함 (C) 뒤에 of가 나오므로 invention이 적절

지도력은 이 변화의 시기에 점점 중요해지고 있다. 많은 지도력 개발 프로그램들이 지도력과 관리 능력을 서로 혼동하는 것에서 비롯되었다. 지도력은 단순히 재정에 관련된 사실들을 기억하고 과거의 전략들을 채택하는 것이 아니다. 훌륭한 지도자는 구성원들이 목표를 공유하도록 하고, 조직 내의 직위와 상관없이 의사 결정 과정에 참여하도록 격려한다. 지도력은 소위 상사와 부하 직원 간의 권위적 관계가 아니라 지도자와 따르는 자들 간에 서로 영향력을 주는 관계이다. 미래의 지도력 개발에 대한 비법은 따로 없지만, 민주적 태도로 지도력의 진정한 본질을 이해하는 것이 당신을 올바른 방향으로 이끌어 줄 것이다.

management 관리 **decision-making** 의사 결정 **status** 지위 **superior** 상사 **subordinate** 부하

UNIT 155~156

Check-up

P. 138~139

155 1. training 2. improving
156 1. predict 2. giving

155

1. devote something to -ing '~을 …에 전념하다'

제시카가 두 아이를 돌봐야 했기 때문에, 그녀는 자신이 2년이라는 시간을 훈련하는 데 전념할 수 있을 지 확신하지 못했다.

2. with a view to -ing '~을 위하여'

우리의 임무는 그들에게 정보를 제공함으로써 무언가를 개선하기 위해 우리의 고객이 투자하는 회사와 연결하는 것이다.

156

1. '이용되다'가 자연스러우므로 동사원형이 적절

이 연구들은 주어진 물리적 상황을 포함하는 실험 결과를 예측하는 데 이용될 수 있다.

2. '익숙해지다'가 자연스러우므로 동명사가 적절

우리 감독관은 투자자들에게 신상품에 대해 발표하는 것에 익숙하다.

EXERCISE

P. 140

01 determine **02** pick **03** warn **04** spending
05 cool and heat **06** eating **07** legalizing
08 shorten **09** giving up **10** discouraging

01 be used to 동사원형 '~에 이용되다'

게임은 동전 던지기와 함께 시작되는데, 이것은 어느 팀이 먼저 갈지 결정하기 위해 이용된다.

02 be used to 동사원형 '~에 이용되다'

백혈구는 신체로 다시 주입되며, 특수 카메라는 인듐-111호로부터 신호를 받는 데 사용된다.

03 be used to 동사원형 '~에 이용되다'

누군가가 막 공격하려고 할 때, 이 도구는 나머지 사람들에게 경고하기 위해서 사용될지도 모른다.

04 look forward to -ing '~하기를 고대하다'

나의 아이들은 이미 하와이의 해변에서 자신의 여름 방학을 보내는

것을 기대하고 있다.

05 be used to 동사원형 '~에 이용되다'

열펌프를 사용함으로써 이러한 일정한 온도가 건물을 시원하게 하거나 따뜻하게 하는 데 이용될 수 있다.

06 be used to -ing '~에 익숙하다'

미셸은 약 2년 째 한국에 머물러 있어서 한국 음식을 먹는 데 익숙하다.

07 be opposed to -ing '~에 반대하다'

도박 중독에 대한 열띤 논쟁이 있어왔고, 많은 사람들은 도박을 합법화하는 것에 반대한다.

08 be used to 동사원형 '~에 이용되다'

예를 들어, 패스트푸드점에서 빠른 템포의 음악은 먹는 시간을 단축시키고 더 많은 손님을 받기 위해 이용된다.

09 come close to -ing '거의 ~할 뻔 하다'

교수님이 나에게 주신 그 과제는 너무 어려워서 나 혼자 완성하기 힘들었고, 그래서 나는 몇 번이나 포기할 뻔 했다.

10 contribute to -ing '~에 공헌하다, 기여하다'

그 법은 사람들이 어떤 잘못된 일을 하는 것을 막는 것에 기여할 것이다.

ACTUAL TEST

P. 141

01 ③ 02 ②

01 ③ ⟨be unaccustomed to -ing⟩ 구문이므로 live가 아니라 living이 돼야 함 ① 생리적인 변화가 겪는 것이 아니라 겪어지는 것이므로 수동, 뒤의 that절은 changes를 선행사로 받는 관계대명사절인데 문장의 맨 뒤에 위치 ② regulate를 수식하므로 부사가 옴 ④ ⟨have trouble -ing⟩ 구문 ⑤ 뒤에 진목적어인 to breathe가 오므로 가목적어 it이 옴

사람이 시원하고 비가 오는 해안 지역에서 덥고 건조하며 산이 많은 지역으로 온다면, 새로운 환경에서 생존할 수 있도록 많은 생리적인 변화가 발생한다. 인간의 신체는 체온을 좀 더 효율적으로 조절하기 위해서 변한다. 심장이 과로하는 것을 피하기 위해서, 신체의 심장 박동수는 느려진다. 게다가 신체는 탈수를 막기 위해서 땀을 덜 배출한다. 게다가 고지대에 익숙하지 않은 사람들은 보통 감소된 산소 때문에 호흡에 어려움을 겪는다. 그래서 인간의 신체는 적혈구를 증가시키며, 이는 사람들이 고지대에서 호흡하는 것을 가능케 한다.

coastal 해안의 physiological 생리적인 undergo 겪다
regulate 규제하다 perspire 땀 흘리다 altitude 고도

02 (A) '만드는 데 이용되다' (B) 뒤에 목적어가 나오므로 동명사가 나옴 (C) used 보다 더 이전 일이므로 might have been이 적절

일리노이 주의 캐럴 스트림에 있는 헤리티지 레이크 스쿨에 다니는 아이들은 환경을 보호하기로 결정했다. 그 학생들은 탄력 있는 운동장 바닥을 만드는 데 사용될 수 있는 낡은 고무 바닥의 신발과 운동화를 모았다. 많은 운동장 바닥은 작은 나무 조각들로 쿠션이 깔려 있다. 학생들은 더 안전하고 좀 더 지구 친화적인 바닥을 만들기 위해서 낡은 신발에서 나오는 고무를 재활용할 수 있다는 것을 배웠다. 그 프로젝트는 작은 나무 조각의 대체물을 만들어 냄으로써 나무를 보호하는 것이었다. 그리고 그 프로젝트는 쓰레기 매립지에 버려질 뻔한 낡은 신발들을 사용하는 것이었다. 그 학교의 학급은 471켤레의 신발을 보냈고 그것은 작은 고무조각으로 잘게 잘렸다. 그 고무조각은 새로운 운동장을 덮었다. 어디에선가 아이들은 캐럴 스트림의 낡은 신발 위에서 놀고 있을 것이다.

replacement 대체물 landfill 쓰레기 매립지

UNIT 157~158

Check-up

P. 142~143

157 **1.** to be used **2.** to be made
158 **1.** how to use **2.** what

157

1. 돈이 사용되는 것이므로 수동

철강업 거물인 앤드류 카네기는 학문적 연구를 위해 사용하라고 자선 단체에 50만 달러를 기부했다.

2. 결정이 만들어지는 것이므로 수동

내일 회의에서 이루어질 한 가지 주된 결정 사항은 이 숲을 보존하기 위한 당신의 제안에 대한 우리의 입장에 영향을 줄 것이다.

158

1. '~하는 방법'이 자연스러우므로 ⟨how to ~ ⟩가 적절

블레어는 그녀의 오빠와 아버지로부터 디지털 카메라를 사용하는 법을 배웠고, 지금은 그것을 잘 다룬다.

2. expect의 목적어가 없으므로 what이 자연스러움

그들의 행동은 또한 예측하기가 쉬우며, 그래서 모든 사람들이 무엇을 기대해야 할지 알고 있다.

EXERCISE

P. 144

01 be memorized 02 represent 03 be installed
04 how 05 be inspected 06 receive 07 be found
08 be roasted 09 be seen 10 whether

01 dialogues가 기억되는 것이므로 수동태가 적절

암기된 스크립트와 대화를 기본으로, 언어 수업은 언어 샘플에 대한 교사 주도적인 설명을 특징으로 한다.

02 인간이 물리적인 환경을 묘사하는 것이므로 능동

지도의 발견은 한 가지를 확실하게 한다. 인간은 오랫동안 자신의 물질적인 환경을 묘사하기를 바라왔다는 점이다.

03 운영 체제가 설치되는 것이므로 수동

컴퓨터가 시작하지 않고 프로그램이 설치되어 있지 않다면, 운영 체제가 다시 설치되어야 할 것이다.

04 이용하는 방법이 자연스러우므로 how가 적절

이 디지털시대에, 그림(이미지)는 정보의 필수적인 구성 단위이며, 효과적으로 사진을 이용하는 방법을 아는 것은 이전보다 더 중요하다.

05 상품이 검사되는 것이므로 수동

시장에 내놓기 전에 모든 상품을 철저히 검사될 필요가 있다.

06 고객이 충분한 정보를 받는 것이므로 능동

자신이 사는 물건에 대한 충분한 정보를 받고 싶은 고객은 콜센터에 그것을 요구할 수 있다.

07 동물이 발견되는 것이므로 수동

동물 보호 구역에서 발견되는 동물들은 야생에서 멸종 위기에 있다.

08 냉동 돼지고기가 구워지는 것이므로 수동

냉동 돼지고기는 갈색이 될 때까지 구워지기 위해서 바로 오븐에 놓여진다.

09 줄리아가 컴퓨터를 다루는 것이 지켜보아 지는 것이므로 수동

줄리아가 아버지가 크리스마스에 사준 새 컴퓨터를 잘 다룰 수 있을지 없을지는 두고 보아야 한다.

10 '~할지 아니면 …할지'라는 의미이므로 whether가 적절

나는 파티 장소로 차를 몰고 갈지, 택시를 탈지 결정할 수 없다.

ACTUAL TEST

P. 145

01 ③ **02** ③

01 ③ expanding과 병렬 구조이므로 work가 아니라 working이 돼야 함 ① 내용상 디즈니 사를 가리키므로 단수가 옴 ② 선행사 cultural misunderstanding을 수식 ④ the lesson을 수식하고 '배우게 될'을 의미하므로 to부정사의 수동태가 적절 ⑤ 뒤에 오는 문장이 완전하므로 관계부사가 옴

마케팅과 브랜드 분야에서 선두주자를 생각할 때 디즈니 사가 가장 먼저 떠오른다. 디즈니 사는 브랜드를 홍보하는 데 있어서 귀재를, 훌륭한 마케팅 전문가를, 놀이공원 산업의 선두주자를, 그리고 널리 인식된 브랜드를 보유하고 있다. 그렇다면 디즈니 사가 홍콩과 아시아 태평양 시장으로 사업 확장을 해나가는 데 있어 도대체 무엇이 문제였을까? 해외 시장으로 진출하여 다른 문화의 나라들과 교류할 때 디즈니 사를 예기치 못한 두통거리와 문제로 이끈 것은 문화적 오해였다. 여기서 배우게 되는 교훈은 해외 시장과 당신이 사업을 하게 될 곳의 문화를 이해하는데 돈과 시간을 투자해야 한다는 것이다.

sector 분야 magnificent 훌륭한 overseas 해외의

02 (A) 뒤에 나오는 문장이 완전하므로 주격 보어절을 이끄는 접속사 that이 적절 (B) 〈의문사+to부정사〉 구문으로 '~하는 방법'을 나타내므로 to부정사가 옴 (C) mask는 '누구인지를 아는' 행위를 방해하므로 〈keep A from -ing〉 구문이 적절

눈을 뗄 수 없게 만드는 광대는 일종의 인식이나 관심을 찾고 있다. 슬픈 것은 그는 남을 위해 바보짓을 하는 것으로만 관심을 받을 수 있다고 생각하는 것이다. 보다 깊이 들어가면, 그는 자신의 역할과 동일시하고 있고, 아무것도 진지하게 생각하지 않음으로써 현실 세계를 무시하려고 애쓸 지도 모른다. 광대 짓을 하는 것은 때론 도피 장치이다. 광대는 심각한 상황에서 자기 자신을 다루는 법을 알지 못하며, 그래서 그는 무책임한 명랑함이라는 태도를 취한다. 다른 사람을 다루는데 있어, 광대 짓은 남들이 자신이 누구인지를 알지 못하도록 하는 충분히 방어적인 가면의 역할을 하고 있다. 그는 인생의 우울한 현실에 직면하기 보다는 오히려 웃고 농담을 한다.

compulsive (너무 흥미로워) 눈을 뗄 수 없는 serve as ~의 역할을 하다 sufficient 충분한 blue 우울한

REVIEW TEST

P. 146

01 for → of **02** makes easier → makes it easier
03 revealing → to reveal **04** producing → produce
05 to not bury → not to bury **06** to sit **07** to detect
08 to write **09** to tell **10** make

01 비난을 의미하는 형용사이므로 의미상 주어 앞에는 of를 붙임

우리 모두가 그 상황에 있었을 때, 당신이 그런 편지를 그녀에게 쓴 것은 경솔했다.

02 뒤에 진목적어인 to recall이 나오므로 가목적어 it이 필요

사실 무엇을 잊는다는 것은 중요한데, 그것은 새로운 기억을 회상하는 것을 더 쉽게 만들기 때문이다.

03 fail은 to부정사를 목적어로 쓰는 동사임

1980년대부터 대부분의 조사는 매칭 교수법이 학습 스타일로서 효과가 있음을 보여 주는데 실패했다.

04 '~에 이용되다'를 의미하므로 〈be used to부정사〉가 적절

새롭게 만들어진 공장은 연간 15만 대의 차량 생산력을 가지고 있으며, 유럽 시장을 위해 특화된 모델을 생산하는 데 사용될 것이다.

05 to부정사의 부정어는 to 앞에 위치

준은 유방암을 겪는 사람들에게 주의 깊은 현실적인 태도를 가지며 스스로를 자신감이라는 허울뿐인 장막 아래 묻지 말라고 충고했다.

06 encourage는 목적격 보어로 to부정사를 사용

유치원 이후로, 교사들은 아이들이 뛰고 돌아다니기보다는 자리에 앉을 것을 장려한다.

07 가주어 it이 문장을 이끌므로 진주어인 to부정사가 필요

맨 눈이 지평선 근처에서 태양의 정확한 위치를 보는 것은 불가능하다.

08 앞에 있는 pen을 수식하는 to부정사가 필요

나는 쓸 수 있는 아무 펜이나 필요했지만 찾을 수가 없었고, 결국 설문지를 채우지 못했다.

09 하지 않은 일이므로 to부정사를 사용

나는 파트너에게 계약에 관한 중요한 어떤 것을 말하는 것을 잊었고, 그래서 나는 다른 회의를 위해 그에게 전화를 해야만 한다.

10 '~에 이용되다'를 의미하므로 〈be used to부정사〉 구문이 옴

최첨단 기법이 싱가포르에 있는 건물의 건축을 위한 성공적인 입찰에 사용되었다.

FINAL CHECK

P. 147~149

01 ① **02** ④ **3** ⑤ **04** ⑤ **05** ② **06** ②

01 ① '태우는 데 이용되다'라는 뜻이므로 to carrying이 아니라 to carry가 돼야 함 ② 〈consider+목적어+목적격 보어〉 구문인데 목적어가 주어 자리로 가고 동사 뒤에는 목적격 보어만 남았으므로 수동태가 적절 ③ Clydesdales를 수식, 뒤에 목적어가 없으므로 과거분사가 옴 ④ 뒤에 완전한 문장이 오므로 관계부사가 옴 ⑤ 주어는 their high-stepping walk로 단수

중세에 말은 주로 방패와 무기로 무장한 전사들을 태우는 데 이용되었다. 당시에 말은 탱크로 여겨졌다. 그 후 사람들은 농사일과 수레를 끄는데 사용하기 위해 말을 길렀다. '짐을 끄는' 말이라고 불리는 클라이스데일은 무거운 짐을 끄는 데 이용되는 대단히 힘센 말이었다. 클라이스데일이란 이름은 이 품종의 말이 개발된 스코틀랜드의 클라이스데일이라는 지명에서 유래했다. 클라이스데일은 1700년대에 수입된 플랑드르의 수말과 스코틀랜드의 암말을 교배시킨 것에서 유래했다. 산업 혁명으로 인해 클라이스데일이 담당했던 운반 기능은 쇠퇴했다. 1950년대에 클라이스데일의 수는 최소치를 기록했다. 클라이스데일은 결혼식과 같은 특별한 행사 때 행진을 하기 위한 말로 복귀했다. 발을 높이 올리며 걷는 클라이스데일의 걸음걸이는 사람들의 시선을 끌며 군중들에게 즐거움을 준다.

armored 무장한 **shield** 방패 **haul** 끌다 **mare** 암컷 말 **bring about** 발생하다

02 (A) 인간의 skeleton을 비교하므로 that of a man이 적절 (B) 주어는 the remains이므로 복수 (C) 5문형으로 뒤에 진목적어인 that절이 나오므로 가목적어 it이 필요

이탈리아 남부에서 발굴된, 서기 1세기로 거슬러 올라가는 해골은 동아시아계 남자의 것으로 확인되었다. 그 기간 동안 이탈리아에 살았던 아시아인에 대한 첫 번째 증거인 이 유물은 바리 지방 근처에 있는 바그나리에 있는 무덤에서 발굴되었다. 남아있는 치아에 대한 산소 동위 원소 조사에서 그 남자가 원래 이탈리아 남부지방 출신이 아니라는 것을 밝혀낸 동시에 그의 DNA에 대한 연구는 그가 동아시아인이라는 사실도 밝혀냈다. 그가 이탈리아에 여행을 왔는지, 아니면 그의 조상이 그곳에 정착했었는지는 알 방법이 없다. 하지만, 무덤의 간결함은 그가 귀족적인 외교관은 아니라는 사실은 명백하게 해주었다. 이러한 발견은 로마 시대의 사람들의 이동과 세계화에 대한 많은 의문을 제기한다.

unearth 발굴하다 **remains** 유물 **ancestry** 가계, 혈통 **isotope** 동위 원소

03 ⑤ need는 to부정사를 목적어로 취하므로 including이 아니라 to include가 돼야 함 ① '눈을 움직이는 것'은 수단이 되어야 하므로 〈by ~ing〉 구문이 적절 ② listeners를 의미하므로 them이 옴 ③ 나머지 하나가 아닌 '다른 하나'를 언급함 ④ to부정사의 부정형

시선 맞추기는 청중의 관심을 유지하는 데 중요한 역할을 한다. 당신의 눈을 한 사람에게서 다른 사람으로 움직임으로써, 당신은 청중에게 당신이 그들에게 개개인 별로 이야기하고 있다는 느낌을 줄 수 있다. 당신은 또한 그들의 얼굴을 바라봄으로써 사람들이 당신의 메시지를 이해하는지 아닌지를 알 수 있다. 많은 사람들과 함께 할 경우, 말하는 동안 당신은 눈을 천천히 방의 한 부분에서 다른 부분으로 옮겨야만 한다. 소수의 사람이나 의장과 같은 단 한 사람에게 집중하지 않도록 주의해라. 당신은 청중들을 똑바로 바라봄으로써 모든 사람을 당신의 관객으로 포함시킬 필요가 있다.

play a role 역할을 하다 **section** 부분

04 (A) 뒤에 완전한 문장이 오므로, belief의 동격절을 이끄는 접속사 that이 옴 (B) 두 팔 중 나머지 하나 (C) 과거에 발생한 사건이므로 〈to have p.p.〉가 옴

노세보 효과는 어떤 것이 아무런 영향이 없음에도 불구하고 그것이 나쁘다고 믿음으로써 생기는 악영향이다. 일본의 연구원들에 의해 시행된 한 실험이 이것을 입증했다. 그들은 57명의 고등학교 소년들의 알레르기를 일으키는 물질에 대한 민감성을 실험했다. 소년들은 옻나무로 겪은 과거의 경험에 관한 설문지를 작성했는데, 이 나무는 가려운 발진을 일으킬 수 있다. 독성이 있는 나무에 대해 심각한 반응이 있다고 보고한 소년들은 눈이 가려졌다. 연구원들은 한 쪽 팔에 옻나무 잎을 문지르고는 소년들에게 그것이 밤나무 잎이라고 말하고, 다른 쪽 팔에는 밤나무 잎을 문지르고, 그것이 옻나무 잎이라고 말했다. 놀랍게도, 소년들이 독성이 있는 나무에 노출되었다고 믿었던 팔에 발진이 생기기 시작했다. 대부분의 경우에 실제 독에 접촉되었던 팔은 아무런 반응이 없었다.

sensitivity 민감도 **allergen** 알레르기 유발 항원 **blindfold** 눈을 가리다 **chestnut tree** 밤나무

05 ② 선행사가 없고, 뒤에 오는 문장에 주어가 없으므로 which가 아니라 what이 돼야 함 ① 주어는 the problem이므로 단수 ③ '언제든지' ④ 주어로 사용되며, 뒤에 doing의 목적어가 없는 불완전 문장이 옴 ⑤ to부정사의 부정어는 to 앞에 옴

천문학 개론 강의 첫 날, 나는 다음과 같은 말을 한다. "분명히 나는 여러분에게 의도적으로 그릇된 정보를 주려는 것은 아닙니다." 그리고, 나는 덧붙였다. "우리 모두의 문제는 우주에 대한 천문학자들의 이해가 너무나 빠르게 변화하기 때문에 오늘날 맞는 것으로서 받아들여지는 지식의 일부가 맞지 않은 것으로 밝혀질 수 있습니다. 나는 지식 체계에서 일어나는 변화에 대해 알게 될 때마다 언제라도 수정할 것입니다." 실제로 수년에 걸쳐 내가 제시해 온 수정된 사항들은 다양한 행성궤도를 돌고 있는 위성의 수, 새로운 성계(星係)의 형성에 관한 것들과 같은 세부 사항들이었다. 내가 이 말을 통해 하고 있는 것은 학생들에게 우주론에 관해 내가 설명하는 것 모두를 절대적 진리로 받아들이지 말 것을 알려주는 것이다.

introductory 입문자를 위한 **announcement** 공고 **cosmos** 우주 **orbit** 궤도를 돌다 **cosmology** 우주론

06 (A) 주어는 the phrase "drill and kill"임 drill and kill을 두 개로 보지 말아야 함 (B) help가 5문형으로 쓰일 때 목적격 보어 자리에 동명사는 올 수 없음 (C) 앞에 사역동사 have가 오므로 동사원형이 옴

'반복 학습'이라는 단어는 잘못된 가르침이라고 여겨진다. 교육적인 환경에서 '반복 학습과 죽이기'라는 구절이 사용되는데, 이는 교사들이 반복 학습 기술을 통해서 학생들이 배우고자 하는 동기를 없앨 수 있다는 것을 의미한다. 사실, 반복 학습 자체는 원래 생각만큼 많이 나쁜 것은 아니다. 심지어 그것은 일부 학생들이 어떤 것을 배울 때 유용할 수도 있다. 우선, 반복 학습은 학생들이 구조적이거나 문법적인 요소들에 집중하도록 도와준다. 또한 그들이 배운 것을 평가하는 방법을 제공할 수 있다. 학생들은 반복 학습을 함으로써 그들이 학습한 것을 쉽게 확인한다. 어떤 교사들은 학생들은 학업적인 면에 능숙하지 못하므로, 그들은 어떤 지식이 자동화가 되도록 할 필요가 있다고 한다. 즉, 학생들은 생각하지 않고 무언가를 할 수 있어야만 한다는 것이다.

motivation 동기 **structural** 구조적인 **automatic** 자동적인

chapter

14 접속사

UNIT 159~160

Check-up P. 152~153

159 **1.** that **2.** What

160 **1.** 여자로서 차이를 만들 수 있었던 것은 나를 기쁘게 한다. **2.** 그가 길을 따라 걷고 있었을 때, 한 무리의 시위자들을 만났다.

159

1. 뒤에 오는 문장이 완전하므로 접속사 that이 자연스러움

실험 결과들은 각각의 수화가 거의 항상 얼굴 표정을 따른다는 것을 나타냈다.

2. 선행사가 없고 worried about 뒤의 목적어가 없는 불완전한 문장이 나오므로 what이 적절

우리가 걱정하는 것은 상황이 그 어느 때보다도 더 악화될 수 있을 것 같다는 것이다.

EXERCISE P. 154

01 whose **02** that **03** which **04** that **05** that
06 Simple as **07** that **08** that **09** that **10** that

01 뒤에 일반명사가 나오며, 집의 지붕을 의미하므로 whose가 적합

집, 지붕이 눈으로 덮여 있는 저 집을 봐.

02 ⟨It ~ that⟩ 강조 구문

비행기가 연착된 것은 바로 폭설 때문이었다.

03 앞에 전치사 in이 있으며 완전한 문장을 이끌고 있으므로 which가 적절

학자들은 사회 내에서의 발전과 사회들이 서로 관련되어있는 방법 모두를 연구하는 것을 통해 인간의 역사를 이해하는 것을 추구한다.

04 The public opinion과 동격절을 이끄는 접속사 필요

사형 제도 폐지되어야 한다는 여론은 점점 강해질 것이다.

05 the fact와 동격인 완전한 문장이 오므로 that이 적절

발음의 정의는 청자의 지각이 중요한 역할을 한다는 사실을 강조한다.

06 ⟨형용사+as+주어+동사⟩ '~임에도 불구하고'

간단한 것처럼 보임에도 불구하고, 지금까지 아무도 이 문제를 풀지 못한다.

07 chances와 동격인 완전한 문장이 오므로 that이 적절

여러분 모두는 영국 비행기에 탄 그들의 사랑하는 사람들이 폭발에서 살아남을 수 있는 기회가 적음을 알고 있다.

08 likelihood와 동격인 완전한 문장이 오므로 that이 적절

광고 빈도를 늘려서, 광고 회사들은 목표 시장의 구성원들이 광고에 노출될 가능성을 늘린다.

09 evidence와 동격인 완전한 문장이 오므로 that이 적절

도시 점검 체계가 공기 질의 차이를 만든다는 증거는 거의 없다.

10 News와 동격인 완전한 문장이 나오므로 that이 적절

나는 수진이가 영어 말하기 대회에서 1등으로 입상했다는 소식을 들었다.

ACTUAL TEST P. 155

01 ③ **02** ⑤

01 ③ be reluctant to 동사원형 '~을 꺼리다'라는 뜻으로 to going이 아니라 to go가 돼야 함 ① 앞의 the idea와 동격인 문장을 이끄는 접속사 that임 ② 사람들이 그의 생각을 따르는 것이므로 능동 ④ something은 형용사가 뒤에서 수식 ⑤ ⟨the 비교급, the 비교급⟩ 구문

몇 년 전 텍사스에서 사람들은 대부분의 석유를 표면 작업에서 얻었다. 그때, 누군가가 더 깊은 곳에 더 많은 석유가 있을 것이라는 생각을 해냈다. 그의 생각을 따라서 사람들은 5천 피트 아래로 유정을 팠다. 놀랍게도 엄청난 분유정이 나왔다. 우리 중 많은 사람들이 표면에서 작업을 한다. 우리는 좀처럼 우리의 놀라운 자원을 발견하기 위해서 더 깊이 가려고 하지 않는다. 다시 말해서 우리는 우리의 능력을 위한 새로운 분야를 찾는데 최선을 다하지 않는다. 우리가 더 많은 시간과 노력을 사용할 때, 우리는 대가로 엄청난 것, 즉 분유정을 얻게 될 것이다. 당신은 성공하기 위해 얼마나 깊이 파 봤는가? 성공하는 사람과 그렇지 못한 사람들 사이에는 큰 차이가 있다. 당신이 깊이 파면 팔수록, 당신은 분유정에 더 가깝게 가는 것이다.

operation 작업 come up with 생각해 내다 oil well 유정 gusher 분유정 do one's best 최선을 다하다

02 (A) 접속사 없이 문장이 연결되므로 관계대명사가 적절 (B) 문장에 주어 those의 본동사가 없으므로 did not tend가 적절 (C) 뒤에 완전한 문장이 오므로 앞의 명사 the new theory의 동격절을 이끄는 접속사 that이 적절

사람들 자신의 개성을 표현하기 위해서 문신이나 피어싱을 한다고 한다. 하지만, 최근의 연구에 따르면 다른 심리학적인 요인이 있다. 폴란드의 연구원들은 약 200명의 남성과 여성을 조사했는데, 그중 반 정도는 신체적 대칭을 위해 귀를 제외한 다른 곳에 문신이나 피어싱을 했다. 이러한 장식을 한 남성들은 그렇지 않는 사람들보다 더 나은 신체적 균형을 보여준 반면 여성에게서는 별 차이가 없었다. 더욱이 덜 균형잡힌 사람들은 문신이나 피어싱을 하려고 하지 않았다. 이러한 연구는 사람들이 신체에 장식을 하는 것은 그들이 외모상의 결점을 감추기를 원해서가 아니라 단지 높은 생물학적인 특성을 보이는 이들은 바늘로 찔려서 감염되는 위험한 행동을 할 여유가 있기 때문이라는 새로운 이론을 제안했다.

symmetry 대칭 drawback 단점 infection 감염

UNIT 161~162

Check-up P. 156~157

161 **1.** because of **2.** because of
162 **1.** Despite **2.** Although

161

1. 명사구 the irrelevant details가 오므로 because of가 적절

화자가 포함하는 연관성 없는 세부 사항들 때문에 만들어지고 있는 주요 사항을 이해하기는 것은 가끔 어렵다.

2. 명사구 the low ~ hygiene가 오므로 because of가 적절

에이즈를 유발하는 바이러스인 HIV는 낮은 교육 수준과 거의 없는 위생 관념 때문에 제3세계에서 빠르게 확산되고 있다.

162

1. 뒤에 명사인 the fact가 오므로 Despite가 적절

소녀들이 소년들보다 더 빨리 성숙하는 경향이 있다는 사실에도 불구하고 나의 딸은 모든 면에서 대부분의 또래들보다 훨씬 뒤떨어진다.

2. 뒤에 주어와 동사를 포함한 문장이 오므로 Although가 정답

비록 가장 잘 알려진 프랜차이즈는 패스트푸드 사업이지만 프랜차이즈는 부동산 중개업이나 비디오 대여점과 같은 많은 산업 분야에서 가능하다.

EXERCISE P. 158

01 Although 02 although 03 Despite
04 Because of 05 because 06 though 07 although
08 because 09 Despite 10 Despite

01 뒤에 문장이 오므로 접속사 Although가 적절

그녀 몸 안의 모든 신경이 그것을 하지 말라고 경고했음에도 불구하고, 그녀는 천천히 문을 밀어서 열었다.

02 형용사 앞에 being이 생략된 분사구문으로 접속사가 적절

그러므로 색채 심리학은 흥미롭기는 하지만, 성격 유형을 분석하는 데 있어서 단지 광범위한 일반화를 제공할 뿐이다.

03 뒤에 명사구가 나오므로 전치사 Despite가 적절

언론의 관심은 피해야 한다는 톰의 요구에도 불구하고, 그의 동료들은 많은 매체와의 인터뷰를 했다.

04 뒤에 명사구가 나오므로 because of가 적절

냄새를 저장하고 발산하는 그들의 능력 덕분에 어떤 꽃들은 곤충을 먹기 위해 곤충을 유혹한다.

05 뒤에 문장이 나오므로 접속사 because가 적절

어떤 단체도 다수에 속하고 지배할 만큼 충분한 사람을 가지지 못하기 때문에 우리는 살아간다.

06 뒤에 분사구문이 오므로 접속사가 적절

그 소떼는 토니 산도스키의 소유임에도 불구하고, 산도스키 가족의 소유물로 여겨진다.

07 뒤에 형용사구가 나오는데, 분사구문 취급하므로 접속사가 적절

예약 제도라는 말은 약속 제도와 아주 유사하지만, 고객이 실제로 그 서비스와 관련된 시설물을 이용할 때 사용된다.

08 뒤에 문장이 오므로 접속사 because가 적절

지난 일요일 밤에 선술집은 사람들이 안쪽으로 가까스로 자리를 끼어 앉아 있어서 작지만 따스했고, 어느 정도 환영하는 분위기였다.

09 뒤에 명사구가 나오므로 전치사 Despite가 적절

전자레인지 오븐에서 진공청소기에 이르는 노동력을 절감시키는 기구가 증가함에도 불구하고 현대의 인간들은 예전 조상들보다 여가 시간이 적은 것 같다.

10 뒤에 명사구가 나오므로 전치사 Despite가 적절

컴퓨터, CD롬 멀티미디어, 인터넷과 같은 발달된 기술의 잠재력에도 불구하고, 일부 작가들은 이러한 기술들이 외국어를 배우는 데는 이상적이지 않다고 주장한다.

ACTUAL TEST P. 159

01 ② 02 ④

01 ② 뒤에 문장이 오므로 because of가 아니라 because가 적절
① let의 목적격 보어이며, 목적어와의 관계가 능동이므로 원형이 옴 ③ '그녀의 공' ④ 과거의 경험을 의미 ⑤ 〈keep from -ing〉 '~하는 것을 막다'

어렸을 때 시씨는 그녀가 가장 좋아했던 게임을 하도록 허용하지 않았던 소년들 때문에 낙심하지 않았다. 그 소년들이 가지고 놀고 싶어 하는 축구공이 그녀의 것이었기 때문에, 결국 그녀는 브라질의 살바도르 거리에서 마음껏 축구를 했다. 그럼에도 불구하고, 그녀는 종종 그 소년들이 보여주었던 부정적인 태도에 좌절감이 커지면 그녀의 공을 가지고 집으로 달려갔다. 시씨는 집 주변에서 발견했던 모든 종류의 물건들을 가지고 연습을 하면서 축구를 배웠다. 그 물건들은 둘둘 말린 양말들과 그녀의 인형 머리들이었다. 그녀의 아버지는 마침내 그녀가 인형들을 망가뜨리지 않도록 그녀가 축구공이 필요하다고 결정했다.

discouraged 낙심한 display 보이다 negative 부정적인

02 (A) 재고가 필요로 하는 것이 아니라 재고를 필요로 하는 것이므로 수동 (B) 뒤에 전치사구가 오는데, 일종의 분사구문으로 볼 수 있으므로 문장 취급하고, 전치사구는 전치사의 목적어가 될 수 없으므로 Although가 적절 (C) 뒤에 목적어가 없으므로 '발생하다'라는 뜻의 자동사 arise가 적절

GE의 사업 부문 대부분은 비효율적인데, 상품배달의 목표 수준을 성취하기 위해 필요한 것보다 더 많은 재고를 유지하기 때문이다. 그들은 독립적인 수요품목들을 위해 안전 재고를 결정하기 위한 ABC 분석과 같은 단순화된 접근법을 종종 이용했는데, 그것은 공급이나 수요의 불확실성, 또는 비용을 무시한 것이었다. 이러한 상황에 대한 해결책은 부품 이용 가능성 목표를 사용하고 가능한 많은 불확실성을 포함하는 정기적 확인 시스템을 개발하는 것이었다. 그 시스템은 P시스템과 원칙적으로 유사하지만 상대적으로 이해하기 쉽고, 재고 간격과 변수를 결정하기 위해 복잡한 방정식을 사용한다. 그러한 복잡성은 안전 재고의 결정에 있어서 수요뿐만 아니라, 공급 면에서의 불확실성을 고려해서 발생한다.

inventory 재고 analysis 분석 stock 재고 periodic 정기적인 availability 이용 가능성 equation 방정식 interval 간격

UNIT 163~164

Check-up P. 160~161

163 **1.** During **2.** while 164 **1.** by creating **2.** but

163

1. 뒤에 명사구 the same period~가 나오므로 During이 적절

원유 가격이 급격하게 증가한 것과 같은 시기 동안, 일본, 스웨덴, 독일에서의 산업 생산은 40% 더 에너지 효율적으로 되었다.

2. 뒤에 전치사구만 나오므로 문장 취급하여 while이 적절

그러한 교육의 피해자는 재학 중 창의적인 재능을 개발하는 교육을 받아야만 한다.

164

1. not by -ing but by -ing의 병렬 구조, '~함으로써가 아니라 …함으로써'

다른 사람들은 우리를 관찰하거나 평가함으로써가 아니라 주의산만을 유발함으로써 우리의 성과에 영향을 미친다.

2. ⟨not A but B⟩ 'A가 아니라 B'

지금 우리에게 중요한 것은 무엇을 먹는 것이 아니라, 어떻게 사느냐이다.

EXERCISE P. 162

01 While 02 During 03 During 04 while 05 During
06 but 07 While 08 but 09 during 10 while

01 전치사구는 문장 취급하므로 접속사 While이 적절

학회 중에 그녀는 영화에서 아시아인에 대한 고정 관념을 깨도록 하는 실험 영화를 접하게 되었다.

02 뒤에 명사구가 나오므로 During이 적절

지난 2주 동안 제니의 건강은 호전되었고, 그녀의 가족은 마음이 편해졌다.

03 뒤에 명사구가 나오므로 전치사 During이 적절

그의 뉴욕 방문 동안, 찰스는 초등학교 시절의 오랜 친구를 우연히 만났다.

04 뒤에 전치사구가 나오므로 접속사 while이 적절

제리는 그녀가 회사에 있는 동안 판매액이 7%에서 12%에 이르는 연매출 증가를 이뤘다는 사실을 보고 놀랐다.

05 뒤에 명사구가 나오므로 전치사 During이 적절

내가 토마스를 가르쳤던 학기 동안, 그는 자신의 포트폴리오에 8학년 물리 수업을 시작했다.

06 ⟨not A but B⟩ 'A가 아니라 B'

당신은 돈과 보석으로 친구를 살 수 없지만, 마음으로 친구를 살 수는 있다.

07 뒤에 전치사구가 나오므로 접속사 While이 적절

감옥에 있는 동안, 그녀는 자신의 경험을 바탕으로 단편 소설을 쓰기 시작했다.

08 ⟨not A but B⟩ 'A가 아니라 B'

우리의 목적은 당신을 위해서 그것을 하는 것이 아니라, 당신 스스로 그것을 하도록 당신을 가르치는 것이다.

09 접속사는 관계사와 같이 쓰이지 못하므로 during이 적절

그 이론에 따르면 두뇌의 양극화가 마무리되면, 인간이 어떤 언어에서 원어민 수준의 발음을 습득할 수 있는 중요한 시기가 끝나게 된다.

10 뒤에 분사구문이 나오므로 접속사 while이 적절

정부는 대표단 사이에 협력 관계를 만드는 동안 고유한 특징과 유산을 강조하는 그룹 활동을 한다.

ACTUAL TEST P. 163

01 ② 02 ③

01 ② 뒤에 문장이 오므로 during이 아니라 while이 적절 ① 분사 chosen을 수식하므로 부사가 옴 ③ '거의' ④ biotech crops가 보는 게 아니라 보여지는 것이므로 수동 ⑤ '대개'

생명 공학은 인류 역사상 가장 빈번하게 선택된 곡물 공학이다. 지지자들은 생명 공학을 점점 늘어나는 인구와 물 자원으로 영양을 공급하는 유한한 경작지에서 우리가 빠져나오는 동안 생산량을 증가시킬 수 있는 유일한 방법으로 생각한다. 산업계는 유전자 조작 작물을 사용한지 거의 20년이 지났는데 전통적인 경작지와 곡물이 평화롭게 공존하는 것을 보여주고 있기 때문에, 먹거리 안전 문제에 대한 관련 증거가 없고 생물의 다양성에도 위협이 없다고 주장한다. 제초제에 항성이 있는 유전자 조작 식물로부터 특성을 받은 수퍼 잡초와 같은 일부 문제점은 발생할 수도 있다. 하지만, 약 10% 정도 살충제 사용을 줄이기만 한다면 지금까지 생명 공학 곡물은 대체적으로 환경에 이익을 주고 있는 것 같다.

farmland 경작지 nourish 영양을 공급하다 biodiversity 생물의 다양성 coexist 공존하다 herbicide 제초제 pesticide 살충제

02 (A) 뒤에 분사구문과 전치사구가 나오므로 while이 적절
(B) devote oneself to -ing '일생을 ~하는 데 바치다'
(C) make의 목적격 보어로 사용되며, him과의 관계가 수동임

많은 사람들이 여행이나 휴가 중에 미래를 위해 그 경험을 보존해 두려고 수많은 사진을 찍는다. 그러나 사진사의 역할이 사실은 현재 순간의 즐거움을 떨어뜨릴 수 있다. 나는 첫 아이이자 외동 아이의 탄생 사진을 찍는 데 진지하게 몰두했던 한 아버지를 안다. 사진들은 아름다웠지만 자기 아들의 삶에서 가장 중요한 첫 번째 순간을 놓쳤다는 생각이 느낀 후에 탄식했다. 카메라 렌즈를 통해 바라보는 것은 그를 현장에서 분리되도록 만들었다. 그는 체험자가 아니라 단지 관찰자였다. 사물을 진심으로 바라보고 무엇이 아름답고 의미 있는지 의식함으로써 계속 진행 중인 경험을 받아들이는 방법으로 카메라를 사용할 수 있도록 스스로 가르쳐라.

detract 감소시키다 earnestly 진지하게 lament 한탄하다 detach 떼어내다 ongoing 지속되는

UNIT 165~166

Check-up P. 164~165

165 **1.** as if **2.** as if 166 **1.** unless **2.** unless

165

1. 앞에 감각동사 look이 있고, 내용상 '마치 ~처럼'이 적절

어떤 것은 마치 오랫동안 잘 돌봐지지 않았던 것처럼 보이지만, 나

는 그것들의 아름다움이 마모된 표면 아래에 여전히 있음을 알고 있다.

2. '마치 ~처럼'

그는 뒤에서 누군가 떨어지는 것을 들었지만, 돌아서서 마치 아무것도 듣지 못한 것처럼 계속 걸어갔다.

166

1. '~하지 않는다면'

예상치 못했던 일이 발생하지 않는다면 평소처럼 그가 말한 것을 따라야 한다.

2. '~하지 않는다면'

애플, HP, 구글과 같은 IT 산업은 우리 미국인들이 기술과 과학에 더 많은 돈을 투자하지 않는다면 그들의 외국 경쟁회사에 의해 빛을 잃을 수 있다.

EXERCISE P. 166

01 as if **02** as if **03** unless **04** even if **05** Even if
06 unless **07** as if **08** even if **09** unless **10** even if

01 seemed 다음에 왔고, 내용상 '마치 ~처럼'이 적절

마치 어느 누구도 전에는 이와 같은 건축물을 만든 적이 없었던 것 같았다.

02 '마치 ~인 것처럼'

그가 그들에게 접근했을 때, 그들은 마치 그가 거기에 없는 것처럼 계속해서 말을 했다.

03 '~하지 않는다면'

그들 모두 그것이 끝났다고 하지 않는다면 그림은 완성되지 않은 것이었다.

04 두 문장의 내용이 대립하므로 even if가 적절

심지어 우리가 다른 나라에서 왔더라도 우리 둘 다 이해하며 고마워할 수 있다.

05 두 문장의 내용이 대립하므로 Even if가 적절

비록 그들이 유언장에 우리에게 돈을 남긴다 하더라도, 우리가 그 돈을 받을 만한 기회는 없다.

06 '~하지 않는다면'

기차는 늘 제 시간에 오니 네가 기차를 놓치지 않는다면 늦지 않을 거야.

07 '마치 ~처럼'

마치 그들이 이벤트를 망치고 있던 것처럼 어두운 하늘은 경기장 위에 비를 퍼부을 조짐을 보이고 있었다.

08 두 문장의 내용이 대립하므로 even if가 적절

10대 소녀들은 심지어 그녀가 나중에 배가 고파지더라도 점심에 양상추 샐러드만을 먹는데, 왜냐하면 그것은 그녀의 친구들이 먹는 것이기 때문이다.

09 '~하지 않는다면'

나의 이웃은 그가 기르는 고양이가 내는 끽끽 소리에 대한 불평을 듣고 싶지 않다면 나의 개가 짖는 것에 대해서 불평하지 않아야 한다.

10 두 문장의 내용이 대립하므로 even if가 적절

만약 어떤 것이 쉽게 수리가 된다면, 이것은 결국 매립지에 버려질 확률을 낮출 것이고, 비록 처음에 돈이 더 들더라도 길게 보면 당신의 돈을 쉽게 절약할 수 있을 것이다.

ACTUAL TEST P. 167

01 ② **02** ④

01 ② '소금이 묻혀져 있지 않다면'이라는 의미가 돼야 하므로 if가 아니라 unless가 적절 ① be의 보어 ③ The standard cookbook이 주어, is가 동사 ④ 뒤에 오는 것이 분사구문이므로 접속사가 필요 없음 ⑤ ⟨It takes 시간/돈 to 부정사⟩ 구문

루마니아는 비만과의 전쟁을 선포했다. 정부는 유럽 최초로 패스트푸드나 사탕, 단 음료수 등에 대한 추가 부담금인 비만세를 도입할 계획이다. 학교에서의 정크 푸드의 판매 또한 금지될 것이다. 다른 유럽 나라들은 이러한 선구적인 조치에 감명을 받았고, 그 결과를 주의 깊게 관찰할 것이다. 하지만, 너무 크게 기대하지는 말아야 한다. 이곳에서는 고기가 빠진 식사는 완벽하다고 생각하지 않는다. 소금을 듬뿍 바르거나 야채를 튀기고 볶지 않으면 음식은 맛이 없다고 생각한다. 몇 대에 걸쳐 가정주부들의 필수 도서가 되어온 권위 있는 요리책은 지방에 대한 공포로 가득 차 있고, 그중 일부는 역겨움에 가깝다. 정부는 문제의 정도를 잘 알고 있다. 우리의 식습관은 망신스러울지도 모르지만, 그러한 식습관을 바꾸기 위해서는 세금 이상의 조치를 취해야 한다.

declare 선언하다 obesity 비만 levy 추가 부담금 trail-blazing 선구자적인 keenly 날카롭게 smother 듬뿍 바르다 obscene 역겨운 disgrace 망신

02 (A) 두 명의 학생 중 나머지 한 명을 의미함 (B) come close to -ing '가까스로 ~하다' (C) look 다음에 나오고 '마치 ~처럼'이라는 의미이므로 as if가 적절

나는 최근에 우연히 두 학생의 대화를 들었다. 한 명은 다른 한 명에게 그가 인터넷에서 에세이를 복사할지 여부를 물었다. 동의한 후에, 그들은 인터넷에서 이용 가능한 에세이에 대한 수요가 너무 많아서 비용이 너무 비싸다고 불평하기 시작했다. 그들이 말한 어느 것도 학술적인 정직성에 관한 윤리적인 면을 거의 인정하지 않다. 과거에 다른 사람에게서 에세이를 훔친 학생은 처벌을 받았지만, 지금은 그들은 다시 숙제를 제출하는 것이 허용된다. 확실히 부정행위자들에게 두 번째 기회를 주는 것은 문제가 있다. 그것은 마치 학술적 절도를 정당화하기 위해서 절차가 존재하는 것처럼 보인다. 그것은 실수가 아니기 때문에 용서도 없어야만 한다.

overhear 우연히 듣다 acknowledge 알다 ethical 윤리적인 resubmit 다시 제출하다 cheater 부정행위자

UNIT 167~168

Check-up P. 168~169

167 **1.** Whether **2.** If **168** **1.** If **2.** whether

167

1. '~인지 아닌지'로 해석되고, 주어로 사용되어 Whether가 적절

우리 회사가 구매자를 위한 비행기 표를 살 수 있는지 없는지는 또 다른 문제이다.

2. '~라면'이라는 뜻의 if가 적절

만약 당신에게 기회가 주어진다면 우리의 제품을 다른 사람들에게 추천할 것입니까?

168

1. '~라면'이라는 뜻의 if가 적절

만약 그들의 자유시간이 과제와 프로젝트로 채워진다면, 아이들은 빠르게 기력을 소진할 것이다.

2. 뒤에 바로 to부정사가 오므로 whether가 적절

엘리너는 돈과 정보를 가지고 관계당국에 갈지 말지 결정할 수 없었다.

EXERCISE

P. 170

01 whether 02 whether 03 whether 04 If 05 Whether
06 if 07 whether 08 If 09 If 10 if

01 뒤에 to부정사가 나오므로 whether가 적절

길고 외로운 여정에 대한 그의 동기는 결혼을 할지 말지를 결정하기 위한 것이었다.

02 전치사의 목적어로 사용되고 있으므로 whether가 적절

린다는 혁신이 정말 습득할 수 있는 것인지 아닌지에 대한 질문은 오래된 논쟁거리라고 말한다.

03 뒤에 or not이 바로 나오므로 whether가 적절

이러한 기술은 보스와나의 사람들이 읽고 쓰는 법을 배우든 배우지 않든 간에 그들에게 친숙하다.

04 가정법 구문이므로 If가 적절

만약 제임슨이 자신의 영화를 홍보하고자 한국을 방문한다면, 나는 기꺼이 그 영화를 볼 것이다.

05 주어절을 이끌기 때문에 Whether가 적절

수학능력에 있어서 실재하는 성별 차이가 있는지 아닌지는 오랫동안 논의되어 왔다.

06 가정법 구문이므로 if가 적절

만약 누군가 어딘가에서 텔레비전 수상기에 이미지를 전달하지 않는다면, 텔레비전 수상기는 거실을 멍하니 바라보게 될 수도 있다.

07 전치사의 목적어이므로 whether가 적절

긴장은 신체적인 접촉, 통제력의 결여와 간지럼 당하거나 다칠지에 대한 두려움 때문에 발생한다.

08 가정법 구문이므로 If가 적절

만약 당신이 누군가 도둑 맞고 있는 것을 본다면 당신은 어떤 문제에도 연관되고 싶지 않기 때문에 다른 방향을 볼 것이다.

09 가정법 구문이므로 If가 적절

만약 도움이 필요한 사람이 당신의 가족 중 한 명이라면 당신은 그냥 지나칠 수 있겠는가?

10 가정법 구문이므로 If가 적절

만약 교사와 부모가 사람들의 창의력에 집중했더라면, 그들은 위대한 예술가나 과학자가 될 수 있었을지도 모른다.

ACTUAL TEST

P. 171

01 ④ 02 ④

01 ④ 뒤에 to부정사가 오므로 if가 아니라 whether가 적절 ① 선수들이 듣는 것 ② flipping a coin을 선행사로 받는 계속적 용법의 관계대명사 ③ 양쪽 팀 중 다른 한 팀을 의미 ⑤ 선수들이 지급을 받는 것이므로 수동

인간 행동의 한 단면은 최후 통첩 게임이라고 불리는 실험에서 잘 나타난다. 이 게임은 다음과 같이 진행된다. 두 명의 선수는 그들이 게임을 할 것이고, 만약 이긴다면 200달러를 받을 수 있을 거라고 듣게 된다. 시작하기 전, 그들은 게임 방법을 배운다. 게임은 동전을 던져서 시작하는데, 이것은 선수에게 A와 B라는 역할을 할당하는 데 사용된다. 선수 A의 임무는 자신과 다른 한 선수에게 200달러의 상금을 나누자는 제안을 하는 것이다. 선수 A가 제안을 한 이후에, 선수 B는 그것을 받아들일지 말지를 결정한다. 만약 그가 받아들인다면, 양 선수 모두 제안에 따라 돈을 지불 받게 된다. 만약 선수 B가 그 제안을 거부하면, 두 선수 모두는 아무 것도 없이 걸어 나온다. 양쪽의 경우에 게임은 그때 끝나게 된다.

aspect 단면 flip 던지다 allocate 할당하다 division 분할

02 (A) on의 목적어이므로 whether가 적절 (B) call의 목적어가 없으므로 선행사를 포함하는 관계대명사 what이 적절, the paradox of choice는 보어 (C) keep은 목적격 보어로 동사원형을 취할 수 없으므로 wondering이 적절

우리는 아이스크림의 그 모든 맛은 말할 것도 없이, 밤마다 저녁으로 무엇을 먹을까부터 시작하여 누구와 결혼해야 하나까지 끊임없이 결정을 내린다. 우리는 우리가 내리는 결정의 상당 부분을 특정한 선호도가 우리의 안녕을 증대시킬 수 있을 것인가 하는 것에 근간을 둔다. 직관적으로, 우리는 우리가 선택권을 많이 가질수록, 궁극적으로 더 잘 살게 될 것이라고 확신하는 듯하다. 그러나 우리의 끝없는 기회로 이루어진 세상은 우리를 행복하게 해 주기보다는 우리를 더욱 구속한다. 한 심리학자가 '선택의 역설'이라고 부르는 것에서, 많은 가능성에 직면하게 되면 우리는 심한 스트레스를 받게 되고 우리가 어떤 결정을 하든지 간에 덜 만족하게 된다. 너무 많은 선택이 주어지는 것은 놓쳐 버린 모든 기회에 대해 궁금 하게 한다.

intuitively 직관적으로 imprison 구속하다 paradox 역설

UNIT 169~170

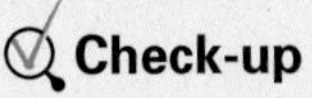

P. 172~173

169 1. why 2. why 170 1. which 2. them

169

1. 앞 문장이 원인/이유, 뒤 문장이 결과이므로 why가 적절

나는 학생들이 놀기 위한 장소가 있다고 믿고 있다. 그것이 바로 내가 나중에 이 문제를 더 다루기 위해서 회의를 열려고 결정한 이유이다.

2. 앞 문장이 원인/이유, 뒤 문장이 결과이므로 why가 적절

내부 반대가 사라짐에 따라, 중요한 논쟁은 사라졌다. 그것이 바로 폭군들의 성공이 보통 반대파를 잠재우고 나서 뒤따라오는 이유다.

170

1. 두 문장의 접속사가 없으므로 which가 적절

몇 개의 장려책이 있는데, 그중 탄력근무제는 강력한 것 중 하나다.

2. 접속사 and가 있으므로 them이 적절

크리스티는 수 년 동안 몇 권의 책을 써왔고, 그중 대다수는 현재 절판되었다.

EXERCISE

P. 174

01 why **02** which **03** why **04** When we actually live **05** because **06** which **07** it **08** beginning **09** Put **10** why

01 앞 문장이 원인/이유, 뒤 문장이 결과이므로 why가 적절

모든 사람들은 사랑 이야기를 좋아한다. 그것이 시인 롱펠로가 순례자에 대해서 말하기 위해서 사랑 이야기를 지어낸 이유이다.

02 접속사 없이 두 문장이 연결되었으므로 which가 적절

에베레스트로의 첫 여덟팀의 원정대는 영국인이었으며, 그들 모두는 산의 북쪽인 티벳으로부터 시도했다.

03 앞 문장이 원인/이유, 뒤 문장이 결과이므로 why가 적절

나는 보통 유사한 상황에서 대부분의 사람들보다 오랫동안 버틴다. 그것이 다른 사람들이 실패했을 때 내가 종종 성공하는 이유이다.

04 문장과 문장이 만나므로 접속사가 필요

그들이 실제로 그들 인생을 살 때, 부의 중요성은 그들의 관계를 평가하는데 있어서 거의 무(無)로 떨어지게 된다.

05 앞에는 좋은 가격의 여행을 찾기 어렵다는 결과가 나오고, 뒤에는 그 원인이 나옴

여행에 있어 좋은 가격을 찾는 것은 너무 복잡하다. 그것은 항공노선이 재고 관리를 위해서 복잡한 공식을 가지고 있고, 그래서 비행기를 채워 이익을 극대화 할 수 있기 때문이다.

06 내용상 [and / which] 다음에 오는 동사의 주어는 앞 문장 전체가 되므로 이를 받는 것은 관계사 which임

실질 소득이 감소한 소비자들은 임금 인상을 요구할 수 있고 이는 생산 비용을 높여 결국 다시 소비자에게 전가될 것이다.

07 it 앞에 접속사가 있으므로 관계사는 올 수가 없음

18홀 골프장은 매일 약 1,000톤의 물을 무료로 사용하는데 이 분량은 평균 50가구가 한 달 동안 사용할 수 있는 양이다.

08 콤마 뒤에 접속사가 없으므로 분사구문이 적절

학생들은 3월에 시작하는 신학기에 맞추어 매년 연말에 선발된다.

09 '행주를 감자 위에 두어라'라는 명령문이 적절

감자를 따뜻하게 하고, 건조하게 유지하기 위해서 증기를 흡수하려면 감자 위에 행주를 덮어 두어라.

10 앞 문장이 원인/이유, 뒤 문장이 결과이므로 why가 적절

경찰과 소방관은 또한 국내 TV 뉴스에서 거의 부정적인 면을 보여주지 않는데, 왜냐하면 기자들은 행정 집행 기관과의 협력 관계를 유지할 필요가 있기 때문이다. 그것이 설사 있다 하더라도 함정 수사나 폭행, 경찰이나 소방관의 실수와 같은 이슈를 시청자들이 거의 보지 못하는 이유이다.

ACTUAL TEST

P. 175

01 ⑤ **02** ②

01 ⑤ 본동사 are scheduled가 나오므로 cover가 아니라 분사인 covering이 적절 ① encourage는 목적격 보어로 to부정사가 오는 동사 ② '~이 예상된다'라는 뜻 ③ 민간분야가 투자를 확대한다는 내용은 앞의 내용의 원인에 해당 ④ opportunities 수식

작년 독일 정부는 젊은이들의 취업 프로그램에서 수십 개의 일자리를 창출하는 목표를 이뤄냈다. 이것은 많은 회사들에게 젊은이들을 고용하라고 격려한 정책의 결과이다. 점점 더 많은 젊은 졸업생들이 새로운 분야에서 일자리를 얻을 전망이다. 이는 중소기업과 대기업이 더 많은 취업 기회를 제공하면서 민간분야가 엄청난 투자를 확대하기 때문이다. 특히 정부는 젊은 여성들의 생계를 보장할 더 많은 복지 정책을 도입할 계획이다. 젊은이들의 복지를 다룰 새로운 입법과 정책은 법률 개정의 결과로 올해 시작될 예정이다.

recruit 채용하다 livelihood 생계 revision 개정

02 (A) 주어는 what이므로 단수 (B) advise는 목적격 보어로 to부정사를 사용 (C) 뒤에 나오는 내용은 앞의 원인

대부분의 사람들은 병 속에 있는 물이 부엌 수도꼭지에서 나오는 물보다 더 깨끗하고 좋을 것이라고 생각한다. 그러나 사람들이 깨닫지 못하는 것은 플라스틱 물병 자체가 사람들에게 해로울 수 있다는 것이다. 물을 플라스틱 용기에 담으면, 플라스틱에 포함된 화학물질이 물 속에 용해될 수 있다. 이러한 화학 물질들은 많은 다양한 인간의 건강 문제들과 연관되어 왔고, 많은 과학자들과 의사들은 사람들에게 유리나 스테인리스 용기에 담겨 있는 물을 마시라고 조언한다. 이는 이러한 용기들이 화학 물질을 포함하는 플라스틱 용기와 달리 물을 안전하게 담을 수 있기 때문이다. 따라서 다음에 물을 마실 때는 당신이 가지고 있는 병이 무엇으로 만들어져 있는지 반드시 확인해야 한다.

store 저장하다 container 용기 dissolve 용해하다

REVIEW TEST

P. 176

01 Despite → Although **02** why → because **03** although → despite **04** what → that **05** if → whether **06** whether **07** despite **08** because **09** Because of **10** although

01 뒤에는 문장이 나오므로 접속사가 필요

테레사 학교에서 뛰어난 학생이었음에도 불구하고, 대학생활에 적응하는 데 심각한 문제를 겪고 있다.

02 뒤에 나오는 내용이 앞의 원인에 해당하므로 because가 필요

최근에 대부분의 광고주들은 광고 모델로 어린 아이돌을 선호한다. 왜냐하면 그들이 팬들로 하여금 광고되는 상품을 사도록 장려할 수 있기 때문이다.

03 뒤에는 명사 the fact가 나오므로 전치사 despite가 필요

한 연구는 패스트푸드에 대해서 생각한 이후, 사람들은 또한 시간을 절약하게 해주는 물건에 보다 더 관심을 가지게 되며 제한 시간이 없다는 사실에도 불구하고, 한 단락을 더 빨리 읽는다는 사실을 보여준다.

04 It ~ that 진주어, 가주어 구문

그에게 자메이카로의 여행에서 그렇게 생기 있고 아름다운 소녀를 만난다는 일은 거의 있을 것 같지 않은 일이었는데 그는 (그런 소녀를) 만났다.

05 바로 뒤에 or not이 오므로 whether가 적절

재스민은 이 주변에서 일하고 먹기 때문에 사용하든 안 하든 상관없이 보통 좋아 보이는 쿠폰을 많이 출력한다.

06 뒤에 or not이 오고, '~인지 아닌지'라는 뜻이므로 whether가 적절

그 프로그램은 자필의 물리적인 특징을 분석함으로써, 그들이 진실을 쓰고 있는지 여부를 판단할 수 있다.

07 뒤에 명사 the time이 오므로 전치사 despite가 필요

이 연구는 운동을 하면 독서나 작문, 수학을 할 시간을 뺏기지만, 운동을 많이 할수록 종종 학교 성적을 향상시킨다는 점에 주목했다.

08 뒤에 완전한 문장이 오므로 because가 적절

몇몇 날쥐들은 물을 마실 필요가 없는데, 그들이 음식으로부터 물을 얻기 때문이다.

09 뒤에 명사 recent progress가 오므로 because of가 적절

신경 과학과 심리학에서의 최근의 진보 때문에 우리는 정서 지능의 중요성에 주목하기 시작했다.

10 빨간 색을 좋아하지만, 노란색 옷을 입었으므로 대조

그녀가 가장 좋아하는 색은 빨간 색이었지만, 그녀는 졸업댄스파티에 노란 색 드레스를 입었다.

FINAL CHECK

P. 177~179

01 ④ 02 ② 03 ① 04 ⑤ 05 ① 06 ④

01 ④ 뒤에 or not이 바로 나오므로 if가 아니라 whether 가 돼야 함 ① elements를 선행사로 받는 관계대명사 ② 가스가 발생되는 것이므로 수동 ③ evidence는 불가산 명사 ⑤ 주어는 determining, 동명사이므로 단수 취급

뉴스는 일부 과학자들이 화성에서 행성의 생물 존재의 가능성을 보여 주는 유기 탄소 성분을 발견했다고 보도했다. 나사에 따르면, 화성에 착륙한 탐사 로봇이 $MClO_4$라고 불리는 과염소산염을 발견했다. 과학자들은 후에 화성과 환경적으로 비슷한 지역인 칠레의 아타카마 사막에서 그 물질을 연구했다. 과학자들은 $MClO_4$를 가진 사막의 모래에 가열을 했다. 이산화탄소나 메틸 클로라이드는 가열에 의해서 만들어진 가스로부터 추출되었다. 이러한 가스는 다른 착륙선이 전에 화성에서 모래를 가열할 때 발생했던 가스와 같은 것이다. 새로운 발견은 화성의 생물체에 대한 많은 증거를 발견해 내는 엄청난 발전을 이뤄냈다. 하지만, 그것이 정말로 화성에 있는 그 물질들로 구성된 생명체의 존재인지 아닌지 확인하기 위해서, 과학자들은 화성으로 또 다른 탐사선을 보낼 것이다. 한 연구팀은 유기원소가 화성에 적합한 요소인지 아니면 다른 행성에 온 운석의 구성 요소인지 결정하는 것은 쉽지 않다고 말했다.

carbon 탄소 **land on** 착륙하다 **substance** 물질 **dioxide** 이산화물 **extract** 추출하다 **compose** 구성하다 **component** 구성 물질 **meteorite** 운석

02 (A) 두 문장이 접속사 when으로 연결되었으므로 대명사 us가 적절 (B) 접속사가 나오지만 주어가 없으므로 분사구문 필요 (C) make가 사역의 의미로 쓰였으므로 feel이 적절

무언가가 우리 기대를 충족시키지 못할 때, 우리 중 많은 사람들은 이런 생각을 하게 된다. "의심이 될 때, 다른 누군가의 잘못임에 틀림 없다." 당신은 이러한 추정이 당신이 보는 거의 모든 장소에서 벌어짐을 알 수 있다. 어떤 것이 사라졌고, 누군가는 그것을 옮겼음에 틀림이 없다. 이러한 탓하는 생각은 우리 문화에서 매우 일반적이다. 하지만, 개인적인 행복의 측면에서 보자면 남을 탓하는 동안 당신은 평화로울 수 없다. 남을 탓하는 것은 엄청난 정신적인 에너지가 필요하다. 그것은 바로 스트레스와 질병을 만드는 '나를 끌어내리는' 마음가짐이다. 비난하는 것은 당신의 삶에 대해 당신을 무기력하게 만든다. 왜냐하면 당신의 행복은 당신이 조절할 수 없는 다른 사람의 행동과 태도를 조건으로 하기 때문이다.

in terms of ~의 면에서 **drag-me-down** 나를 끌어내리는 **contingent** ~을 조건으로 하는 **behavior** 태도, 행동

03 ① '마치 ~처럼'이라는 의미이므로 as if가 와야 함 ② 동사 enable은 to부정사를 목적격 보어로 취함 ③ 주어와 동일하게 octopuses를 가리킴 ④ 문어가 눈을 위로 세우는 것이므로 능동 ⑤ '거의'

일반적인 믿음과는 반대로, 대부분의 문어들은 수영을 잘 하지 못한다. 예를 들어, 문어들은 보통 비다 바닥을 따라 기어가기 위해 다리를 사용한다. 하지만 그것들은 마치 열쇠 구멍을 통해 방 사이를 드나드는 것처럼, 작은 구멍을 통해서 비집고 다닐 수 있다. 몸에서 유일하게 딱딱한 부분인 부리가 바다 속 바위들의 좁은 틈 사이를 비집고 다닐 수 있게 해준다. 그들은 또한 모래나 진흙 속에 자기의 몸을 묻을 수도 있다. 문어들 중 일부는 심지어 잠수함의 잠망경처럼 눈을 내밀어 모래 속을 수영해 다닐 수도 있다. 어떤 문어들은 자신들이 만든 껍데기를 타고 바다 속을 수영하면서 그들의 삶을 보내기도 하고 껍데기들을 거의 카누처럼 이용한다.

crawl 기다 **squeeze** 짜내다 **stick up** 삐죽 내밀다 **periscope** 잠망경 **submarine** 잠수함

04 (A) 명사를 수식하므로 alive는 오지 못함 (B) indulge와 병렬구조 (C) whether A, B, or C의 구조, 'A 하든, B 하든, 또는 C하든' 이라는 뜻

일단 여러분이 타이완의 문화 관광지를 탐험하고 타이완 자연의 아름다움을 발견하는 것을 끝내면, 놀라운 요리가 기다리고 있습니다. 활기찬 야시장에서 맛있는 전통 음식을 맛보고, 매운 시추앙의 맛과 숨겨진 휴식처인 하카 특산물에 빠져보거나, 아니면 최상급 호텔에서 세계적인 멋진 저녁 식사를 경험해 보세요. 타이완은 다양한 예산과 선호를 위한 미각이 존재하는 미식가의 천국입니다. 여러분이 이 맛있는 전통 음식의 맛을 보든, 문화적인 다양성에 놀라든, 아니면 산과 정글로 탈출을 하든 확실히 당신의 기대 이상일 겁니다.

culinary 요리의 **savor** 맛보다 **indulge** 탐닉하다 **delicacy** 맛있는 것 **haven** 휴식처 **gourmand** 미식가 **relish** 맛보다 **exceed** 초과하다

05 ① 뒤에 동격의 접속사 that의 수식을 받는 명사 concerns가 왔으므로 because가 아니라 because of가 돼야 함 ② 주어는 precious little evidence로 단수 ③ 전치사 by의 목적어로 동명사가 옴 ④ 세 그룹 중 나머지 하나를 의미 ⑤ 과거 이전의 내용을 설명하고 있음

수 년 동안 우리는 휴대폰이 방출하는 방사선이 암을 유발할 수도 있다는 걱정 때문에 휴대폰으로 너무 오랫동안 통화하는 것에 대한 경고를 받아 왔다. 하지만, 과학자들은 그것에 대한 어떠한 증거도 없고, 지금 전자기선은 알츠하이머병을 방지하는 등 두뇌에 이익을 줄 수 있을 것처럼 보인다고 밝혔다. 그들은 첫 번째는 알츠하이머병에 걸린 것과 같은 상태고, 두 번째는 유전적으로 그 병에 걸리기 쉽고, 세 번째는 정상적인 세 그룹의 쥐에 똑같은 빈도수의 휴대폰에서 발생되는 것과 동일한 전자기파를 노출시켰다. 그들은 정신적인 퇴보의 신호를 찾고 있었지만, 8개월 후 모든 쥐는 기억력 테스트에서 전자기파에 노출되지 않았던 설치류들보다 더 잘 수행했다.

electromagnetic 전자기의 genetically 유전적으로
prone ~하기 쉬운 deterioration 퇴보 rodent 설치류

06 (A) '비록 ~일지라도' (B) children이 주어이므로 복수 (C) 분사인 reacting을 수식하므로 부사가 적절

조건화는 간접적으로 일어나는데, 그것은 우리에게 그 영향력을 증가시킨다. 예를 들어, 다른 사람이 전기 충격을 받는 것을 목격했다고 치자. 충격이 전달되기 전에 매번 (전기 충격의) 신호를 나타내는 등이 들어온다. 자신이 충격을 받는 것은 아니지만 당신은 곧 그 신호에 대해 감정적 반응을 보이게 된다. 부모님이 천둥에 반응하는 것을 목격함으로써 천둥에 대한 두려움을 알게 된 아이들도 비슷한 조건화를 겪는다. 공포 영화가 우리에게 영향을 끼칠 수 있다면 부모님, 친구들, 친척들의 감정은 훨씬 더 많은 영향력을 가지고 있음을 예상할 수 있을 것이다. 예를 들어, 도시에 사는 아이가 어떻게 뱀을 두려워하고 단지 그 그림만 보고도 감정적으로 반응하겠는가? "뱀은 위험해"라고 들은 것만으로는 그 아이의 감정적 반응을 설명할 수 없을 것이다. 아마, 다른 사람들이 뱀이라는 단어나 텔레비전에 나오는 뱀의 모습에 벌벌 떨며 반응하는 것을 그 아이가 이미 목격했을 것이다.

mere 단순히 react 반응하다

chapter 15 가정법

UNIT 171~172

Check-up P. 182~183

171	1. be	2. were
172	1. had not attempted	2. had prepared

171

1. 현재 사실에 대한 가정이므로 가정법 과거가 적절

우리 회사가 만약 그 프로젝트에 대해 3배 더 많이 지불한다면, 우리는 파트너로 선택될 텐데.

2. 현재 사실에 대한 가정이므로 가정법 과거가 적절

만약 태양에서 더 멀리 떨어져 있거나 가깝다면 지구는 아마 덥고, 건조하고, 생물이 살 수 없는 불모의 행성일 것이다.

172

1. 과거 사실에 대한 가정이므로 가정법 과거완료가 적절

내가 그것을 시도하지 않았다면 되었을 사람보다 더 낫고 행복한 여자가 되었을 것이다. (시도해서 더 낫고 행복했다.)

2. 과거 사실에 대한 가정이므로 가정법 과거완료가 적절

만약 그때 정부가 태풍에 대해 준비했다면 사상자와 부상자의 수가 감소할 수 있었을 텐데.

EXERCISE P. 184

01 would 02 have been 03 have left 04 hadn't
05 had fallen 06 have been 07 have been
08 had said 09 have lost 10 tied

01 현재 사실에 대한 가정이므로 가정법 과거가 적절

그들이 맞아야만 해. 그렇지 않다면, 그들은 자신들의 목숨을 구할 수 없을 거야.

02 과거 사실에 대한 가정이므로 가정법 과거완료가 적절

만약 내가 감각이 있었다면, 그것은 이틀짜리 이야기가 아니라 하루짜리 이야기였을 텐데.

03 과거 사실에 대한 가정이므로 가정법 과거완료가 적절

만약 당신이 17세기경에 살았다면, 당신은 고국을 떠나 미국으로 왔을까?

04 과거 사실에 대한 가정이므로 가정법 과거완료가 적절

만약 클라우스가 그렇게 빠르고 결단력 있게 반응하지 않았다면, 한 명이 아닌 두 명의 익사자가 나왔을 것이다.

05 과거 사실에 대한 가정이므로 가정법 과거완료가 적절

그는 엄청나게 운이 좋다고 느꼈다. 만약 그가 다르게 떨어졌다면, 그의 목이 부러졌을지도 모른다.

06 과거 사실에 대한 가정이므로 가정법 과거완료가 적절

만약 3일 전, 그의 용기가 없었다면, 내 다섯 살짜리 아들은 그때 차에 치였을 것이다.

07 과거 사실에 대한 가정이므로 가정법 과거완료가 적절

만약 그 당시에 사람들이 그것들을 이해했다면, 사람들이 고통 받았던 그 질병들은 쉽게 처리될 수 있었을 텐데.

08 과거 사실에 대한 가정이므로 가정법 과거완료가 적절

만약 내가 아버지에게 학교 운동장에 가서 함께 야구를 하자고 물었다면, 그는 "그래"라고 했을 텐데.

09 과거 사실에 대한 가정이므로 가정법 과거완료가 적절

만약 수영복만 입은 사람들로 실험을 했다면, 머리를 통해서 체열의 겨우 10% 이상은 잃지 않았을 것이다.(머리로 빠져나간 열이 신체 열의 10%를 넘지 않았을 것이다.)

10 현재 사실을 반대로 가정한 것이므로 가정법 과거가 적절

만약 그녀가 로프의 한쪽 끝을 기둥에 묶고, 다른 한쪽 끝에는 차를 묶은 다음 그것을 구부리기 위해서 차를 몬다면, 그 목수가 위로 뻗어서 고양이를 구할 수 있을 텐데.

ACTUAL TEST P. 185

01 ② 02 ③

01 ② 과거 사실에 대한 가정이므로 studied가 아니라 would have studied가 적절 ① 내용상 뒤에 나오는 것이 나중에 나오므로 followed by가 옴 ③ 사람 주어일 경우 감정동사는 과거분사로 사용 ⑤ 주어는 no follow-up이므로 단수

많은 사람들은 비판할 때, 일반적인 칭찬으로 시작하고 다음에 "하지만"이라는 단어를 사용한 다음 비판적인 말을 하며 끝을 맺는다. 예를 들어, 공부에 대한 아이의 무심한 태도를 바꾸고자 할 때, 당신은 이렇게 말할 지도 모른다. "톰, 나는 네가 수학 점수를 올려서 정말 자랑스러워. 하지만, 네가 영어를 좀 더 열심히 공부했었더라면 성적이 더 좋았을 거야." 이 경우, 톰은 "하지만"이라는 단어를 듣기 전까지 고무되었을지도 모른다. "하지만"이라는 단어를 듣고 나서는 칭찬이 단지 립서비스가 아닐까 궁금해 할지도 모른다. 신뢰성은 무너질 것이고 아마도 당신은 톰의 학습 태도를 바꾸는 데 성공하지 못할 것이다. 이것은 "하지만"이란 단어를 "그리고"로 바꾸면 쉽게 해결될 수 있다. "나는 네가 수학 성적을 올려서 정말로 자랑스러워. 그리고 영어에도 같은 성실한 노력을 기울인다면 너의 영어 성적도 다른 과목처럼 오를 거야" 이제 톰은 칭찬을 받아들일 것이다. 왜냐하면, 실패에 대한 어떠한 함의도 없기 때문이다.

credibility 신뢰성 tear down 부서지다 inference 함의

02 (A) 다른 임대인이 나오므로 티나는 마지막 임대인이 아님 (B) 현재 사실에 대한 가정이므로 가정법 과거가 적절 (C) 그녀가 여겨지는 것이므로 수동, a housing expert는 목적격 보어

당신은 일 년간 아파트를 임대해 왔는데, 집주인 아주머니는 당신에게 그녀는 임대료를 한 달에 500달러 인상하겠다고 말한다. 어느 날, 당신은 같은 건물에 사는 다른 임차인인 티나를 복도에서 만나게 된다. 당신은 그녀에게 집주인 아주머니와의 문제에 대해 말해준다. 티나는 당신에게 조언을 해준다. 몇 주 후에, 티나로부터 당신의 상황에 대해 들어서 알고 있는 다른 임차인인 프랭크를 만나게 된다. 프랭크는 당신에게, "이봐, 이건 내 일은 아니지만, 내가 너라면 나는 집 문제에 관해서 티나의 조언을 받아들이지 않을 거야. 그녀는 지난번 아파트에서 쫓겨났거든."이라고 말한다. 사실, 티나가 그녀의 지난번 아파트에서 쫓겨났기 때문에 프랭크가 하는 말은 상당히 이치에 맞는 것처럼 보일 수 있다. 그러나 그렇지 않다. 왜냐하면 프랭크는 티나의 조언에 대해 비난하는 것이 아니기 때문이다. 그 대신, 그는 그녀의 조언을 단지 감정적으로 비난하고 있다. 사실, 그녀는 매우 심각한 집 문제를 겪었으므로, 주택 전문가로 여겨질 수도 있다. 당신이 그녀를 좋아하는지 안 하는지는 그녀가 좋은 충고를 했는지 여부와는 별개의 문제이다. 충고의 신뢰성은 편견이 없는 것에 근거해야 한다.

landlady 여자 집주인 tenant 임차인 evict 쫓아내다
bias 선입견 freedom from ~이 없음

UNIT 173~174

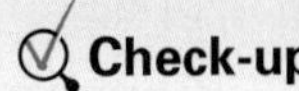
Check-up P. 186~187

173 **1.** enjoy **2.** do **174** **1.** changed **2.** have gone

173

1. 주절이 현재 사실의 가정이므로 가정법 과거가 적절

만약 소설이 그때 번역되지 않았다면, 지금 그의 소설을 즐겨 읽지 못할 것이다.

2. 주절이 현재 사실의 가정이므로 가정법 과거가 적절

만약 당신이 그때 내 말을 듣지 않았다면, 지금 이처럼 그 일을 할 수 없을 거야.

174

1. 현재 사실에 대한 가정이므로 가정법 과거가 적절

만약 우리가 회의 날짜를 바꾼다면 더 편안해질까?

2. 과거 사실에 대한 가정이므로 가정법 과거완료가 적절

만약 어제 날이 맑았다면, 우리는 동물원으로 소풍을 갈 수 있었을 텐데.

EXERCISE P. 188

01 would be **02** please **03** be **04** be **05** have been **06** be **07** be **08** be **09** have been **10** be

01 주절이 현재 사실의 가정이므로 가정법 과거가 적절

만약 그때 내가 그녀에게 프로포즈를 했다면, 지금 그녀와 함께 있을 텐데.

02 주절이 현재 사실의 가정이므로 가정법 과거가 적절

만약 이 여행이 2주만 일찍 이루어졌다면, 이 모든 것이 지금 그들의 눈을 기쁘게 할 텐데.

03 주절이 현재 사실의 가정이므로 가정법 과거가 적절

만약 당신이 한 차례의 거창한 식사 대신 여러 번의 간단한 식사를 했다면, 당신은 지금 좀 더 신경을 써서 당신의 몸을 대하고 있을 것이다.

04 현재 사실에 대한 가정이므로 가정법 과거가 적절

만약 직원이 개인 보상이 가능하다는 것을 안다면, 그녀는 아마도 기대보다 더 나은 일을 하려고 할 가능성이 많을 것이다.

05 과거 사실에 대한 가정이므로 가정법 과거완료가 적절

물론 그런 적은 없었지만, 제이크가 그렇게 말했다면, 그건 거짓말이었을 것이다.

06 주절이 현재 사실의 가정이므로 가정법 과거가 적절

네가 그런 멍청한 짓을 하지 않았다면, 지금 너는 행복할 텐데.

07 주절이 현재 사실의 가정이므로 가정법 과거가 적절

정부가 2000년대 중반에 가난한 사람들을 위해 더 많은 집을 지었다면, 지금 그 나라의 몇몇 지역에서 주택 문제가 그렇게 심각하지 않을 텐데.

08 주절이 현재 사실의 가정이므로 가정법 과거가 적절

그녀가 한 시간 전에 그 샌드위치를 먹었다면, 그녀는 지금 시간에 그렇게 배가 고프지 않을 텐데.

09 과거 사실에 대한 가정이므로 가정법 과거완료가 적절

만약 새로운 관리자가 첫 번째 조사에서 나온 모든 결과를 수정할 필요를 느끼지 않았다면, 작년 12월에 보고서가 나오지 않았을 것이다.

10 주절이 현재 사실의 가정이므로 가정법 과거가 적절

만약 숀 켄트가 과감히 인공 심장 이식을 시도하지 않았다면, 인공 심장의 발전은 오늘날 이루어지지 않았을 것이다.

ACTUAL TEST

P. 189

01 ② 02 ④

01 ② 주어는 the ways이므로 is가 아니라 are가 돼야 함 ① 뒤에 완전한 문장이 오므로 〈전치사+관계사〉는 올 수 있음 ③ what they should do를 의미하므로 소유대명사가 옴 ④ 주절이 현재 사실의 가정이므로 가정법 과거가 적절 ⑤ 선행사가 없고 뒤에 call의 목적어가 없는 불완전한 문장이 옴. social structure는 목적격 보어

사회화 과정을 통해서 인간은 자신이 태어난 가족과 학교, 동료, 사회에서의 사회적 역할을 배우고 그들을 둘러싸고 있는 사회적 관계를 이해하게 된다. 예를 들어 교사와 학생이 상호작용하게 되는 방식들은 대개 '교사'와 '학생'의 역할로 언급된다. 교사들은 사범 대학에서 그들이 해야만 하는 것을 배우며, 학생들은 학교나 매체에서 그것들을 배우게 된다. 사람들은 매우 안정적인 기존의 관계의 세계 속에 들어온다. 만약 그들이 그 세계를 만들었다면, 그들은 지금 부여된 역할을 배울 필요가 없을 것이다. 이것을 하향식 시스템이라고 부른다. 하지만, 이런 시스템은 빈번히 사람들의 도전을 받게 된다. 다른 사람들과 상호작용을 함으로써, 그들과 협상을 하게 된다. 협상 과정에서 우리가 소위 사회 구조라는 부르는 것을 만들고 재창조한다.

socialization 사회화 pre-existing 기존의 assign 부여하다
top-down 하향식의 be confronted with ~에 직면하다

02 (A) known to '~에게 알려진' (B) 과거 사실에 대한 가정이므로 가정법 과거완료가 적절 (C) 견딜 수 없었을 것이라는 의미가 돼야 하므로 could not이 적절

1965년 4월 12일, 야구는 휴스턴에 해리스 카운티 돔경기장을 개장함으로써 경기장의 건축 세계를 바꾸었다. 그것은 휴스턴 아스트로돔으로 세계에 더 잘 알려졌다. 그것은 세계 최초로 밀폐되고 냉방 시설을 갖춘 야구 경기장이었다. 돔경기장이 존재하기 전에 휴스턴의 야구 선수들은 모기로 가득 찬 습기가 많은 날씨에서 그리고 때로는 폭염 속에서 야외 경기를 했다. 돔경기장이 만들어지지 않았더라면, 프로 야구선수뿐만 아니라 열정적인 야구선수들마저도 불쾌한 날씨를 견딜 수 없었을 것이기 때문에 메이저리그 야구 경기는 휴스턴에서 살아남을 수 없었을지도 모른다.

enclose 둘러싸다 humidity 습기 endure 견디다

UNIT 175~176

Check-up

P. 190~191

175 **1.** Had we known **2.** Should he fail
176 **1.** Supposing **2.** Provided

175

1. if 생략 구문으로 Had가 도치되어 앞으로 나감

만약 TLC사가 유동성 부족을 겪고 있다는 사실을 알았다면, 우리는 돈을 투자하지 않았을 것이다.

2. if 생략 구문으로 Should가 도치되어 앞으로 나감

만약 그가 실패한다면, 그의 어머니는 그 결과에 실망할 것이다.

176

1. if가 없는 문장에서 Supposing이 if를 대신할 수 있음

만약 용광로 온도가 충분히 높다면, 그것은 철을 쉽게 녹일 것이다.

2. if가 없는 문장에서 Provided가 if를 대신할 수 있음

당신이 돈을 현명하게 사용하면, 돈은 우리에게 많은 혜택을 줄 수 있다.

EXERCISE

P. 192

01 Had he 02 Should two vehicles meet 03 Provided
04 Had she 05 Suppose 06 Provided 07 In case
08 Had they 09 Were only some sections of wheel
10 Had they been

01 문장과 문장이 만나는데 접속사가 없으며, 가정법 내용이므로 if가 생략된 구문, 따라서 주어와 동사가 도치됨

만약 그가 나에게 자동차 열쇠를 주었다면, 나는 집으로 운전해서 왔을 것이고 우리는 그 사고를 피할 수 있었을 것이다.

02 문장과 문장이 만나는데 접속사가 없으며, 가정법 내용이므로 if가 생략된 구문, 따라서 주어와 동사가 도치됨

흔히 그러듯이 만약 두 개체가 만나면, 하나의 개체는 다른 개체가 지나가도록 제일 가까운 빈 공간으로 되돌아 가야 할 것이다.

03 if 대신 사용된 가정법, Provided가 if를 대신함

만약 우리가 테러와의 전쟁에서 패한다면, 우리의 후손들은 우리처럼 행복한 삶을 살 수 없을 것이다.

04 문장과 문장이 만나는데 접속사가 없으며, 가정법 내용이므로 if가 생략된 구문, 따라서 주어와 동사가 도치됨

만약 그 자동차사고로 그녀가 죽지 않았다면, 지금 나와 함께 대학에 다니고 있을 텐데.

05 문장은 두 개인데 접속사가 없으므로, if를 대신하여 Suppose나 supposing을 사용할 수 있음

만약 우리가 어제 놀이공원에서 그녀를 만났다면, 그때 우리는 무엇을 했을까?

06 문장은 두 개인데 접속사가 없으므로, if를 대신해 Provided를 사용할 수 있음

시간이 충분하다면, 우리 회사는 이번 달 말까지 모든 물건을 보낼 수 있을 것이다.

07 뒤에 문장이 왔으므로 if의 대용인 in case가 옴. 〈in case of+명사〉

세제가 하나도 없을 경우, 나는 밤 동안 옷들을 세탁해서 말릴 수 없을 것이다.

08 문장과 문장이 만나는데 접속사가 없으며, 내용상 가정법 내용이므로 if가 생략된 구문, 따라서 주어와 동사가 도치됨

눈보라가 그렇게 심할 줄 알았다면, 등산객들은 적절한 장비 없이 산을 오르지 않았을 것이다.

09 문장과 문장이 만나는데 접속사가 없으며, 가정법 내용이므로 if가 생략된 구문, 따라서 주어와 동사가 도치됨

만약 바퀴의 겨우 일부만 수리가 된다면, 그것을 사용하는 것은 현명한 일이 아닐 것이다.

10 if 생략 구문으로 과거 사실에 대한 가정이므로 가정법 과거완료가 적절

만약 그들이 스스로 선택을 할 수 있었다면, 가장 성공한 사람 중 일부는 그들이 돈을 버는 방식과는 다른 직업을 선택했을 것이다.

ACTUAL TEST

P. 193

01 ⑤ 02 ③

01 ⑤ 부정어인 barely가 앞으로 나왔으므로 주어와 동사가 도치되어 you can이 아니라 can you가 돼야 함 ① 시간을 나타내므로 much가 옴 ② help의 목적격 보어 자리이므로 동사원형이 옴 ③ gaining과 병렬 구조 ④ if가 생략되어 주어와 동사 도치

우리는 골프장에서 경제나 정치 지도자들이 사업 거래를 포함한 몇 가지 이슈에 대해서 이야기하는 것을 듣거나 본다. 다른 선수들과 마찬가지로 그들은 골프장에서 변덕스러운 골프공을 찾는 데 많은 시간을 보낸다. 하지만, 골프 자체가 당신이 더 많은 개인적 관계를 형성하는데 도움을 주는 것은 사실이다. 그것이 골프를 하는 한 가지 이유이다. 그리고 그것은 가장 중요한 200번째 이유가 될 수도 있다. 더 중요한 이유는 친구들과 시간을 보내는 것과 승진하는 것, 아름다운 풍경으로부터 즐거움을 얻는 것, 많이 이야기하는 것을 포함하는데, 아마도 경기보다 말을 하는데 더 많은 시간을 소비할 지도 모른다. 게다가 인생을 위한 게임이기도 하다. 당신은 고등학교에서 축구나 농구를 했을 수도 있다. 하지만, 만약 당신이 40세나 60세라면, 당신이 여전히 공을 차고 리바운드를 할 수 있겠는가? 그래도 경기를 하는 가장 중요한 이유는 골프는 중독성이 심하다는 것이다. 당신이 골프의 세계로 들어올 때 골프 없는 인생을 상상도 할 수 없을 것이다.

capricious 변덕스러운 corporate ladder 기업체의 계층적 서열 scenery 풍경 barely 거의 ~ 하지 않는

02 (A) 접속사 but이 있으므로 관계대명사는 올 수 없음 (B) 본동사 provide가 있으므로 주어를 수식하는 분사구문이 적절 (C) if가 생략되어 주어와 동사가 도치

우리의 경험은 부분적으로는 우리가 느끼는 어떤 감정들로 이루어져 있고 부분적으로는 우리가 생각하는 사고들로 이루어져 있을지도 모르지만, 대부분 우리의 경험은 감각 인상의 집합일 것이다. 예를 들면 어느 봄날의 감각 인상은 파란 하늘과 흰 구름, 싹트는 잎과 수선화를 보는 것으로 이루어질 것이다. 그래서 봄날의 경험을 표현하고자 하는 시인은 엄선된 감각 인상을 제공한다. 이와 유사하게, 겨울날을 나타내기 위해 셰익스피어는 그의 시 겨울에서 올빼미의 침울한 "부엉부엉" 소리뿐만 아니라 매달려 있는 "고드름," "언" 우유, 그리고 마리안의 "빨갛고 얼얼한" 코와 같은 표현을 제시 한다. 그가 그렇게 하지 않았다면, 그는 이런 감각을 수반하는 겨울날의 감정을 불러 일으킬 수 없었을 것이다. 그때, 그 시인의 언어는 일상 언어보다 더 감각적이다. 그것은 비유적 표현이 더 풍부하다.

accompany 동반하다 sensuous 감각적인

UNIT 177~178

Check-up

P. 194~195

177	1. realized	2. had met
178	1. hadn't met	2. is

177

1. wish 다음에 나오는 문장은 가정법

네가 어제 했던 실수를 깨닫는다면 좋으련만

2. wish 다음에 나오는 문장은 과거 사건일 경우 과거완료 사용

그녀가 그때 당신보다 일찍 나를 만났다면 좋으련만.

178

1. 과거 사실에 대한 가정이므로 가정법 과거완료가 적절

에머슨에게는 모든 사람들이 마치 전에 본 적이 없었던 것처럼 낯설게 보인다.

2. 고등학교에서 수학을 가르쳤다고 들은 적이 있는 것 같으므로 지금도 선생님일 가능성이 있음, 따라서 직설법이 적절

멜린다는 마치 선생님처럼 보인다. 그녀가 고등학교에서 수학을 가르쳤다고 들었던 것 같다.

EXERCISE

P.196

01 were 02 looked 03 had written down 04 had come 05 had never seen 06 had happened 07 found 08 were 09 would 10 had studied

01 wish 가정법으로 현재 바라는 것이므로 과거형이 적절

케네디가 오늘날에도 산다면 좋으련만.

02 wish 가정법으로 현재 바라는 것이므로 과거형이 적절

내가 너에게 말을 하려고 할 때, 나를 바라보면 좋겠어.

03 wish 가정법으로 과거의 내용을 말하므로 과거완료가 적절

지난 회의에서 줄리의 전화번호를 받아 적어 놨으면 좋으련만.

04 wish 가정법으로 과거의 내용이므로 과거완료가 적절

그 남자들은 친구들과 함께 런던으로 여행을 갈 수 있었기를 바라면서 친구들을 부러워했다.

05 과거 사실에 대한 가정이므로 가정법 과거완료가 적절

짐은 그가 마치 전에 나를 본 적이 없다는 듯이 바라보았는데, 이것이 나를 약간 당황스럽게 만들었다.

06 과거 사실에 대한 가정이므로 가정법 과거완료가 적절

캐서린은 마치 아무 일도 일어나지 않은 듯 샤워를 했고, 진흙을 씻어 버리고, 자기 할 일을 했다.

07 현재 사실에 대한 가정이므로 가정법 과거가 적절

우리는 마치 미래가 너무 느리게 온다고 생각하고, 미래를 재촉하려 노력하고 있는 것처럼 미래를 기대한다.

08 현재의 상황을 이야기 하고 있으므로 가정법 과거 사용

네가 말하고 사람들을 즐겁게 하는 방식 때문에 모두가 너의 프레젠테이션을 좋아했어. 나의 프리젠테이션 반만큼이라도 좋다면.

09 현재 사실에 대한 바람/유감이므로 가정법 과거가 적절

그저 앉아서 아무것도 안 하지 있지 말고 무언가 말하기를 바라.

10 과거 사실에 대한 유감/바람이므로 가정법 과거완료가 적절

내 친구들은 대학 시절에 경영학과 경제학을 공부했기를 바란다.

ACTUAL TEST

P. 197

01 ② **02** ④

01 ② 그가 자극을 받는 것이므로 stimulating이 아니라 stimulated가 돼야 함 ① 뒤에 완전한 문장이 오므로 how가 옴 ③ 뒤에 나오는 to lose가 진주어로 가주어 it이 사용됨 ④ 뒤에 concerned가 생략되어 be동사만 남음 ⑤ as if 구문으로 뒤에 현재 사실에 대한 가정

어떤 상황을 해석하려는 사람은 주로 자신이 어떻게 행동해야 하는지 알아보기 위해서 주변의 사람들을 살펴본다. 만약 다른 사람들이 차분하고 무관심하면, 그도 그렇게 하려고 할 것이고, 다른 모든 사람들이 격하게 반응을 하면, 그는 자극적으로 되기 쉽다. 그러나 때로 다른 사람들의 반응은 잘못된 정보를 제공할 수 있다. 예를 들어, 치과의 대기실에서 환자들의 태연한 척하는 행동은 그들의 내적 불안을 잘 보여주지 않는다. 공공연히 '침착함을 잃는' 것은 당황스러운 것으로 간주된다. 그렇게 되면 잠재적으로 심각한 상황에서도, 모든 사람들은 그들이 실제로 느끼는 것보다 덜 걱정하는 것처럼 보일 것이다. 군중은 일이 긴박한 것이 아니라고 암시함으로써 구성원들에게 가만히 있을 것을 강요할 수 있다. 그러한 군중 안에 있는 어떤 개인이라도 사안이 심각한 것처럼 행동함으로써 바보처럼 보일지도 모른다는 것을 두려워한다.

severe 엄격한 inaction 활동하지 않음

02 (A) 앞 문장이 부정문이며, 뒤의 문장과 연결되므로 부정을 나타내는 nor가 적절 (B) 앞의 as는 〈describe A as B〉에 사용되는 as임 앞의 형용사가 비교급이므로 뒤에는 than이 옴 (C) as if 구문으로 현재 사실에 대한 가정

정치학은 두 가지 분야, 윤리학과 정치학으로 나누어진다. 아리스토텔레스에게 있어서 윤리학은 사회적이며, 정치학은 윤리적이다. 그는 그의 저서 '윤리학'에서 개인은 본질적으로 사회의 구성원이라는 사실을 잊지 않았고, 그의 저서인 '정치학'에서 국가의 행복은 시민의 행복에 기반을 둔다는 사실도 잊지 않았다. 그는 전자의 구절은 후자와 다름을 확신한다. 윤리학의 서두에서 그는 국가의 행복은 개인의 행복보다 더 위대하고 더 완벽하다고 생각한다. 즉, 그는 만약 우리가 전자를 이루지 못하다면, 후자는 견뎌야 하는 것이라고 생각했다. 하지만, 책의 말미에서 그는 마치 국가가 개인의 생활에 종속하는 것처럼 말한다.

the former 전자 the latter 후자 subordinate to ~에 종속하다

UNIT 179~180

Check-up

P. 198~199

179 **1.** took **2.** had **180** **1.** if any **2.** if ever

179

1. 〈It's time+가정법 과거〉 구문

우리가 필수과목으로 기하학 수업을 들을 시간이다. 이것은 나의 마지막 수업이다.

2. 〈It's time+가정법 과거〉 구문

이제 내 아들이 머리카락을 자를 때다. 머리카락이 너무 길다.

180

1. 명사(funds)를 강조하므로 if any가 적절

검찰에 따르면, 만약 BFC의 비자금과 연관이 있는 은행 거래가 있다면 자세히 살펴봐야 한다고 한다.

2. 동사(neglected)를 강조하므로 if ever가 적절

엄청난 존경을 받을 만한 정치인은 드물며 설사 있다 하더라도 살아있는 동안에 완전히 무시되는 일은 거의 없다.

EXERCISE

P. 200

01 turned **02** any **03** put **04** any **05** ever **06** had **07** happened **08** any **09** ever **10** realized

01 〈It's time+가정법 과거〉 구문

지금은 그들이 눈을 다른 세상으로 돌릴 시간이다.

02 명사를 받으므로 any가 적절

만약 금이나 다이아몬드가 있다면 은행으로 가져오세요. 그러면 금고에 넣어 놓을 수 있어요.

03 〈It's time+가정법 과거〉 구문, put one's money where one's mouth is '말을 행동으로 옮기다'

당신의 말을 행동으로 보여주기 좋은 때이다.

04 명사를 받으므로 any가 적절

설사 있다 하더라도 한국 역사에 대한 그의 생각에는 오해가 거의 없다.

05 동사를 받으므로 ever가 적절

설사 있다 하더라도 제니퍼는 오빠 없이 다른 남자애들을 거의 만나지 않는다.

06 〈It's time+가정법 과거〉

이제 도서관에서 열심히 기말고사 공부를 할 시간이야. 왜 아직도 여기에 있니?

07 〈It's time+가정법 과거〉

우리가 그 계획을 위해 회의를 할 시간이야. 예정보다 늦었어.

08 명사를 받으므로 any가 적절

설사 있더라도 한국의 전기 회사들 사이에는 유사성이 거의 없다.

09 동사를 받으므로 ever가 적절

너의 사촌인 러셀은 식당에서 음식 값을 거의 내지 않는 구두쇠이다.

10 〈It's time+가정법 과거〉 구문

너는 정말 자기중심적이구나. 이제 이 세상에 너 혼자가 아니란 걸 깨달을 시간이야.

ACTUAL TEST P. 201

01 ③ 02 ④

01 ③ 주어는 The idea로 단수이므로 are가 아니라 is가 돼야 함 ① 〈It's time+가정법 과거〉 ② 현수막이 학생들에 의해 만들어지는 것이므로 수동 ④ 5문형 구문으로 뒤에 진목적어인 to see가 있으므로 가목적어 it이 옴 ⑤ see를 수식하므로 부사가 옴

이제 우리가 레이크 문화 센터를 구하는 것에 대한 이야기를 할 때이다. 센터 외벽의 한 면을 대형 그림 현수막으로 가리려는 계획이 진행 중이다. 현수막은 근처 지그문트 예술 대학의 학생들이 만들 것이다. 학생들의 미술 작품을 전시함으로써 그들에게 자신감을 준다는 생각은 충분히 이해된다. 그러나 그 계획에는 이상할 만큼 우스꽝스러운 점이 있다. 센터를 디자인하는 데 5천 5백만 달러를 쓰고, 새로 지은 건물의 대부분을 현수막으로 가리다니. 그것은 명백한 돈 낭비이다. 그 계획은 즉시 철회해야 한다. 사실상 건물 안 사람들이 밖을 제대로 내다보기도 어렵고 반대의 경우도 마찬가지다.

exterior 외관 banner 현수막 underway 진행 중인 exhibit 전시하다 withdraw 철회하다 vice versa 반대로

02 (A) 비교 대상이 brain이므로 이를 지칭하는 소유대명사가 적절 (B) 선행사는 내용상 앞 문장 전체이므로 단수 취급 (C) 〈It's time+가정법 과거〉

아이들에게 애정을 주고 아이들을 돌보는 것은 엄마를 더욱 인지적으로 만들어준다. 아빠의 경우는 어떨까? 한 연구는 아버지에게도 똑같은 효과가 있음을 밝혀냈다. 아빠 쥐와 총각 쥐에게 실험을 해서, 아빠 쥐가 더 나은 수렵가이며 더 편안하고 덜 스트레스를 받는 상태를 보인다는 것을 입증했다. 그 연구는 아빠 쥐의 뇌에 총각 쥐의 뇌보다 더 많은 전기적 신호가 있다는 것을 밝혀냈다. 아빠 쥐는 또한 돌보는 행위와 관련된 호르몬인 바소프레신을 더 많이 배출한다. 다른 연구에서는 원숭이가 아빠가 되었을 때, 그의 뇌 구조가 복잡하게 되고, 뉴론으로 밀집하게 되는데, 이는 그를 더욱 인지적이게 만든다. 이러한 결과는 엄마를 대상으로 한 실험과 동일하지만, 아빠의 경우 그들이 임신을 하지 않는다는 점에서 더 중요하다. 이제 아빠들은 더 똑똑해지기 위해 아이들을 돌볼 때다.

bachelor 총각 caregiving 돌봄 dense 밀집한

REVIEW TEST P. 202

01 engaged 02 had taken 03 would have cooperated with 04 would know 05 hadn't met 06 is granted 07 had not been 08 moved onto 09 would not find 10 had come in

01 현재 사실에 대한 가정이므로 가정법 과거가 적절

그 연구 결과는 교육가들이 모든 학생들의 감각을 사로잡는다면, 아이들은 더 잘 배울 뿐만 아니라 더 잘 사고할 수 있다는 것을 암시한다.

02 과거 사실에 대한 가정이므로 가정법 과거완료가 적절

닉과 팀은 둘 다 그들이 만약 그때 다른 행동을 취했다면 5천 달러까지 더 이익을 취할 수 있었음을 깨달았다.

03 과거 사실에 대한 가정이므로 가정법 과거완료가 적절

만약 그들이 나에게 도움을 요청했다면 나는 경찰과 협력했을 것이다.

04 현재 상황에 대한 가정이므로 would know가 옴

만약 당신이 나를 잘 안다면, 당신은 내가 모든 칭찬을 액면 그대로 받아들이고 그들이 단지 아첨하는 것이라고 생각하지 않을 만큼 부끄러움을 모른다는 것을 알 것이다.

05 과거 사실에 대한 가정이므로 가정법 과거완료가 적절

내가 피터 잭슨을 만나지 않았다면, 나는 영화와 연극에 대한 내 열정을 발전시키지 못했을 것이다.

06 '만약 …하지 않으면'

만약 공보실에서 허가가 나지 않으면 플래시를 터트리는 사진 촬영은 박물관 내에서 허용되지 않는다.

07 과거에 대한 가정이므로 과거완료 구문이 옴

지난 일요일에 바쁘지 않았다면 좋으련만. 그랬다면 너와 함께 그 문제를 해결했을 텐데.

08 〈It is time+가정법 과거〉

아직도 같은 문제를 풀고 있니? 시간이 없어. 다른 문제로 넘어갈 때야.

09 주절이 현재 사실을 가정하므로 가정법 과거가 적절

만약 캐서린이 어제 주의 깊게 그 문제를 검토했다면, 그녀는 지금 아무 문제가 없을 텐데.

10 과거 사실에 대한 가정이므로 가정법 과거완료가 적절

만약 그녀가 지난번 인터뷰에 왔다면, 우리는 그녀에게 그 일자리를 주었을 텐데.

FINAL CHECK P. 203~205

01 ① 02 ⑤ 03 ③ 04 ② 05 ⑤ 06 ③

01 ① as if 가정법이므로 if절의 동사는 is가 아니라 were가 적절 ② universities가 주어, what department and disciplines가 group의 목적어 ③ 두 문장이 접속사 없이 연결되었으므로 which가 옴 ④ 완전한 보어절을 이끄는 접속사 ⑤ 〈dedicate to〉 '~에 전념하다'

우리는 사회과학이 마치 하나의 개체인 것처럼 이야기한다. 그러나 사실은 그렇지 않다. 실제로 어떤 것들이 사회과학인 것인가? 그 질문에 대답하는 한 가지 방법은 대학이 사회과학이라는 이름 아래 어떤 학과와 학문을 분류하는지를 보는 것이다. 사회과학부는 보통 인류학과, 경제학과, 정치학과, 사회학과를 포함한다. 왜 사회과학부는 자신의 발전을 위해, 사회과학에서 개념과 방법론을 차용한 법학, 교육학, 경영학, 사회 복지학, 행정학과 같은 학과들을 포함하지 않는가? 그 이유는 그 전에 언급된 학과들은 대학 안에서 보통 일어나는 활동인 인간 사회의 체계적인 지식을 추구하는 데에만 오로지 전념하는 반면에, 이러한 학문들의 주요한 목적은 대학 밖의 전문적인 일을 훈련시키는 것이기 때문이다.

entity 개체 discipline 학문의 부분, 학과 anthropology 인류학

02 (A) 주어는 our growth이므로 단수 (B) 현재 사실에 대한 가정이므로 가정법 과거가 적절 (C) 5문형 동사인 call 뒤에 목적어가 없으므로 called가 옴, bicycle riding은 목적격 보어

사물의 새로운 질서를 도입할 때 주도권을 잡기란 매우 어렵다고 어떤 철학자가 말했다. 사실, 뭔가 새로운 일을 하는 것은 두렵

다. 그러나 태어나서 제 역할을 하는 인간으로 성장하는 것은 변화와 새로운 환경에 얼마나 잘 적응하는가에 달려 있다. 만약 넘어지는 것에 대한 두려움을 극복하지 못하면 결코 일어서는 법을 배울 수 없다. 우리들 중 많은 사람은 무릎에 자전거 타기라는 새로운 기술을 익히고자 하는 열망으로 몸에 상처를 입을 때까지도 끈질기게 해냈다는 것을 입증하는 상처가 있다. 그러나 우리가 그 기술을 배웠을 때 얼굴에 스치는 바람을 느끼는 일은 얼마나 흥분되는 것인가. 우리는 두려움을 극복했고 그로 인해 얻게 된 느낌은 정말로 대단한 것이었다.

function 기능하다 **persist** 지속하다 **conquer** 정복하다

03 ③ 현재 사실에 대한 가정이므로 are lowered가 아니라 were lowered가 적절 ① 〈the same as〉 '~와 같은 것' ② 주어는 the industry's production cost이므로 단수 ④ '제안된'을 의미하므로 수동형인 과거분사가 옴 ⑤ 〈동사+대명사+부사〉 구문으로 get과 back 사이에 옴

음반 업계는 10대들이 유료 웹사이트로부터 음악을 다운로드 받기를 바라지만 그들은 음악을 다운로드 받을 때 지불하는 높은 가격이 음악 시디를 사는 것만큼의 비용과 같다는 것을 알지 못한다. 음악 시디를 만드는 업계의 생산 가격이 낮더라도 10대에게 판매되는 가격은 개당 20달러로 상당히 높은 수준이다. 만약에 개당 가격을 최고 10달러까지 낮춘다면 아마도 10대들은 불법적으로 음악을 다운로드 받으려고 애쓰지 않고 상점에서 음악을 살 수 있을 것이다. 실현 불가능하다고? 가능하다. 세계에서 가장 큰 음반회사는 지난 10월 음악 시디의 권장 소비자 가격을 12.98달러로 낮추었다. 여러분은 할인점에서 10달러짜리 음악 시디를 찾을 수 있을 것이다. 음악을 불법적으로 다운로드 받는 이들을 비난하기보다 음반업계는 정상적인 길로 그들이 돌아올 수 있도록 도움의 손길을 내밀어야 한다.

maximum 최대치 **retail** 소매의 **extend** 확장하다

04 (A) 〈It's time+가정법 과거〉 (B) '죽은 피부세포를 제거하기 위해서' 마사지를 받음 (C) almost like '거의 ~같은'

이제 곧 여름이고, 이제 해변에 갈 때입니다. 여러분은 바다로 뛰어들기 전에, 바디 스크럽과 Elemis Visible Brilliance Facial 프로그램을 포함하는 Tone Me Up 피부 관리를 선택하셔야 합니다. 죽은 피부 세포를 제거하고 피부를 생기 있게 하기 위해서, 우선 부드럽게 마사지를 받게 되실 겁니다. 그러고 나서 피부 관리사가 진흙을 당신의 다리에 바르고 호일로 감싸면, 진흙이 피부를 부드럽게 만들고 영양분을 공급하게 됩니다. 얼굴을 스크럽하고 씻어내고, 마사지 하면 이제 거의 필 마스크 같은 진흙을 제거할 시간입니다. 당신은 편안해 지고, 피부는 눈에 띌 만큼 더 부드럽고 매끄러워집니다. 이제 당신은 여름을 즐길 준비가 되었습니다!

invigorate 활기 띠게 하다, 기운 나게 하다 **apply** 바르다
nourish 영양분을 공급하다 **noticeably** 눈에 띄게

05 ⑤ as if 가정법 구문이므로 eat가 아니라 ate가 적절 ① 주어는 the acid이므로 단수 ② worn out을 수식하므로 부사가 옴 ③ 앞 문장 전체를 받는 관계대명사 which가 옴 ④ 〈~인 때〉를 나타냄, 보어절을 이끄는 접속사

영양이 풍부한 음식을 먹고 운동을 하는 것은 여러분을 정신적, 육체적으로 건강하게 유지하도록 도와준다. 일부 음식과 음료수의 산이 치아와 만날 때, 치아의 단단한 에나멜 표면은 일시적으로 부드러워진다. 우리가 그 직후 이를 닦을 때, 에나멜은 보다 쉽게 닳게 되며 시간이 지날수록 부드러워지는데, 이는 산부식이라고 알려져 있다. 이런 산부식으로부터 치아를 보호하는 간단한 방법이 있다. 이런 상황을 피하기 위해서는 산성 음식을 먹은 후 이를 닦기 전 가능한 한 오래 기다려라. 왜냐하면 이 기간이 에나멜이 가장 약할 때이기 때문이다. 또 다른 것은 껌을 씹는 것이다. 그것은 마치 여러분이 무언가를 먹는 것처럼 침 생산을 자극하므로 산성을 중화시킨다.

acid 산성 **temporarily** 일시적으로 **worn out** 닳은 **erosion** 침식 **neutralize** 중성화시키다 **saliva** 침

06 (A) wish 가정법, 현재 사실에 대한 바람/유감을 나타내므로 had가 적절 (B) 〈spend+시간/돈+-ing〉 ~하는 데 시간/돈을 쓰다 (C) 앞의 have는 사역동사가 아닌 일반동사, 뒤에 나오는 내용은 '목적'에 해당하므로 to부정사의 부사적 용법이 옴

당신은 당신을 어디론가 태워다 줄 누군가 있었으면 하고 바라거나 당신이 필요할 때 도와줄 사람을 바란 적이 있는가? 우리 중 많은 이들은 우리를 도와줄 친구와 이웃, 가족들이 있지만, 그들이 항상 도움이 필요할 때 함께 있을 수는 없다. 타임 뱅킹 공동체 안에서 누군가는 항상 당신과 함께 할 것이다. 그것은 대가족을 가지는 것과 같다. 타임 뱅킹은 처음 보는 낯선 사람을 친구로 바꿀 것이다. 타임 뱅킹은 단순히 당신의 공동체에 있는 누군가를 위해 무언가를 하려고 시간을 쓰는 것에 관한 것이다. 그 시간은 타임 달러로 타임 뱅크에 들어간다. 그러면 당신을 위해 무언가를 하는 누군가를 가지는데 쓸 수 있는 타임 달러를 가지게 된다. 타임 뱅킹은 공동체를 구성하는데 강력한 영향력을 발휘한다.

community 공동체 **extended family** 대가족

chapter
16 강조, 도치

UNIT 181~182

Check-up P. 208~209

181 **1.** was **2.** was

182 **1.** 라이벌이라고 불리는 사람은 바로 이야기에서 영웅을 괴롭히고, 다치게 하고, 못살게 하는 인물이다.
2. 아프리카 난민이 그 도시에서 탈출하도록 우리나라가 도와야 한다고 제안한 사람이 바로 대통령이었다.

181

1. 〈It ~ that〉 강조 구문으로 주어 a skinny kid가 단수

제주도의 바위 투성이 해변에서 낚시를 하고 있는 사람은 바로 두 개의 밀짚 모자를 쓰고 있는 깡마른 아이였다.

2. the students가 주어처럼 보여도 It ~ that 강조 구문이므로 동사는 단수형이 적절

그 사람에게 계란을 던지고 그를 조롱했던 사람이 바로 웨스트사이드 고등학교의 학생들이었다.

EXERCISE

P. 210

01 that 02 It 03 It 04 that 05 that 06 that
07 where 08 that 09 It 10 determine

01 ⟨It ~ that⟩ 강조 구문, 장소가 아닌 사람을 강조

좋아 보이는 것은 호주의 사람들만이 아니다.

02 ⟨It ~ that⟩ 강조 구문, not because ~ wisdom을 강조

우리는 단지 지혜 때문만이 아니라 우리의 짜증나는 문제 때문에 정신적, 영혼적으로 성장한다.

03 ⟨It ~ who⟩ 강조 구문, our parents를 강조

우리에게 옳고 그름에 대한 지각, 사랑에 대한 이해, 우리가 누구인가에 대한 앎을 준 사람들이 바로 우리 부모님들이다.

04 ⟨It ~ that⟩ 강조 구문, which는 완전한 문장을 이끌 수 없음

캐서린이 남편이 될 사람과 처음 데이트를 한 곳이 바로 그 놀이동산이었다.

05 ⟨It ~ that⟩ 강조 구문으로 while 시간부사절을 강조

그가 앤더슨을 두 번째로 만난 것은 바로 뉴욕에서 공부하고 있을 때였다.

06 ⟨It ~ that⟩ 강조 구문, 뒤에 완전한 문장이 와서 which는 불가능

사람들이 스포츠의 새로운 경험에 마음의 문을 열 수 있는 시기는 바로 스포츠와 일상생활의 차이가 인지될 때이다.

07 in the book을 강조하므로 장소를 나타내는 where가 옴

내가 그의 발견에 관해서 읽었던 곳은 바로 네가 작년에 나에게 사준 책에서였다.

08 ⟨It ~ that⟩ 강조 구문, 시간을 강조하므로 which는 올 수 없음

현대의 신문이 발간된 것은 바로 1860년과 1868년 사이였다.

09 ⟨It ~ that⟩ 강조 구문, ⟨not until~⟩구문이 강조됨

바로 그 사건이 일어나고 나서야 비로소 제임스는 그의 어리석음을 깨닫게 되었다.

10 ⟨It ~ that⟩ 강조 구문, the uses ~ is put이 강조되는데, determine의 주어는 the uses로 복수임

사회에 대한 그 가치를 결정하는 것은 바로 그 장치가 어떻게 사용되느냐이다.

ACTUAL TEST

P. 211

01 ③ 02 ③

01 ③ 전치사 through의 목적어가 되고, 도둑이 전선을 파는 것이므로 sold가 아니라 selling이 적절 ④ ⟨It ~ that⟩ 강조 구문, without any security라는 부사구를 강조 ① metal items를 지칭 ② ⟨become+비교급⟩ 구문 ⑤ ask의 목적격 보어

물품과 금속 절도는 전국적으로 특이한 문제 중 하나가 되었다. 예를 들어 마약 사용자들이 건물에서 구리나 알루미늄관 같은 금속물품을 훔치고 약을 사기 위한 돈을 벌기 위해 폐품으로 그것들을 판다. 그리고 유타주의 고속도로는 종종 밤에 평소보다 더 어두워지는데, 도둑들이 반복적으로 가로등의 전선을 훔치기 때문이다. 정부는 도난 당한 전선을 대체하기 위해 수만 달러의 돈을 지출한다. 하지만 도둑은 전선을 팔아서 백 달러나 그보다 적게 번다. 또한 건축 자재나 도구도 종종 절도의 표적이 되는데 이것은 바로 그것들이 종종 건축 현장에서 경비 없이 방치되어 있는 것이 발견되기 때문이다. 이러한 상황을 막기 위해서, 일부 주는 금속 딜러들에게 그들에게 금속을 파는 사람들의 인적 정보를 기록할 것을 요구하는 법을 통과시켰다.

commodity 물품 copper 구리 scrap 폐품 construction material 건축 자재

02 (A) 주어는 one이므로 단수 (B) It으로 시작하며 that이 나오면 ⟨It is thought that~⟩ 구문, 주어가 사람이 아니면 think는 수동형이 옴 (C) a manner of speaking을 강조하는 ⟨It ~ that⟩ 강조 구문

우리말에서 가장 평가 절하된 단어 중 하나는 사랑이다. 우리는 사랑을 어디에나 사용한다. 우리는 가족을 사랑하고, 새로운 아이폰을 사랑하며, 축구와 비틀즈, 그리고 혼자 있는 것을 사랑한다. 우리는 먼저 생각하고 그리고 나서 우리의 생각을 표현할 단어를 찾는다고 여겨진다. 실제로 사실은 그 반대이다. 예를 들어 우리는 우리가 애인을 사랑하는 것과 같은 방법으로 가족을 사랑하지는 않는다. 우리는 우리가 피자를 좋아하는 개념으로 신을 사랑하지 않는다. 우리는 애완동물을 사랑하는 방식대로 나라를 사랑하지는 않는다. 이러한 언어의 차이를 만드는 것이 바로 말하는 방식이다. 우리가 사용하는 단어는 우리가 생각하는 것을 통제한다. 그것이 바로 우리가 보통 슬로건이 표현하는 명확한 실체보다는 슬로건에 의해 행동을 취하는 이유다.

devalue 평가 절하하다 sweetheart 애인 verbal 말의 embody 표현하다

UNIT 183~184

Check-up P. 212~213

183 1. that 2. that
184 1. did he know 2. did Jack violate

183

1. ⟨It ~ that⟩ 강조 구문, 이유를 강조하고 있어 who는 부적절

우리가 그를 찾아야만 하는 이유는 바로 그 편지들이 제임스에게 온 것이기 때문이다.

2. ⟨It ~ that⟩ 강조 구문, 앞에 강조 받는 부분(일종의 선행사)이 있으므로 what은 부적절

우리가 이번 재판에서 이기기 위해서 필요한 것이 바로 이 사건과 관련있는 증거이다.

184

1. not until이 없는 절이 도치가 됨

그가 결승점을 통과하고 나서야 그는 100미터 경기에서 우승했음을 알게 되었다.

2. not only가 있는 절이 도치가 됨

잭이 법을 위반했을 뿐 아니라 이사회도 그의 위반을 막지 못했다.

EXERCISE

P. 214

01 that 02 did he begin 03 do the employees of the factory want 04 she arrived 05 not until 06 a monkey is 07 that 08 did Beethoven compose 09 the lack of a national pension became 10 did my pause give

01 not until 구문을 강조하는 ⟨It ~ that⟩ 강조 구문

그녀가 시를 쓰기 시작한 것이 바로 45세 때였다.

02 not until 구문이 앞으로 나갔으므로 주절의 주어와 동사가 도치

그가 변호사를 만나고 나서야 그는 그가 공원에서 목격한 것을 이야기하기 시작했다.

03 not only가 있는 절의 주어, 동사가 도치

공장의 근로자들은 급여 인상뿐만 아니라 근로 시간 단축도 원한다.

04 not until 안에 있는 문장은 도치하지 않음

그녀가 어제 도착하고 나서야 우리는 회의를 시작하고 회사의 문제에 대해 논의할 수 있었다.

05 '~하고 나서야 …하다'는 뜻의 not until이 적절

우리가 결혼하고 나서야 비로소 나는 그가 이런 어떤 사람인지 깨닫게 되었다.

06 not until 안의 문장은 도치가 이루어지지 않음

원숭이들이 어느 정도 나이가 되었을 때, 비로소 그 원숭이는 어미로부터 독립할 징후를 보이기 시작한다.

07 ⟨It ~ that⟩ 강조 구문, around ~ details를 강조

성인과 아이들 사이의 대화는 바로 이러한 세부적인 사항에서부터 시작된다.

08 not until 구문이 문두로 나가서 주절의 주어와 동사가 도치

베토벤이 30살이 되어서야 첫 번째 교향곡을 작곡하게 되었다.

09 ⟨It ~ when⟩ 강조 구문, not until에 걸리는 문장이 아니므로 주어, 동사가 도치 되지 않음

2007년이 되어서야 비로소 국민연금의 부족이 젊은이들과 노인들 사이에 큰 이슈가 되었다.

10 not only 구문의 주어, 동사는 도치됨

중간 휴식은 학생들에게 내가 무슨 말을 했는지 생각할 시간을 주었을 뿐 아니라 나에게도 무슨 말을 할 것인지 생각할 시간을 주었다.

ACTUAL TEST

P. 215

01 ③ 02 ④

01 ③ ⟨not only ~ but also⟩ 구문은 but also 뒤에서 도치 일어나지 않으므로 do they가 아니라 they do가 적절 ① ⟨so ~ that⟩ 너무 ~해서 …하다 ② 이번 예가 마지막이라는 근거가 없으므로 '또 다른'을 의미하는 Another가 올 수 있음 ④ 주어는 The combined effect이므로 단수임 ⑤ some work가 이루어지는 것이므로 수동

보통의 화학 물질 중 다수는 너무 독성이 강해서 포유동물과 다른 동물들에게 나쁜 영향을 끼친다. 예를 들어 알킬페놀라 불리는 한 종류의 화학 물질은 호르몬 체계와 성장을 방해할 수 있다. 알킬페놀는 종종 샴푸에서 발견된다. 프틸레이트라는 또 다른 화학 물질은 생식계에 해로운데 이것은 비닐 바닥재에 널리 사용된다. 이런 화학 물질들은 유해할 뿐 아니라 쉽게 자연 분해되지도 않는다. 즉, 그들은 아주 오랫동안 지구에 있을 것이다. 이런 속성들이 결합된 화학 물질은 흔히 "잔류성 유기오염물질" 혹은 POP라고 알려져 있다. POP가 우리의 건강과 환경에 미치는 효과는 점점 더 연구되고 알려지고 있다. POP의 사용을 통제하기 위해 몇몇 연구들이 이루어졌지만 현재 소수의 화학 물질만이 정부의 통제를 받고 있다.

interfere with 방해하다 **reproductive** 번식의 **biodegrade** 자연 분해되다 **a handful of** 소량의 **fall under** ~의 영향을 받다

02 (A) 전치사가 앞에 있으므로 that은 오지 못함 (B) not until 부사구가 문두에 있으므로 주절의 주어와 동사는 도치
(C) thought의 주어가 되는 주격 관계대명사가 필요

비록 소크라테스는 정의에 대한 정확한 지침을 생각해 내지는 않았지만, 그는 '소크라테스 방법'이라고 알려지게 된 것을 활용했다. 어떤 용어에 대한 진짜 정의에 도달하기 위해서, 소크라테스는 그 용어를 이해한다고 주장하는 사람과 대화를 시작하곤 했다. 그는 계속해서 주의 깊게 탐구하고, 계속해서 질문을 했다. 마침내 그들이 정확한 설명에 도달했을 때, 비로소 소크라테스는 상대방으로부터 모든 종류의 정의들을 이끌어냈고, 그들의 부족함과 결함을 보여주곤 했다. 당연히 이러한 접근법은 그가 그 문제에 대해 함께 논의했고, 자신있게 자기가 모든 것을 안다고 생각했던 이들을 짜증나고 굴욕감을 느끼게 했던 것 같다.

enter into 시작하다 **probe** 탐구하다 **persistently** 바득바득 우기는 **elicit** 이끌어내다 **opponent** 상대편 **inadequacy** 부족함

UNIT 185~186

Check-up

P. 216~217

185	1. was	2. is
186	1. beautiful is	2. is the problem

185

1. 문두에 Among ~ Awards가 있으므로 주어, 동사 도치, the lovely ~ Marilyn Monroe가 주어

   아카데미 상을 받은 영화배우들 중에 사랑스러운 금발여인 마를린 몬로가 있다.

2. 문두에 Just ~ sites가 있으므로 주어, 동사 도치, a castle이 주어

   유적지 바로 바깥쪽에 돌벽과 키 큰 나무들로 둘러싸인 성이 있다.

186

1. So beautiful이 앞으로 나가서 주어, 동사 도치

   그 여인이 너무 아름다워서 나는 한눈에 그녀와 사랑에 빠졌다.

2. So great가 앞으로 나가서 주어, 동사 도치

   오염에 관한 문제가 너무 심각하기 때문에, 우리는 오염을 줄이기 위해 무언가를 해야만 한다.

EXERCISE

P. 218

01 have **02** you can see **03** are **04** So **05** is a collection **06** was a huge box **07** was one hundred-dollar bill **08** was **09** was this element **10** did I notice

01 So 도치 구문으로 주어는 the ways이므로 동사는 복수형

여기서의 삶의 방식이 거의 바뀌지 않아서 15세기로 거슬러 올라가 있는 자기 자신을 상상하는 건 쉽다.

02 Under the see가 앞으로 나갔지만, 부사구 뒤에 콤마가 왔으므로 도치가 일어나지 않음

바다 아래에서 당신은 많은 물고기와 해마와 거북이, 해파리 등과 같은 많은 바다 생물을 볼 수 있다.

03 so 도치 구문으로 주어는 the world~wakefulness로 복수

수면의 세계와 각성의 세계는 많이 달라서 모든 사람이 두 개의 세상에 살고 있다고 한다.

04 〈so ~ that〉 도치 구문

과학은 아주 많이 발전해서 우리는 우리 몸 안의 신체 상태를 매일 검사할 수 있는 로봇을 가지게 될 것이다.

05 장소 부사구가 문두에 나왔으므로 주어와 동사는 도치

LA에 있는 SST 박물관에는 중세와 르네상스 시대의 미술 작품이 있다.

06 Next to the piano가 문두에 있으므로 주어와 동사는 도치

그 피아노 옆에는 역시 나무로 만들어진 큰 상자가 뚜껑이 열린 채 있었는데 그 안에는 여러 장의 악보가 들어있었다.

07 On the couch가 문두에 있으므로 주어와 동사는 도치

그 교재 안에 100달러짜리 지폐 한 장이 있었다.

08 Observing the ~ students가 앞으로 왔으므로 주어, 동사 도치, 관계대명사 who와 선행사 Detective John Smith가 가까이 있기 위해 도치가 일어남

학생 중 한 명이라도 범죄를 목격했을지도 모른다는 생각을 한 존 스미스 형사는 지역 고등학생들을 지켜보고 있었다.

09 〈so+형용사〉가 문두로 나가 주어와 동사는 도치

이 성분은 너무 중요해서 일부 과학자들은 연구를 위한 실험을 하는데 그것들을 이용하기도 했다.

10 앞에 Only then이 있으므로 주어와 동사 도치

각각의 귀에 있는 공기주머니에서 유스타키오관이라고 불리는 관이 이어지는데, 이는 비강과 귀 바깥쪽을 연결한다.

ACTUAL TEST

P. 219

01 ⑤ **02** ②

01 ⑤ 〈so+형용사〉가 문두로 나가 주어, 동사 도치되므로 the difference가 아니라 is difference가 적절 ① '~으로 나눠진다' ② 문장을 연결하는 접속사가 없으므로 관계사가 옴 ③ 주어가 what절이므로 단수 ④ 〈형용사+enough〉의 어순

미국의 중산계층은 다음과 같이 새로운 세 개의 그룹으로 나눠진다. 경제 성장의 이득을 보지 못하는 하위 계층, 빠른 변화에 대해 사회적으로나 경제적으로 안정된 상위 계층, 고용되어 있지만 미래에 대해 걱정하는 사람들로 대부분 이루어진 불안 계층. 이들을 분류하는 것은 정규교육 수준이다. 1990년대가 돼서야 대졸 남성이 고졸 남성보다 49퍼센트를 더 벌었다. 물론 꽤 많은 차이이긴 하지만 이 차이는 두 사람 모두가 중산층이라고 불릴만한 영역에 도달할 수 있을 만큼 작기도 하다. 2009년에 대졸 남성은 고졸 남성인 동료보다 95%를 더 벌었다. 그 차이는 너무 커서 그들은 더 이상 공통적인 영역에 속하거나 공통적인 가능성을 공유할 수 없다.

underclass 하위 계층 **shift** 변화 **overclass** 상류 계층 **categorize** 분류하다 **formal** 정규의 **sizable** 상당한 **territory** 영역 **outearn** ~보다 많이 벌다

02 (A) 주어는 The convention이므로 단수 (B) 뒤에 always가 나오므로 almost가 옴, '거의 ~ 항상' (C) not until이 문두로 나왔으므로 주절의 주어, 동사는 도치

과학자들 사이에 의사소통 관례는 공식적이고 복잡하다. 만약 새로운 발견이 다른 과학자들에 의해 진지하게 받아들여지려면 분명하고 엄격한 기준이 충족되어야 한다. 이는 새로운 결과가 발표되고 받아들여지기 전에 실험이 승인된 절차에 따라 반복되고 증명되어야 한다는 것을 의미한다. 그 다음에 그 결과는 거의 항상 공식적인 과학 연구 논문이나 학회지 논문을 통해 의사소통이 이루어진다. 가장 중요한 새로운 결과물들은 모든 과학자들의 공통 관심사인 사이언스지나 네이쳐지 같은 저널에 실릴 수 있다. 두 저널 다 저널 편집자와 두세 명의 익명 심사위원의 검증을 거고 나서야 그 논문은 출간이 될 것이다. 이는 공식적인 과학에 대한 가장 광범위한 안전 장치 중의 하나이다.

convention 관례 **take A seriously** A를 진지하게 생각하다 **verify** 증명하다 **undergo** 겪다 **referee** (논문 등의) 심사위원

UNIT 187~188

Check-up

P. 220~221

187 **1.** does she realize **2.** do doctors save
188 **1.** have I **2.** nor

187

1. Little이 문두에 있으므로 주어와 동사는 도치

그녀는 자신이 처한 위험을 거의 깨닫지 못한다.

2. Nowhere ~ America가 문두에 있어 주어와 동사 도치

미국의 어떤 곳에서도 의사들이 아이들을 구하거나 신문사들이 정직한 뉴스를 인쇄하지 않는다.

188

1. nor가 앞에 있으므로 도치

나는 지난 회의 이후로 그를 만나본 적도 없고, 통화한 적도 없다.

2. 앞 문장이 부정문이므로 nor가 옴

줄리안은 미국인이라는 사실을 부끄러워하지 않고, 미국의 국기를 입은 것도 부끄러워하지 않는다.

EXERCISE P. 222

01 had I **02** everyone is **03** have the dead **04** it means **05** should he **06** is a computer **07** have I felt **08** is the atmosphere **09** are curveballs **10** he offered

01 No sooner가 문두에 있으므로 주어, 동사 도치

나는 그를 보자마자 눈물을 터뜨렸다.

02 Not everyone '모두가 ~한 것은 아니다', 부분 부정을 의미

모든이가 이 문제가 처리되어야 하는 방식에 반대하진 않을 것이다.

03 not only 문장 내에서 도치가 이루어짐

죽은 이들이 살아 돌아왔을 뿐 아니라, 게다가 식인종이 되었다.

04 but 이하는 도치가 이루어지지 않음

그 어휘는 '그녀가 빨리 달리다'에서와 같이 '급하고 빠르게 움직이는 것'을 의미할 뿐만 아니라, '그 창문은 꽉 껴 있다'에서와 같이 '절대로 움직이지 않는'을 의미하기도 한다.

05 nor 다음에는 도치가 이루어짐

신사 신원처럼 욕을 하지 않으며, 새벽 2시에 술을 마시러 나가지도 않아야 한다.

06 Rarely가 문두에 있으므로 주어와 동사가 도치

컴퓨터가 동일한 지리적 혹은 환경적인 요소들을 관리하는 데 있어서 인간보다 더 민감하거나 정확한 경우는 드물다.

07 Never ~ 가 문두에 있으므로 주어, 동사 도치

다른 때에는 전혀 느끼지 못한, 심지어 내가 가장 큰 승진을 한 후에도 느낀 적이 없는 커다란 행복감을 내 딸이 태어나서 느꼈다.

08 hardly가 앞에 나갔으므로 주어와 동사가 도치

디트로이트에 있는 나의 이웃은 다소 음침하고 분위기는 평화로운 생각에 거의 도움이 되지 않는다.

09 not only 문장 내에서 도치가 이루어짐

그 자체가 선물이기도 한 커브볼은 우리를 깨어있게 하는 우주의 방법일뿐 아니라, 우리에게 놀라움을 가져다 주는 방법이기도 하다.

10 but also 다음에 오는 문장은 도치가 이루어지지 않음

당신도 알다시피 그는 답장을 썼고 그가 나를 대했던 방식을 사과했을 뿐만 아니라, 나에게 내 차에서 거래할 것을 제안했다.

ACTUAL TEST P. 223

01 ⑤ **02** ④

01 ⑤ Nor가 문두에 있으므로 Nor many가 아니라 Nor did many가 돼야 함 ① '거의 항상' ② materials를 수식하는데 둘의 관계가 수동이므로 과거분사가 옴 ③ 〈the 비교급, the 비교급〉 구문 ④ combining을 수식하므로 부사가 옴

새로운 아이디어나 갑작스러운 깨달음은 거의 항상 어떤 문제에 대해 머리가 무의식적으로 작동한 산물인데 이는 오랜 학습과 의식적인 사고를 통해 축적된 자료들을 이용하는 것이다. 지식의 창고가 더 크고 범위가 더 넓을수록 당신은 더 창의적이 될 것이다. 당신이 가지고 있는 다양한 지식의 상호작용은 너무 미묘하고 복잡해서 그 결과를 예측할 수가 없다. 새로운 발명품들은 다양한 종류의 지식을 창의적으로 결합함으로써 만들어진다. 벤자민 프랭클린이 전기의 속성을 연구하기 위해 폭풍 속으로 연을 날렸을 때, 그는 그의 발명에 관심이 많은 미래의 사람들이 만들어낼 세탁기, 전자렌지, 텔레비전 같은 위대한 발명품들을 예상하지 못했다. 그 발명가들 중 많은 사람들도 프랭클린의 업적을 연구할 때 이런 것들을 예견하지 못했었다.

storehouse 창고 **subtle** 미묘한 **sophisticated** 복잡한 **property** 속성 **foresee** 예상하다

02 (A) 부정어구인 nor가 문두에 있으므로 주어, 동사 도치 (B) 뒤에 오는 문장이 완전하므로 notion과 동격절을 이끄는 접속사 that이 옴 (C) 앞뒤 내용이 대립관계이므로 even if가 옴

보물 찾기와 도굴, 땅 속이나 물 밑에서 금을 움켜쥐는 것, 부자가 되기 위해 누군가의 신성한 조상일 수 있는 무덤을 파헤치는 행위는 오늘날 고고학자들이 하는 일이 아니다. 고고학자들은 우스꽝스러운 모자를 쓰지도 않고 채찍이나 권총을 들고 다니지도 않으며, 나치나 국제 밀수업자들과 싸우지도 않는다. 모든 고고학이 흥미진진하다는 생각은 많은 서류 작업과 그에 수반되는 따분한 실험실 절차를 생각할 때 근거 없는 것이다. 사실 당신은 모르는 것에 대한 환상을 가지고 있다. 혹여 그것이 1950년대의 콜라병이라 할지라도 그 발굴이 무엇을 밝혀낼지는 절대 모를 것이다. 어떤 고고학자들은 어떻게 통속 문화가 직업을 묘사하는지를 연구한다. 책과 인터넷 사이트는 영화와 심지어 고고학 관련 장난감들에서의 모든 재미거리들 가운데 잘못된 부분들을 지적하고 있다.

excavate 발굴하다 **whip** 채찍 **pistol** 권총 **smuggler** 밀수꾼 **groundless** 근거 없는 **amid** 가운데

UNIT 189~190

Check-up P. 224~225

189 **1.** was this frontier spirit **2.** must the window
190 **1.** what I can **2.** wind is used

189

1. 부정부사어구인 in no other heart가 앞에 있으므로 도치

그 어떤 사람들의 마음에도 어릴 적 제이피 모건의 개척 정신보다 강렬하게 주입되어 있지는 않았다.

2. 부정부사어구인 under no circumstances가 앞에 있어 도치

어떠한 경우에라도 창문은 열려있어야 한다.

190

1. 간접의문문이므로 〈의문사+주어+동사〉의 어순

나는 나의 독특한 목소리로 어떤 생각들을 좀 더 받아들이기 위해서 무엇을 할 수 있는지 궁금하다.

2. 간접의문문이므로 〈의문사+주어+동사〉의 어순

목관악기의 소리는 얼마나 많은 바람이 사용되느냐에 따라서 더 크게, 아니면 더욱 부드럽게 만들어 질 수 있다.

EXERCISE

P. 226

01 who I was **02** they could **03** what she was **04** has he **05** how the body is **06** will Sports Fitness Advisor **07** would I **08** does it say **09** who stole the golden ball **10** what kinds of boys her brothers were

01 간접의문문의 어순은 〈의문사+주어+동사〉

나는 내가 단지 내 남편뿐 아니라 내 공간, 즉 내 삶의 방식과 내가 누구였는지도 잃어버렸음을 발견했다.

02 간접의문문의 어순은 〈의문사+주어+동사〉

한 실험에서 연구원들은 참가자들에게 실험을 위해 주어진 어떤 과제를 얼마나 많이 통제할 수 있는지 예측해볼 것을 요청했다.

03 간접의문문의 어순은 〈의문사+주어+동사〉

짐이 그녀에게 그녀가 무엇을 하고 있었는지를 물었을 때, 그녀는 우울해 보였고 그때 무언가를 쓰고 있었다.

04 부정어가 포함된 부사구가 문두로 나왔으므로 주어, 동사 도치

그가 여기에 온 이래로, 그는 단 한마디도 하지 않았다.

05 간접의문문의 어순은 〈의문사+주어+동사〉

그들은 연구에서 신체가 스포츠에서 어떻게 훈련되고, 단련되며, 조작되는지에 대한 중요한 질문을 하고 있다.

06 문두에 부정어가 포함된 전치사구가 있으므로 주어, 동사 도치

스포츠 피트니스지의 고문은 이 웹사이트나 그곳에 포함된 조언 때문에 발생할 지도 모르는 어떤 부상이나 문제에 결코 책임을 지려 하지 않을 것이다.

07 문두에 부정어가 포함된 전치사구가 있으므로 주어, 동사 도치

어떤 경우에도 나는 남의 안위를 희생할 지도 모르는 그런 비열한 짓을 하지 않을 것이다.

08 문두에 부정어가 포함된 전치사구가 있으므로 주어, 동사 도치

그 책 어디에도 고대 일본 왕국이 한국의 영토를 점령했었다는 언급은 없다.

09 who가 주어, the golden ball은 목적어이므로 간접의문문 어순임

우리는 이 탐정이 누가 황금공을 훔쳤는지 밝힐 수 있기를 바란다.

10 her brothers가 주어, kinds of boys는 were의 보어로 what과 함께 이동, 〈의문사+주어+동사〉의 간접의문문 어순

노엘은 그녀의 가족을 방문하기 전에, 그녀의 형제들이 어떤 사람들인지 알기를 원했다.

ACTUAL TEST

P. 227

01 ④ 02 ③

01 ④ 선생님이 신체에 손을 올려놓는 것이므로 placed가 아니라 placing이 돼야 함 ① 뒤에 완전한 문장이 오므로 관계부사가 옴 ② 주어는 Alexander Technique이므로 단수 ③ 간접의문문의 어순은 〈의문사+주어+동사〉 ⑤ '당신의 신체를 더 잘 알게 되고, 그래서 안 좋은 신체적 습관을 피하는 법'을 의미하므로 앞의 to become과 병렬 구조

브룸스베리가(街)에 있는 현대식 건물에는 도움이 안 되거나 해로운 습관들을 스스로 방지하면서 운동하는 방법인 알렉산더 기법을 20년 이상 동안 가르쳐 온 알렉산더 센터가 있다. 이 운동의 목적은 우리가 일상적인 활동에서 몸을 사용하는 방법을 바꾸는 것이다. 관절이나 근육통 환자에게 있어서, 이 운동은 자세를 개선할 수 있고 움직임이 용이해지게 할 수 있다. 최근 연구는 이 운동이 단지 6개의 수업으로 만성적인 등 통증으로 고생하는 환자들에게 지속적인 편익을 준다는 것을 알아냈다. 한 수업에서는 선생님이 신체 상태에 대한 충분한 정보를 얻기 위해서 손을 당신의 신체에 올려 놓으면서, 당신의 자세와 움직임을 관찰한다. 또한 당신이 자신의 신체에 대해서 전체적으로 뿐만 아니라 부분적으로도 더 잘 알게 되고, 그래서 나쁜 신체적 습관을 피하는 법을 알려준다.

self-prevention 자기 방지 joint 관절 posture 자세 aware of ~을 아는

02 (A) getting과 병렬 구조 (B) 간접의문문으로 〈의문사+주어+동사〉의 어순 (C) 선행사는 앞 문장 전체, which가 주어이므로 단수

미국에는 성공하기 위해 다른 나라로부터 온 많은 이민자들이 있다. 그들은 직업을 구하거나 영어를 말하도록 노력하는 것과 같이 많은 부분에서 어려움을 겪고 있기 때문에 그들의 자녀들이 더 성공하도록 하기 위해서 학교에서뿐만 아니라 집에서도 영어고 말하기를 원한다. 따라서 몇몇의 이민 2세대들은 다른 인종 집단들 사이에서 그들이 누구인지를 잃어버렸다. 심지어 영어가 유창하지 못한 자신의 부모를 무시하고 있으며, 이는 가족 안에서 의사소통을 부재를 낳는다. 이민자 부모들은 자녀들로부터 무시당하지 않기 위해서 그들에게 자기 민족의 언어를 가르쳐야 한다. 또한 공통된 언어로 의사소통하는 것은 자식들이 그들의 유산을 이해할 수 있도록 도와줄 수 있다.

immigrant 이민자 ethnic group 인종집단 ignore 무시하다

UNIT 191~192

Check-up

P. 228~229

191 **1.** So do I **2.** So was I **192** **1.** are **2.** did

191

1. 앞의 내용을 받는 so 도치

"나는 논문에 대한 충분한 자료를 조사하지 않았어. 나는 더 많은 시간이 필요해." "나도 그래. 교수님이 시간을 더 주셨으면 해."

2. 앞의 동사 was asked를 받으므로 so was I가 정답

존은 길거리에서 연구를 위한 양식을 작성해달라고 부탁 받았고, 나도 그랬다.

192

1. 앞의 동사 are dying를 받으므로 are가 정답

점점 더 많은 새와 물고기가 오염된 물 때문에 죽어가고 있다. 그리고 우리의 숲도 그렇다.

2. 앞의 동사 claimed를 받으므로 did가 정답

로빈슨은 탐이 많은 실수를 했다고 주장했다. 다른 사람들도 그렇게 주장했다.

EXERCISE

P. 230

01 were **02** are **03** are we **04** So do **05** is
06 does Australia **07** did **08** did **09** would **10** is

01 앞의 was used를 받으므로 were가 적절

그는 그의 안 좋은 상태에 익숙해 있었고, 내 친구들도 그러했다.

02 앞의 is를 받으므로 are가 적절

음악은 일상적으로 아름답다고 인식된다. 마찬가지로 소나무의 속삭임과 고양이의 부드러운 그르렁 거림 같은 소리 또한 그러하다.

03 ⟨so ~ that⟩ 구문 도치

우리는 너무 경솔해서 우리는 우리의 것이 아닌 시간 속에서 방황하고, 우리에게 속하는 시간이라고 생각하지 않는다.

04 앞의 동사 depends를 받아서 do가 옴

그것은 완전히 다른 상품에 의존한다. 또한 다른 것과 결합되었을 때만 작동하는 녹음기나 냉장고, 수천 개의 다른 상품도 그러하다.

05 앞의 is를 받음

올해의 대회 우승자는 수진인데 그녀의 딸은 귀엽고 똑똑하며, 그녀의 아들도 마찬가지이다.

06 so 도치

뉴질랜드는 관광과 교육 산업에서 발생한 수입에 상당히 의존하는데, 호주 또한 마찬가지이다.

07 앞의 동사 signed를 받으므로 did가 옴

서울시는 SKS사와 용산에 도자기 박물관을 짓기로 계약을 체결했으며, 부천시도 마찬가지다.

08 앞의 동사 used를 받으므로 did가 옴

지난 주말에 개봉한 그의 영화는 다수의 화려한 특수 효과를 사용했는데, 이는 그의 다른 영화들도 마찬가지다.

09 앞의 would raise를 받아서 would가 옴

그들이 링에 들어왔을 때, 포맨은 그의 팬들과 함께 손을 들었고, 타이슨 또한 그러했다.

10 앞의 동사 is를 받으므로 be동사가 옴

잭슨은 어떤 면에서 주류에서 너무 멀리 떨어져 있고, 그의 가장 친한 친구인 찰리 역시 그러하다.

ACTUAL TEST

P. 231

01 ④ **02** ①

01 ④ so가 문두로 나가 주어, 동사가 도치되므로 has permanent show가 돼야 함 ① 뒤에 목적어가 없으므로 수동태가 적절, 뒤에 나오는 것은 목적격 보어 ② 뒤에 완전한 문장이 오므로 ⟨전치사+관계사⟩가 옴 ③ 앞에 접속사가 있으며, 뒤에 본동사가 없으므로 분사구문 absorbing ~이 옴 ⑤ 뒤에 나오는 내용이 앞에 나오는 내용의 결과임

온실 효과는 보통 지구 온난화의 주된 이유로 간주된다. 그러나 이것은 대기의 자연스럽고 필수적인 과정이며, 이것 없이는 우리 행성에 인간이 살 수 없게 될 것이다. 대부분의 온실가스는 대기층에 의해 반사되는 몇몇의 광선을 흡수하는 동시에 태양 광선을 통과시키며, 이는 지구 표면의 온도를 조절한다. 문제는 인간이 이러한 상황을 악화시키고 있다는 것이다. 지난 십 년 동안 지구의 빙하는 감소했고 만년설도 그러하다. 산업 발전 때문에 인류는 지구가 처리할 수 있는 것보다 더 많은 온실가스를 배출했다. 그것이 온실 가스가 이런 악명을 얻게 된 이유이다.

greenhouse effect 온실 효과 simultaneously 동시에
release 배출하다 notorious 악명 높은

02 (A) 선행사 things가 있어 what은 올 수 없음 (B) '어떻게 호두나무가 자랐는지'를 의미하므로 how가 옴 (C) 앞의 동사 can do를 받으므로 can이 나옴

호두를 지구상에서 자라는 아름답고 흥미진진한 것들과 비교하면 이것은 놀라운 창조물처럼 보이지 않는다. 호두는 흔하고, 거칠고, 특별히 매력적이지도 않고, 확실히 그렇게 가치가 있지는 않다. 게다가그것은 작다. 호두의 성장은 그것을 둘러싸고 있는 딱딱한 껍질, 즉 그것이 평생 동안 결코 탈출하지 못하는 껍질에 의해 제한을 받는다. 물론 그것은 호두를 판단하는 잘못된 방법이다. 호두 하나를 깨서 열고 안을 들여다 보아라. 호두가 어떻게 사용 가능한 모든 구석을 채웠는지를 보아라. 그것은 껍질의 크기나 모양에는 결정권이 없었다. 그러나 그 제한점들을 고려해 보면 그것은 완전히 성장했다. 우리가 호두처럼 우리에게 주어진 인생의 모든 면에서 꽃을 피우고 번영한다면 얼마나 운이 좋은 것인가. 용기를 내라! 호두가 할 수 있다면, 여러분도 할 수 있다.

walnut 호두나무 marvelous 굉장한 judge 판단하다
blossom 꽃을 피우다 bloom 번영하다

UNIT 193~194

Check-up

P. 232~233

193	**1.** Neither	**2.** So
194	**1.** can you	**2.** do young students give

193

1. 앞의 문장이 부정문이므로 neither가 적절

갑자기 잭은 그가 좋아하는 패스트푸드를 만드는 회사 이름을 말할 수 없었다. 나 역시 그럴 수 없었다.

2. 앞의 문장이 긍정문이므로 so가 적절

대부분의 텔레비전 방송국들은 광고 구매를 더욱 매력적으로 만들기 위해서 그들의 가격을 구축한다. 다른 매체들도 마찬가지다.

194

1. ⟨only+시간 부사어⟩가 앞에 있으므로 도치

오직 경기 전후에만 경기장에서 선수들을 인터뷰 할 수 있다.

2. ⟨only+장소 부사어⟩가 앞에 있으므로 도치

오직 한국에서만 어린 학생들이 노인들에게 자리를 양보한다.

EXERCISE
P. 234

01 could she 02 did our ally join 03 were they 04 is a life of value 05 so 06 neither 07 does 08 can we 09 neither 10 so

01 Neither 다음에 나오므로 주어와 동사 도치

그녀는 마찬가지로 스스로 춤을 잘 춘다고 말할 수 없었는데, 그것은 명백히 사실이 아니기 때문이다.

02 Only 부사구 다음에 나오므로 주어와 동사 도치

우리의 동맹군이 합류한 바로 그때, 우리는 공공의 적을 물리치기 위해 협력했다.

03 Only 부사구 다음에 나오므로 주어와 동사 도치

그가 죽고 난 후에야 그들은 그가 그들의 국가를 위해 했던 것을 인정할 수 있었다.

04 〈only+when절〉이 문장의 앞에 나왔으므로 주어와 동사 도치

그가 흔쾌히 노력을 하고 있을 때 비로소 가치 있는 인생이 가능하다.

05 앞의 문장이 긍정문이므로 so가 옴

인간은 시간의 흐름과 함께 변화하며, 동물과 식물을 포함한 자연도 그러하다.

06 앞의 문장이 부정문이므로 neither가 옴

컴퓨터가 작동하지 않았기 때문에 나는 아무 일도 할 수가 없었고, 내 동료들도 그러했다.

07 〈only+시간부사구〉가 문두로 나가 도치된 구문으로 주어는 Catherine이므로 3인칭 단수

오직 토요일과 일요일만, 캐서린은 친구들과 영화를 볼 수 있다.

08 〈only+when절〉이 문장의 앞에 나왔으므로 주어와 동사 도치

오직 그 환자가 안정될 때, 우린 그녀를 수술할 수 있다.

09 앞의 문장이 부정문이므로 neither가 옴

리버풀 팀은 단 8명의 선수로 싸울 수가 없고, 첼시 팀도 그러하다.

10 앞의 문장이 긍정문이므로 so가 옴

당신은 그것에 대해서 반대 의견을 제시할 수 있었지만, 선택은 존의 몫이고 결과 또한 마찬가지일 것이다.

ACTUAL TEST
P. 235

01 ④ 02 ⑤

01 ④ 문두에 only then이 나오므로 its novelty will이 아니라 will its novelty가 돼야 함 ① force는 목적격 보어로 to부정사를 가짐 ② start는 to부정사와 동명사 모두를 목적어로 취함 ③ be associated with '~와 연관되다' ⑤ 주어는 expressions로 복수

누군가 "인생은 한 잔의 커피이다"라고 말한다면, 당신은 전에 이 표현을 들어본 적이 없을 것이다. 하지만 이것의 참신함은 당신을 이것의 의미에 대해 생각하게 만들 것이다. 여기서 사용된 은유의 매개체인 커피 한 잔은 일상생활의 흔한 물건이므로 그 인생에 대해 생각하기 위한 자료로 쉽게 인지할 수 있다. 이 은유는 당신이 신체적, 사회적, 그리고 커피 한 잔과 연관된 다른 속성들의 유형에 관해서 인생에 대해 생각하는 것을 시작하도록 한다. 하지만 이 은유가 통용되기 위해서는 오랫동안 다른 많은 사람들의 마음을 사로잡아야 한다. 이 은유의 참신함이 진부해지면 그때서야 "인생은 음료다." 같은 새로운 개념의 은유에 대한 기초가 탄생하는 것이다. 그 다음에, "인생은 한 잔의 차다", "인생은 한 병의 맥주다", "인생은 한 잔의 우유다"와 같은 표현들이 인생의 다양한 관점을 제공하면서 유사하게 이해된다.

novelty 참신함 vehicle 매개체 perceivable 인지할 수 있는 metaphor 은유 compel 강요하다 attribute 속성 worn out 진부한 conceptual 개념의 perspective 관점

02 (A) 분사구문으로 주어는 he이며, 그가 얼굴을 찡그리는 것이므로 능동 (B) only then이 문두에 와서 주어와 동사 도치 (C) feel 다음에 오고, '마치 ~처럼 느껴졌다'는 뜻이므로 as if가 적절

"이봐요"라고 조나단이 말했는데, 그의 목소리 때문에 두 마리 작은 새들이 날아갔다. 그 여자는 그를 전혀 인식하지 않은 채 계속해서 스케치를 했다. 얼굴을 찌푸리면서, 그는 좀 더 크게 "이봐요, 아가씨"라고 말했다. 이번에도 그 여자는 그를 인식하지 않았고, 조나단은 그녀가 청각 장애인이 아닌지 궁금해지기 시작했다. 그는 그녀에게 자신의 뒷마당에서 떠나라고 말하려는 의도를 가지고 그녀에게 걸어갔다. 그녀는 심지어 그가 그녀에게서 2피트 정도 이내에 설 때까지도 그를 올려다보지 않았다. 그제서야 비로소 그녀는 그를 올려다보았다. 잠시 동안 조나단은 그가 그때까지 보았던 것 중 가장 멋진 녹색 눈에 마음이 끌렸다. 그는 입을 열었지만 그가 고함지르려 했었던 날카로운 명령 대신에 "누구세요?"라고 조용히 질문했다. 그 여자는 미소를 지었고 그는 마치 그녀가 자기 주변을 둘러싼 세상을 환하게 비추는 것처럼 느꼈다.

frown 얼굴을 찌푸리다 be struck by ~에 끌리다
light up (불을) 밝히다

REVIEW TEST
P. 236

01 nor you should → nor should you 02 both sets of pigs were exposed → were both sets of pigs exposed 03 we were → were we 04 why do many people → why many people 05 children can → can children 06 were their math grades 07 have scientists begun 08 did Jameson notice 09 did I dream 10 can patients be

01 nor가 문장 앞으로 왔으므로 주어와 동사 도치

당신과 캐서린은 미래를 함께 할 수도 있지만, 당신은 그것을 사실로 간주해서는 안 되며 그녀를 기다리면서 당신의 사회 생활을 보류해서도 안 된다.

02 〈not only ~〉 구문 안의 주어와 동사는 도치

연구원들은 두 환경의 돼지들 모두 같은 행동 증상을 보여줄 뿐만 아니라, 그 행동들은 두뇌 영역에서 항체 부분과 연결되어 있는 것 같다는 것을 발견했다.

03 〈not only ~〉 구문 안의 주어와 동사는 도치

우리는 커다란 조각상의 조각들에 놀랐을 뿐만 아니라, 또한 우리는 그 무덤이 인공적인 것임을 발견했다.

04 간접의문문이므로 〈의문사+주어+동사〉의 어순

왜 많은 사람들이 그들의 소득 내에서 생활하는 데 어려움을 겪는지 이해하고자 할 때, 우리는 높은 이자율과 같은 요인들로 원인을 돌리는 경향이 있다.

05 among objects가 문장의 앞에 나와 주어와 동사 도치

심지어 매우 어린 나이이며 언어의 발달 이전에도 아이들은 사물들을 자연스럽게 구별할 수 있다.

06 〈not only~〉 구문 안의 주어와 동사는 도치

그들은 수학 성적이 올랐을 뿐만 아니라, 그들 중 많은 이들은 자신이 정말로 수학을 좋아한다는 것을 깨달았다.

07 〈only+시간부사구〉가 주어와 동사 도치

비록 장난감과 인형의 조작에 대한 인지적인 혜택이 잘 알려져 있지만, 겨우 지난 십 년 동안 과학자들은 아이들에게서 더 왕성한 신체 활동과 지능 사이의 연관성을 발견하기 시작했다.

08 〈Not until〉 구문이 문두에 있으므로 not until이 없는 절의 주어와 동사 도치

마지막 순간에 되어서야 제임슨은 누가 골키퍼인지 깨달았다. 바로 그의 선생님이었다.

09 Little이 문두에 있으므로 주어와 동사 도치

나는 이 만남이 나의 동창인 제인과의 결혼에 이르게 할 거라고는 꿈에도 생각 못했다.

10 〈Not until〉 구문이 문두에 있으므로 주어와 동사 도치

우리가 이 약을 개발하고 나서야 많은 환자들이 끔찍한 고통에서 벗어날 수 있다.

FINAL CHECK

P. 237~239

01 ④ **02** ① **03** ③ **04** ② **05** ① **06** ④

01 ④ the visitor has는 주어(The first impression)를 수식하는 관계사절로 본동사가 필요하므로 been이 아니라 is가 적절
① Located ~ arcades가 문장 앞으로 나가 주어와 동사 도치됨, 주어는 a new and exciting cafe이므로 단수 동사 is가 옴 ② 선행사가 없고 주어가 없는 불완전한 문장이 나오므로 what이 옴 ③ 주어인 A curry colored wall을 수식하는 분사구문
⑤ 5문형 동사 make의 목적격 보어이므로 형용사가 옴

상가들에 둘러싸인 곳 중 한 곳에 위치해 있는 새롭고 흥미로운 카페는 동아시아의 길거리 음식을 특징으로 한다. 2층에 있는 카페는 현재의 P.E. District에 위치해 있고, 1층 높이에 있는 형형색색의 간판으로 재미가 시작된다. 밝은 노란색과 흰색 그리고 네온으로 윤곽이 그려진 글자들은 붉은색, 핑크색, 노란색으로 배경에서 조명받는 판넬과는 구별이 된다. 엘리베이터로 통하는 카레색 벽은 윗층 벽에서 다시 나타날 아시아 가면들로 강조된다. 안으로 들어가면 카페는 활기찬 색과 질감으로 재미난 혼합물로 밝고 에너지가 넘친다. 방문객이 가지는 첫 번째 인상은 빛나는 등들의 거대한 불빛으로 가득 채워진 높은 공업용 천장이다. 카운터쪽에는 분위기를 보다 현대적으로 만드는 다수의 매달려 있는 특이한 모양의 등들로 강조된다.

enclosed 둘러싼 **shopping arcades** 상가 **situate** ~을 놓이게 하다 **stand out** 두드러지다 **mural** 벽의 **luminous** 빛나는 **suspended** 매달린

02 (A) occur는 자동사로 수동태 불가 동사 (B) enter이 '들어가다'로 사용될 경우 전치사 into를 사용하지 못함 (C) 〈형용사 as 주어+동사〉

뉴턴은 빛은 색깔이 없으며 따라서 색깔은 우리의 두뇌 속에서 발생해야만 함을 지적한 첫번째 사람이었다. 그는 "빛의 파장 그 자체는 색깔이 없다"라고 기록했다. 그가 살던 시대 이후로 우리는 빛의 파장이 다양한 진동수로 특징지어진다고 배워 왔다. 빛의 파장이 관찰자의 눈에 들어올 때, 연쇄적인 신경 화학적 현상을 유발시키며, 그 최종 산출물은 우리가 색깔이라 부르는 내적인 정신적 이미지다. 여기에서 중요한 것은 우리가 색깔로 지각하는 것이 색깔로 구성되어 있지 않다는 점이다. 사과는 빨갛게 보일지도 모르지만 그것의 원자들 그 자체가 빨간 색은 아니다.

characterize 특징짓다 **frequency of vibration** 진동수 **set off** 유발하다 **atom** 원자

03 ③ Not only가 문두로 나왔으므로 office design determines가 아니라 does office design determine이 돼야 함 ① 주어는 the character이므로 단수 동사가 옴 ② '무엇이든지 간에' ④ Rarely가 문두에 왔으므로 주어, 동사가 도치 ⑤ 앞의 내용이 결과에 해당하며 뒤로는 원인이 나오므로 because가 적절

사람들의 개인적인 작업 환경의 특징이 그들의 성취도에 크고 놀라운 차이를 만든다. 책상의 배열, 자연광 수준과 사무실의 소음은 당신의 편안함과 만족도, 특히 생산성에 대한 주요한 지표가 된다. 직원들은 가령 조그마한 식물이나 아이들 사진과 같은 자신들을 가장 편안하게 느끼게 하는 무엇이든지 간에 보기에 알맞은 대로 그들의 주변 환경을 꾸미는 것을 격려 받을 때 최고의 성과를 낸다. 사무실의 디자인이 직원들의 목을 아프게 하는지 아닌지 결정할 뿐만 아니라, 그들이 얼마나 성취하는 지와 직업 만족도에도 영향을 미친다. 사장들은 거의 이러한 심리학적인 면은 고려하지 않지만, 고려해야 한다. 그것은 작업 공간의 디자인에 좀 더 신경을 쓰는 것이 직원들의 복지와 생산성을 최소의 비용으로 향상시킬 수 있기 때문이다.

performance 성취도 **predictor** 지표 **contentment** 만족도 **productivity** 생산성

04 (A) 부사절을 이끄는 whatever가 적절 (B) belong은 수동 불가 동사 (C) 간접의문문이므로 〈의문사+주어+동사〉의 어순임

우리가 어떤 상품을 구매하던 간에, 우리가 선택하는 것은 근본적으로 상표가 아니라 문화이거나 오히려 그 문화와 연관이 있는 사람들이다. 당신이 찢어진 청바지를 입는 것을 좋아하든 시를 암송하기를 좋아하든, 그렇게 함으로써 당신은 한 무리의 사람들에 속해 있다는 것을 말한다. 우리가 누구인지 믿는 것은 우리가 비슷해지기를 원하는 사람에 대하여 만드는 선택들의 결과이며, 그 결과, 다양하고 종종 미묘한 방법으로 다른 사람들과 비슷해지려는 마음을 표현하게 된다. 이런 과정은 인위적이지만, 이것은 우리의 '정체성', 즉 우리가 나 자신과 다른 사람들을 식별하는 모든 피상적인 차이들에 기초한 정체성이 되는 것이다. 결국, 우리가 쇼핑을 하는 것은 우리가 누구인지 아는 것인 자아 정체성을 위한 것이다.

recite 암송하다 **subsequently** 그 결과 **demonstrate** 설명하다 **subtle** 미묘한 **artificial** 인공적인 **superficial** 피상적인

05 ① 〈It ~ that〉 강조 구문이므로 which가 아닌 that이 와야 함

② 주어가 동명사 Making이므로 단수 동사가 옴 ③ '무엇이건 간에' ④ 뒤에 본동사(will dry)가 나오며, 목적어를 가지므로 능동 분사구문이 옴 ⑤ 미래의 사건이지만, if절 안이므로 현재형으로 표현됨

작곡가들은 그들의 사적인 세계를 바로 소리의 사용을 통해서 묘사한다. 그러한 묘사를 구체적이고 세부적으로 하는 것은 영감뿐만 아니라, 어떤 유용한 도구와 기술을 필요로 한다. 작곡하는 곡의 양식이 무엇이건 간에, 당신은 강약, 속도, 화성과 리듬의 사용을 이해할 필요가 있다. 또한 악기의 음역과 성능, 사람 목소리의 가능성과 음감의 문제를 알 필요가 있다. 당신이 듣고 싶은 것이 무엇인지 음악가들에게 전달할 수 있는 청사진을 고안할 수 있어야 한다. 이러한 기술 훈련에서 작곡가로서의 역할을 하기 위해 서둘러 지름길로 가는 젊은 작곡가는 매우 빠르게 밑천이 드러나고말 것이다. 만약 당신이 언젠가 제대로 된 기술을 배운다면, 열정은, 그것이 진심이라면, 해낼 것이다.

description 묘사 inspiration 영감 acoustics 음향 blueprint 청사진 passion 열정 genuine 진실한

06 (A) 비교 대상이 인간과 네안데르탈인의 DNA이므로 that of modern humans가 적절 (B) 준 것이 밝혀진 것보다 먼저 일어난 일이므로 완료형이 적절 (C) 앞에 부정어인 never가 나와 있으므로 주어와 동사가 도치됨

네안데르탈인은 진화 계보 상 우리에게 가장 가깝다고 알려진 친척이다. 그들은 약 13만 년 전에 유럽과 아시아에서 살았다. 하지만, 약 3만 년 전에 그들은 사라졌다. 그들에게 무슨 일이 벌어진 것일까? 과학자들은 최근에 네안데르탈인의 화석에서 DNA를 발견해서 그것을 현대 인간의 DNA와 비교했다. 그들은 우리에게 고유한 어떤 유전자 적응이 의사소통이나 사회적 기술, 지각 감각과 같은 인지적 기능들에서 점진적인 이점을 주었을 수도 있다는 사실을 밝혀냈다. 역설적으로, 이런 똑같은 유전자들의 변종이나 과발현은 때때로 자폐증이나 다운 증후군과 연관되어 있다. 하지만 네안데르탈인들은 완전히 사라진 것은 아니다. 유전적인 증거는 네안데르탈인이 언젠가 아프리카에서 이주한 이후, 인간이 그들과 섞였다는 것을 보여준다. 당신의 DNA 중 4% 정도는 먼 네안데르탈인 조상에게서 비롯되었을지도 모른다.

evolutionary 점진적인 cognitive 인지적인 perceptual 지각의 associate with ~와 연관된 emigrate 이주하다

chapter 17 병렬 구조

UNIT 195~196

Check-up P. 242~243

195	1. participating	2. mathematical
196	1. that	2. that of boy students

195

1. 앞의 going과 병렬 구조

다른 인기 있는 일하면서 보내는 휴가는 고고학 유적지에서 발굴하러 가거나 지역 공동체 개발에 참여하는 것을 포함한다.

2. 앞의 형용사 architectural, astronomical과 병렬 구조

중앙아메리카의 고대 아즈텍은 건축적이고 천문학적이고 수학적인 지식을 가지고 있었다.

196

1. 앞의 단수 명사 The proportion을 받음

'과거 경험'을 고려하면서 직업을 고르는 경향이 있는 남자들의 비율이 여자들의 비율보다 더 낮다.

2. 비교 대상이 the number이므로 대명사 that이 필요

특히 서울 같은 도시에서, 심지어 초등학교에서도 여학생 수는 남학생 수를 훨씬 초과한다.

EXERCISE P. 244

01 the Earth's **02** endure **03** those of the victim **04** mark **05** reaching **06** that of the other countries **07** hacking **08** burying **09** enjoying **10** sitting

01 수성의 velocity와 지구의 velocity를 비교하고 있음

수성의 회전 속도는 지구의 회전 속도보다 훨씬 빠르다.

02 support와 병렬 구조

이러한 초기 모델 대부분은 무거운 무게를 지탱하지 못했고, 강한 물살도 견디지 못했다.

03 서로의 소망을 비교하고 있음

피해자 가족들의 소망은 피해자의 소망보다 더 중요한가?

04 circle, underline와 병렬 구조

그들이 그것에 동그라미를 치고, 밑줄을 긋고, 어떻게든 표시할 때 그들은 기억 속에 정보를 입력하고 있다.

05 taking, watching, having, watching과 병렬 구조

그것은 당신에게 갑판에서의 휴식, 영화 보기, 음료 마시기, 멋진 풍경 보기와 다음 목적지에 도착하기의 선택을 제공한다.

06 아르헨티나에서의 비율과 다른 나라의 비율을 비교하고 있음

아르헨티나에서 기존의 씨앗 비용에 대한 유전자 이식 씨앗 비용의 비율은 다른 나라의 비율보다 더 높다.

07 by에 걸려 sending, using과 병렬 구조

일부 사용자들은 스팸 메일을 보내고, 다른 사람들을 욕하기 위해 이메일을 사용하고, 정부나 회사의 시스템을 해킹함으로써 이 특권을 이용하고 있다.

08 by에 걸려 sealing과 병렬 구조

농부들은 종종 씨앗을 흙으로 만든 항아리에 밀봉하거나 그것들을 재로 덮인 바구니에 묻음으로써 저장된 씨앗을 곤충들이나 동물들로부터 보호한다.

09 앞의 enjoying과 병렬 구조

이러한 경향은 모든 음식 종류에 걸쳐 동일하게 발견되었는데, 만약 어렸을 때 야채를 많이 먹었다면 어른이 되어서도 야채를 즐길 것이고, 만약 고기가 어린 시절의 주요 섭취물이었다면 주로 고기를 즐기게 될 거라는 것이다.

10 '일 하러가서 앉아 있는 걸 즐기다'가 되어야 자연스러우므로 going to work와 병렬 구조가 되어야 함

집에서 많은 육체 노동을 해왔던 여성은 실제로 일 하러가서 잠시 동안 앉아 있는 것을 즐길지도 모르며, 이는 그녀의 뇌가 활동을 하고 그녀의 등이 휴식을 취하도록 한다.

ACTUAL TEST

P. 245

01 ① 02 ⑤

01 ① 〈contribute to -ing〉 '~에 기여하다'이므로 create가 아니라 creating이 돼야 함 ② '~로 대체되다' ③ 주어는 The rule이므로 단수 ④ 〈not only A but also B〉 구문 ⑤ 주어는 three가 아닌 Less이므로 단수

"옛날 옛날 한 옛날에..." 한국의 모든 동화들은 그렇게 시작한다. 이러한 반복은 이야기에 안정되고 차분한 어조를 만드는 데 도움을 줄 뿐만 아니라 한국 동화에 나타난 "삼회 반복"의 규칙을 반영한다. 그 "옛날"의 마지막 반복은 이따금 "호랑이 담배 피던 시절에"와 같은 것으로 대체될 수 있지만 이것이 완전히 삭제되어서는 안 된다. 3의 규칙은 시작 문장에만 적용될 뿐만 아니라 이야기 전반의 다양한 요소들에도 적용된다. 예를 들어, 한국판 신데렐라 이야기인 '콩쥐, 팥쥐'에서 콩쥐의 계모는 콩쥐에게 불가능한 세 가지 집안일을 시킨다. 그리고 '해님 달님이 된 오누이' 이야기에서는 도움을 주는 세 가지가 번갈아 가며 호랑이의 괴롭힘으로부터 불쌍한 오누이를 구해준다. 셋 이하는 너무 적으며 셋 이상은 케이크 위에 설탕을 너무 많이 입힌 것과 같다.

narrative 이야기 **reflect** 반영하다 **substitute** 대체하다 **omit** 빼먹다 **stepmother** 계모 **tormenting** 괴롭힘

02 (A) 주어는 the Two ~ things이므로 복수 (B) 추상적인 내용이므로 widely가 적절 (C) 앞의 place와 병렬 구조

구근을 심는 것은 간단하다. 시작하기 전에, 당신은 반드시 적당한 화분을 선택해야 한다. 구근을 심을 때 알아야 할 가장 중요한 두 가지는 적절한 깊이에 구근을 두는 것과 그 구멍 안에 똑바로 구근을 두는 것이다. 당신의 정원에 구근을 심기 위한 몇 가지 팁이 있다. 튤립, 히아신스, 수선화처럼 잘 자라고 널리 이용할 수 있는 다양한 것들부터 시작하라. 구근 식물들은 땅이 얼기 직전 가을에 심을 수 있다. 구근을 구근 크기의 세 배만큼 깊은 구멍에 넣고 뿌리가 자랄 수 있도록 물을 충분히 주어라.

bulb 구근 **reliable** (식물 등이) 잘 자라는 **variety** 다양함

UNIT 197~198

Check-up

P. 246~247

197	1. lowering	2. get
198	1. dispatching	2. being

197

1. 앞의 making과 병렬 구조

이것은 식량 공급을 원활하지 않게 하고, 세계 어느 지역에서 삶의 질을 떨어뜨리는 것에 대한 전체적으로 의도되지 않은 결과이다.

2. to complete, make와 병렬 구조, make 앞의 to가 생략되었으므로 get이 적절

당신은 스스로를 격려할 필요가 있는데, 왜냐하면 당신이 프로젝트를 끝내고, 스케줄을 작성하고, 아니면 정각에 일어나게 해 줄 사람은 없기 때문이다.

198

1. 〈from A to B〉 구조로 prohibiting과 병렬 구조

몇몇 아프리카 정부들은 숲에서의 밀렵을 금지하는 것부터 경찰관을 파견하는 것에 이르는 환경을 보존하는 것과 관련된 정책들을 고려하고 있다.

2. 〈from A to B〉 구조로 taking과 병렬 구조

나는 어머니를 돌보는 것에서부터 부양하는 것까지를 하는 데 감정적으로 지쳐 있다.

EXERCISE

P. 248

01 learning 02 sliding 03 evaluate 04 playing
05 farming 06 respond 07 saying 08 reveals
09 highlight 10 humming

01 앞의 having과 병렬 구조

콘스탄틴 씨 수업의 학생들은 즐거워하고 있었으며 동시에 배우고 있었다.

02 앞의 depressing과 병렬 구조

지하철에서 당신은 버튼을 누르거나, 레버를 당기거나, 문을 옆으로 밀어서 스스로 문을 열어야만 한다.

03 앞에 있는 analyze와 병렬 구조

서평가로서 당신은 이야기를 어떻게 전개하는지에 대해 책을 분석하고, 글쓰기와 구성의 질을 평가한다.

04 앞에 있는 testing, challenging, asking과 병렬 구조

그러므로 당신은 가설을 실험하고 그 규칙을 의심하며, 가정하는 질문을 하거나 그 문제를 두루 생각하는데 시간을 거의 투자하지 않을 것이다.

05 〈from A to B〉 구문으로 foraging과 병렬 구조

어떤 사회는 실제로 채집에서 농경으로 변화했기 때문에, 당신은 모든 사회가 그래야만 한다라고 생각하는 경향이 있을 수 있다.

06 the capacity of에 to check와 함께 내용상 걸려있음. to는 생략 가능

컴퓨터와 뇌는 둘 다 그들의 환경을 점검하고, 그들의 환경을 다루기 위해서 다양한 반응에 응답할 수 있는 능력을 가진다.

07 becoming, narrowing과 병렬 구조

당신은 점점 더 구체적으로 만들고, 당신의 주제를 좁히고 당신이 의미하는 바를 정확하게 말하면서 그것을 발전시켜야만 한다.

08 〈not only A but also B〉 구문으로 contributes와 병렬 구조

고래의 피부 조각에서 추출한 DNA는 집단에서 개개의 고래를 구별할 뿐만 아니라 서로 간의 관계를 드러낸다.

09 앞의 underline, take와 병렬 구조

그들이 읽기 시작하자마자, 그들은 요점에 밑줄 치며, 여백에 필기를 하고 키워드나 중심 어구를 자신만의 상징 부호로 강조한다.

10 앞의 seeing, gossiping, listening과 병렬 구조

우리는 친구를 만나고 그들 중 몇몇에 관한 소문을 이야기하며, 자동차 라디오로 음악을 듣고 그중 오래된 곡을 콧노래로 부를 것을 행복하게 기대하고 있다.

ACTUAL TEST

P. 249

01 ③ **02** ⑤

01 ③ 〈from A to B〉 병렬 구조로 to는 전치사이므로 to develop이 아니라 developing이 돼야 함 ① 〈have trouble -ing〉 구문 ② 가족과 함께하는 식사에 대한 흥미로운 이점들을 현재까지 쭉 발견해온 것이므로 현재완료가 적절 ④ 뒤에 완전한 문장이 오므로 주격 보어를 이끄는 접속사 that이 옴 ⑤ when 뒤에 분사구문이 옴

우리의 일정이 바빠 그 어려움을 극복하기가 힘들어서, 많은 가족이 함께 식사하기 위한 시간을 찾는 데 어려움을 겪는다. 그러나 우리는 가족 식사의 중요성을 인식할 필요가 있다. 과학자들은 그러한 식사에 대한 흥미로운 이점을 알아냈다. 과학자들에 따르면, 매주 평균 5회에서 7회 정도 식구들과 함께 식사를 하면 식이 장애를 줄이는 것부터 아이들의 언어를 발전시키는 것에 이르는 다양한 혜택을 누리게 된다. 한 가지 더 말하고자 하는 것은 야채는 틀림없이 그들의 건강에 중요하고, 아이는 가족과 함께 식사할 때 그것을 더 많이 섭취한다는 것이다. 대부분의 사람들처럼, 아마 당신도 일정이 바쁠 것이다. 그럼에도 불구하고, 가족과의 저녁 식사는 분명 시간을 들일 충분한 가치가 있다.

eating disorder 식이 장애 dine 저녁 식사를 하다 nevertheless 그럼에도 불구하고

02 (A) in addition to의 to는 전치사이므로 동명사가 적절 (B) 내용상 '요구하고 연구하다'가 되어야 하므로 asking과 병렬 구조 (C) 뒤에 완전한 문장이 오므로 접속사 that이 적절

과학자들은 남성들과 여성들이 재미있어하는 것을 관찰하기 시작했으며 사람들이 무엇을 재미있다고 여기는지에 대해 조사하기 시작했다. 이 연구에 따르면, 흥미로운 유형들이 나타났다. 1990년대 이전의 논문은 농담의 공감에 초점을 맞췄다. 이는 연구자가 실험자에게 농담을 제시하고 그 다음에 그들의 반응을 기록했던 인위적인 상황이었다. 실험은 유머를 지어내는 것을 보고, 실험자들에게 농담을 제시할 것을 요구하거나 실제로 사람들이 어떻게 서로를 웃게 만드는지를 연구하기 시작했다. 이 실험은 무슨 일이 일어나고 있는지에 대해 훨씬 더 정확한 설명을 보여 주었다. 여성들은 그 호의에 보답하기 위해 자신들이 준 것의 두 배로 즐겁게 해줄 수 있는 상대를 찾는 반면, 남성들은 그들이 필요로 한 것보다 3분의 1정도 더 많은 유머를 제공한다는 것을 밝혀냈다. 이러한 결과는 남녀가 각각 유머에 대해 다른 관점에서 접근한다는 것을 보여 준다.

literature 논문 appreciation 평가 subject 피실험자 document 기록하다 seek 구하다 whereas 반면

UNIT 199~200

Check-up

P. 250~251

199 **1.** anything **2.** have **200** **1.** By living **2.** To find

199

1. think의 경우 주절의 부정문은 사실상 종속절(that절)의 부정문이므로 부정어가 다시 나와서는 안 됨

조사원들은 폭풍이 카메라의 움직임에 관련이 있다고 생각하지 않는다.

2. 부정 부사인 hardly가 이미 있으므로 부정어는 올 수 없음

길들여지지 않은 말들을 조련하는 방법은 지난 10세기 동안 거의 변하지 않았다.

200

1. 수단이 나와야 하므로 By living이 자연스러움

제이콥의 친구들과 잠시 같이 살며 여가 비용을 과감하게 줄임으로써, 그들은 3년 안에 적당한 집을 사기에 충분한 돈을 저축하기를 원했다.

2. 목적을 나타내므로 To find가 적절

이러한 유적지를 찾기 위해서, 많은 고고학자들은 오늘날 체계적인 조사, 그리고 다양한 첨단 도구와 기술에 의존한다.

EXERCISE

P. 252

01 any **02** anything **03** By copying **04** anything **05** By passing **06** anything **07** can **08** if **09** any **10** anywhere

01 앞에 부정어 not이 있으므로 no는 오지 못함

여행은 어떤 동행들에게 그들이 더이상 어떤 집단에도 속하지 않는다는 기분을 느끼도록 해준다.

02 앞에 부정어 couldn't가 있으므로 nothing이 오지 못함

에이미는 오직 두 개의 빛나는 눈만 제외하고 그 모양이나 크기 중 어느 것도 전혀 볼 수가 없었다.

03 내용상 수단의 내용이 나와야 함

그녀는 상사의 목소리를 흉내내서 가까스로 시스템에 접속하여 필요한 정보를 얻을 수 있었다.

04 앞에 부정이 not이 있으므로 nothing은 오지 못함

많은 그림은 어떤 것에 관한 것이 아니라, 단지 예쁜 패턴일 뿐이다.

05 수단이 나와야 함

자격 시험에 통과함으로써 당신은 캘리포니아 대학에 입학하기 위한 시험을 볼 기회를 얻을 수 있다.

06 앞에 부정어 didn't가 있으므로 nothing은 오지 못함

제임슨과 그의 동료들은 폭풍이 해발 1,500 피트 아래에 있으므로 로봇의 움직임에 어떤 관련이 있을거라고 생각하지 않았다.

07 뒤에 부정부사어 hardly가 나오므로 cannot은 올 수 없음

누군가 나보다 앞서 잡지를 빌려가서 나는 요즘 거의 도서관에서

잡지를 손에 넣을 수가 없다.

08 뒤에 don't라는 부정어가 있으므로 unless는 올 수 없음

비록 그와의 대화는 즐겁지 않았지만, 당신이 그것을 하지 않는다면 바뀌는 것은 없을 것이다.

09 앞에 not이 있으므로 no는 올 수 없음

나는 아들에게 만약 계속해서 나쁜 짓을 한다면 쇼핑하는 데 더는 데려가지 않을 것이라고 분명하게 말했다.

10 앞에 부정어인 doesn't가 있으므로 nowhere는 올 수 없음

그의 아들이 죽었고 지금 그가 갈 곳이 없다는 사실을 받아들이는 것은 제임스를 아주 많이 아프게 한다.

ACTUAL TEST

P. 253

01 ② **02** ④

01 ② no one이 앞에 있으므로 didn't take가 아니라 took이 돼야 함 ① consider가 5문형 동사로 사용됐고 뒤에 목적격 보어가 왔으므로 수동태가 옴 ③ of가 왔으므로 명사가 옴 ④ '교수들'이라는 뜻의 복수 ⑤ 형용사로 사용되며 matters를 수식

점성학은 과학적이거나 학문적인 것이 아닌 대중 문화의 한 영역으로 간주되어 왔다. 즉, 학계의 누구도 그것을 심각하게 받아들이지 않았다. 그러나 영국의 몇몇의 연구자들이 이러한 상황을 변화시키기 위해 노력하고 있다. 캠브리지 대학의 연구자들은 '점성학의 비평적 고찰'이라는 논문을 시작했다. 그들은 과학, 역사, 종교에서 점성학의 역할을 공부하는 대학 수준의 강의 도입을 추진하려고 노력하는 중이다. 그러나, 교수들의 대부분은 이러한 추세에 비관적이다. 사우샘프턴 대학의 데이비드 맥케이 교수는 "점성학은 요정들과 같은 범주에 속한다"라고 말했다. 그는 대학들이 그들의 돈과 시간과 노력을 다른 것, 즉 좀 더 중요한 문제에 투자해야 한다고 생각한다.

astrology 점성학 **skeptical** 회의적인

02 (A) 치즈가 상하는 것을 막아야 하므로 〈keep from -ing〉이 적절 (B) 뒤에 명사가 오므로 because of가 적절 (C) '속도변화 측정'은 '치즈를 묘사'하기 위한 수단

때때로 좋은 치즈가 상하는 것을 막는 데 필요한 것은 경청이다. 프랑스의 연구원들은 치즈가 숙성할 때 치즈의 소리를 듣고 치즈 제조자들에게 결함을 경고해 주는 초음파 감지기를 개발해냈다. 치즈 제조자들은 발견되지 않은 결함 때문에 그들의 생산품 중 5분의 1까지 품질을 낮추어야 한다. 만약 새 기기가 잘 작동한다면, 그러한 문제는 감소될 것이다. 그 기술은 낮은 주파수의 초음파 신호를 치즈에 통과시켜 다른 쪽의 센서에 보내는 것을 포함한다. 나타나는 신호의 속도와 크기의 변화를 측정함으로써, 치즈의 수분과 구멍이 발견될 수 있다.

sympathetic 동정어린 **come up with** ~을 생각해 내다 **ultrasonic** 초음파 **mature** 익다 **defect** 결점 **undetected** 발견되지 않은 **emerge** 나타나다

UNIT 201~202

Check-up

P. 254~255

201	**1.** Like	**2.** Unlike
202	**1.** pick them up	**2.** called me up

201

1. 내용상 두 내용이 비슷하므로 Like가 자연스러움

사람이 걱정을 느낄 수 있었던 이러한 상황들처럼 시험에 대한 공포는 복통과 긴장성 두통을 유발한다.

2. 블랙홀과 웜홀은 서로 다르므로 Unlike가 적절

어떤 곳으로의 통행을 허용하지 않는 블랙홀과는 달리, 웜홀은 입구뿐만 아니라 출구로서의 역할도 할 수 있다.

202

1. 〈동사+대명사+부사〉

나는 서울역에 갈 것이기 때문에 거기에 그들을 태울 것이다.

2. 〈동사+대명사+부사〉

내가 침대에 누워있을 때, 잭이 나에게 전화를 해서 수지가 수업에 들어오지 않았다고 말했다.

EXERCISE

P. 256

01 blow it up **02** Unlike **03** pick them up
04 push herself up **05** Like **06** Unlike
07 write it down **08** Unlike **09** cut it down **10** Unlike

01 〈동사+대명사+부사〉

그들은 운석에 구멍을 내야하고 핵무기로 그것을 날려버려야만 한다.

02 뒤에 나오는 것과 다르다는 내용이므로 Unlike가 옴

다른 아시아 국가와는 달리, 어떠한 외국 회사도 북한에서 노동자를 자유롭게 고용할 수 없다.

03 〈동사+대명사+부사〉

나는 사업차 공항에 들러야 하므로 그들을 무료로 태울 수 있다.

04 〈동사+대명사+부사〉

눈물을 흘리거나, 놀라지 않고 에이미는 스스로 분발하며 다시 한 번 노력할 것이다.

05 뒤에 나오는 것과 비슷하다는 내용이므로 Like가 옴

인간과 마찬가지로, 대부분의 원숭이는 도구를 사용하고 문제를 처리하기 위해서 동료들과 협동할 수 있다.

06 뒤에 나오는 것과 다르다는 내용이므로 Unlike가 옴

당신이 양파를 자를 때 나오는 눈물과는 달리, 웃음을 포함한 눈물은 특이하게 당신이 스트레스를 느낄 때 발산하는 단백질을 기반으로 한 호르몬이 풍부하다.

07 〈동사+대명사+부사〉

필기를 하는 것은 주의를 기울이고, 들은 것을 이해하고 그것을 받아 적을 정도로 충분히 오래 작동 기억 장치에 저장하는 사람의 능력에 달렸다.

08 뉴잉글랜드의 대부분의 지역은 비가 오며 보스톤은 비가 안 오니 Unlike가 나옴

많은 비가 예상되는 뉴잉글랜드의 대부분의 지역과는 달리, 보스톤은 맑고 화창할 것입니다.

09 〈동사+대명사+부사〉

이웃나라에서 재정적 도움을 요청했을 때, 정부는 그것을 거절했다.

10 대부분의 일본 십대와 다른 것이므로 Unlike가 적절

대부분의 일본 십대와는 달리, 미츠키는 비디오 게임을 하거나 첨단 기술로 만들어진 장난감을 가지고 노는 것을 좋아하지 않는다.

ACTUAL TEST

P. 257

01 ④ 02 ②

01 ④ 〈동사+대명사+부사〉 구조이므로 turned off them이 아니라 turned them off가 돼야 함 ① 콤마 뒤에 나오며, 본동사가 앞에 있고, 접속사가 보이지 않으므로 분사구문이 오며, 뒤에 목적어가 있으니 현재분사가 옴 ② 주어는 Vampire energy ③ 앞에 are에 걸려 진행형을 나타냄 ⑤ 주어는 the sum으로 단수

당신은 뱀파이어가 밤이나 할로윈 기간에만 등장한다고 생각할지도 모른다. 정말 그럴까? 그들은 도처에 있으며 24시간 내내 활동하면서 당신 가정의 에너지를 사용한다. 대기 전력이라고도 불리는 뱀파이어 에너지는 가전 제품이 꺼졌거나 사용되고 있지 않은 가전 제품에 의해 소비되는 전력을 가리킨다. 당신은 가전 제품을 껐다고 생각하지만, 그것들은 여전히 작동 중이다. 가전제품에서 낭비되는 대기 전력은 보통 매우 적지만 가정 내에서 이러한 기구들의 대기 전력 총합은 매우 크다. TV, VCR, DVD 플레이어, 컴퓨터, 전자레인지, 커피 머신 등은 일상적인 뱀파이어 에너지의 은밀한 사용자이다.

standby 대기하는 consume 소비하다 typically 전형적으로

02 (A) 주어가 〈the+형용사〉인데 '수줍어 하는 사람들'을 의미하므로 복수가 됨 (B) 뒤에 완전한 문장이 오므로 〈전치사+관계사〉가 옴 (C) 아이들은 놀이에서 '실제 생활'과는 다르다는 내용이므로 unlike가 옴

아이들은 연극을 통해 다양한 방법으로 실제생활의 역할의 여러 행동들을 표현할 수 있다. 연극은 그들이 실제 생활에서 맡고 있는 역할을 바꿀 기회를 준다. 예를 들어, 소심한 아이가 사자나 호랑이가 될 수 있다. 놀이에서 소심한 아이들은 이런 동물들의 일반적인 특징을 띠게 되어 두려움이 없어지고, 공격적이며, 자부심이 강해진다. 그, 또는 그녀는 겁먹은 척 하며 흩어지는 놀이 상대를 향해 달려가거나 뛰어들 수 있다. 놀이를 통해 아이는 소심하다기 보다는 강해지고 용감해진다. 연극은 또한 아이들에게 다른 상황이었다면 용납되지 않았을 충동을 발산하는 기회를 주기도 한다. 아이는 화가 나서 공을 찰 수도 있고, 경찰과 강도 연극, 즉 공격성과 갈등이 용납되고 실생활과 다르게 어른들의 나무람을 두려워할 필요 없이 감정을 드러낼 수 는 활동을 하면서 놀 수도 있다.

reverse 거꾸로 하다 timid 소심한 aggressive 공격적인 self-sufficient 자부심이 강한 scatter 흩뿌리다 impulse 충동 conflict 곤란 manifest 조작하다 censure 비난하다

UNIT 203~204

Check-up

P. 258~259

203 **1.** or **2.** and **204** **1.** stir **2.** check

203

1. 앞의 명령문 내용을 따르지 않을 경우가 나오므로 or가 적절

당신의 과제를 마감 기한까지 제출해라, 그렇지 않으면 교수님한테서 D를 받을 수도 있다.

2. 앞의 명령문 내용을 따를 경우의 내용이 나오므로, and가 적절

암세포에서 발견된 패턴들을 정상적인 세포에서 나온 것들과 비교해라, 그러면 당신은 결국 그 차이점을 알게 될 것이다.

204

1. 앞에 명령문(Add)이 있는 병렬 구소로 동사원형 stir가 와야 함

반죽에 밀가루를 조금 추가하고 걸쭉해질 때까지 저어라.

2. 주절에 주어가 없고 동사만이 있으므로 명령문으로 봐야 함

당신이 (자기 집 차고에서 하는) 중고 물품 판매 전에, 팔지 말아야 할 것을 확인해라.

EXERCISE

P. 260

01 make 02 lean 03 To discover 04 By using 05 Making 06 Read 07 Make 08 Begin 09 make 10 be

01 명령문으로 뒤의 skim과 병렬 구조

당신이 집중하도록 돕기 위해서 스스로 질문을 만들고 해답을 찾기 위해 훑어보아라.

02 본동사가 없으므로 명령문이 적절

만약 당신이 칸막이 줄에 앉아 있고 충분한 공간이 있다면, 당신의 상체를 당신의 짐에 기대라.

03 '~하기 위해서'를 뜻하는 to부정사

당신 자아상을 발견하기 위해서, "나는 어떤 사람인가?"라는 질문에 어떻게 대답할 지 생각해 보아라.

04 뒤에 문장이 나오는데 접속사가 없고, 내용상 수단이 나오는 게 자연스러우므로 By using이 적절

컴퓨터를 사용함으로써 우리는 웹사이트를 검색하고 친구들과 이메일을 교환한다.

05 뒤에 본동사 requires가 나오므로 동명사 Making이 적절

그런 묘사를 구체적이고 자세하게 만드는 것은 영감뿐만 아니라 어떤 실용적인 도구와 기술을 필요로 한다.

06 〈명령문+and 문장〉 구조

첫 번째 문장이나 문단을 아주 주의 깊게 읽어라, 그러면 그것들이 작가가 이야기 하고자 하는 것에 대한 몇 가지 아이디어를 줄 것이다.

07 뒤에 본동사가 나오지 않으므로 명령문인 Make가 적절

얼어 있는 떡은 항상 다소 딱딱하고 맛이 없는 인상을 주기 때문에 떡을 먹기 전에 꼭 상온에 두어라.

08 뒤에 오는 check와 병렬 구조

당신의 지역 동전 상점을 방문하는 것부터 시작하고 그들의 실제 등급과 당신이 기대하는 등급이 일치하는지 아닌지를 알기 위해 동전들 중 몇 개를 확인해 봐라.

09 뒤에 본동사가 나오지 않으므로 명령문인 make를 선택

당신이 테이블에 있는 동안, 도움에 대한 감사함을 표현하기 위해서 값이 비싸지 않은 동전을 의례적으로 구매해라.

10 so로 연결된 절에 동사가 없으므로 be가 적절

우리는 지금 유럽에서 가장 훌륭한 박물관 중 하나에 입장하고 있어요. 그러니 제발 어떤 귀중한 예술 작품에도 손대지 않도록 조심해 주세요.

ACTUAL TEST

P. 261

01 ⑤ 02 ③

01 ⑤ 〈명령문+and〉 '그러면', 〈명령문+or〉 '그렇지 않으면', and가 아니라 or가 돼야 함 ① 완전한 문장을 이끄는 관계부사 ② 주어와 목적어가 several immersion schools로 동일 ③ four weeks를 하나의 단위로 보아 단수 취급 ④ 추천되는 것이므로 수동

한 연구는 언어가 사용되는 나라에서 언어에 몰입하는 것이 언어를 익히는 가장 확실하고 빠른 방법이라고 밝혔다. 현재 몇몇의 이머전 스쿨은 극도로 집중적인 단기 언어 과정을 제공함으로써 바쁜 전문직 종사자들에게 스스로를 광고하고 있다. 예를 들자면, 프랑스에 있는 파리 교육 커뮤니티에서는 시간이 부족한 학생들이 주말에 집중 언어 프로그램에 참여할 수 있다. 하지만 전문가는 외국어에 있어서 훌륭한 기초를 위해서는 적어도 4주의 기간이 적정하다고 얘기한다. 현지인처럼 말하는 것은 서서히 일어나지 않는다. 특히 유대감이 있을 시 벗어나기 위한 결연한 노력을 해야한다. 방해 요소를 덜 마주칠 것 같은 작은 마을에서 프로그램에 참여하는 것을 권장한다. 일단 다른 언어에 유창해지고 나면, 규칙적으로 사용하고 연습해라. 그렇지 않으면 그것을 잊어릴 것이다.

immerse oneself in ~에 몰입하다 **pick up** 익히게 되다 **market** 광고하다 **optimal** 최적의 **concerted** 결열한 **connectedness** 유대감 **encounter** 직면하다

02 (A) 아이가 단어를 사용하는 것이므로 능동 (B) '그녀가 듣지 못했다'는 내용과 '말을 시작한다'는 내용은 대립이 됨 (C) 실수를 함으로써 문법을 더 깊이 이해하고 있다는 것을 보여 주는 것이므로 By making이 적절

부모들은 때로 자녀들의 문법이 점점 나빠지기 시작하는 것을 보고 놀라게 된다. 어린이가 문장을 사용하기 시작할 때는 문법이 꽤 정확하다. 예를 들어, 한 번도 다른 사람이 그런 말을 쓰는 것을 들은 적이 없었더라도 mice라는 말을 썼던 아이가 mouses라고 말하기 시작할 수도 있을 것이다. 약간 더 나이가 들면, 똑같은 아이가 실수를 더 많이 하기 시작한다. 만약에 여러분의 자녀에게서 이와 같은 유형의 오류를 보게 되더라도 걱정하지 말아라. 아동 발달 전문가들은 그것은 사실상 좋은 징조라고 말한다. 이러한 실수를 함으로써 어린이들은 문법에 대한 더 깊은 이해를 보여 주고 있는 것이다.

get worse 악화된다 **reasonably** 비교적

REVIEW TEST

P. 262

01 unique → uniqueness 02 look → looking
03 Like → Unlike 04 America → that of America
05 hearing → hear 06 storing 07 makes
08 improve 09 delivering 10 placing

01 〈not only+명사 but also+명사〉 구조

원본의 가치는 그것의 독특함뿐만 아니라 복제품이 만들어지는 원천이 된다는 점에서 발생한다.

02 본동사 offer가 나오므로 New eateries를 수식하는 분사가 적절

홍보를 하고 싶어하는 새 식당들은 샨과 킴과 같은 단골 비평가에게 공짜로 식사를 제공한다.

03 대부분의 다른 젊은 가수와는 다르다는 의미, Unlike가 적절

대부분의 다른 젊은 가수들과는 달리, 그의 팬들은 특정 연령대에 국한되지 않는데, 그들은 범위가 7살에서 나이든 여자까지 이른다.

04 중국과 미국의 시장을 비교하므로 that of America가 적절

미국인들은 때때로 중국의 시장이 그들의 시장보다 더 개방적으로 보이는 것을 알고 놀란다.

05 understand와 병렬 구조

이 장치는 사용자들이 시끄러운 환경 속에서 입술을 읽을 필요없이 연설을 이해할 수 있도록 하고, 심지어 다양한 상황에서 강의를 들을 수 있도록 해준다.

06 learning, forming과 병렬 구조

두뇌는 새로운 정보를 학습하고, 공간적인 기억을 형성하며, 단기 기억을 장기기억으로 저장하는데 중요한 역할을 한다.

07 creates와 병렬 구조, 〈not only A but also〉 구문

이것은 감독을 위한 개선된 기술의 사용을 만들어낼 뿐만 아니라, 운동 선수들 사이에 스포츠 과학 사고방식을 만든다.

08 sharpen, enhance와 병렬 구조

연구팀은 아이들을 더 많이 움직이게 만드는 것은 지능을 향상시키며, 창의성과 계획 능력을 높이며, 수학과 독서 성취도를 개선시킬 수 있다는 결론을 내렸다.

09 from A to B, finding과 병렬 구조

우리 사무실은 잃어버린 고양이나 강아지를 찾는 것에서부터, 러브레터를 배달하는 것에 이르는 다양한 문제를 다룰 수 있다.

10 capable of에 걸리는 operating과 병렬 구조

인간은 그러한 도구를 올바르게 이용하고 그것들을 적당하고 유용한 장소에 위치시키는 것을 더 잘 할 수 있다.

FINAL CHECK

P. 263~265

01 ① 02 ③ 03 ② 04 ① 05 ④ 06 ①

01 ① 선행사가 없고, learning의 목적어가 없으므로 that이 아니라 what이 돼야 함 ② attending, sitting, taking과 병렬 구조 ③ Not only가 문두로 나와서 도치된 구문 ④ didn't가 왔으므로 either가 옴 ⑤ apply A to B 'A를 B에 적용하다'

누가 배우는 것은 교실에서 해야 한다고 말하는가? 일을 떠나서 따로 시간을 가지라는 것은? 글쎄, 그럴 필요는 없다. 사실, 연구는 당신이 배운 것을 일에 적용할 때 더 많이 배운다는 것을 보여 준다. 우리 모두는 수업에 출석하고, 긴 수업 시간 동안 앉아 있고, 방대한 양의 노트 필기를 하고, 그 다음에 일자리로 돌아가서는 그 노트를 책꽂이에 끼우고 다시는 보지 않았던 기억들이 있다. 우리는 소중한 시간을 소비했을 뿐 아니라 실제로 직업적으로 발전하지도 않았다. 새로운 기술이나 정보를 바로 일상생활에서 하고 있는 것에 접목시키는 것이 낫지 않겠는가? 만약 당신이 직업적으로 발전하려고 노력으로부터 진짜로 배우고 성장한다면 멋지지 않겠는가?

apply A to B A를 B에 적용하다 **lecture** 강의 **precious** 소중한 **endeavor** 노력 **copious** 방대한

02 (A) '문맥을 이용하는 방법'이라는 뜻으로 how가 적절 (B) The use가 주어이므로 is가 적절 (C) 〈from A to B〉 구문으로 using과 병렬 구조

문맥에서 모르는 단어의 의미를 추측하는 것은 독해의 전략과 기술, 두 가지 모두에 포함될 수 있다. 독자가 이러한 개념을 처음으로 만나고 익숙하지 않은 어휘의 의미를 찾아내기 위해 문맥을 이용하는 방법을 연습할 때, 그들은 몇 가지 전략들을 사용한다. 그들이 배우고 연습하는 동안 이러한 전략들의 사용은 완전히 의식적인 것이다. 모르는 단어를 문맥에서 추측하는 능력이 자동화될 때, 독자는 의식적인 전략을 사용하는 것에서 무의식적인 기술을 사용하는 것으로 넘어갈 수 있다. 이 기술의 이용은 독자의 직접적인 의식 밖에서 일어난다. 다시 말해, 명백한 전략 설명의 교육은 독자를 독해 전략의 의식적인 통제에서 독해 기술의 무의식적인 사용으로 옮겨가게 하는 것이다.

concept 개념 **conscious** 의식있는 **utilize** 활용하다 **unconscious** 무의식적인 **objective** 목적 **explicit** 명백한

03 ② Our mission is various from 뒤에 나오는 delivering과 병렬 구조 ① 뒤에 목적어가 바로 나오지 않으므로 동명사가 아닌 명사가 옴 ③ 앞에 선행사가 없고 뒤에 주어가 없으므로 주어 역할을 하는 What이 적절 ④ 앞의 fairs를 수식하는 분사구문 ⑤ help의 목적격 보어

킴즈 그룹은 국제적인 사업과 세계 정세에 대한 분석의 선도적인 정보원입니다. 우리의 임무는 신문이나 잡지 배달하기부터 여러 회의를 개최하는 것까지 다양합니다. 우리를 하나로 묶어주는 것은 우리 의견의 객관성과 통찰력의 독창성, 전 세계적인 경제, 정치적 자유에 대한 옹호입니다. 우리는 후원자와 대표자들을 함께 모시고 경영 교육과 같은 우리 고객과 관련된 분야에서 온라인 박람회를 하기 위한 새로운 사업을 구축하고 있습니다. 우리는 이와 비슷한 이벤트에서 성공한 전적이 있고, 현재의 서비스를 확장하고 개선하려는 기술을 사용하는 데 중요한 상업적 기회를 인지하고 있습니다. 우리는 곧 이 사업을 시작할 예정이며, 우리의 상업적 야심을 실현하는데 도움을 줄 야심차고 역동적인 팀을 구성하는 중입니다.

analysis 분석 **objectivity** 객관성 **originality** 독창성 **insight** 통찰력 **advocacy** 옹호 **sponsor** 후원자 **delegate** 대표 **perceive** 인지하다 **commercial** 상업적인 **launch** 시작하나 **ambitious** 야심찬 **dynamic** 역동적인

04 (A) 앞의 standing과 병렬 구조 (B) 뒤에 분사구문이 오므로 접속사 while이 적절 (C) '그들의 권리'를 의미해야 하므로 theirs가 와야 함

단호한 태도는 당신의 권리를 옹호하고, 타인의 권리를 침해하지 않는 직접적이고 적절한 방식으로 당신의 생각과 감정을 표현하는 것을 포함한다. 단호한 태도를 보여 주는 사람들은 원만한 대인 관계를 유지하면서도 갈등 상황을 손쉽고 확실하게 처리할 수 있다. 이와는 대조적으로, 공격적인 행동은 생각과 감정을 표현하고 타인의 권리를 드러내 놓고 침해하는 방법으로 자신의 권리를 보호하는 것을 포함한다. 공격적 행동을 보여 주는 사람들은 다른 사람들의 권리는 자신들의 권리에 종속되어야만 한다고 믿는 것 같다. 따라서 그들은 원만한 대인관계를 유지하는 데 어려움을 겪는다. 그들은 지배권을 유지하기 위해 끼어들고, 빨리 말하며, 다른 사람들을 무시하기 쉽다.

assertive 단호한 **exhibit** 보여주다 **assurance** 확신 **subservient** ~에 종속하는 **interrupt** 방해하다

05 ④ it will appear에 뒤따라오는 lighter와 병렬 구조 ① 접속사 뒤에 주어가 없으므로 분사구문이 옴 ② 원칙이 기초가 되는 것이므로 능동 ③ 요청받는다는 뜻 ⑤ '거의 모든 유형'이라는 뜻

야구 선수들은 워밍업 스윙을 하기 전에 종종 자신의 배트에 무게가 나가는 고리를 끼운다. 그들은 반복적으로 더 무거운 배트를 휘두르는 것이 고리를 끼우지 않은 배트를 비교적 더 가볍게 느끼도록 해준다고 말한다. 이 효과에 내재해 있는 주요 원리는 지각적 대조라고 알려져 있다. 간단히 요약하면, 물체의 특징들은 다른 것들과 비교해서 지각된다는 것이다. 당신이 체육관에서 10파운드짜리 아령을 들도록 요구 받았을 때, 먼저 20파운드짜리 아령을 들었다면 10파운드짜리 아령이 더 가볍게 느껴지고 5파운드짜리 아령을 먼저 들었으면 더 무겁게 느껴질 것이다. 10파운드짜리 아령은 그것에 대한 당신의 지각을 제외하고는 실제로는 아무 것도 변한 것이 없다. 이러한 심리적 과정은 당신이 내릴 수 있는 거의 모든 유형의 판단에 유효하다. 모든 경우에 있어 지각하는 과정은 똑같은데, 전의 경험이 지각에 영향을 끼치기 때문이다.

weighted 무거운 **in comparison to** ~와 비교해서 **underlie** ~의 기초가 되다 **gymnasium** 체육관 **perceptual** 지각 있는 **color** 영향을 끼치다

06 (A) 조건을 나타내는 if가 와야 함 (B) 주절에 주어가 없으므로 명령문이 와야 함 (C) 새로운 프로그램을 만들기 위해서 멈추는 것이 아닌 만드는 행위 자체를 멈춘다는 내용이 오므로 stop -ing가 옴

당신의 아이가 왜 모든 문장의 끝을 질문하듯이 올리는지, 고등학교에 가는 것에 대해 얘기하고 비상시 999보다 911에 전화할 것 같은지 알고 싶다면 TV 편성표를 살펴보아라. 영국은 지난 십여 년 동안 어린이 텔레비전에 있어서 글로벌 리더였지만, 미국 수입물이 인계 받았다. 한 연구가 이번 주에 밝힌 것과 같이 2003년 이후로 어린이 텔레비전에 대한 투자는 48%로 감소한 반면 영국의 독창적인 프로그램은 일년에 1,900시간에서 900시간으로 줄어들었다. 부분적으로 이는 어린이 방송 시간 동안의 정크 푸드 광고금지의 결과이다. 새로운 채널의 확산으로 인해 이미 타격을 입은 광고 업계는 급락했고, 큰 상업 채널들은 새로운 프로그램을 만들기를 중단했다. 오직 BBC만이 여전히 프로그램을 의뢰하고 있으며 쥐꼬리만한 요금에 경쟁력은 거의 없나.

interrogative 의문의 **upbeat** 상승 **emergency** 응급 상황 **revenue** 수익 **proliferation** 확산 **plummet** 곤두박질 치다 **commission** 의뢰하다 **paltry** 하찮은

구문을 알면 독해가 저절로!

구문 독해 204

204개의 핵심 구문을 통한 직독직해 완전정복!

BOOK 2

SENTENCE STRUCTURE+READING

혼돈하기 쉬운 구문의 비교 학습

2000여 개에 달하는 풍부한 문제를 통한 반복 학습

어법부터 독해까지 한 권으로 끝내는 학습 구조

NEXUS makes your next day
www.nexusbook.com | 책에 대해 궁금한 사항은 넥서스 홈페이지 독자 게시판을 이용하세요.

NEXUS Edu

LEVEL CHART

	초1	초2	초3	초4	초5	초6	중1	중2	중3	고1	고2	고3
VOCA	초등필수 영단어 1-2 · 3-4 · 5-6학년용											
VOCA					The VOCA + (플러스) 1~7							
VOCA			THIS IS VOCABULARY 입문 · 초급 · 중급					고급 · 어원 · 수능 완성 · 뉴텝스				
VOCA							WORD FOCUS 중등 종합 5000 · 고등 필수 5000 · 고등 종합 9500					
Grammar			초등필수 영문법 + 쓰기 1~2									
Grammar			OK Grammar 1~4									
Grammar			This Is Grammar Starter 1~3									
Grammar					This Is Grammar 초급~고급 (각 2권: 총 6권)							
Grammar						Grammar 공감 1~3						
Grammar						Grammar 101 1~3						
Grammar						Grammar Bridge 1~3						
Grammar						중학영문법 뽀개기 1~3						
Grammar						The Grammar Starter, 1~3						
Grammar									구사일생 (구문독해 Basic) 1~2			
Grammar									구문독해 204 1~2			
Grammar								그래머 캡처 1~2				
Grammar									[특급 단기 특강] 어법어휘 모의고사			

초1	초2	초3	초4	초5	초6	중1	중2	중3	고1	고2	고3

Writing

- 공감 영문법+쓰기 1~2
- 도전만점 중등내신 서술형 1~4
- 영어일기 영작패턴 1-A, B · 2-A, B
- Smart Writing 1~2

Reading

- Reading 101 1~3
- Reading 공감 1~3
- This Is Reading Starter 1~3
- This Is Reading 전면 개정판 1~4
- This Is Reading 1-1 ~ 3-2 (각 2권; 총 6권)
- 원서 술술 읽는 Smart Reading Basic 1~2
- 원서 술술 읽는 Smart Reading 1~2
- [특급 단기 특강] 구문독해 · 독해유형

Listening

- Listening 공감 1~3
- The Listening 1~4
- After School Listening 1~3
- 도전! 만점 중학 영어듣기 모의고사 1~3
- 만점 적중 수능 듣기 모의고사 20회 · 35회

TEPS

- NEW TEPS 입문편 실전 250+ 청해 · 문법 · 독해
- NEW TEPS 기본편 실전 300+ 청해 · 문법 · 독해
- NEW TEPS 실력편 실전 400+ 청해 · 문법 · 독해
- NEW TEPS 마스터편 실전 500+ 청해 · 문법 · 독해